Research in
MUSIC EDUCATION

Research in
MUSIC
EDUCATION

An Introduction
to Systematic Inquiry

EDWARD L. RAINBOW
HILDEGARD C. FROEHLICH

SCHIRMER BOOKS
A Division of Macmillan, Inc.
NEW YORK

Collier Macmillan Publishers
LONDON

Schirmer Books
A Division of Macmillan, Inc.
866 Third Avenue, New York, N.Y. 10022

Collier Macmillan Canada, Inc.

Library of Congress Catalog Card Number: 87-9870

Printed in the United States of America

printing number
1   2   3   4   5   6   7   8   9   10

Library of Congress Cataloging-in-Publication Data

Rainbow, Edward L.
    Research in music education.
    Bibliography: p.
    Includes indexes.
    1. Music—Instruction and study—Research.
I. Froehlich, Hildegard C.   II. Title.
MT1.R26   1987   780'.01   87-9870
ISBN 0-02-870320-0

Contents

List of Figures

List of Tables

PREFACE

This book is a reflection of our collective experiences in teaching research to both beginning and advanced graduate music education students. These experiences include introducing master-level students to basic concepts of research, developing skills of critical analysis in doctoral students, and guiding doctoral candidates in dissertation work. In all these situations it appears that the main problem in bringing research close to the minds of the students lies in their diverse views of what music education is.

For many, the content of music education consists of the methodologies and skills employed in teaching music to people from 5 to 18 years of age. For others, the content is found in the acquisition of knowledge about appropriate music and teaching literature. A third group tends to equate music education with any form of music teaching wherever it occurs—in schools, universities, church programs, camp activities, or private studios.

Because of the diverse goals most music education students have set for themselves, a research book in music education should have a two-fold aim: to train the future researcher and to make those who do not wish to conduct research comfortable with the role of disciplined thinking in music education. The book should be general and specific at the same time. *Research in Music Education* attempts to be that book.

In this book, a description of the field of music education is integrated into the concept of research as disciplined inquiry. The thought processes inherent in that inquiry take precedence over the specific techniques of how to conduct research. This focus reflects our contention that the logic of specific research techniques tends to become clear once the logic of the research process itself has been understood.

Music educators often categorize research according to the primary methodology utilized in an investigation. A study may thus carry the label of experiment, descriptive survey, quantitative-analytical investigation, sampling, speculative, historical, or qualitative-analytical research. The classification refers to both the investigative techniques employed in an investigation and the purpose for which the techniques are being utilized. As a result of that dual reference, the categorization of research has become somewhat confused. After all, a study may be historical, yet use quantification techniques; an investigation may be experimental and also employ a questionnaire in order to assess attitudes and perceptions of different groups of people.

It is hoped that the categorization of disciplined inquiry into three modes— historical, philosophical, and empirical—helps to clear up some of the misconceptions about the types of research found in music education. Each of the modes of inquiry represents an established view or perspective from which one looks at a problem. Since each of the modes has its own acknowledged set of rules, guidelines, and limitations, the chosen perspective ultimately determines the type of findings that provide the answer to a given question.

This book should not be taught in its entirety in one course. Such an undertaking is likely to be unrealistic and impractical. Instead, the instructor should make a judgment as to what sections or chapters to use. Parts 1 and 2 (chapters 1 to 5), along with the suggested additional reading and some written work, are intended as the basis for teaching the aspect of understanding the thought processes of research. Depending on the instructor's focus, these chapters could provide the major content of a quarter or semester course on an introduction to research in music education. Only selected chapters of Part 3 (chapters 6 to 10) would in that case be included in such a course. An instructor might wish to look at all three modes of inquiry (historical, philosophical, and empirical), or one mode might be emphasized over the others. Criteria that pertain to skills in critical reading and research evaluation are addressed in chapters 5 to 9. If the focus of a course centers on research techniques, then an in-depth study of chapters 6 to 10 would be appropriate. Part 4 (chapter 11) is intended primarily for the master's or doctoral candidate who is writing a thesis or dissertation.

Some of the chapters are lengthy. In many instances the subsections of a chapter were therefore written in such a way that they would stand by themselves and allow for specific reading assignments of manageable proportions. Also, the often lengthy lists of references included in the text should be viewed as an invitation to the students to begin the reading process that becomes the foundation of all research. The references should not be treated as material that must be covered in a course. Wherever appropriate, a chapter concludes with a number of suggested readings that we would call "thinking books." It is unreasonable for any or all of these books to be assigned or made mandatory reading. Many of the publications simply represent good reading since the authors have often looked at the usual in an unusual way. The books provide food for thought and represent some of the "spirit" of research.

A word about questions for discussion. First, it has been customary for textbook writers to present at the end of each chapter a series of questions by which the material in the chapter is reviewed. We have found that these questions seldom meet the rules of a specific class since the students themselves usually generate better questions than the author. Second, the kind of questions to ask depends entirely on the focus the instructor has chosen for the overall course. Because the book seeks to be useful for a variety of teaching situations, we have decided not to pose too many specific discussion questions. Instead, we have listed a few topics from which questions could be developed. But even these topics are only suggestions. It is our opinion that the instructor should teach "around" the book, not "by" the book.

We wish to extend gratitude and thanks to our students at North Texas State University. They used and critiqued preliminary drafts of the text and made many excellent points. All of the comments were appreciated and, where appropriate, incorporated into the present version of the text. As research is an ongoing process, so is writing: We do not claim that this version has reached the stage where one could call it final any more than one would consider the performance of a musical composition in recital to be the final product in one's career as a musician. Music performance is the process of moving toward the goal of perfection; it is of secondary importance whether that goal is ever reached. The same holds true in research and writing: A research result or a written report is never more than a step in the process of searching for knowledge. With each step, one hopes to gain more knowledge, yet more questions and, consequently, more plans for further work arise.

Finally, several specific thank yous are in order: To Alton Chan, Graduate Research Assistant, for his many hours of legwork without which the manuscript could not have been completed; and to our faculty colleagues in music education for their support during the time the manuscript was prepared. Special mention must be made of Dr. David McGuire and Dr. William May for their help in providing constructive criticism and encouragement.

E.L.R. and H.C.F.
Denton, Texas

Research in
MUSIC
EDUCATION

PART ONE

The Researcher and The Research Process

Chapters 1 and 2 serve as an introduction to the research process in music education. In chapter 1, the role of research in music and music education is discussed. In chapter 2, the attributes of those who pursue research activities are described in general. Music education is viewed as a field of study with an emerging body of knowledge. Thus, the role of research is suggested to be the same as that in other fields of study: the application of disciplined inquiry to questions pertaining to a body of knowledge.

Inquisitiveness is considered the key to the development of all knowledge. Other attributes characterizing a good researcher are suggested to be: (a) the ability to plan in a disciplined way new approaches and perspectives by which to study an issue; (b) an awareness of ideas and events in fields other than one's own; and (c) a willingness to communicate one's ideas and findings to the profession at large. All these attributes together form what may be called the mind-set of the researcher.

C h a p t e r   O n e

The Role of Research in Music Education:
Establishing a Body of Knowledge

1.1 Introduction

Music has been an area of intellectual pursuit for many centuries. Early documents discussing the music of Chinese people are believed to have been written prior to 1000 B.C. (Cho, 1975). Cho refers to early writings on the music of China dating back to about 122 B.C., and specifically cites the book *Shi Chih*, in which Ssu-ma Ch'ien (97 B.C.) describes the pentatonic pattern and the twelve semitones within the octave (Cho, 1975, p.16). We have knowledge of the relationship of mathematics and music as it is believed to have existed in India, ancient Egypt, the early Greek culture, and the Arab world (see, among others, McClain, 1978; Pfrogner, 1981; Sachs, 1943, 1953).

Regarding early writings on Western music and aesthetic thought, hardly anyone fails to acknowledge the works of Pythagoras (ca. 500 B.C.) and Plato (427–347 B.C.) as the beginning of modern concepts of music (e.g., Backus, 1977; Farnsworth, 1969; Helmholtz, 1954; Lippman, 1977; Margolis, 1978; Rowell, 1983; Sachs, 1955; Winckel, 1967). Both Pythagoras and Plato sought to describe physical aspects of sound in terms of arithmetic relationships. It was Plato, however, who went so far as to speculate on the manifestation of the beautiful and its relationship to the moral development of the human character.

For many centuries the general emphasis of inquiries into the subject of music continued to focus on a description of the arithmetic and physical properties of sound and existing tonal systems (Farnsworth, 1969; Pfrogner, 1981; Sachs, 1955). Observations were organized, and reports about them served as the body of knowledge from which specific musical laws were developed. The outcome of such systematic study may be said to have resulted in the science of music—that is, musicology in its truest sense (Sachs, 1955).

The accumulation and preservation of knowledge as well as the continued study of the various aspects of the science of music have enabled music to remain an important field of study for over 25 centuries. During this time span the field of music has evidenced a similar division and growth of investigative interests as have fields in the physical and natural sciences. Research in music is no longer confined to the examination of the physical properties of sound. Historical-chronological musicology (music history) has evolved with a research focus that differs significantly from earlier scientific pursuits in music. Today, music historians are primarily concerned with the study of musical composition and the people responsible for the development of the art.

Closely connected to research in music history is research in music theory, an area that addresses foremost the analysis of structural devices in musical compositions and how these devices determine musical style. Music theorists are somewhat less involved in the study of particular individuals who have contributed to the history of the musical art. Instead, they are more interested in the study of music from an "architectural" point of view. Inevitably, concerns of music history and theory are in some cases the same, so that a clear distinction between both areas of study is not always easy or possible.

Other music-related areas of study have emerged in response to the many questions historical musicology and theory failed to address in a systematic way. These areas include systematic musicology, ethnomusicology, music therapy, the art of composition and performance, pedagogy, and music education. Each area has defined its own scope of research, developed its own questions, and determined its own research methodologies by which to answer the questions.

Despite the specifics of different methodologies, scholars in music tend to agree on certain attributes that characterize a good researcher. Foremost among these attributes is the ability to probe the accuracy of accepted fact and seek answers to the unknown (Farnsworth, 1969; Lippman, 1977; Smith, 1976). Questions must be raised about the nature and process of composing musical works, of performing and perceiving musical sound, and of becoming musically educated through formal and informal instructional settings. Another attribute is the ability to find answers to a given question in a manner acceptable to the community of scholars. That ability must be coupled with the person's willingness to share any found answer with the profession at large. Adhering to the attributes described means to adhere to principles of disciplined inquiry.

1.2 The Nature of Disciplined Inquiry

Scholars of many different fields have addressed and continue to address the function of disciplined inquiry in the pursuit of human knowledge. To list even a small sample of these efforts would fill pages of this book. Thus, a brief introductory statement as to what constitutes the nature of disciplined inquiry must suffice. This statement is a synopsis of many writers' efforts, among them Good, Barr, and Scates (1941); Buchdahl (1969); Fischer (1971); Dessel, Nehrich, and Voran (1973); Agnew and Pyke (1978); Sax (1979); Broudy, Ennis, and Krimerman (1973); Russell (1976); Kline (1985); and Leedy (1985).

Disciplined inquiry emanates from an attitude of curiosity about the unknown. Such inquisitiveness can generally be found in people who believe in a universal truth behind everything that exists. That truth is believed to become visible through discernable laws that govern the universe. The discovery of any one of these laws through research contributes to knowledge and is considered instrumental in explaining the structure of the world as a place of order rather than chaos. The inquisitive mind therefore searches for the universal truth of things by attempting to attach order to what appears chaotic and by finding logical explanations for things and phenomena that seem unclear (Breisach, 1983; Burke, 1978; Kuhn, 1975; Lovejoy, 1978; Popper, 1968; Russell, 1945; Toynbee, 1972).

Searching for Truth

The desire to find answers to questions may lie not only in a basic curiosity about life but also in the fact that knowledge tends to provide one with a sense of security, whereas the unexplained may trigger fear. To illustrate: In early history, people searched for explanations about things they did not understand primarily by asking persons who were believed to possess wisdom and/or political power (Dessel, Nehrich, & Voran, 1973; Good, Barr, & Scates, 1941). In instances where the wise authority (e.g., the priest, king, medicine man, chief of the tribe) seemed to have little control over nature, people reasoned that control of the universe rested in someone or something outside the immediate environment. Tales of supernatural beings—animals and creatures who were part human, part animal—served as explanations for observed environmental phenomena. Supernaturals were said to control the weather, military battles, and life itself. They became the gods believed to guide all aspects of human life. Today we label those explanations myth, legends, or fairy tales. We know about them through artistic objects of the past, such as hieroglyphs, sculptures, paintings, and epic poems. In our own time, the Bible, the Koran, or other sources of religious belief are similar documents of how generations of people have explained and continue to explain the existence of the human species and the reasons that people function the way they do.

Aside from spiritual truth and the word of the wise men, observations about the physical world were a second way of explaining the nature of things. People noted and kept records about the portion of the universe that was immediately visible to them—the stars and planets. By recording perceived movements of the celestial elements and by sharing that knowledge with others, people began to develop an empirical base for attempting to explain how parts of the universe worked. The recorded observations led to the discovery of patterns in the movement of the stars, in the cycle of the moon, and in the ratio between the amount of light and darkness in a day. Order and patterns were also established for the cycle of the seasons and the cycle of life.

The description of observed patterns in the physical world resulted, among other things, in accurate predictions of the "movements" of the planets and stars as well as those of seasonal changes. From such rather humble beginnings, astrology and then astronomy may be said to have developed as a field of study. Human ability to predict seasonal changes, however, led to agriculture as an integral part of people's life. Human curiosity—the willingness to record observations and to share them with others—has resulted in major advances of human knowledge.

A third avenue toward searching for truth has been the power of reasoning. Systems of logical argumentation were employed in order to regulate and organize the way in which to find satisfactory answers to important questions. Russell (1945) has traced the history of those systems of thought in a most straightforward manner in his book *A History of Western Philosophy*. He points out clearly how any one system of thought may exercise control over what is considered to be the truth. One such example is the debate between Socrates and a gathering of teachers called Sophists (see Guthrie, 1971, pp. 1–26).

To state the argumentative positions briefly: In debating the truthfulness of assumptions, beliefs, values, and ideas, Socrates separated statements as either true or false, yes or no. The Sophists, on the other hand, included in their perception of the world the possibility of truth as expressed in a "maybe." They believed that answers to questions did not always fall into the dualistic category of either-or but that they could lie in the middle of both. As Guthrie points out, the Sophists have been recorded as having lost that debate, as a result of which the Socratic system of logical reasoning was left to govern the argumentative way of Western civilization until the latter part of the 19th century.

A fourth way of finding answers to questions about the universe has been that of common sense perceptions. Throughout the history of civilization, this source of explaining the nature of things has had some remarkable clashes with spiritually, empirically, and philosophically derived truths. For example: Based on centuries of observation and what now appears to us to be a limited knowledge about the environment, people concluded that the earth was flat and that it was the center of the universe. Technological advances, observations, and logical reasoning helped Galileo and others to come to an opposing conclusion—namely, that the earth was not the center of the universe and not flat, but round. In effect, these research-based conclusions were opposed to the common sense perceptions of the time.

Galileo's empirically derived truth also resulted in a conflict with truth as represented by Roman Catholic Church doctrine, the foundation of which rested in dichotic Socratic logic. This doctrine, based on common sense perception as well as authoritarian decree, was diametrically opposed to the truth as suggested by Galileo's findings. In the end, power politics won out—Galileo was made to recant his observations. While all of Galileo's observations have not remained completely true, his initial truths led to substantial changes in our understanding of the planetary system. This understanding has even caused a belated change in the perception of truth among Roman Catholic Church leaders, when in 1980 the Vatican reviewed the 347-year-old heresy conviction of Galileo for advocating that the earth was flat (*New York Times,* 1980); and again in 1983, when Pope John Paul II stated that the Vatican was still examining the "heresies" of Galileo (*New York Times,* 1983).

It should be mentioned that a loop exists in this example of searching for truth according to Socratic and Sophist logic. This loop has been created by the works of Isaac Newton, Albert Einstein, Max Planck, and other 20th century mathematicians and physicists. Current thought suggests that many areas of physical existence work on probabilities that certain events will transpire. Answers to questions may not always be yes or no; they do not necessarily follow principles of either-or, but may instead lie in the gray area of maybe. Perhaps we are, at least those of us in Western civilization, back to the Sophists' system of thought.

Sources of Truth

In his discussion of sources of knowledge, Sax (1979, pp. 1–5) refers to appeals of common sense, authority, intuition, and revelation. In the illustrations presented in the previous section, five different, though not mutually exclusive, sources have been identified that have been employed in the search for understanding of the laws that govern humanity, its thoughts and actions, and its physical environment. These sources may be labeled (a) expert opinion, (b) common sense, (c) systematic observations, (d) the power of logical argumentation, and (e) authoritarian verdict and decree. Whatever label one wishes to attach to these sources of truth and knowledge, they have been with humanity since the earliest of time and appear to be with us today.

Expert truth emanates from individuals or groups of people who, due to their position of acknowledged expertise in a specific subject matter, are believed to have more accurate answers to questions than anyone else. That expertise results in accepted authority. Therefore, depending on the nature of the question, one turns to physicians, lawyers, theologians, psychologists, physicists, teachers, or one's own parents for an answer. One attaches to the answer the label of truth because of the trust one has in the expert. Once that trust diminishes, one's faith in the person's answer also tends to diminish.

Common sense truth, too, serves an important purpose in human inquiry. In it, tradition, expertise, and intuition work together and help us to arrive at a solution to everyday problems. Those solutions may often be the best recourse we have for action. After all, "what grandmother says" often is true and can serve us well in our daily lives. But, what grandmother says must also be subjected to rigorous testing. A reliance on personal experiences that are assumed to represent absolute truth can hinder progress and blind a person to both reality and the search for more accurate facts.

Empirical truth is knowledge obtained by means of systematic observation and experimentation. One gains an understanding of how the universe and life on earth are structured by carefully observing the actions and movements that are hypothesized to determine their course. The observations allow one to establish patterns of actions, to experiment with specific variables, and to establish from the results the evidence that supports the answers to one's questions.

Logical truth comes from the application of the power of rational thought and reasoning to ideas and observed phenomena. It is rooted in common sense truth as well as in empirical truth since all conclusions are based on known facts and empirical evidence about the hitherto unknown. We infer the truth about the nature of things by attempting to explain the unknown through what is already known.

Authoritarian truth comes from opinions and beliefs imposed by people with political power, and often through intimidation. That truth is decreed, not suggested; it therefore differs from expert truth. Facts are manipulated in order to support a particular point of view or to strengthen the status quo of value systems and beliefs. Imposing such beliefs on others without providing avenues of questioning their factual basis frequently stifles curiosity. We hinted at the use of authoritarian truth in the example of Galileo's work. We can point to Stalin, who decreed Lysenko's biology doctrine to be truth. This decree was nearly a disaster for the study of biology in the Soviet Union. In the United States, political force can create authoritarian truth when State School Boards have the power to order censorship over ideas in textbooks.

Authoritarian truth and the dogma surrounding it represent obstacles to the spirit of individualized inquiry. Both the gathering and the transmittal of truth can be stifled. However, authoritarian sources of truth should not be considered the sole villain in stifling the search for answers to the unknown. Rather, sole reliance on any one source of truth may put blinders on one's inquiry. How the answer to a question is derived effects a person's perception of truth, and the relativity of that perception should always be acknowledged.

The Nature of Facts in Research

People generally accept the answer to a question as truthful only to the degree it completely satisfies their curiosity. A satisfactory answer is expected to account fully for what one wishes to know. It should also confirm one's belief that things are organized according to principles that do not contradict the laws of reason or those of one's own belief system. If either of these conditions is met, an answer tends to be given the status of truth; the answer becomes factual and, thus, the basis for knowledge and understanding. If a person ceases to trust an expert, if an answer explains a question only partially, or if personal experiences prove accepted facts to be wrong, more questions are raised and information is sought to enable one to arrive at better answers to those questions. To the degree that facts change, understanding changes.

Factual knowledge may be defined as evidence that can be corroborated or verified. Observations of same events that produce similar findings under the same or only slightly altered circumstances result in factual knowledge. Historical interpretation that can be supported by primary documents may be considered facts; findings of empirical research can provide facts when the investigations are replicated under similar conditions. In the continuous testing of such facts lies the heart of research. Once a research area has a certain quantity of factual information to its credit, the area may be called a field of study with an emerging body of knowledge.

As knowledge expands in a field of study, researchers often devote their energies to the in-depth study of subportions of that field. Biology is one such example in which many investigative areas have been spawned. Mycology, virology, and genetics are some of those areas that have become fields of study in their own right but belong to the broad field of biology. However, just as the discovery of new facts may lead to the establishment of new fields of study, a field may also disappear because new factual evidence proves accepted knowledge to be false.

Throughout history, fields of knowledge have emerged and disappeared, indicating that the facts supporting a discipline today may with tomorrow's new discoveries undergo radical alteration, if not abandonment (Berger & Luckmann, 1967; Kuhn, 1975). Indeed, one may say that the activity of conducting research is historically rooted in the dissatisfaction of some people with the answers they have received about specific questions regarding human existence, the nature of the universe, and the causation of environmental phenomena. Thus, the answer to a question serves not so much the purpose of "knowing something once and for all" but as a stimulant to additional questioning. No single answer gives the full truth. Rather, it is the process of continuously searching for better and more complete answers by which we may be brought nearer to a truth. We may never rest in a state of fully knowing the real truth, but searching for it may eventually bring us closer to it.

To summarize:

1. All sources for seeking answers to questions may produce truth and facts. Myths and legends, common sense perceptions and spiritual insights, logical reasoning, expert opinion and systematic observation—all may serve as such sources and help in the development of factual information.

2. As facts may change over time, there is no guarantee they will remain permanent. New technologies and investigative methodologies, different perspectives and new factual information from external fields may contribute to a reevaluation of traditionally accepted facts.

3. Methods of seeking truth, such as logic, observation, and expert knowledge, may all be valid approaches in the search for answers to specific questions. However, the very method employed in seeking to establish facts as truth carries with it inherent limitations that should be considered in the evaluation of the facts.

4. Factual evidence should be constantly corroborated by additional evidence. It is wise to subject expert opinion to systematic observation. It is wise to employ empirical means wherever possible for the verification of philosophical truths. It is wise to apply common sense to empirically derived truths. A truth that cannot be verified should be rejected or, if one is not fully satisfied with the employed methods of testing, that truth should be investigated by new means. Under no circumstances, however, should a researcher allow false dogma to prevail in the acceptance of what may be true.

5. Ideas and thoughts that run counter to authoritarian dogma can result in personal rejection by one's peers. Facts and new perspectives of what is believed to be the truth will always create some counterreactions, but life is dull without some adventure and the taking of risks is an integral part of inquisitiveness.

Through inquisitiveness an area of interest develops. Efforts at procuring answers to specific questions result in a field of study in which knowledge is accumulated. Through the process of challenging and testing the answers to any given question, factual knowledge is obtained. Although the facts may, over time, undergo change, they are the working body of knowledge in the field of study on which all its operations are based. The more observations confirm that knowledge, the greater the certainty that the knowledge is valid.

1.3 The Testing of Theories

Knowledge can never be more than a well thought out idea of what might be true. Scientists therefore conduct research in order to support or refute certain views they hold regarding how and why things work the way they do. The systematic development of such views is an integral part of the scientific method and, when codified, is commonly referred to as a theory. A scientific theory is meant to account for complex and seemingly unrelated observations and should predict the occurrence of future events and developments. Theories should simplify and enlighten rather than obscure one's understanding of the nature of things. Thus, a theory that is more complicated than the question that triggered it is likely to be confusing instead of enlightening.

To test a theory, data are gathered to serve as evidence of its accuracy. The more data corroborate previous findings, the stronger the theory becomes: The theory has validity. If scientifically based research indicates repeatedly that the data will not support the theory, the theory may be said to be in error: The theory is invalid. Either new evidence must be found or the theory must be revised, if not abandoned. The task of scientific research lies thus in the continuous testing of proposed theories that may aid humans in their understanding of themselves, the environment, and their role in it.

The development of theories about human behavior or the testing of their validity often leads researchers to knowledge in fields other than their own.

Such knowledge may contradict or at least question the researcher's own notions about how things relate to each other. It should also be acknowledged that the subject area under study may adhere to a different perceptual framework than is accepted by the professional in the area the researcher belongs to. Specialized knowledge may, indeed, alter perception. In other instances, the results of existing studies that have supported a particular theory may be of limited value due to poor subject control, error, or improper research technique. In all these cases it may become necessary for the researcher to refute an accepted way of thinking and acknowledge the need for the development of a new theory that may more accurately explain the phenomenon under question. Scientists thus contribute to theory formation by (a) continuously corroborating extant knowledge; (b) acknowledging that new information may falsify accepted theory; and (c) presenting the newly obtained information in a clear and prescribed manner. These three steps are the prerequisites to what is referred to as the scientific process.

The Scientific Process

The credibility of scientifically gathered knowledge hinges on the corroboration and/or verification of evidence. For that evidence to become part of the body of knowledge of the field, all research results must be communicated to the profession in such a way that other researchers can replicate the study and that all conclusions can be easily followed and understood by the reader. To meet both demands, there are certain steps all scientifically minded researchers should adhere to: A study should have a clearly stated purpose. Depending on the nature of that purpose, questions *(research problems, hypotheses)* should delineate the specific aspects under investigation. All steps essential to arriving at answers to the questions should be clearly described and justified *(methodology)*. The answers should be reported as the *results of the study* and presented in the order in which they were posed. From the results, *conclusions* should be drawn and related to already existing knowledge in the field.

Generally, the more detailed a research report, the easier it is for colleagues in the field to follow the conclusions of the study and judge the trustworthiness of the results. Additionally, the more thorough the research report, the more likely it is that the investigation can be replicated and the results of both the original and the replicated study be compared with each other.

1.4 Music Education as a Field of Study

Music education in the form of music teaching and as an area of interest has been in existence for centuries. As an area for research, however, it is still relatively young. For example, only within the past three decades has there been the opportunity for music educators to disseminate research-based in-

11

formation in journals that are specifically geared toward the field of music education.

To illustrate: The first issue of the *Journal of Research in Music Education* was published by the Music Educators National Conference in the Spring of 1953. In 1963 the first issue of the *Bulletin of the Council for Research in Music Education* was published under the supervision of the College of Education and School of Music of the University of Illinois and the Office of the Superintendent of Public Instruction, Urbana, IL. Both journals have been instrumental in providing music educators with a forum of their own and an avenue through which they may disseminate information pertinent to the research community. Prior to the existence of these journals, the vehicles of communication for music educators were journals geared toward education, psychology, or musicology/music theory.

A third publication that may be considered a symbol of music educators' efforts to establish their own field of study is *Basic Concepts in Music Education* (Henry, 1958). This book contains a selection of articles that describe the scope of concerns paramount to and typical of music education as a field of study. Specifically, the book acknowledges the multidisciplinary characteristic of the field, stressing the relationship of music education to such disciplines as philosophy, psychology, and sociology.

The relatively novel view of music education as a field of study suggests the basing of teaching techniques in music on a clearly defined body of knowledge. To do this, music educators must develop valid theories of the various processes that lead to the most efficient instructional strategies in music. Since theory formation needs the corroboration of evidence, it becomes the task of music educators to provide that evidence through research and teaching. An important trademark of all those who call themselves music educators should therefore be a thorough knowledge of the mental and physical processes by which the learning and teaching of music takes place. That knowledge should guide the development of all instructional strategies so that the activity of teaching is not the result of personal experience alone but also an outcome of the systematic study of musical behavior. Music education, then, may be defined as the discipline in which the learning and teaching of music is systematically studied and its body of knowledge applied to music instruction.

This definition has important ramifications for all research in music education. It determines (a) the scope and the boundaries of the field; (b) the questions that should be asked about its body of knowledge; and (c) the methods by which such questions might have to be investigated. The definition also guides the content of the rest of this book.

Scope and Boundaries of the Field of Music Education

If one defines music education as the study of the learning and teaching of music, the components of concern to the music educator become the learner,

Figure 1.1   Determinants of Music Education as a Field of Study: The Learner, The Teacher, and Music

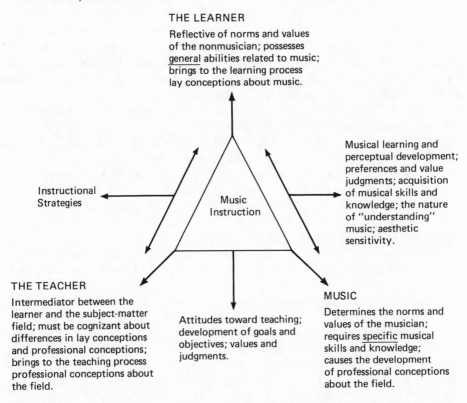

THE LEARNER

Reflective of norms and values of the nonmusician; possesses general abilities related to music; brings to the learning process lay conceptions about music.

Instructional Strategies

Music Instruction

Musical learning and perceptual development; preferences and value judgments; acquisition of musical skills and knowledge; the nature of "understanding" music; aesthetic sensitivity.

THE TEACHER

Intermediator between the learner and the subject-matter field; must be cognizant about differences in lay conceptions and professional conceptions; brings to the teaching process professional conceptions about the field.

Attitudes toward teaching; development of goals and objectives; values and judgments.

MUSIC

Determines the norms and values of the musician; requires specific musical skills and knowledge; causes the development of professional conceptions about the field.

the teacher, the subject matter (music), and the interrelationships among these three components. Figure 1.1 visualizes this relationship as an equilateral triangle in order to display the interdependence of and interconnection between the teacher, the learner, and the subject matter of music.

To illustrate: Music as a subject reflects the skills and knowledge characteristic of the accomplished musician. The purpose of all musical instruction is to develop in the learner the appreciation, if not mastery, of those very skills and knowledge. The inexperienced learner tends, however, to exhibit musical preferences and behavior typical of the nonmusician—that is, the musically untrained. Thus, lay conceptions of music largely determine the learner's attitude toward music. It becomes the music teacher's task to work with these conceptions in order to bring the learner closer to musical behaviors typical of and expected by trained musicians.

If the task of the music teacher consists of moving the learner more or less gradually toward the use and understanding of skills and knowledge typical of the musically trained person, then it seems imperative that music teachers be as thoroughly familiar with the learner's characteristics and musical behavior as they are with those of the musician. Teaching strategies and methods might then be defined as the steps the teacher takes to overcome the differences between the learner's perceptions of music and those of the trained musician. To improve music instructional methods, one task of research in music education would be to determine the characteristics of the learner at any given level of musical training. Music educators need information about how musical learning actually takes place.

Knowledge about the nature of musical learning might include information about the physical, perceptual, and aesthetic properties of music. Insights may also be needed into the physiological, psychological, and sociological conditions of learning. Such knowledge should logically go hand in hand with insights into the professional socialization of the music teacher. One would have to investigate the processes that guide the development of professional norms and values, and also study the impact of music teachers' professional self-concepts on their teaching effectiveness. One could ask how their mastery of musical skills and knowledge may relate to their role as performers and/or educators. Knowledge about the interaction between the teacher and learner would develop from questions on how the learner views the teacher and how the teacher structures the student–teacher relationship.

Research on the interaction between music and the learner should facilitate information about the learning process itself: One could study, for example, how the learner perceives music at differing age levels and levels of training and exposure. Within that context one might investigate the relationship between specific perceptual tasks and the means (learning tools) by which the students are asked to demonstrate what they hear. Are the evaluating tools appropriate or are they more difficult to comprehend than the task itself? From such information, instructional procedures may be developed that facilitate learning in the most efficient way. The effectiveness of those procedures should be continuously tested and related to extant knowledge about music instructional processes.

1.5 The Body of Knowledge in Music Education

The greatest amount of factual information currently available on the learning and teaching of music lies, thanks to music historians and theorists, in the music component of the triangle "music, learner, teacher." Music educators have at their disposal a substantial amount of information about composers, dates of compositions, musical styles, proper chord progressions, and how to perform on a variety of instruments. If we possessed only half as much information about the learner's perception of and responses to music as we have about the subject of music itself, the teaching process might be less guess work than seems to be the case at present.

Thus far, music educators do not have a comprehensive theory of music instruction. The profession has not reached the point of sharing an agreed upon explanation for specific musical behaviors that typically describe the music instructional process. There is, however, a substantial amount of research literature that may be viewed as the initial body of data from which laws about the learning and teaching of music may eventually be derived. A person who wishes to employ disciplined inquiry for the purpose of contributing to the development of a theory of music instruction must be familiar with that body of knowledge.

Currently, the research literature in music education covers a wide range of questions and addresses past events, present-day observations, as well as predictions for future developments. Research has been conducted on the sequence of learning tasks appropriate to children of different age groups as well as on the measurement of musical ability and achievement. Issues of aesthetics and aesthetic education have been addressed by a varied group of scholars in various disciplines; questions of musical preferences and taste have been investigated by music psychologists, educators, sociologist, and philosophers. Theories exist of how the brain functions and how it may process musical stimuli. The theories come from studies directly related to music as well as from studies in such areas as psychology, education, medicine, and neurology.

Modes of Inquiry

Over the years, music educators have approached research from three different perspectives. Each perspective reflects a particular mode of inquiry within which questions have been asked and techniques were developed to answer the questions. In this book, these modes are referred to as philosophical, historical, and empirical inquiry. They will be discussed in detail later. Suffice it to say here that whereas there are important differences in the techniques employed in each research mode, all of them share some striking commonalities.

The first is that of the basic meaning behind all three terms. All the terms have a reference to learnedness, wisdom, and experience. According to *The American Heritage Dictionary of the English Language* (1970), the Greek term *philosophos* means loving wisdom (philos: loving; sophos: wise). The Latin term *histor* means learned man. Empirical can be traced from the Latin *empiricus* or from the Greek *empeirikos, empeira,* and/or *empeiros,* all of which refer to experience in something—more specifically, the experiences that come from the senses (as opposed to experience from studying the past). A second shared characteristic between the three modes is that someone who wishes to employ any of them in an investigation is expected to adhere to the principles of logical thinking and to the verification or corroboration of evidence.

It should be noted that there are other classifications for the modes of inquiry than those proposed here. In 1972, Sidnell reviewed several of the classification systems researchers had proposed to use for studies in music education. Subsequently, he suggested four types of research, all of which were derived from the methodologies employed in the studies reviewed. The classifications were historical, descriptive, experimental, and philosophical. Phelps (1986) has suggested adding a fifth category—aesthetic inquiry. We believe that any of the classifications suggested by other writers are fully accounted for in the three categories proposed here.

Philosophical inquiry in music education has traditionally contributed to the analysis of musical thought and has raised questions about human behavior in relationship to music. Philosophers in music education have probed the constructs of aesthetic and creative thought, argued about the meaning of value in music, and attempted to develop "philosophies" of music education— that is, justifications and rationales for music as a subject in the schools and as a field of study (e.g., Reimer, 1970; Saffle, 1983; Schwadron, 1973; 1984). Frequently, such justifications and rationales have been positioned within the framework of music education as aesthetic education.

Historical inquiry in music education has been directed to the description of past music programs in the schools of various states, counties, and cities. It has traced the lives of particular music educators and has attempted to assess the effect those individuals have had on the advancement of music in the United States. Informative descriptions of the nature and content of that kind of research have been provided by Turrentine (1973) and Heller and Wilson (1982). A series of studies in comparative education have described educational systems across the world and determined their impact on music teaching in various countries in order to compare those findings with music education in the United States.

Empirical inquiry has been devoted to the study of the nature of musical talent, ability, achievements, attitudes, and preferences (for an overview of this kind of research, see Leonhard & Colwell, 1976). Attempts have been made to determine major characteristics of different teaching styles and effectiveness by systematic observation of music classrooms "in action." The relative merit of various teaching methods and techniques has thus been explored. Many empiricists in music education have investigated students' perceptions of sound, compared musically trained and untrained listeners' responses to music, and studied the effect of the socioeconomic background of the learner on musical achievement, preferences, and taste. Particularly in the area of perceptual research, several psychologists and systematic musicologists have contributed to the field of music education (Clynes, 1982; Deutsch, 1982; Dowling & Harwood, 1986; Moore, 1982; Pierce, 1983). Because of the multidisciplinary nature of music education, such efforts should be viewed as an important dimension of research in the field.

There are various survey articles published in the *Bulletin of the Council for Research in Music Education (CRME)* that give helpful insights into the current state of research in various areas pertinent to music education. Klemish (1973) reviewed research in elementary music education; Greenberg (1976) provided a review of research in early childhood education; Rainbow (1973) surveyed the status of research on instrumental music and Gonzo (1973) provided a similar synopsis for choral music; Nelson (1983) did the same more specifically for string teaching and performance. Similar reviews exist for research on

16

educational technology (Deihl & Partchey, 1973); evaluation (Whybrew, 1973); attitude and preference (Wapnick, 1976); creativity (Richardson, 1983); and child development (Andress, 1986; Katz, 1986; Simons, 1986; Zimmerman, 1986).

From the number of research publications currently available in music education it seems safe to say that the field does have a developing body of knowledge. However, because the field is still young its body of knowledge resembles that of other young fields: It appears as unordered bits and pieces of a giant puzzle rather than as the outline of the picture the puzzle is eventually to become. Much more time may have to pass before researchers in music sort out the pieces and attach principles of order to the myriads of seemingly unrelated observations. But, as with other fields of study, music educators have an obligation to try to explain the workings of their field and to expand their body of knowledge by the systematic analysis of human behavior in the realm of the learning and teaching of music.

Suggested Activities

1. Select an article of your choice that surveys the current status of research in a particular area within music education. Describe *in your own words* the essence of the article.

2. Choose one journal article from those referenced by the authors and determine the accuracy with which the author paraphrased the content of the publication.

3. Develop a list of issues in music education for which you can find reviews of research.

4. Identify some "sources of truth" from which current music teaching methods seem to have been developed.

5. Identify up to 10 statements about the teaching and learning of music that may be considered facts as agreed on by the profession.

Topics for Discussion

1. The common factors in all forms of research.

2. Discoveries throughout history that have altered our perspective of the universe.

3. Discoveries that have had an effect on music research.

4. The various ways of seeking the truth. The strengths and weaknesses in each approach.

5. The subject matter of music education.

6. Differences between theory and opinion.

Suggested Readings

Abeles, H. F., Hoffer, Ch. R., & Klotman, R. H. (1984). *Foundations of music education.* New York: Schirmer Books.

Allen, W. D. (1962). *Philosophies of music history: A study of general histories of music 1600–1960.* New York: Dover.

Barnes, S. H. (1982). *A cross-section of research in music education.* Washington, D.C.: University Press of America.

Behague, G. (Ed.) (1984). *Performance practice: Ethnomusicological perspectives.* Contributions in Intercultural and Comparative Studies, No. 12. Westport, CT: Greenwood Press.

Butts, R. E., & Hintikka, J. (Eds.) (1975). *Historical and philosophical dimensions of logic, methodology and philosophy of science.* Part 4 of the Proceedings of the Fifth International Congress of Logic, Methodology, and Philosophy of Science, London, Ontario, Canada, 1975. Dordrecht, Holland and Boston, U.S.A.: D. Reidel Publishing Company.

Cady, H. L. (1969). A conference on research in music education. *Council for Research in Music Education, 18* (Fall), 10–21.

Critchley, M., & Henson, R. A. (Eds.) (1978). *Music and the brain: Studies in the neurology of music.* London: William Heinemann Medical Books Limited.

Crocker, R. (1963/1964). Pythagorean mathematics and music. *Journal of Aesthetics and Art Criticism, 22,* 189–198; 325–335.

Dasilva, F. B., Blasi, A., & Dees, D. (1984). *The sociology of music.* Notre Dame, IN: University of Notre Dame Press.

Downs, R. (1982). *Landmarks in science: Hippocrates to Carson.* Littleton, CO: Libraries Unlimited.

Falck, R., & Rice, T. (Eds.) (1982). *Cross-cultural perspectives on music.* Toronto: University of Toronto Press.

Goldstein, M., & Goldstein, I. (1984). *The experience of science: An interdisciplinary approach.* New York: Plenum Press.

Losee, J. (1980). *A historical introduction to the philosophy of science* (2nd ed.). Oxford: Oxford University Press.

Lundin, R. W. (1986). *An objective psychology of music* (3rd ed.). Malabar, FL: Robert E. Krieger Publishing Company.

***Musik und Zahl* (1976).** Interdisziplinäre Beiträge zum Grenzbereich zwischen Musik und Mathematik. Herausgegeben von Günter Schnitzler. Bonn: Verlag für systematische Musikwissenschaft GmbH.

Peters, G. D., & Miller, R. F. (1982). *Music teaching and learning.* New York: Longman.

Pirsig, R. M. (1974). *Zen and the art of motorcycle maintenance: An inquiry into values.* Toronto: Bantam Books.

Reimer, B. (1985). Toward a more scientific approach to music education. *Council for Research in Music Education, 83* (Summer), 1–22.

Sachs, C. (1962). *The wellsprings of music.* (J. Kunst, Ed.). The Hague: Martinus Nijhoff.

Warnock, G. J. (1967). *The philosophy of perception.* London: Oxford Press.

REFERENCES

Agnew, N. Mck., & Pyke, S. W. (1978). *The science game: An introduction to research in the behavioral sciences* (2nd ed.). Englewood Cliffs, NJ: Prentice-Hall.

The American Heritage Dictionary of the English Language (1970). (4th ed.). New York: American Heritage Publishing Co.

Andress, B. (1986). Toward an integrated developmental theory for early childhood music education. *Council for Research in Music Education, 86* (Winter), 10–17.

Backus, J. (1977). *The acoustical foundations of music* (2nd ed.). New York, NY: Norton.

Berger, P. L., & Luckmann, T. (1967). *The social construction of reality: A treatise on the sociology of knowledge.* Garden City, NY: Doubleday.

Breisach, E. (1983). *Historiography: Ancient, medieval, and modern.* Chicago: University of Chicago Press.

Broudy, H. S., Ennis, R. H., & Krimerman, L. I. (Eds.) (1973). *Philosophy of educational research.* New York: John Wiley.

Buchdahl, G. (1969). *Metaphysics and the philosophy of science: the classical origins. Descartes to Kant.* Oxford: Blackwell.

Burke, J. (1978). *Connections.* Boston: Little, Brown.

Cho, G. J. (1975). *Some non-Chinese elements in the ancient Japanese music: An analytic-comparative study.* Unpublished doctoral dissertation, Northwestern University, Evanston, IL.

Clynes, M. (Ed.) (1982). *Music, mind, and brain: The neuropsychology of music.* New York: Plenum Press.

Deihl, N. C., & Partchey, K. C. (1973). Status of research: Educational technology in music education. *Council for Research in Music Education, 35* (Winter), 18–29.

Dessel, N. F., Nehrich, R. B., Jr., & Voran, G. I. (1973). *Science and human destiny.* New York: McGraw-Hill.

Deutsch, D. (Ed.) (1982). *The psychology of music.* New York: Academic Press.

Dowling, W. J., & Harwood, D. L. (1986). *Music cognition.* New York: Academic Press.

Farnsworth, P. R. (1969). *The social psychology of music* (2nd ed.). Ames, IA: Iowa State University Press.

Fischer, R. B. (1971). *Science, man and society.* Philadelphia: W. B. Saunders.

Galileo's 'heresies' still under study, Pope says (Rome, Reuters). (1983, May 10). *New York Times,* p. A12.

Gonzo, C. (1973). Research in choral music. *Council for Research in Music Education, 33* (Summer), 21–33.

Good, C. V., Barr, A. S., & Scates, D. E. (1941). *The methodology of educational research.* New York, NY: Appleton-Century-Crofts, Inc.

Greenberg, M. (1976). Research in music in early childhood education: A survey with recommendations. *Council for Research in Music Education, 45* (Winter), 1–20.

Guthrie, W. K. C. (1971). *The Sophists.* Cambridge, England: Cambridge University Press.

Heller, G., & Wilson, B. (1982). Historical research in music education: A prolegomenon. *Council for Research in Music Education, 69* (Winter), 1–20.

Helmholtz, H. L. F. von (1954). *On the sensations of tone as a physiological basis for the theory of music* (2nd English ed.; trans. A. J. Ellis). New York, NY: Dover.

Henry, N. B. (Ed.) (1958). *Basic concepts in music education.* The 57th yearbook of the National Society for the Study of Education. Chicago, IL: The National Society for the Study of Education. Distributed by University of Chicago Press.

Katz, L. (1986). Current perspectives on child development. *Council for Research in Music Education, 86* (Winter), 1–9.

Klemish, J. (1973). A review of recent research in elementary music education. *Council for Research in Music Education, 34* (Fall), 23–40.

Kline, M. (1985). *Mathematics and the search for knowledge.* Oxford: Oxford University Press.

Kuhn, T. S. (1975). *The structure of scientific revolutions* (2nd ed., enl.; 6th impr.). Chicago: University of Chicago Press.

Leedy, P. D. (1985). *Practical research: Planning and design* (3rd ed.). New York: Macmillan; London: Collier Macmillan.

Leonhard, Ch., & Colwell, R. (1976). Research in music education. *Council for Research in Music Education, 49* (Winter), 1–30.

Lippman, E. A. (1977). *A humanistic philosophy of music.* New York, NY: New York University Press.

Lovejoy, A. O. (1978). *The great chain of being* (14th printing). Cambridge, MA–London, England: Harvard University Press.

Margolis, J. (Ed.) (1978). *Philosophy looks at the arts. Contemporary readings in aesthetics* (rev. ed.). Philadelphia: Temple University Press.

McClain, E. G. (1978). *The myth of invariance. The origin of the gods, mathematics and music from the Rg Veda to Plato.* (Intr. S. Levarie; Ed. P. A. Heelan). Boulder and London: Shambhala.

Moore, B. C. J. (1982). *An introduction to the psychology of hearing* (2nd ed.). New York: Academic Press.

Nelson, D. J. (1983). String teaching and performance: A review of research findings. *Council for Research in Music Education, 74* (Spring), 39–46.

Pfrogner, H. (1981). *Lebendige Tonwelt: Zum Phänomen Musik.* (2. durchgesehene Auflage). München: Langen Müller.

Phelps, R. (1986). *A guide to research in music education* (3rd. ed.). Metuchen, NJ: Scarecrow Press.

Pierce, J. R. (1983). *The science of musical sound.* New York: Scientific American Books.

Popper, K. R. (1968). *Conjectures and refutations: The growth of scientific knowledge.* Harper Torchbooks. New York: Harper and Row.

Rainbow, E. L. (1973). Instrumental music: Recent research and considerations for future investigations. *Council for Research in Music Education, 33* (Summer), 8–20.

Reimer, B. (1970). *A philosophy of music education.* Englewood Cliffs, NJ: Prentice Hall.

Richardson, C. P. (1983). Creativity research in music education: A review. *Council for Research in Music Education, 74* (Spring), 1–21.

Rowell, L. E. (1983). *Thinking about music: An introduction to the philosophy of music.* Amherst, MA: University of Massachusetts Press.

Russell, B. (1945). *A history of Western philosophy* (14th paperback printing). New York, NY: Simon and Schuster.

Russell, B. (1976). *Human knowledge. Its scope and limits.* (Copyright renewed 1976 by Alton Felton.) New York, NY: Simon and Schuster.

Sachs, C. (1943). *The rise of music in the ancient world.* New York, NY: Norton.

Sachs, C. (1953). *Rhythm and tempo: A study in music history.* New York, NY: Norton.

Sachs, C. (1955). *Our musical heritage: A short history of music* (2nd ed.). Englewood Cliffs, NJ: Prentice-Hall.

Saffle, M. (1983). Aesthetic education in theory and practice: a review of recent research. *Council for Research in Music Education, 74* (Spring), 22–38.

Sax, G. (1979). *Foundations of educational research* (2nd ed. of book formerly titled: *Empirical foundations of educational research*). Englewood Cliffs, NJ: Prentice-Hall.

Schwadron, A. A. (1973). Philosophy in music education: State of the research. *Council for Research in Music Education, 34* (Fall), 41–53.

Schwadron, A. A. (1984). Philosophy and aesthetics in music education: A critique of the research. *Council for Research in Music Education, 79* (Summer), 11–32.

Sidnell, R. (1972). The dimensions of research in music education. *Council for Research in Music Education, 29* (Summer), 17–27.

Simons, G. (1986). Early childhood musical development: A survey of selected research. *Council for Research in Music Education, 86* (Winter), 36–52.

Smith, F. J. (Ed.) (1976). *In search of musical method.* London: Gordon and Breach Science Publishers.

Toynbee, A. (1972). *A study of history.* (New edition revised and abridged by the author and Jane Caplan). New York, NY: Weathervane Books.

Turrentine, E. M. (1973). Historical research in music education. *Council for Research in Music Education, 33* (Summer), 1–7.

Vatican reviews Galileo's conviction for heresy (Rome, United Press International). (1980, October 23). *New York Times,* p. A5.

Wapnick, J. (1976). A review of research on attitude and preference. *Council for Research in Music Education, 48* (Fall), 1–20.

Whybrew, W. E. (1973). Research in evaluation in music education. *Council for Research in Music Education, 35* (Winter), 9–17.

Winckel, F. (1967). *Music, sound and sensation. A modern exposition.* (Trans. from German by T. Binkley). New York, NY: Dover.

Zimmerman, M. Pflederer (1986). Music development in middle childhood: A summary of selected research studies. *Council for Research in Music Education, 86* (Winter), 18–37.

Chapter Two

The Researcher

2.1 Introduction

As stated in chapter 1, researchers in music education have traditionally contributed to the field by means of historical, philosophical, and empirical inquiry. Thus, in addition to being teachers, music educators may also be philosophers, historians, and/or empirical researchers. They search for knowledge about the nature of musical behavior, look inquisitively at the learning and teaching processes in music, wonder about those processes, and ask questions about them.

The perspective from which the inquisitive person poses a question or finds its answer generally determines which of the three research modes is chosen in order to conduct an investigation. Philosophers study ideas and constructs of thought and employ logic and rhetoric in order to reason out answers to their questions. Historians ask questions about human behavior from a perspective of the past and seek to determine causes and effects of historically significant individuals and events. Empirical researchers, sometimes referred to as empiricists, investigate human behavior from the standpoint of present-day actions, behaviors, and events that are visible and, thus, observable.

Although there are important differences between the three modes of inquiry, the thought process is roughly the same in all of them—a cycle that moves from looking and guessing to examining the truth of an answer in a systematic way. From such an examination, a revision of the initial research question might become necessary. The revision, however, may lead to the development of additional questions. This research loop of looking, guessing, examining, and revising is the essence of scientific inquiry. Its method employs observation (*look*), hypothesizing (*guess*), description and/or experimentation (*examine*), and conclusions (*revise*). Regardless of what specific methodology researchers choose, the search for knowledge should always be rooted in the cycle of asking questions and examining the truthfulness of their answers. It is this cyclical nature of asking questions that makes research a process rather than an activity with a definite ending point.

In developing methodologies appropriate to their questions, good researchers employ equally intuition, analytical skills, technical skills and knowledge, imagination, and personal experience. In doing so, they should define their terms clearly and classify all observations pertinent to the question according to explicitly stated principles. The results obtained are to be presented in an organized manner and conclusions drawn from them should then be related back to the research purpose.

Philosophers, Historians, and Empiricists in Music Education

If all good research can be characterized by the degree to which it adheres to modes of scientific inquiry, one might consider it an unfortunate trend among music education researchers that information provided by one group of researchers tends to be considered irrelevant to the work of another group. Empiricists often criticize the methodological "sloppiness" of philosophers and historians, while philosophers call empiricists narrow minded because they study only what is observable. Historians point to the fact that empiricists may "reinvent the wheel" when they study old questions using new methods. Such trivial bickering among researchers in music education can only bring harm to the profession. Good researchers ignore all narrow-minded debates over whether one mode of inquiry is better than another. Instead, they employ the best of all knowledge available to them to investigate the laws and principles governing a field of study.

Philosophers explain their own understanding of the causes of things through methods of logically stringent argumentation. In such argumentation, the strictest rules of axiomatic reasoning are utilized as much as the powers of rhetoric, dogma, speculation, and persuasion. Bertrand Russell (1945) places the philosopher somewhere between the theologian and the scientist when he calls philosophy

> . . . something intermediate between theology and science. Like theology, it consists of speculations on matters as to which definite knowledge has, so far, been unascertainable; but like science, it appeals to human reason rather than authority, whether that of tradition or that of revelation. All *definite* knowledge— so I should contend—belongs to science; all *dogma* as to what surpasses definite knowledge belongs to theology. But between theology and science there is a No Man's Land, exposed to attack from both sides; this No Man's Land is philosophy. (p.xiii)

The historian inquires not so much about ideas, as does the philosopher, but about observable things of the past. The nature of past events is examined and attempts are made to establish cause-and-effect relationships between them. Known facts, statements, and actions of previous times, documented through written evidence or the spoken word of witnesses, serve as the data base from which historical knowledge is derived and conclusions about actions and behaviors of preceeding generations are drawn. Therefore, a good historian should master both the methods of logic and the methods of empirical research, just as a good philosopher should also be a good historian.

Rather than investigating past events, the empiricist assesses the nature of present-day actions, behaviors, and statements of people by conducting observations about them. The term *observation* generally has two connotations:

1. An observation may be any form of evidence that supports the truthfulness—that is, the factuality of a statement. The evidence can be based on test or survey measurements, common sense reporting, or shared experience.

2. An observation may refer to a specific technique in which overt behavior may be recorded according to prescribed procedures. This type of observation is generally referred to as systematic observation.

To distinguish between the two types of observation in research, we will always refer to the second type as systematic observation.

Traditionally, observations about musical behavior have been gathered not only by music educators but also by researchers with training in such disciplines as physics, psychology, education, and sociology. In the first half of this century, important contributions were made by Seashore (1938), Mainwaring (1947), and Jersild and Bienstock (1931)—all of them psychologists by training and profession.

The reasons for the early interdisciplinary efforts in music education research may lie in the way music education developed as an area within which doctoral degrees were granted. For much of the early part of this century, the study of music education in the United States took place either at a two-year normal school or at a four-year teachers college. Advanced degrees in music were largely reserved for musicologists. Thus, persons who expressed interests in nonhistorical research activities related to music had to pursue degrees and research in other fields. The advanced degree in music education and, with it, research in areas other than history was a creation of the late 1930s, and was accelerated after 1945. A research journal for music education did not exist until 1953, although Seashore began the publication of *Iowa Studies in the Psychology of Music* as early as 1932. With the advent of college graduate degrees in music education came the training of research skills in that field.

Music education, however, is not necessarily in a unique position when it acknowledges that major contributions to its body of knowledge have come from people outside the field. The sharing of information across areas occurs in many other disciplines as well. An early example in the history of the United States is that of Benjamin Franklin, a printer by trade, who contributed significantly to the understanding of electricity as well as to the flow of the gulf stream currents (see Clark, 1983, pp. 54, 269, 300, 415–416). An example more closely related to educational concerns is that of Jean Piaget, who was trained as a biologist, proclaimed himself to be a genetic epistemologist and, in that role, contributed considerably to the advancement of educational psychology.

Both Franklin and Piaget shared the common bond of wanting to know things that resided outside their primary area of employment or training. Rather than waiting for answers from "the experts," curiosity and inquisitiveness compelled them to seek the answers on their own. More importantly, neither Franklin nor Piaget shied away from publishing what they considered to be the correct answers. Both men possessed the three most important prerequisites for conducting research: they had inquisitive and disciplined minds, sensed relationships between various areas or fields of knowledge, and they shared their insights in writing.

Even if researchers in music education have not yet reached the stature of people like Franklin or Piaget, the field has had, and still has, a group of people—historians, philosophers, and empiricists alike—who have exhibited over the years the very attributes (described in the previous paragraph) that characterize good researchers.

2.2 The Development of an Inquisitive and Disciplined Mind

As suggested in chapter 1, answers given by experts in the field generally reflect what a profession has accepted to be true. Inquisitive persons tend not to be satisfied with the status quo of knowledge as passed on by the experts. Instead, inquisitive individuals probe the truth of expert opinion by relying on their own expertise when investigating a given problem. Such self-reliance on and trust in one's own abilities are important personal traits in the research process. These personal traits are not always adequately fostered in the professional training of musicians.

A substantial proportion of the people who work in the music profession—either as teachers, performers, music therapists, music theorists, or musicologists, or as teachers of teachers—have devoted significant amounts of time and effort learning to sing or play one or more musical instruments. Many hours have been spent in both classroom and practice room developing skills of keyboard harmony, sight singing, dictation, part writing, and conducting. If one calculates all the time spent in this type of skill development, it is probably safe to say that the professional training of a musician focuses far more on the development of musical-technical skills than on the skills necessary for critical thinking and reasoning.

Typically, the training of technical skills in music takes place in a teacher-student relationship that resembles the master-apprentice situation common to many areas of the skilled trades. From medical surgery to tool and die making, from plumbing to gourmet cooking, the master accepts an apprentice or intern, with the obligation to guide that person in the development of skills considered essential for the successful execution of specific tasks. In music, the applied lesson is one such situation where the task of seeking answers and solutions to specific performance problems is delegated to the teacher. The student is the apprentice who is guided by the teacher (master) in the acquisition of performing skills. In the lesson, the student performs and the teacher critiques that performance in order to improve it. The student accepts the critique as long as there is a bond of trust with the teacher. Learning is taking place. The apprentice believes and trusts in the master because the master—in due time—will be instrumental in turning the apprentice into a master as well.

Learning from the word of experts is also possible in the many workshops that music educators sponsor, workshops that are designed to permit the master teacher to demonstrate classroom instructional techniques and to suggest appropriate student activities. As long as those who attend the workshops have faith in the authority of the clinician, they will assume they have acquired the truth about how to teach music to children. Indeed, if the information offered is based on or supported by systematically gathered evidence, learning from an authority or expert can be a very efficient and direct way to acquire information. It is not unusual, however, that the information provided by the experts via workshops and master classes is at best supported by common sense reasoning and, more frequently, supported only by personal opinion.

These illustrations are not intended to be a critique of applied music instruction and what transpires within the teaching studios, nor is it a criticism of in-service workshops. Rather, we wish to point out how skill learning in music may tend to make musicians accept as fact the word of the authority. Because of the conditioned admiration of and respect for the expert, musicians sometimes find it difficult to trust their own judgments and insights into things. They hesitate to break away from the mold of expert experiences and to raise questions about the veracity of an authority statement or one derived from common sense.

There is little doubt that the pedagogical system musicians have used for gaining information and developing performance skills and knowledge has in many instances worked well. But the system has also carried with it a serious danger: the risk of believing that the master musician or master teacher knows everything there is to know about music, music performance, and music teaching. Over the past few decades, various music subjects have frequently been taught as a collection of irrefutable facts never to be questioned or changed. Educational institutions, such as universities and colleges, have focused their teaching more on what appears to be hard-core fact than on how much is uncertain; little is done to develop a student's skill to explore and seek answers to the multitude of questions that still characterize the body of knowledge in most, if not all, fields of study.

Whereas skill training in music does not seem comparable to the acquisition of an intellectually inquisitive mind, it does seem comparable to the acquisition of a disciplined mind because most music students and experienced musicians recognize the necessity of the daily routine of practice. At its best, daily practice helps musicians improve techniques and skills vital for an acceptable level of performance; at its worst, practice helps stem the tide of decay.

Good musical practice is a constant search for improved performance quality through self-evaluation. One listens critically to one's own performance, demands one's own best efforts, and continuously employs realistic judgment about the quality of one's work. When errors occur, one asks why they happened and how they might be remedied. So it is with disciplined thinking. It, too, demands constant self-criticism and self-evaluation. And just as performance outcome is the yardstick for successful musical practice, so quality rather than quantity of effort is the yardstick for successful intellectual pursuits.

A second similarity between the musically disciplined mind and the intellectually disciplined mind lies in the way an experienced musician prepares a composition for performance and a researcher prepares a project. Performers must understand the overall purpose of a composition, possess or be able to acquire the techniques necessary to "bring it off," discern the focal point or peak of the work, then have a plan of action to interpret what they believe to be the composer's intent. So it is with researchers. They must know the purpose of their study and the specific questions to be answered; they must have a plan for finding the answers; and they must have the skills to transmit the findings to others. All these aspects require careful and critical attention if a researcher is to gain the approval of his or her colleagues.

Most musicians have attended recitals where a performer's technique was dazzling, yet somehow the results of the performance made little musical sense. The ability to *do* stood in the way of the performer's ability to *say* something. A similar situation is often found in research where a person may provide reams of historical data but does not seem to find a way to piece things together in a logical cause-and-effect relationship. Or an investigation may shine with the brilliant execution of a seemingly complicated statistical analysis, providing yards of printed-out tables and numbers, but offering no conclusions. In both music performance and research, good technique is important, but it should never override the idea one wishes to communicate. Additionally, enthusiasm and personal integrity are as important in carrying out a research project as they are in the presentation of a good musical performance.

2.3 The Ability to Sense and Seek Relationships Between Various Areas or Fields of Study

In the introduction to this chapter, reference was made to psychologists Seashore, Mainwaring, Jersild, and Bienstock, who contributed significantly to the body of knowledge in music education. Since the time their contributions were made, the relationship between music education research and music psychology has continued to be very close. Research findings in music psychology are almost automatically accepted as important for the advancement of the field of music education because both fields look at rather similar questions about human behavior. Equally close connections may be said to exist between music education and general education, educational as well as developmental psychology, as scholars in each of those fields have contributed important ideas to music education. The Ann Arbor Symposia I, II, and III are cases in point. Their purpose was to bring together psychologists and music educators so that they might discuss the significance of cognitive theories for formulating a theory of musical development. Such a theory, it was hoped, would have the potential of leading toward a theory of music instruction.

Aside from intentionally developed relationships between closely aligned disciplines, relationships may also emerge by chance. Such is the case when an invention, made yet ignored in one century, is rediscovered decades later and becomes a major link in advancing scientific discoveries. An example of this point is the story told by Burke (1978) about the contributions a scholar in the second century made toward advancing technology in the 9th century.

The scholar was Ptolemy (AD 122–151), who developed a measuring tool called the astrolabe. With it, the same star could be located and observed regardless of changes in the viewer's geographical positioning. Ptolemy wrote a 13-volume treatise on the stars as documentation of his observations. All but one copy of the treatise was lost to the Western world during the sacking of Rome (4th–6th centuries). The one surviving copy was transported to a monastery in Jundi Shapur, Iran, and translated into Arabic. In the mid-13th century, Alfonso the Wise, a Christian king of Spain, set up a school in Toledo to translate the Arabic books into Latin; 700 years after Ptolemy developed his astrolabe and made his observations about the constellation of the stars, his work was rediscovered and his measuring tool as well as his measurements were made available to navigators in the Western world.

Whether good ideas generated in one field of study find their way into other fields by serendipitous findings or by carefully planned design, music educators should remain open to both possibilities since they are likely to encounter both of them in the process of conducting research. But even though different fields of study may share common concerns and observations about human behavior, the methods by which to investigate such concerns may differ from one field to another. Thus, if researchers from one discipline want to investigate questions from the perspective of another discipline, they must learn to master the technical know-how of that discipline.

Sensing Commonalities Between Observations and Events

It does not always take a highly trained researcher to sense commonalities between things. Sometimes, commonalities may be found while one is browsing through museums and libraries, maintaining an open and inquisitive mind and a curiosity for relationships extant in the concerns of people of past civilizations and those expressed in current times.

To illustrate: The British Museum holds a substantial Sumerian collection. In that collection are some display cases containing several small clay tablets with cuneiform writing on them. The tags identifying the holdings describe the tablets as legal letters and documents. According to the translation provided by the Museum staff, one of those letters is a legal document sent by a young man to his wife. In it he announces that their marriage of one year is to be terminated and how he intends to divide their common property. The ancient document reflects concerns of Sumerian life that are remarkably similar to those currently experienced by many people in the 20th century. Likewise, the Egyptian collection of the British Museum contains, among other things, papyrus scrolls that document the writings of an Egyptian physician from about 1000 B.C. The writings are in fact a long treatise on the development of remedies to cure—hemorrhoids!

Those who watch television commercials may sense relationships between the concerns of modern people and their predecessors nearly 3,000 years ago. Is there any reason to hold the parochial view that the concerns of people in former times differ from our problems in the 20th century?

In his three-volume history, the French historian Fernand Braudel (1981–1982) illustrated most admirably the commonalities of concerns in different centuries by focusing his description of the time from the 15th century to the 18th century not on wars and politicians but on the psychological concerns of the *people* of the time. All three volumes are fascinating chronicles of the everyday life in those times as Braudel shows the similarity of human needs then and now. From reading such literature and from one's own encounters with one's cultural heritage, one could tentatively ask the broad question: Is there stability in both the psychological needs and concerns of all people throughout all ages? As stated, this question may be too broad to research, but if one senses relationships between things, one should not hesitate to ask even the biggest and most daring questions about them. Such an inquiring attitude may in many instances lead to more specific questions from which important research endeavors and findings may result.

The most direct way of learning about commonalities of thought among several disciplines is staying abreast of the literature in various fields of study. Because music education has so many concerns and is so broad in scope, researchers need to become familiar with those fields of study that interact with their own. In the course of reading, informed music educators should therefore be well-read in the fine arts, the liberal arts, and the social and natural sciences. While beginning researchers in music education may argue that they have barely time to read the literature in their own field, much less that in another, the problem is not insurmountable as curiosity tends to transcend being curious about a single issue. Reading in a wide range of fields can be both pleasurable and informative. One takes mental and written note of all the reviewed materials, collects and files the insights gained from that reading, and observes over time some of the consistent patterns of thought that may exist in seemingly unrelated areas. Many insights and research ideas have come from such reading across the disciplines.

Seeking Contacts with Colleagues in Other Disciplines

Since music education is a very broad field of study, its research concerns are, in most instances, interdisciplinary in nature. For example, a person wishing to investigate the properties (elements) of sound may be working in the areas of music as well as physics; someone interested in how music teachers perceive their role in society will be working in an area of sociological inquiry; a researcher wishing to investigate a muscle response to a perceived sound will of necessity deal with some of the concerns of neurology. Any investigation in music education that touches on the concerns of another field of study must be conducted in a way that meets professional criteria acceptable to both music education and the external area. This might entail a researcher's training in specific techniques that pertain to the method of inquiry used in the external area. Extensive reading or even the taking of courses in the external area may be advisable. For example, the intensive study of interview techniques may be necessary for the purpose of oral history. Studies in anatomy may be essential if the investigation identifies muscular responses to music; the knowledge of acoustical measurement may be mandatory if a study centers on qualitative differences in musical sound. Likewise, training in philosophical discourse is necessary if a person attempts to tackle research problems involving the use of logical inference.

When pursuing research on interdisciplinary topics, music educators should not only be familiar with the literature in the external area and know its standard research methods; they should also seek contacts with active researchers in that area. In fact, it is generally a good idea to discuss a research project with colleagues inside and outside one's own field. A critical discussion is likely to improve the quality of the final product; in addition, interested colleagues tend to offer expertise and the use of sophisticated technology if they can also gain information from the investigation. For example, the studies of Isley (1972), Newton (1972), and White (1972) could not have been undertaken without the assistance of an interested physician-researcher. In a similar situation a neurologist aided Wallace (1985) in his investigation, while an otolaryngologist provided the medical expertise and advanced technical equipment to aid Peters' study (1984).

All the studies mentioned provided useful information to all the parties who were actively involved in the pursuit of knowledge. After all, research is a quest for an explanation of our being and our universe. Understanding the work of others and searching for commonalities and similarities within and among the findings of other researchers can aid in the search for that explanation.

2.4 The Sharing of Ideas: The Publication

The third trademark of a researcher—that of publishing one's research results and conclusions—is a responsibility as well as a professional obligation. While many people criticize the so-called "publish or perish" syndrome, publishing remains the main avenue for the dissemination of information. It may be compared to the professional musician's responsibility to perform in public. Public performances are displays of abilities, and they carry with them the risk of failure. On the other hand, the musician gains approval if other musicians recognize the person's musicianship and high level of performance skills.

Researchers who display, in writing, their skills of critical thinking look for the same peer approval as do professional musicians. Submitting one's work to critical judgment by peers indicates a willingness to share publicly mistakes as well as successes. That willingness takes courage and personal persistence, attributes that, when coupled with curiosity and the desire to search continually for quality, become the hallmark of a good researcher. Because the primary purpose of publishing is the communication of ideas, it is also important for researchers to express themselves in a precise and straightforward manner. This may be achieved if simple language is used and if all trains of thought are logically cohesive.

Leedy (1985) has advised:

> Cliches, colloquialisms, slang, jargon and the gibberish of any group or profession usually obscures thoughts. The evidence of the lazy mind is the irresponsible use of professional jargon. Those who employ it do so usually because they feel that it impresses or that it adds importance to what they are saying.

> The thought's the thing. And when it is most clear, it is clothed with simple words, concrete nouns, and expressive verbs. Every student would do well to study how the great writers and poets set their thoughts in words. They have much to say by way of illustration to those who have trouble in putting their own thoughts on paper. (p.58)

Newman (1976, p. 6) hypothesizes that simple things tend to be made more complicated than necessary by the employment of jargon. There is, after all, always a chance that others outside the field may understand how simple things really are! Jargon, Newman contends, thus becomes a protective device to keep the uninitiated on the outside from looking in.

In our view, a difference should be made between jargon, or verbiage, and what can be described as the technical language of a field. Technical language derives from the subject matter under consideration and carries rather precise definitions for those who work within that field. People in music, for example, generally understand the meaning of the terms pitch, timbre, or barline. The field of study has defined these terms. To say that something is significant in a statistical sense is technical language because it is defined and precisely understood by those who work with statistics. To talk about creativity, aesthetic or "meaningful" experiences, appreciation, "a heavy player," the "whole" child, or the production of a "full, pure tone" is to employ jargon if these terms have either not been defined at all, have been inadequately defined, or are misused.

Research articles, textbooks, opinion-based articles, and even philosophical treatises abound with that type of jargon in which unclear thinking is disguised by the use of "big" terms that intimidate the readers. For fear of exposing what may be their own ignorance, readers tend to shy away from criticizing jargon. One feels foolish not to understand, when in fact the lack of understanding stems from the writer, who should have been clear, defined all terms, and employed unambiguous language.

All fields use jargon, and it is perhaps difficult for anyone to omit it completely. But it would be wise for writers to describe and explain their ideas as clearly and precisely as possible. If the ideas are of value, the language used to transmit them should be intelligible to all who have a potential interest in that field. Moreover, most good research ideas are simple in content even though the efforts to study them may be complicated.

2.5 Summary

Ideally, researchers in music education share important bonds regardless of whether they favor the philosophical, historical, or empirical mode of inquiry. They conduct research as a complementary activity to teaching; they take a disciplined and analytical approach toward the discovery of how people of all ages learn and respond to music; and, most importantly, they love the pursuit of knowledge. We therefore stated in chapter 1 that philosophers, historians, and empiricists in music education share with their colleagues in the social and natural sciences the desire to know the unknown and to probe the accuracy of accepted facts. The questions music educators raise seek to address knowledge about the learning-teaching process in music. Answers to the questions are sought in ways that are acceptable to the research community. In sharing found answers with the interested public, a person may contribute to the body of knowledge in music education. Any research that adds information to and helps confirm already existing knowledge about the learning-teaching processes in music may therefore be called a contribution to music education.

Contributions to the body of knowledge in a field of study demand careful and critical attention to *all* aspects of an investigation. A brilliant technical display demands an equally brilliant intellectual conclusion or interpretation. The inception of the purpose of the investigation, guided by a combination of intuitive and analytical thinking, the selection of the techniques to be employed in carrying out the investigation, and the interpretation of the findings, must be quality-controlled because all aspects must be in balance if a project is to be successful.

Suggested Activities

1. Develop a list of disciplines other than music that can contribute to knowledge about the learning and teaching of music. State broad topics

that are subjects of research in those disciplines but may also be considered crucial to the body of knowledge in music education.

2. Browse through some professional journals not in music and music education and determine the degree of difficulty you may have in understanding the technical language in those journals.

3. Analyze a variety of journals/magazines in music and music education with regard to the degree to which they employ technical language versus verbiage. Where, in your judgment, verbiage was used, develop some alternative ways of wording the content in question.

4. Keep a daily log of the amount of time you practice your instrument.

5. Keep a daily log of the amount of time you devote to reading both for school and for fun.

Topics for Discussion

1. The disciplined mind.
2. Connecting links between music education and other fields.
3. The importance of professional dialogue.
4. Factors that influence investigative methods in music education.
5. Interdisciplinary efforts in research.
6. Techniques versus ideas.

Suggested Readings

Froehlich, H. C., Paul, S. J., & Rainbow, E. L. (1983). Researchers and teachers in music education: Where is the connection? *UPDATE*, 2 (1), 17–21.

Hofstadter, D. R. (1979). *Gödel, Escher, Bach: An eternal golden braid.* New York: Vintage Books.

Lefrancois, G. R. (1982). *Psychological theories and human learning: Kongor's report* (2nd ed.). Monterey, CA: Brooks/Cole.

Thomas, L. (1983). *Late night thoughts on listening to Mahler's ninth symphony.* New York: Viking Press.

REFERENCES

Braudel, F. (1981–1982). *Civilization and capitalism, 15th–18th century.* (S. Reynolds, trans., rev.). (Vol. I: The structures of everyday life: The limits of the possible. Vol. II: The wheels of commerce. Vol. III: The perspective of the world. [©1984]). New York, NY: Harper and Row.

Burke, J. (1978). *Connections.* Boston: Little, Brown.

Clark, R. W. (1983). *Benjamin Franklin: A biography.* New York: Random House.

Isley, C. L. (1972). A theory of brasswind embouchure based upon facial anatomy, electromyographic kinesiology, and brasswind embouchure pedagogy (Doctoral dissertation, North Texas State University, 1972). *Dissertation Abstracts International, 33* (8), 3956A.

Jersild, A. T., & Bienstock, S. F. (1931). The influence of training on the vocal ability of three-year-old children. *Child Development, 2,* 292–298.

Leedy, P. D. (1985). *Practical research: Planning and design* (3rd ed.). New York: Macmillan.

Mainwaring, J. (1947). The assessment of musical ability. *British Journal of Educational Psychology, 17,* 83–96.

Newman, E. (1976). *A civil tongue.* Indianapolis: Bobbs-Merrill.

Newton, W. J. (1972). The activity of certain facial muscles in the B^b clarinet embouchure: An exploratory study utilizing electromyography (Doctoral dissertation, North Texas State University, 1972). *Dissertation Abstracts International, 33* (8), 4460A.

Peters, J. (1984). *An exploratory study of laryngeal movements during performance on an alto saxophone.* Unpublished master's thesis, North Texas State University, Denton, TX.

Russell, B. (1945). *A history of Western philosophy* (14th paperback printing). New York, NY: Simon and Schuster.

Seashore, C. E. (1938). *Psychology of music.* New York, NY: McGraw-Hill.

Wallace, J. (1985). *An investigation of extrinsic laryngeal muscle response to auditory stimulation.* Unpublished doctoral dissertation, North Texas State University, Denton, TX.

White, E. A. (1972). A comparison of labial mouthpiece pressure and electromyographic potentials of selected facial muscles in trumpet playing (Doctoral dissertation, Columbia Teachers College, 1972). *Dissertation Abstracts International, 33* (8), 3977A.

PART TWO

The Stage of Orientation and Planning

Part 2 addresses orientation and planning, the first step in doing research. In this phase, one becomes thoroughly familiar with the content of the field and identifies questions about its body of knowledge. Skills of critical reading must be applied to a large selection of professional literature. A thorough familiarity with all university library resources, references, indices, and techniques of computer data searches is therefore mandatory. Techniques of note taking should be mastered.

Following this phase of broadening one's knowledge of the field, the researcher needs to focus all subsequent reading on the selection of a research area and purpose. That procedure is a continuous exercise of reading and reflecting about increasingly more narrowly defined research ideas. It is a funneling process from the general to the specific. To the degree that the researcher's knowledge of the field broadens, so the research area and subsequent purpose become increasingly more defined and narrower in scope.

In preparing one's research, the activities of reasoning and writing go hand in hand with those of reading. The rationale for the purpose of study is thought out and the research problems/questions are formulated. The purpose, rationale, and research problems serve as the intellectual foundation of the intended investigation. Thoughts about what mode of inquiry to employ are incorporated into that foundation. Consequently, in the final phase of the orientation and planning stage the researcher must consider some methodological issues pertinent to the research purpose. Along with the purpose statement and problems the researcher should define all terms and state any other delimitations that are not accounted for by the research problems/questions. As an outgrowth of this planning phase, the researcher ideally emerges as an expert in a specific subject area and is prepared to embark on the actual "doing" of the project.

C h a p t e r   T h r e e

Prerequisite for Conducting Research
Becoming Familiar With the Body of
Knowledge

3.1 Introduction

The ideas for research often originate from questions generated by experiences in work and daily life. Most scholars, however, agree that reading is the first formal step in all practice toward doing research. One must become familiar with the content of the field in which one wishes to conduct an investigation. Professional books and magazines, research journals, monographs, and papers provide the pool of materials by which one may gain that familiarity. The purpose of this kind of reading is to become knowledgeable in the field so that one may identify the questions the profession appears to have answered and the questions that are in need of resolution.

Reading for the purpose of identifying researchable questions in a field differs substantially from the kind of reading most students engage in during their university studies and which they may commonly refer to as research— that is, finding printed materials to write a term paper or, as the student would call it, a research report. Reading for the purpose of producing a term paper is necessary, but one must be aware of a few common pitfalls that often trap the reader. Looking up a few facts and writing them down in a documented paper does not constitute research, as Leedy (1985) points out:

> Such activity is, of course, no more than *fact-finding* and *fact-transcribing*. No amount of mere transfer of information from one place to another—even though the act of transportation is done with benefit of note card and is acknowledged by proper footnote form—can be defined by the term *research*. *Transfer of information, transportation of fact from one place to another* are what their activities suggest, nothing more! (p. 3)

The type of activity described by Leedy cannot be called research because it seldom proceeds from a question, does not produce new facts, nor does it develop new interpretations of old facts. While fact transferral cannot be called research per se, it certainly constitutes an integral part of the research process. Knowledge of the printed word serves to strengthen the researcher's reasoning in conducting an investigation, in designing an appropriate methodology, and in interpreting the results of the investigation in light of extant knowledge. Thus, the purpose of reading in the context of conducting research is to compare different writers' thoughts and work on a specific issue with one's own thoughts and work.

To illustrate: Almost all music teachers have made certain observations during the periods when they provided musical instruction in elementary or secondary school general music, or during band, choir, or orchestra rehearsals. The elementary music specialist may have observed children's reactions to different musical compositions; band directors may have observed a marked difference in their students' motivational drive to improve their technical skills on the instrument; choral directors at the junior-high level of teaching may have noticed that not only boys go through voice changes but that girls also may exhibit difficulties in singing they had not encountered before puberty.

When observing the behavior of their students, experienced music teachers may utilize what they have seen in the improvement of their teaching techniques. The band director may try new ways of challenging the students through drill; the choral director may try to select literature that accommodates the vocal ranges of the girls during their time of voice change. Thus, a teacher may rethink established teaching/rehearsal strategies and inquire about ways to address the problems observed more adequately. In the process of searching for new teaching approaches, some teachers may even wonder whether their colleagues have made similar observations and whether they too have changed their methods of instruction. Aside from personal conversations among colleagues, the best way of finding out how other people have addressed and attempted to solve problems related to the teaching of music is by consulting the professional literature in music education.

In the situation described, reading becomes a two-fold activity: (a) publications are located that appear to address the question one is interested in, and (b) one searches within that pool of publications for the most satisfactory answer. If a satisfactory answer cannot be obtained, one has the choice of terminating the frustration of reading or of enlarging the pool of publications from which to draw additional information. The enlarged resource pool may lead to the discovery of a usable answer to a question. However, such a reading process can be tedious because it is rare that a personal concern will be precisely matched by concerns expressed in the literature. Moreover, rarely does it happen that an answer given by one person fully satisfies or suits another person's needs and problems.

If an individual chooses to pursue rather than terminate the reading process, the groundwork is laid for becoming acquainted with the body of knowledge in music education. The boundaries of personal interest may widen as publications are found that address only peripherally the question that triggered the initial search. Eventually, one may even begin to read books and articles whose titles have nothing in common with the question originally posed.

When reading the professional literature without having a specific question in mind, one browses in order to find out about the issues people in the field have addressed and about which they have written. Ideally, such reading leads to the development of a good overview of what is accepted knowledge in a field and what questions still await answers. Frequently, however, this type of reading appears to be aimless and endless. The reader may literally wander around in the library.

The most pleasurable reading experience is that of reading for fun. It resembles the playing of an instrument for fun: For many a music student, doodling plays a favored role in practicing an instrument. But if doodling was the extent of one's musical aspirations, it would not be necessary to develop all the skills essential for mastering the instrument. So it is with the activity of reading in the research process. Keeping a proper balance between focused reading and reading for fun is the best assurance that one will obtain a comprehensive view of the body of knowledge in music education. Ideally, reading should be treated like practicing one's instrument: It should become a daily routine.

Regardless of what type of reading one engages in, printed words should be viewed as nothing more than a writer's published reflections on a specific issue. Such reflections may be based on personal opinion, educated guess work, or common sense experience; they may also be the result of systematically gathered observations and otherwise controlled research. Whatever the source of those reflections and no matter how authoritatively presented, thoughts may be challenged and observations may be refuted by further evidence. Therefore, a publication simply serves the purpose of informing the profession at large about the author's work. The printed word is not "the gospel" in which absolute answers to specific questions are "carved in stone."

Because the printed word has the potential of being wrong, the activity of reading has a three-fold purpose: (a) getting acquainted with the thoughts expressed in a publication; (b) assessing the degree to which writers provide evidence for the truth of their thoughts; and (c) comparing such thoughts with one's own ideas in order to identify agreements and disagreements between all of them. Such reading, also referred to as critical reading, may then lead to the identification of areas in need of (further) investigation. The more thoroughly a researcher is familiar with the areas in need of study, the easier it is to identify questions suitable for research.

3.2 The Use of the Library

The efficient use of a professional library requires, first, being at ease with the physical layout of the buildings, the way the holdings are arranged, and the procedures of where and how to look up publications and other documentary materials. Second, students should learn to compile and reference bibliographies as well as annotate their contents.

"Getting Around" in the Library

The use of a professional library begins by acquainting oneself with its general floor plan and holdings. Universities differ in the organizational structure of their libraries. Some universities have separate facilities for undergraduate and graduate students; others have humanities and science libraries or may provide each discipline with its own separate library building. A newcomer to a university must find out which organizational structure the library follows. Most universities employ trained personnel who are willing and usually efficient in helping students to become familiar with the library system. In the effort to become a skilled user of a library, one should not hesitate to seek that help.

In spite of many different types of arrangements on campuses across the country, all respectable university libraries are likely to have card catalogues and/or computerized catalogue terminals, general and special collections, reference rooms, facilities for the reproduction of materials, and interlibrary loan and computer facilities. They have publication indices for most disciplines and, within the disciplines, for a variety of subjects. To provide easy access to standard dictionaries, encyclopedias, dissertation and master's theses abstracts, professional yearbooks, and proceedings, these publications are generally located in central places within the library.

In addition to being comfortable with the physical arrangements and locations of card catalogues, collections, reference rooms, and past and current periodicals, students should also familiarize themselves with the procedures for interlibrary loan, computer-based searches, and the viewing of microfilm and microfiche. Finally, locating books and articles on both broad and very specific topics by means of publication indices is another skill that needs practicing before one engages in research activities.

The Systematic Search for Publications: Making Use of Publication Indices

Publication indices play an important role in the search for literature because they provide an initial insight into the quantity of work that has already been done on a particular topic. Figure 3.1 provides a selection of some of the bibliographical indices that music education students should consult in the beginning stage of searching for publications pertinent to research in their field. The indices are: *Music Psychology Index, Music Index, Music Article Guide,* the index of the *Library of Congress, Dissertation Abstracts International, Educational Resources Information Center, Repertoirs International de Literature Musicale,* and *Bibliographie des Musikschrifttums.* Additional, equally important indices outside the field of music and music education are the *Psychology Index,* the *Education Index,* and the *Current Index of Journals in Education.* Beyond these are numerous

Figure 3.1 Selected Subject Headings in Bibliographical Indices Related to Music and Music Education

Music Psychology Index

The international interdisciplinary index of influence of music behavior: references to the literature from the natural and behavioral sciences and the fine and therapeutic arts. Organized by name and title. Terms are crosslisted.

Selected Subject Headings:

Ability	Music Classses
Accountability	Music Concepts
Achievement	Music Curriculum
Acoustics	Music Education (Curricula)
Aesthetics	Music(al) Instruction,
Art	Music(al) Learning
Auditory Perception	Music Lessons
Choral Art	Music Listening (Experience, Skills)
Choral Rehearsal	Music(al) Perception,
College	Music Preference
College Music Educators	Music Reading Skills
Communication	Music Teacher Training
Education (Elementary)	Music Teaching Success
Education (Secondary)	Musical
Instrumental Music	Musicianship
Kodaly Approach	Pedagogy
Motivation	Philosophy
Music	Physiology
Music(al) Achievement	Psychology of Music
Music Activities	Response (Musical)
Music Appreciation	School
Music(al) Aptitude	Sociology
Music Attitude	Technology
Music Business	

Music Index

Authors of articles, names, and subjects—interfiled in one alphbetical listing. Terms are crosslisted.

Selected Subject Headings:

Appreciation of Music	Philosophy
Arts	Psychology
Choral Music	Schools
Colleges and Universities	Schools of Music
Education	Sociology
Esthetics	Study and Teaching
Instrumental Music	Tests and Measurement
Perception	Voice

Figure 3.1 *(Continued)*

Music Article Guide

Annotated quarterly reference guide to selected, significant signed feature articles in American music periodicals. Subject headings are listed alphabetically and differ for each issue. Terms are not crosslisted.

Selected Subject Headings:

Acoustics	Music Education
Aesthetics	Music Listening
the Arts	Music Reading
Choral Art	Music Tests
College (Jr. College)	Musicianship
College (Universities)	Orff Schulwerk
College (Professional School)	Pedagogy
Elementary School Music	Psychology and Music
Instrumental Music	Technology in Music Education
Kodaly (Zoltan)	Sight Reading
Motivation	Student Teaching
Music Appreciation	Voice
Music Aptitude Tests	

Library of Congress

Literature on music and such related materials as libretti and music textbooks included in the various catalogues. Also, a selected bibliography of works including recordings. Terms are crosslisted.

Most Pertinent Subject Headings:

> Education
> Education (Musical)
> Music in Education
> Music—Instruction and Study

Dissertation Abstracts International

Listings grouped into A: The Humanities and Social Sciences; B: The Sciences and Engineering; C: European Abstracts. Lists in alphabetical order the principal subject categories of the dissertations. Authors listed alphabetically within each category. Terms are not crosslisted.

Most Pertinent Subject Headings:

> Humanities
> Education (Music)
> Music

Educational Resources Information Center

Listings by subject and author. Terms are crosslisted.
Selected Subject Headings:

Accountability	Music
Achievement	Music Activities
Aesthetic Education	Music Appreciation
Arts Education	Music Education

Auditory Perception	Music Reading
Education	Music Teachers
Humanities	Music Techniques

Repertoirs International de Literature Musicale

Abstracts all significant literature on music that is indexed by computer. Included are books, articles, essays, reviews, catalogues, dissertations, iconographies, etc. Terms are not crosslisted.

Most Pertinent Subject Headings:
Music and Other Arts
Music and Related Disciplines
Pedagogy

Bibliographie des Musikschrifttums (in German)

Comprehensive bibliography of music publications. Terms are crosslisted.

Selected Subject Headings:
Akustik [acoustics]
Philosophie Ästhetik [aesthetics]
Musikpädagogik und Didaktik [music
education and didactics]
Physiology
Psychology
Sozialforschung [social psychological
research in music]

---

indices to various other disciplines that may prove beneficial to research in music education.

Figure 3.1 illustrates the kind of subject headings and terminology a person must become comfortable with if a publication search is to be fruitful. As the figure reveals the subject headings are unfortunately not the same for all indices and may cause confusion for the researcher. For example, one subject heading in the *Music Index* is "Study and Teaching," whereas the *Library of Congress* lists its holdings of books on music education under "Music—Instruction and Study." The subject headings in *Repertoirs International de Literature Musicale (RILM)* are very general, the ones in the *Music Psychology Index* very specific. In fact, the latter publication's descriptors resemble key terms more than general subject headings. This specificity makes it easier for a reader to locate publications on relatively well-defined issues. The same holds true for the *Educational Resources Information Center (ERIC)*, an educational clearinghouse of research papers and articles.

Most of the major indices in education, music, and other disciplines contain the name of the author of a publication, its title, source, year of publication and, in some indices, a brief content synopsis. The number of volumes per year differs from index to index, and ranges from semiannual to monthly publication. Some indices provide yearly lists of all articles, dissertations, or research papers that appeared during the last year. Such a summary, usually also referred to as an index, is generally cross-listed by subject and author.

A relatively new form of publication index is the computerized search, a service most, if not all, libraries offer to the university community. This kind of search provides the reader with a printout of published books, articles, and research papers that contain in their titles any of the key terms, or descriptors, the researcher has selected as appropriate for the topic under investigation. The basis for all such searches is the indices discussed in the last paragraph. The advantage of utilizing computerized data lies in the accessability of a wide array of disciplines in which specific publications may be located. The disadvantage lies in its relative cost and in the nonselective nature of the search. For example, if one enters the descriptor *music* into the computer, the printout will contain *all* publications that contain music in their title, regardless of whether the title itself relates to the reader's topic of interest. It is therefore important to prepare a computer search carefully. If a reader has already done some preliminary work on the best suitable key terms and existing publications, the computer printout is likely to contain much more usable information than would be the case if key terms are selected "cold" and with very little preparation.

A computerized data base is not necessarily complete as it simply reflects the extent to which the information of standard indices has been programmed. Thus, these searches should never be considered the most exhaustive of all efforts to locate a list of publications. Rather, a computer search should be viewed as only one step among many a person must take in order to compile as complete a record of publications from as many sources as possible. (For a list of selected research journals pertinent to music education, see Appendix A.)

When to Stop the Search

If a person is at the very beginning of a research "career," it frequently happens that pertinent literature seems to be difficult to find. In such a situation the immediate reaction of many students tends to be the termination of the library search altogether. However, rather than stopping at that point, it is advisable to extend the search to other key terms even if they appear to be only remotely related to the chosen topic area. In many instances the sources appear limited only because the reader has not explored all the avenues from which an issue may be examined.

In cases where the sources are indeed limited because the researcher enters a relatively new territory of exploration, it may become necessary to look for literature in external disciplines more closely aligned to the new territory of research. If that search also produces limited evidence, the researcher should document that lack of evidence and develop a plan of action, preferably together with colleagues from other disciplines, in order to set up feasible research questions and possible investigative procedures.

Generally, however, and particularly for the inquisitive mind, the process of searching for literature on a given topic rarely stops! Although this prospect may discourage many music students from getting seriously involved in research activities, the task of locating and perusing professional literature pertinent to a specific topic of interest is not as frustrating or difficult as it may initially seem. After all, a single subject heading in the card catalogue or in any of the indices mentioned lists a multitude of publications; one article among those publications alone is likely to contain a bibliography of additional writings. A glance through several of those sources may lead to other bibliographies that refer to even more materials. When trying to locate a specific book in the stacks, a person should be encouraged to browse through other books nearby. Similarly, a person should browse through the contents and/ or bibliographies of research articles, monographs, dissertations, and dissertation abstracts.

Many publications in music education contain references that go beyond the field of music. Thus, while perusing periodicals and books to learn more about a topic of interest, writings on related issues in disciplines other than music or music education may be found. Even if a person's topic does not seem to call for the consultation of publications in other disciplines, it is advisable to get acquainted with writings in other fields. Reading articles in scientific, philosophical, historical, or art and theater journals may considerably broaden a person's mind and lead to interesting insights into parallels as well as conflicts in the thought processes of various disciplines, be they the humanities or the social or natural sciences. Because the libraries for each of these disciplines may be located at different sites on or off campus, it will require some effort to become familiar with their whereabouts.

Note Taking

When reading, the researcher should become familiar with a wide variety of articles and books. The reading list should include both articles that are primarily based on speculation and personal opinion and those that follow a clearly described research methodology. Some writings will be easy, others rather cumbersome in style and presentation of content. Whatever the quality, format, and style of the printed word, getting acquainted with the spectrum of the professional literature should equip a person to assess the scope of issues pertinent to the field.

The act of reading is, in a way, a "silent dialogue," or exchange of ideas, between the reader and the various authors. The reader engages in a mental discussion about perceptions of and solutions for specific problems posed by the authors. For the discussion to be effective and ongoing, the reader should take diligent notes, not only about who said what but also about the quality of what was said.

45

The process of note-taking consists of three steps: (a) the identification of a publication, (b) the description of its content, and (c) an evaluation of content and format of the publication. Whereas the first step is the same for all note taking, the next two steps change in depth and specificity depending on the purpose for which the information will be used. If the purpose of reading is to obtain an overall view of the extant body of knowledge in a field, the notes should contain all information necessary to identify the publication, briefly describe its content, and indicate whether it seems to be based on opinion or documented evidence. If the reading is to aid one in the finding of a research purpose, the notes must be in-depth and should describe and assess the quality of a publication in detail. To record information, note cards (many people use a 5 by 7 inch format), leaflets in a spiral binder, a note book, or computer data files may be used.

Identifying a Publication. The identification of any publication entails the author's full name, the complete title, place of publication, publisher, year and—in the case of articles in magazines, journals, and books—the first and last page number of an article. At the top of the note card, page, or data file the last name of the author, the *full* first name, and initials of the middle name are entered. This should be followed by the title of the publication, location, publisher, year of publication and, if applicable, page numbers. In the case of books, some researchers prefer to record also the library call number.

Figure 3.2 shows several examples of how to identify a publication on a note card. The examples do not reflect fully any one of the referencing styles currently favored by the social sciences or humanities. Instead, each card contains *all* information according to which references, notes, and bibliographies may be documented in any style format requested by a publisher or a university. The titles of books, monographs, journals, journal supplements, magazines, and newspapers are generally underlined. We recommend this practice.

The most frequently cited style manuals currently in use in the social sciences and/or humanities are those published by the American Psychological Association (APA) (1983) and the University of Chicago Press (1982). Additional manuals are those by Turabian (1973) and the Modern Language Association (Gibaldi & Achtert, 1980). Substantial differences in style can be found among them. Disagreements exist primarily about the order in which all information is presented and whether that information appears as a footnote, endnote, or reference. Changes also occur periodically within the style manuals themselves, and it is advisable to stay abreast of such changes in order to meet new demands set forth by various communities of scholars.

A note on the documentation of a dissertation: According to the APA style manual, referencing a dissertation by its appearance in *Dissertation Abstracts International* (DAI) is permissible. It may happen, however, that the abstract will be published long after the dissertation has been completed. Both dates—that of the completion of the dissertation and that of the abstract— are needed in a proper reference. Therefore, information about where and when the degree was obtained should also be included on one's note card.

Figure 3.2   Identifying a Publication-Step 1 in Note Taking

Book

> Dretske, Fred I.
> *Seeing and Knowing*
> Chicago
> University of Illinois Press
> 1969

Article/Chapter in Book

> Forsythe, Jere L.
> "The Effect of Teacher Errors on
> Student Attentiveness:
> Music versus Classroom Teachers"
> *Research in Music Behavior: Modify-*
> *ing Music Behavior in the Classroom*
> Eds. Clifford E. Madsen, R. Douglas
> Greer, and Charles H. Madsen, Jr.
> New York and London
> Teachers College Press, 1975,
> pp. 49–55.

Dissertation

> Zwissler, Ruth N.
> "An Investigation of the Pitch Discrim-
> ination Skills of First Grade Children
> Indentified as Accurate Singers and
> Those Indentified as Inaccurate Sing-
> ers"
> Unpublished Ph.D. Dissertation
> University of California at Los Angeles
> *D.A.I.*, 1972, *32*, 4056A.

Journal Article

> Eisner, Elliot W.
> "The Role of the Arts in Cognition and
> Curriculum"
> *The Canadian Music Educator*
> Vol. 23, No. 1, 1981, pp. 7–22.

Unpublished Paper

> Heller, George N.
> "Music Education in Kansas before
> before the Civil War."
> Paper presented at the Southwest
> Division of the Music Educators
> National Conference
> Colorado Springs, Colorado
> February 2, 1979.

Describing the Content of a Publication.   The taking of notes should always be "complete enough not only to be useful but also to save researchers from having to reexamine the same item for information overlooked the first time" (Phelps, 1980, p. 102). But reading for the purpose of getting acquainted with a wide range of professional literature is likely to result in a less-specific content description than the in-depth reading of literature in a narrowly defined area of research. As the purpose for which one reads changes over time and according to the project one is working on, there should remain enough space in the section on content description to add further details and additional notes as the need arises.

If students read primarily to familiarize themselves with the scope of publications and to obtain an overview of the field, they might wish to note only briefly the general area of concern addressed by a publication. It is often helpful to indicate in the right-hand corner of the note card the most pertinent subject heading and/or key terms a title pertains to. For a brief description of books, it might be advisable to copy a book's table of contents and excerpt those statements the author considered to be the conclusions of the work. Page numbers should accompany all such excerpts. In some instances it might be wise to attach to the note card a photocopy of important pages or more lengthy paragraphs that proved to be of particular interest to the reader. A dissertation might be briefly described by writing a synopsis of the dissertation abstract.

If a reader takes notes in order to look for researchable ideas, a more detailed content description than that just suggested is most important. Notes on research articles and dissertations should include major points of the research rationale, purpose, problems (and/or hypotheses), methodology, results, and conclusions. To obtain that information, dissertation abstracts are seldom sufficient, and the reader must consult the actual dissertations. Since the methodological steps in opinion-based books and articles tend to be less specific, excerpting their content is generally not as clear cut as is the description of research-based publications. One should be able, however, to identify the purpose of a publication, major points of argumentation, and the most important conclusions. If those items cannot be easily identified in a publication, a note to that effect should appear in the content section of the bibliographical card.

A thorough content description of dissertations, chapters of books, complete books, or any kind of articles is a time-consuming activity and requires from the reader a great deal of diligent work and concentration. Excerpting the contents of professional literature demands self-discipline as there is nothing more tempting than speeding up the process of note taking simply by leafing through an article or book and recording one's own subjective evaluation prior to having fully understood the content of the publication.

Evaluating the Content of a Publication. The third step in note taking—evaluating the content of a publication—is by far the most subjective and, possibly, the most difficult task in the whole process of reading. But it is also one of the most crucial skills in a person's preparation as a competent researcher. It improves over time as a researcher's involvement in both research and publication increases.

Based on the purpose for which one is reading, the evaluation of the content of a publication may differ in depth and focus. Those who wish to gain that earlier mentioned bird's-eye view of knowledge in music education may simply state the way in which a publication corresponded to their own topic of interest. Readers who intend to develop research expertise in a specific problem area must determine for all publications the purpose, the procedures by which the evidence was provided, and the conclusions that were drawn. A research-based article should be evaluated using the following questions:

1. Is the purpose clearly defined?

2. Are the research problems, questions, or hypotheses appropriately derived from the research purpose?

3. Does the methodology accurately describe all steps necessary for the investigation of all research problems, questions, or hypotheses?

4. Are the results reported clearly and in correspondence with the problems, questions, or hypotheses?

5. Are the conclusions derived logically from the reported results (findings) and are they discussed in the light of already existing literature in the field?

Whether scanning the literature or reading specific publications in depth, it is always necessary to take note of the degree to which a publication is based on either personal speculation or the systematic gathering of evidence and the use of logical reasoning. Probable fact should be winnowed from unsupported opinion, the systematic (or logical) development of ideas from unsupported generalizations, and wisdom from foolishness. Undoubtedly, such an assessment becomes easier the more versed a reader is in accepted scholarly practice and methodology.

3.3 The Skill of Critical Reading

The suggestion was made in chapter 2 that music students may not always be at ease with thinking inquisitively because of the nature of their professional training. Similarly, the nature of musical study may also make it difficult to understand clearly what constitutes critical reading. Applied music instruction, often perceived as the most important and certainly the most prolonged learning experience a musician has, tends to be an authoritative experience because the teacher generally tells the student how to produce a sound, how to phrase a musical line, how to play in tune, how to memorize. When the student is no longer satisfied with the teacher's advice, it is a common practice among many music students to consult another teacher who may follow a different but equally authoritative plan of instruction. Used to being told what is right and wrong or how to improve a performance, a "music person" may find it difficult to rely entirely on personal judgment and understanding when it comes to the reading and assessment of research literature.

Since publications should be viewed simply as a written report about an individual's ideas and work on a particular issue, critical reading should be applied to all types of publications, be they the most impressive editions of hardcover books or inexpensive, weekly pamphlets. Faulty content and weak scholarship can appear everywhere, and ideas expressed in books are not necessarily developed or researched anymore carefully than those that appear in journals and periodicals.

Going beyond the marking of misspellings, typos, or grammatical errors, the skill of critical reading develops from informed judgment about the degree to which all written statements that claim to be more than speculation are supported by systematic and logical evidence. In the words of Barzun and Graff (1985, p. 367), "all novel or startling assertions and all distinct elements in a demonstration or argument" must have been properly documented. The proper documentation of evidence lies in the verification of the sources of such evidence.

Verifying Sources of Evidence

The verification of evidence to support a writer's thoughts occurs primarily in two contexts: Either the writer makes use of quotations—that is, ideas of other writers; or a writer provides evidence for the support of given statements through observation and measurement or logical argumentation. It is the reader's task to assert (a) that the references used for quotations are accurate and can be trusted; and (b) that all other supportive evidence is provided by established and agreed upon criteria of disciplined inquiry.

Verifying Printed References. The documentation of all written statements is done through sources of reference. If reference is made to the very first document in which an idea was expressed, that source is called the *primary* source. If a second source refers to the original document and is being used as the source of reference for the original, it becomes the *secondary* source. *Tertiary* sources, accordingly, are references that themselves utilize second-hand information about an original source.

Theses and dissertations are considered primary source materials; so are articles that are based on dissertations and carry the researcher's name. For the critical reader it is always advisable to consult the actual dissertation rather than the article since the latter is a less comprehensive source.

Although good scholarship is generally characterized by the exclusive use of primary source materials, it is not uncommon that secondary, sometimes even tertiary, references are utilized in publications. Many reviewers of dissertations in music education have taken to task some researchers' careless use of secondary sources when primary sources were available and should have been consulted (see, for example, Cowden, 1971; Hornyak, 1974; Radocy, 1980; Rainbow, 1976; Ralston, 1973; Schwadron, 1975; Turrentine, 1968; Zimmerman, 1974). The reviewers pointed out how a researcher's use of proper reference sources would have enhanced the reader's trust in the research project and thus in the research results.

Verifying Other Sources of Supportive Evidence. After carefully checking the accuracy of references in a publication, the critical reader must assess the presence of other, albeit related, sources of evidence by which a researcher's statements or findings are supported. Such sources are any data-gathering devices other than printed material: statements of people, measurement devices (e.g., tests, observational systems, attitudinal and rating scales), questionnaires, and interviews. To the degree that a researcher/writer has documented the *reliability* and *validity* of all such data-gathering devices, the evidence obtained through those sources may be called reliable and valid. Information is considered reliable if it can be replicated. Information is valid when it does what it is supposed to do—that is, when it is convincing. Thus, the validity of evidence can only be determined if the purpose for which the information was gathered is known.

In addition to looking for the reliability and validity of evidence, a reader should also critically assess the degree to which a writer makes use of logical reasoning as a means of proving the truthfulness of research conclusions. Logical reasoning is generally said to be divided into a priori (deductive) and a posteriori (inductive) reasoning. A priori reasoning proceeds from general statements (theories, systems of belief) to the existence of particular facts and observations; a posteriori reasoning proceeds from specific, observed phenomena (accepted facts, results of experiments, common sense experiences) to general theories and systems of thought. As long as a field of study acknowledges that it is governed by principles of logic, both approaches are needed in a researcher's effort to come to verified findings and conclusions about the nature of human behavior. (This issue is discussed at greater length in chapter 7.)

Application of Critical Reading to Philosophical, Historical, and Empirical Research in Music Education

Critical reading for the purpose of conducting research exceeds the verification of sources of evidence, goes beyond the determination of their reliability and validity, and transcends an assessment of the overall logic that holds an argument together. Critical reading for the purpose of doing research requires the reader to separate good investigations from bad investigations, complete evidence from incomplete evidence, and convincing procedural approaches from questionable ones. Such an evaluation of existing research must be based on clear principles of scholarship as established by the research community in music education. Undoubtedly, there seems to be more agreement about what good empirical research is than what may constitute good philosophical or historical research. But the application of principles of disciplined inquiry to the critical reading of all three modes of research can certainly provide the reader with safe, helpful guidelines by which to separate good studies from weak studies and speculation from logically sound argumentation.

A publication that adheres to principles of disciplined inquiry has very distinct characteristics that set it apart from other types of writing. As Cronbach (1973) has described it,

> The argument can be painstakingly examined. The report does not depend for its appeal on the eloquence of the writer or any surface plausibility. The argument is not justified by anecdotes or casually assembled fragments of evidence. Scholars in each field have developed traditional questions that serve as touchstones to separate sound argument from incomplete or questionable argument. . . . The mathematician asks about axioms, the historian about the authenticity of documents, the experimental scientist about verifiability of observations. . . . [The researcher] institutes controls at each step of information collection and reasoning to avoid the sources of error in his conclusions. . . . The report of a disciplined inquiry . . . displays the raw materials entering the argument and the logical processes by which they were compressed and rearranged to make the conclusion credible. (p.7)

When applying Cronbach's description of disciplined inquiry to the critical reading of philosophical studies, one should look, first, for a clear purpose and a reason for that purpose. Second, one should search for support and verified evidence of all statements the researcher has used to draw the final conclusions. A plan of logical reasoning should be present that describes the vantage point, or philosophical position, from which the researcher approached the study. All statements that are part of the argumentation should appear in sequential order. All terms utilized in the argumentation should be clearly defined.

In good historical investigations, the reader should expect a multitude of questions posed by the researcher at the outset. A plan of action should be present that details how all primary source materials were located and validated, be they public records, newspaper clippings, birth or death certificates, bills of sale, or similar documents. The report should provide a complete picture of the person or event described; both negative and positive traits or good and bad characteristics should have been used in that description. Selectivity, if indicated by a bias of reporting, ought to make the reader criticize the investigation as being unscholarly. Above all, a critical reader of historical research should look for conclusions and interpretations of the reported events because the heart of historical research lies in the interpretation of reported events. Chronology may be viewed as the data of historical inquiry; a good historical study will try to suggest their causes and effects.

When reading empirical research reports, one should look for the relationship between the purpose statement and problems and the methodology employed in the study. The design of the study should be clearly described and should include the number of subjects used, the variables measured and, if applicable, the steps taken to control the variables. A well-documented study also contains a thorough description of all measurement tools—both standardized devices and newly developed ones. In the latter case, the report should contain a section on how the tools were constructed. The reader should look for reliability and validity scores for all those tools. In addition, a statement regarding all statistical techniques employed in the data analysis should be present. The tables should be unambiguous and clear to the reader and should be explained in the text. Finally, the reader must examine the interpretation of the findings to determine if the conclusions of the study are in line with the reported results, or if they are speculative and far exceed what the researcher actually investigated.

3.4 Summary

Reading for the purpose of getting acquainted with the body of knowledge in music education may be compared to the process of practicing a musical instrument: There is no point at which one can say practice is no longer necessary. Like music practice, library work should become the subject of regular and daily practice. Increased practice will result in the sharpening of one's critical mind and in the improvement of the ability to separate scientifically based knowledge from guesswork and wishful thinking. In addition, the continuous reading of the professional literature may result in the discovery of more knowledge in several fields of study. That knowledge can in turn contribute to a better understanding of one's own area of expertise.

The process of reading is divided into three steps: (a) the location of appropriate sources, (b) the taking of notes while reading those sources, and (c) the determination of the quality of each source read. The latter should be the application of scholarly-scientific criteria, set forth by the research community, to the evaluation of the professional literature. Such an assessment, if based on a thorough understanding of scientific thought processes, is as crucial in the preparation of a research project as the execution of the project itself.

The quality of a research report is judged primarily by the technical excellence with which the research has been executed. Thus, a detailed, step-by-step description of the investigation is essential for its proper evaluation. Additionally, the reader needs to have a degree of knowledge about what actually constitutes technical excellence in research. All three modes of inquiry—philosophical, historical, and empirical—possess somewhat different criteria for judging technical excellence. However, they do share a common basis, that of disciplined inquiry. Consequently, in spite of important differences in the techniques employed by each mode, good research can be judged by the presence of a clear purpose; stated questions, problems or hypotheses; a description of the logic and techniques by which the questions or problems were resolved; and the inclusion of all evidence that led to the conclusions presented by the investigator. It is a critical reader's task to assess the degree to which a research report contains all these attributes of disciplined inquiry.

Suggested Activities

1. Locate in the library the major indices relevant to research in music education.
2. Initiate a computer search for references.
3. Locate some of the research periodicals listed in Appendix A and develop a list of additional research periodicals that may be of potential value for music education.
4. Read five articles from the research journals and evaluate them according to the criteria described in this chapter.

Topics for Discussion

1. Characteristics of critical reading.
2. Observations about note taking and the critical evaluation of articles.
3. A comparison of similarities and differences in the contents in the *Music Educators Journal, The Instrumentalist,* the *Journal of Research in Music Education,* and the *Bulletin of the Council for Research in Music Education.*

REFERENCES

American Psychological Association. (1983). *Publication manual of the American Psychological Association.* (3rd ed.). Washington, D.C.: American Psychological Association.

Barzun, J., & Graff, H. F. (1985). *The modern researcher* (4th ed.). New York: Harcourt Brace Jovanovich.

Cowden, R. L. (1971). Norman Earle Dawson: A study of the roles of music supervisors in selected school districts. *Council for Research in Music Education, 24* (Spring), 50–53.

Cronbach, L. J. (1973). Disciplined inquiry. In H. S. Broudy, R. H. Ennis, and L. I. Krimerman (Eds.), *Philosophy of educational research* (pp. 6–16). New York: John Wiley.

Gibaldi, J., & Achtert, W. S. (1980). *MLA Handbook for writers of research papers* (Student edition). New York: Modern Language Association.

Hornyak, R. R. (1974). A. S. Rumbelow: Music and social groups: An interactionist approach to the sociology of music. *Council for Research in Music Education, 40* (Winter), 11–17.

Leedy, P. D. (1985). *Practical research: Planning and design* (3rd. ed.). New York, NY: Macmillan; London: Collier-Macmillan.

Phelps, R. P. (1980). *A guide to research in music education* (2nd ed.). Metuchen, NJ: Scarecrow Press. [Quote is not contained in 3rd ed., 1986.]

Radocy, R. E. (1980). W. B. Montgomery: Basic aural discrimination: Third grade children's perception of changes in music. *Council for Research in Music Education, 63* (Summer), 43–47.

Rainbow, E. L. (1976). Louise R. Mandell: The effects of three types of music on group test performance. *Council for Research in Music Education, 49* (Winter), 40–48.

Ralston, J. L. (1973). Marcia Wilson Lebow: A systematic examination of the *Journal of Music and Art* edited by John Sullivan Dwight: 1852–1881, Boston, Massachusetts. *Council for Research in Music Education, 31* (Winter), 12–18.

Schwadron, A. A. (1975). Dwight D. Killiam: Aesthetic realization: Rationale and structure of a new approach in music education. *Council for Research in Music Education, 44* (Fall), 33–43.

Turabian, K. L. (1973). *A manual for writers of term papers, theses, and dissertations* (4th ed.). Chicago: University of Chicago Press.

Turrentine, E. M. (1968). David Paul Swanzy: The wind ensemble and its music during the French Revolution (1789–1795). *Council for Research in Music Education, 14* (Fall), 43–48.

University of Chicago Press. (1982). *The Chicago Manual of Style.* (13th ed., rev. and exp.). Chicago: University of Chicago Press.

Zimmerman, M. P. (1974). Ronald Lee Larsen: Level of conceptual development in melodic permutation concepts based on Piaget's theory. *Council for Research in Music Education, 38* (Summer), 44–46.

Chapter Four

Finding a Research Purpose

4.1 Introduction

Knowledge is a degree of certainty about how and why things work the way they do. This certainty is expressed in the form of theories that attempt to explain the nature of human behavior and its relationship to the environment. The more evidence one has to support a theory, the more certain one may be about the validity of that theory and, consequently, the accuracy of one's knowledge. Any aspect of a theory for which evidence is to be gathered and whose validity is to be tested provides the reason for conducting a study. We call this reason the purpose of a study. Other researchers have referred to it as the research problem. Whatever the label, the research purpose/problem is the objective of a specific investigation toward which one initially directs all research efforts. The purpose provides the criterion according to which all subsequent methodological decisions are made. As such, the research purpose guides not only the investigator in conducting the study, but also the reader in understanding the reason why the study was carried out.

It is quite common for novice researchers in music education, particularly those who are in the process of finding a thesis or dissertation topic, to search for a research technique prior to having formulated a research purpose. They look for a method of investigation before they have finalized the question. When a novice researcher says "I have developed this questionnaire; can I now do my research?", the answer should be "You are putting the cart before the horse! What is the purpose of your study?"

The research purpose develops logically from an assessment of what is known in music education and from what is not known. It reflects the specific question the researcher has proposed to answer within the framework of a given theory. The wording of the purpose statement should be formulated before the study is undertaken, clearly identified as the purpose of the study,

Figure 4.1   Zeroing in on a Research Purpose: The Reading Process

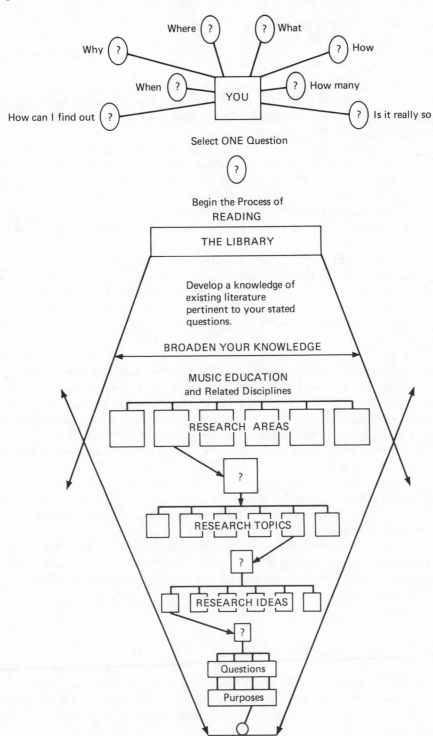

and be consistent throughout a research report. If a researcher does not explicitly state the purpose of a study, or if the same wording is not maintained throughout the research report, an important criterion of good scholarship has been violated.

Following the definition of music education as the study of the learning and teaching of music, research purposes in music education should develop from questions about the learner, the teacher, the nature of music, and the interactions among these three components. Such questions may deal with past or present events typical of the music instructional process, with thoughts about music, or with the nature of musical behaviors. Whatever the method by which a researcher develops such questions—be the modes of inquiry philosophical, historical, or empirical—relations between verifiable actions, phenomena, and ideas are to be assessed; underlying causes of how people learn music need probing; and assertions about the meaning of such knowledge should be developed.

The process of finding a research purpose is best divided into at least two separate parts. First, a person must learn to identify broad areas of concern within the total field of music education. Second, one of those concerns must be transformed into a research purpose that is specific enough for its investigation to be properly carried out within the parameters of the investigator's ability.

Figure 4.1 depicts the steps of finding a research purpose as a two-fold activity. A specific concern triggers a reading process that leads to a broadening of knowledge in the field(s) of study pertaining to the reader's interests. At what point this "inverted funnel process" is terminated is hard to pinpoint. Usually, time and other related factors make such a decision necessary. From there on, the actual funnel process takes place: From a general knowledge of the literature one moves back to the formulation of a specific, researchable purpose statement.

The actual purpose statement may or may not bear a resemblance to the first question that triggered the whole endeavor. In the process of reading, questions change, interests shift, and insights into the literature cause a revision of initially important concerns. Within those areas of concern, several research ideas may be identified. Each idea is likely to carry with it a variety of topics, each of which may have the potential for several specific research questions. One of those questions may then be transformed into the actual purpose statement.

4.2 The Identification of Areas of Concern

Areas of concern in any field of study are best identified by asking questions about what is or is not known. Personal experiences as well as knowledge gained from the reading of professional literature ought to guide the researcher in this process.

Personal Expertise as the Starting Point for Asking Questions

All music teachers, at the public school level and the university level alike, are challenged daily to find solutions to problems that arise in the music classroom or rehearsal hall. Take, for example, Teacher X, who we will call "Mike." Mike is an experienced and successful elementary general music teacher who is highly regarded by his colleagues. His teaching schedule is reasonable and there is ample space in the music room. Classroom instruments of all ranges are readily available and Mike has been able to purchase the newest edition (including the recordings) of two of the leading music series—with lavish pictures and pretty covers.

With all these favorable conditions, Mike notices that some of his students still show no particular interest in music. Many of them cannot talk intelligently about music, sing in tune, walk to the beat of the music, clap in rhythm, or sight read simple tone patterns. Furthermore, those children who are the least able to carry out such musical activities appear to misbehave the most. Mike believes that these misbehaving students are a major source of distraction for the rest of the class, and he feels that if that distraction could be eliminated, his teaching would be more successful. He takes the first step toward solving the problem by asking for the reasons behind the students' observed misbehavior and lack of adequate musical response. He asks: "Why do my students misbehave, not sing in tune, walk to the beat, or match pitches? Why do they show a lack of motivation? How could they be motivated? Why do they not respond to music instruction the same way the other students do?" Mike is asking good questions, and it is quite likely that similar questions are raised every day in most music rooms around the world. These kinds of questions may actually serve as the starting point for the identification of areas of concern in the field of music education.

When asking questions based on observations in one's work, a differentiation should be made between genuine questions and pseudoquestions. A genuine question truly seeks an answer, whereas a pseudoquestion expects no answer, cannot be answered, or has an answer that is already known to the person asking the question. For example, the question "Why do my students exhibit a lack of motivation?" may often be meant as a statement: "My students exhibit a lack of motivation!" The true question would be whether the students indeed exhibit a lack of motivation or whether it is a lack of something else, and what the nature of that something else is. To find out, one would have to ask: "What behaviors allow me to conclude that other students are motivated?" One might ask whether all students labeled "not motivated" exhibit like behaviors, or whether the absence of such behaviors in other students allows one to conclude that they are motivated. Finding answers to such questions would require a careful study of the various current theories on motivation. One would need to study these theories and test their validity. Likewise, the question of why so many students sing out-of-tune may be specified by asking what is meant by "many" and "out-of-tune." One

Table 4.1   Selected Problem Areas in Music Education As Discussed in Articles Published in *CRME*

Problem area	Location (Bulletin No.)	Author
Accountability	36 (special issue)	Cooksey
Aesthetics and aesthetic education	74; 46, 79	Saffle; Schwadron
Attitudes and preference	48	Wapnick
Choral music	33	Gonzo
Child development	86	Katz
Children's voices	86	Atterbury
Competency-based teacher education	40; 46	Holt; Mountford
Creativity	74	Richardson
Early childhood	45; 86	Greenberg; Andress; Simons
Educational technology	18; 35	Lincoln; Deihl and Partchey
Elementary music	34	Klemish
Evaluation	35	Whybrew
Instrumental music	33; 74	Rainbow; Nelson
Jazz education	82	Bash and Kuzmich
Middle childhood	86	Zimmerman
Piagetian research	62	Serafine
Secondary music	27	Glenn
Special education/ music therapy	35; 57	Jellison; Krebs
Teacher education	81	Colwell; Leonhard; Meske

might wonder if those people who sing out-of-tune also have other characteristics in common.

All the questions asked here refer to such subjects as motivation, in-tune singing, and musical ability and achievement, issues of great importance to music education. The next step in the search for a research topic would be to read the literature that is most pertinent to these and other related areas of concern. Several survey articles in the *Council for Research in Music Education* may serve the novice researcher as a starting point for becoming familiar with extant research in a variety of areas in music education. Table 4.1 lists a few of those areas and the issue numbers in which they are discussed.

Knowledge of the Field of Music Education as the Starting Point for Finding a Research Purpose

Figure 4.2 provides an overview of selected areas of concern in the field of music education about which a researcher should develop insights when critically reading the professional literature. This figure corresponds to Figure 1.1 (chapter 1) because the areas reflect the interrelatedness of knowledge about the learner, the teacher, and music. Although it is usual to study each

Figure 4.2   Selected Investigative Areas Pertinent to Knowledge in the Field of Music Education

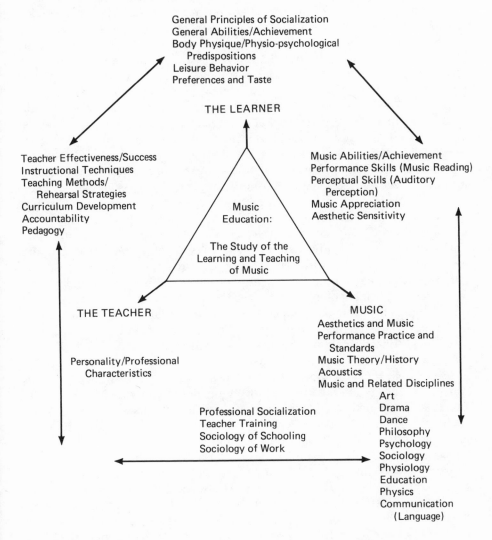

General Principles of Socialization
General Abilities/Achievement
Body Physique/Physio-psychological
      Predispositions
Leisure Behavior
Preferences and Taste

THE LEARNER

Teacher Effectiveness/Success
Instructional Techniques
Teaching Methods/
    Rehearsal Strategies
Curriculum Development
Accountability
Pedagogy

Music
Education:

The Study of the
Learning and Teaching
of Music

Music Abilities/Achievement
Performance Skills (Music Reading)
Perceptual Skills (Auditory
    Perception)
Music Appreciation
Aesthetic Sensitivity

THE TEACHER

Personality/Professional
    Characteristics

Professional Socialization
Teacher Training
Sociology of Schooling
Sociology of Work

MUSIC
Aesthetics and Music
Performance Practice and
    Standards
Music Theory/History
Acoustics
Music and Related Disciplines
    Art
    Drama
    Dance
    Philosophy
    Psychology
    Sociology
    Physiology
    Education
    Physics
    Communication
    (Language)

component of the triangle separately by raising questions specifically geared to the understanding of any one of the areas shown in Figure 4.2, each area may also be seen as being bonded to several other areas.

To illustrate: A researcher might be interested in matters of acoustics where the purpose of the study might be to investigate the relationship between the physical and psychological properties of pitch. That purpose has seemingly little to do with the study of teaching methods or curriculum development; however, questions concerning how an individual perceives different pitches may be closely connected to knowledge about the music abilities of the learner.

The assessment of musical abilities, in turn, has often been said to be related to the learner's general abilities and learning experiences. The study of a person's educational and economic background may thus also be seen in relationship to issues that would fall under the general principles of socialization.

Similarly, the assessment of music achievement may be viewed in the context of teacher and student characteristics and their impact on teaching style; teacher characteristics, on the other hand, may depend on the teacher's professional socialization. Learning disabilities and musical behavior may be affected by the learner's home environment as well as by the use of specific teaching methods. Sociopsychological areas, such as the sociology of schooling and musical taste, deal also with questions about musical responsiveness, music appreciation, and preference. Furthermore, to investigate the nature of value and quality in music one should know studies in aesthetics and philosophy as well as in sociology. Questions about perceptual skills and aesthetic sensitivity may refer to the physiopsychological predispositions of the learner in addition to the techniques and methods used in general music instruction. In short, whatever the nature of a chosen area of concern turns out to be, its link to other areas of study should be clearly seen when critically reading the professional literature and when deciding on a research purpose. Aesthetic education does have a link to concerns of teacher effectiveness and the effectiveness of a variety of instructional techniques. Similarly, a music educator's knowledge of the acoustical properties of sound should tie in with knowledge of student characteristics or such general traits as intelligence or musicality.

When critically reading the literature, a researcher should assess what questions have been raised by other researchers in a variety of areas of concern in several fields of study; how these questions have been investigated; whether conclusive answers to the questions were obtained; and whether the results supported or refuted accepted theories in the realm of music instruction. From such an assessment the researcher should develop his or her own research ideas and, ultimately, research purpose and methodology.

Currently, the field of music education abounds with questions about constructs of aesthetic thought, the meaning of value in music, and the development of rationales or justifications for music education. So far, a commonly accepted theory of music instruction is nowhere in sight. Many questions exist on how people perceive sound, how musical stimuli are processed by the brain, and what the responses are. Current knowledge about the physiology of music performance and proper vocal and instrumental playing techniques is not as solidly supported by insights from controlled research as would be desirable. "Good teaching" continues to escape a comprehensive definition. More information is needed on the nature of student-teacher interactions in the classroom, evaluation of teaching techniques, measurement of performance skills, and assessment of music preferences and attitudes. Investigations should be conducted on the comparative development of public school music in the United States and in foreign countries. Information is needed about the effect certain people have had on the development of music education both in the United States and abroad.

In reviewing the status of music education research up to 1976, Leonhard and Colwell (1976) posed 12 questions that they believed warranted investigation. The questions evolved from a review of research literature pertaining to such diverse areas of concern as music teaching and learning, development and maturation, perception and psychoacoustics, training, attitudes, automated learning, creativity, and psychological theory. Obviously, the quantity of research studies in music education has increased since 1976, but it appears that the broad questions Leonhard and Colwell suggested as areas of concern in music education are still with us today:

1. What is music as art?
2. What constitutes aesthetic responsiveness to music?
3. How does aesthetic responsiveness to music relate to aesthetic responsiveness to other arts?
4. What is the basis for aesthetic responsiveness to music?
5. What is the basis for musical perception?
6. What is the influence of aptitude on the development of musical responsiveness and perception?
7. What is the influence of maturation on the development of musical responsiveness and perception?
8. To what extent can a growth gradient be established for the development of musical responsiveness and perception?
9. How can aptitude for musical responsiveness and perception be measured?
10. How can achievement in musical responsiveness and perception be measured?
11. How does achievement of performance skills, listening skills, and skills in analyzing compositional devices and stylistic characteristics affect the development of music responsiveness and perception?
12. What types of experience with music contribute to the development of musical responsiveness and perception? (p.22)

Leonhard and Colwell's questions are so broad and touch on so many areas within the field of music education that it is not possible to find answers to them unless we break each question into many subquestions. For example, instead of asking what music is as art and what constitutes aesthetic responsiveness to music, one should inquire about the nature of specific constructs of aesthetic thought, the meaning of value in music, the development of musical taste and preferences, and/or music appreciation. For each of these subject headings, a large body of literature can be found whose critical assessment may lead one to further and more narrowly defined questions.

The process of narrowing down a broad question is continued until a question has become so focused that its potential answer may be considered a contribution to knowledge in music education. This may be the case if the answer will either provide practical solutions to specific problems encountered in the teaching of music or if the answer will give basic explanations for the causes of observed behaviors or events. Results that appear to fall into the first of the two categories may be said to come from applied research. Investigations whose findings explain rather than solve everyday teaching problems are often labeled basic research.

Examples of applied research are the comparison of two or more teaching methods, the investigation of approaches toward motivating students for music, studies dealing with discipline problems in the classroom, and the development of more efficient ways to teach specific musical skills and knowledge. Basic research is concerned not only with finding the causes of problem behaviors but also with the investigation of all other behaviors related to musical learning. Wanting to understand how things work precedes one's specific efforts toward solving any of the particular problems of teaching. In the eyes of the nonresearcher, basic research often seems of little use since the applicability of basic research to concrete concerns of the teaching profession appears remote, if not nonexistent.

In our view, a research question is useful when its answer supports or refutes accepted theories of knowledge in a field. As such, all good research has the potential to affect music instruction in the schools. Applied research may have a more immediate bearing on daily decisions in the classroom than basic research, but the strength of the latter lies in the foundation it provides for developing concrete information about how people learn and respond to music. Viewed from that perspective, the impact of basic research on music education may be longer lasting and more consequential to the development of the overall body of knowledge in music education than the impact of applied research.

4.3 The Transformation of a Concern Into a Research Purpose

Earlier in this chapter it was suggested that the transformation of a personal concern into a research purpose takes place at four levels of increasing specificity. For the sake of clarity, these levels may be labeled research area, idea, topic, and question/purpose, respectively. Not all researchers are likely to make use of all the levels of specification prior to finalizing a purpose statement. On the other hand, there may be some researchers who find it necessary to go through even more levels of refinement than the four suggested here. The point is simply that an initially posed concern must pass through several stages of in-depth reading, reflecting, and asking questions before a research purpose may be formulated. Seldom is one's very first question specific enough to serve also as the actual research purpose.

Tables 4.2 to 4.5 describe how one may transform a concern into a research purpose. The tables are intended as guidelines, not as hard and fast rules to which everybody must adhere at all times. To illustrate the use of these tables we will refer back to the situation of Teacher X, Mike, who was concerned about the poor musical response of some of his elementary students. Beginning with that concern, we follow the teacher through the research process as he selects an investigative area, defines a general research idea, refines it into a research topic and, finally, formulates a purpose statement.

Level 1: The Selection of a Research Area (Table 4.2)

As previously discussed, concerns about the learning-teaching process in music may develop from personal observations and teaching experience or from insights gained by reading the professional literature. One observes and reads about specific behaviors and speculates about their causes (Step 1.1) As there are many reasons why people act the way they do, there are also many possible explanations about such behaviors and equally as many avenues by which the explanations may be tested.

The first task in reading the literature (Step 1.2). consists of finding out how others in the profession have studied and/or explained the nature of musical behaviors. Insights are gained into the various perspectives by which music educators have viewed the learning-teaching process in music. In reading the literature and in reflecting on the reasons why the students behaved the way they did, one begins to contemplate the causes that may provide the best explanations for the observed behavior (Step 1.3). Each possible cause is worded in the form of a question.

Any of the questions formulated may have an equal chance of becoming the avenue by which concerns about the learning-teaching process can be investigated and by which a better understanding of students' musical and social behavior may be gained. The selection of one question from among the many should be guided by an informed judgment about the scope of professional literature extant in any of the areas of concern identified by the researcher (Steps 1.4 to 1.6).

At this level of reading, the literature still covers a broad scope of issues since many alternative approaches exist by which observed behaviors can be explained and workable solutions to problem behaviors may be studied. It is therefore possible for the scope of the literature covered to become substantially broader than one's initial question seemed to suggest.

What Teacher X Did

The poor musical response of some students in the classroom caused Mike concern. He speculated about reasons for their behavior and looked for ways to change it. He began his search by asking whether all the students had consistently shown the same degree of poor musical response, and whether he had done anything in his teaching that made it difficult for the students to follow the instructions or to understand his explanations. He also began to wonder about the behavior of the other children in the classroom: Did they behave properly because they truly understood the subject matter or because they were too polite (or too grade-conscious) to indicate boredom or frustration? Did they imitate

Table 4.2   Level 1: The Selection of a Research Area

Step	What To Do	Examples
1.1	*Identify* personal concerns about the learning-teaching process in music.	(a) Some students do not sing in tune, walk to the beat of the music, clap in rhythm, or read/sing at sight. (b) Some students are not attentive. (c) Some students seem to lack an understanding of teacher instructions.

1.2	*Read* literature on the concerns identified under 1.1.	Subject headings may be[1]:
		For (a): Pitch-Matching Behaviors, Pitch Perception, Sight-Singing Skills, Rhythm Responsiveness, Rhythmic Perception.
		For (b): Attentiveness, Attention Span, Motivation.
		For (c): Any of the terms above, as well as: Instructional Analysis, Instructional Methods, Instructional Sequence.

1.3	*Specify* your concerns by asking "true" questions about them.	What do students fail to understand? Is that failure the same for all of the observed students, a majority, a few? How should one measure student learning? Should one distinguish between memorization/imitation and understanding? What do the students actually hear compared with what you think they hear? How would one assess such listening skills? What do those skills have in common with motivation and discipline? What sociological and/or psychological factors may contribute to the students' learning gains, their motivation, and their overall attentiveness? Did you account for such factors in the planning of the instructional sequence?

Table 4.2 (*Continued*)

Step	What To Do	Examples
1.4	*Reflect* on which of the questions under 1.3 interest you the most and/or what question, if answered, might contribute to the solution of your initial concern.	
1.5	*Select* one question as stated under 1.3 and *identify* areas in music education that deal with that question from an angle that interests you.	For example, how do you determine/measure student learning? Related areas may be: Teacher effectiveness Student learning Measurement of learning Acquisition of skills and knowledge in music Objectives in music education Aesthetic education History of music education
1.6	*Read* literature on the areas identified under 1.5.	Key terms may be: Teacher language Teaching style Teacher success Accountability Curriculum development and evaluation Teaching materials Learning sequence Instructional techniques Teaching methodologies Music aptitude and achievement Concept learning and perception Motivation Student maturation and gender Student socioeconomic, ethnic, home, and school environment
1.7	*Reflect* on how the issues may relate to teaching methods used by you or advocated in music teaching textbooks. *Identify* contradictions of beliefs in various publications, and note similarities in thoughts.	Is the sequence suggested in books working? What is the impact of age and maturation on musical learning? Is there a hierarchy in which musical elements are perceived? What does the literature say about these questions? What do method books say? Are there discrepancies?

Table 4.2 (Continued)

Step	What To Do	Examples
1.8	*Select* one area identified under 1.5 that you feel pertains the most to your initial concerns.	For example, student learning.
1.9	*Collect* bibliography of Steps 1.2 to 1.6 and write down your reflections on the chosen area up to this point.	

[1]Subject headings are taken from *Music Psychology Index*.

him rather than showing actual learning? These and similar questions prompted Mike to want to know more about learning responses in general—that is, how they could be assessed and how they could best be defined. Additionally, he began to question some of his own teaching goals and those of the profession.

Questions about the relationship of motivation, discipline problems, and teaching effectiveness came up: Should Mike not judge learning by what the students actually knew rather than by the way they showed attentiveness in the classroom? Was he more interested in long-term or short-term learning results? How would one assess both types of learning, and what role would sociopsychological factors play in such assessments and comparisons?

In reading articles and books on topics related to these questions, Mike found some articles that addressed to what extent the students' sociopsychological problems might be the source of misbehavior. Other studies established a direct relationship between the students' behavior and their difficulties in understanding teacher instructions or in following a particular style of teaching. Some educators suggested that the students might not be interested in music because they did not see the need to know what they were expected to know.

Mike realized that student behavior could be studied from the viewpoint of improving instructional methods as well as from the viewpoint of studying musical perceptions and the students' ability to perform specific learning tasks in music. For each of these issues he found many books and research- and opinion-based articles that examined such aspects as teacher language, teacher success, accountability, curriculum development, curriculum evaluation, teaching materials, learning sequence, instructional techniques, teaching methods, music aptitude, music achievement, music perception, concept learning, motivation, and teacher-student interaction.

In consulting various method books on instructional strategies, Mike

Table 4.3   Level 2: The Selection of a Research Idea

Step	What To Do	Examples
2.1	*Read* publications related to the area selected under 1.8.	*Student learning* Key terms may be: Children's responses to music Musical perception and processing of auditory stimuli The relationship of language learning to learning in music The relationship of chronological age to musical learning The application of learning theories to music
2.2	*Select* one key term from those under 2.1 for further reading.	For example, children's responses to music.
2.3	*Read* publications specifically related to the aspect chosen under 2.2.	Related issues may be: Preferences and attitudes of children to music Perceptual responses to specific tasks (pitch, rhythm, harmony, tone color) Hierarchical structure of perceptual tasks Development of listening skills Definition of *perception* as suggested by various authors and researchers
2.4	*Select* one issue from those under 2.3 for further study	For example, children's perceptual responses to specific musical tasks.
2.5	*Reflect* on how research on the selected issue may contribute to a better understanding of your initial concern (see 1.1). *Identify* specific factors (variables, constructs) that may need researching.	Perceptual responses to specific tasks may depend on: (a) The response mode used—i.e., kinesthetic, lingual, visual. (b) Chronological age, and/or exposure/experience, (e.g., perception may be effected more by exposure/experience than by chronological age).
2.6	*Select* one or two of the factors identified under 2.5 as your research idea.	Your research idea may be: to study children's perceptual responses to specific tasks in music in relation to their age and exposure to and experience in music.
2.7	*Collect* bibliography of Steps 2.1 and 2.3 and take notes about reflections up to this point.	

noticed that they offered somewhat contradictory statements about what should be taught as the first, second, and third steps in an instructional sequence. He began to wonder whether the concept of sequence as reflected in the textbooks was the same as that suggested by several research studies in music education. He also agreed with writers in the field that skills taught in early grades did not seem to serve as a foundation for additional learning. He discovered that the profession seemed to know very little about what constituted an appropriate learning sequence in the elementary music curriculum. He found an area much written about but lacking in evidence about what the correct sequence of learning tasks might be.

Level 2: The Selection of a Research Idea (Table 4.3)

This table describes the process of selecting one research idea from the many that may be found within a chosen research area. An idea is the result of thinking. It demands the act of reflection and the ability to consider alternatives. In the context of finding a research purpose, we therefore define a research idea as the hunch, or notion, about what should be investigated in the confines of a more broadly defined research area. That idea is developed by choosing a previously identified key term for further reading and study (Step 2.1).

By reading publications pertinent to the chosen key term (Steps 2.2 and 2.3), it will once again become apparent that each term is still broad in scope (Step 2.4). The decision of how to delimit the scope should be guided by (a) one's area of expertise, (b) the personal interest one has in a particular mode of research, and (c) one's ability and/or opportunity to work with children and/or adults. Other considerations should be the quantity and quality of existing studies pertinent to each of all possible research avenues, as well as the kind of variables that would need investigation (Steps 2.4 to 2.6).

What Teacher X Did

In Step 1.8, Mike had chosen as his research area the question of how students learn music. To narrow that question down to several research ideas, he acquainted himself with a variety of publications that looked at different ways of describing the process of musical learning. He read publications on the mastery of certain performance techniques as well as on the assessment of instrumental or vocal sight reading abilities and achievements; he located studies on the measurement of shifts in musical preference, on music appreciation, and on the relationship between musical ability and specific sociopsychological factors that contribute to learning in music. He learned about researchers who had described their observations of children's responses to music at different age levels.

Other researchers had applied theories of language learning to the study of learning in music. Numerous attempts had been made to apply general learning theories to music. Mike became slightly confused about those theories and attempted to understand more about them. He read publications on the relationship of chronological age to musical perception in the process and found references to Jean Piaget, Jerome Bruner, and Benjamin Bloom. He decided to learn more about these people.

Soon it became apparent to Mike that Piaget, Bruner, and Bloom had been of great influence to research in music education although they had not specifically investigated aspects of musical learning. Instead, they had formulated various theories about learning in general, and music educators seemed to have adopted those theories in their own efforts to formulate explanations about how children learn music.

Mike also noticed that music education researchers held differing views on how general learning theories might affect the development of theories on musical learning. Some of these researchers seemed to believe that the same general principles of learning held true for all subject areas; others suggested that musical learning and perception differed enough from other types of learning that an adaptation of general learning theories to research on musical behavior was not warranted. Those researchers believed it necessary to gather enough data to develop learning theories that were fully based on the observation of musical learning rather than on the observation of learning in other fields.

Of the various approaches music education researchers had employed in the investigation of the nature of musical learning, the study of *children's responses to music* appealed to Mike because he found it to be a logical way to study the nature of musical learning in the classroom. His initial area of concern originated from observations in the classroom, and he felt at ease with that type of environment. He therefore focused his reading on such topics as the development of specific performance tasks and/or skills of music listening at various age levels; preferences and attitudes of children to music; and children's listening habits at different age levels. He noticed that many different "chunks" of variables had been considered by researchers who investigated the nature of children's responses to music. One group of investigators had studied children's understanding of the musical elements (e.g., pitch vs. rhythm, harmony vs. tone color). Other researchers had attempted to develop theories about which of the elements in music were the easiest to perceive and which the most difficult.

A large group of studies addressed questions of music appreciation as well as attitudes toward and preferences for music. A fewer number of researchers had described step by step how they systematically observed the responses of learners to specific learning tasks in music, and how such responses varied with different ages and with regard to other, albeit related, variables. This survey of the the literature led Mike to conclude that children's responses to music had been studied primarily from the viewpoints of *musical perception* or *appreciation and preference*. He also noticed that both avenues would result in the development of distinctly different research ideas. Mike decided to follow the viewpoint of musical perception.

Specifically, he wanted to know how children would respond to a variety of musical tasks because he relied heavily on that type of listening in his instructional methods. He wanted to know how children labeled their perceptions of high and low sounds and fast and slow and long and short phrases. He wished to find out how children responded to tasks in which they were to discriminate same from different phrases, patterns, and motives. Such knowledge, Mike reasoned, would enable him to design teaching strategies that were truly based on a sequence that came from what the learner actually knew rather than from what the teacher thought the learner knew.

In his readings Mike came across the idea that musical understanding may be demonstrated by the execution of specific musical tasks. Such tasks often center around a child's ability to label certain tone patterns according to appropriate musical terminology. The proper execution of such tasks is then interpreted in the research literature as a reflection of the musical concept a child has developed. This idea intrigued Mike and he decided to pursue research that would address the relationship of a child's ability to execute musical tasks to the child's musical and developmental background. Specifically, Mike chose to compare the effects of chronological age on musical learning relative to the effects of exposure to and experience in music. He wished to know the effect of the teaching environment on tasks of musical learning, and he was interested in the impact the mode of response (verbal, aural, or tactile-kinesthetic) had on children's ability to perform selected musical tasks. He wondered about the relationship between the successful completion of musical tasks and the length of those tasks.

In raising these questions and in reading the related literature, Mike noticed a scarcity of conclusive evidence about the relationship between age and exposure to musical perception. He reasoned that the answer to that question would have major implications both for music education as a field of study and for the development of specific teaching methods. He thus became interested in the investigation of musical perception as related to chronological age versus musical exposure and experience. He had decided on one research alternative from among the many ideas that came to his mind once he had chosen to investigate children's perceptual responses to specific musical tasks.

Level 3: Defining the Research Topic (Table 4.4)

Although a research idea gives the investigator a fairly clear idea of the direction a research study might take, the parameters within which that idea is to be investigated have not yet been specified. The idea has not been compared with the step-by-step procedures other researchers have employed in the investigation of the same or similar idea. The research idea has not been

Table 4.4 Level 3: Defining the Research Topic

Step	What To Do	Examples
3.1	*Read* in detail studies pertaining to the research idea selected under 2.6. Focus exclusively on research-based publications.	See, for example: Bennett, 1981; Deutsch and Roll, 1974; Klemish, 1973; Lenz, 1978; Ramsey, 1983; Rimm, 1966; Sergeant and Roche, 1973; Shatzkin, 1981; Taylor, 1972; Webster and Zimmerman, 1981.
3.2	*Identify* major points of argument and/or discussion in the studies. Assess the quality of the various research methods and designs, such as strength of rationales, methodologies, findings, and conclusions.	Things to look for: *Rationale*: cohesiveness of theoretical basis, use of primary sources, inclusion of most studies pertaining to the idea under study. *Methodology*: use of appropriate measurement tools, size of sample, appropriate data analysis. *Conclusions*: close relation to reported results, confidence in data collection.
3.3	*Reflect* on: (a) Does a need exist for additional verifiable support for given research results? (b) Do the results of related studies support or contradict each other? (c) Does a need exist to relate newly discovered information or insights to previously made conclusions?	
3.4	*Formulate* several research topics based upon your reflections under 3.3.	Topics may be: (a) To determine the difference in children's ability to perceive simple tonal elements separated from melodic context and incorporated into melodic context. (b) To question the nature of testing materials used to measure children's responses to music—to test the feasibility of using same–different, alike–not alike as sole response modes.

Table 4.4   (continued)

Step	What To Do	Examples
		(c) To compare constructs of musical perception described in textbooks with the findings of pertinent research studies.
		(d) To compare abilities of pitch and rhythmic perception to gender, age, and musical exposure.
		(e) To assess differences in the perception of familiar and unfamiliar melodic patterns.
3.5	*Select* one research topic from those listed under 3.4 and *reflect* on whether the investigation of that topic will (a) aid you in the understanding of the nature/cause of your initial concern(s), and (b) will have to be studied *after* some other aspects have been looked at first.	E.g., Example (a) under 3.4: to determine the difference in children's ability to perceive tonal elements separated from melodic context and those incorporated into melodic context.
3.6	*Collect* bibliography of Step 3.1 and take notes of your reasoning up to this point.	

placed within existing theories about musical behavior, nor has much thought been given to how those theories compare with each other. From such in-depth analysis, however, the research topic develops. It specifies the research idea and demands a critical and detailed analysis of investigations pertinent to that idea.

At this level of reading (Step 3.1), each study must be analyzed according to its research purpose, research problems, research design, mode of inquiry, and the employed methodological techniques. The conclusions must be shown to be truly based on the data and results of the study; weaknesses and strengths in each of the investigations must be determined; and the degree to which each study has made a contribution to one's own research idea must be ascertained (Step 3.2). In some investigations, major flaws in sampling procedures may be found; other studies may seem to be on the right track but have weaknesses in carrying out the research design or in analyzing the data. Whatever the strong or weak points in an investigation, each of them has the potential of contributing to the definition of one's own topic. Flaws in a study might prevent one from falling into some pitfalls, and strong studies may serve as models for one's own research efforts.

Step 3.3 in Table 4.4 lists three points of reflection that should be applied to the critical analysis of research studies and that might help a person develop several research topics pertinent to a given research idea. These points are: (a) whether there is a need for additional evidence because of small sample size, poor documentation of evidence, or faulty argumentation; (b) whether various studies contain research results that contradict each other; and (c) whether one's personal insights into the topic suggest a change in the designs of the studies. Answers to these questions provide an array of possible investigative topics (Step 3.4).

After having identified several research topics, one topic must be selected as the basis for the actual investigation (Step 3.5). The selection should be guided by the same considerations that held true for selecting a research area and a research idea: (a) the quantity and quality of existing research on each respective topic; (b) the researcher's resources and investigative expertise; and (c) considerations about which topic may contribute the most to answering the first general concern that triggered the search for the purpose statement. Also, as one topic might have to be investigated prior to others, the researcher should determine in which order several studies might have to be conducted in order to follow a logical sequence of thought.

What Teacher X Did

Mike's research idea was to study children's perceptual responses to specific tasks in relation to chronological age and exposure. His reasoning was as follows:

Need for Additional Evidence
Studies on children's perceptual responses to music generally dealt only with small groups of children. More evidence for how children behaved "musically" was needed before final conclusions could be drawn. Mike formulated as one possible research topic the replication of a particular study using a different group of children.

Supportive or Contradictory Research Results in Several Studies
1. According to Bennett, Ramsey, and other researchers, different children prefer different response modes for showing what they hear. Mike's question, therefore, was whether the restriction to one response mode in several of the designs of existing studies on perceptual responses could have adequately shown children's abilities in musical perception. A modified replication of an existing investigation might be necessary that utilized a variety of response modes and children of different ages and musical exposure.
2. Some researchers made children respond to short but abstract rhythm and pitch patterns, whereas in other studies children identified

short melodic excerpts within which various pitch and rhythm patterns were imbedded. The results of those studies suggested that the perception of rhythm and pitch patterns in separation from each other was not the same as the perception of such patterns in melodic context. There was, however, disagreement among the researchers whether musical perception was dependent on one's perception of melodic patterns or on the perception of pitch patterns isolated from rhythm patterns. In addition, results on rhythmic abilities of children seemed to outnumber studies on pitch perception. Mike questioned whether those two elements were sufficient constructs of musical perception. He therefore defined as a third possible research topic the investigation of constructs of musical perception. He thought about approaching such a topic using either an empirical or a philosophical mode of research.

Personal Insights in Relation to Existing Research Designs

Mike questioned the approach by which perceptual responses of young children had been investigated separately for tasks on pitch perception and tasks on rhythm perception. He reasoned that such logic followed that of trained musicians, who have learned to discriminate among the musical elements as the "building blocks" of music and, thus, the basis of auditory perception. Results reported in some research literature as well as Mike's own teaching experience suggested that young children found it difficult to separate pitch from rhythm structures. As the sequencing of learning steps was said to move from the familiar to the unfamiliar, from the simple to the complex, and from the concrete to the abstract, easy should be what was familiar and concrete to the child, not the musician. Mike felt that certain research designs violated that premise when investigators asked young children to separate pitch from rhythm in perceptual tasks. Such a task should come more appropriately at a later point in the learning sequence. Mike reasoned that musical perception should be measured by tasks that used melodic patterns in their entirety, not separated into pitch and rhythm patterns. Many research topics and related activities resulted from that reasoning, some of which were:

1. To provide proof for the reasoning that children's ability to perceive tonal elements isolated from each other develop later than their ability to perceive and identify melodic patterns.

2. To question the procedure of measuring children's responses according to same–different, alike–not alike, and/or to question the nature of testing materials used by various educators to measure children's perceptual responses to music.

3. To investigate children's responses to melodic perception in relation to pitch/rhythm perception, or children's responses to rhythmic perception in relation to age and exposure/experience.

4. To investigate the difference between children's ability to perceive tonal elements separated from melodic context and in melodic context.

5. To assess differences in the perception of familiar and unfamiliar melodic patterns.

Table 4.5   Level 4: Formulating the Research Purpose

Step	What To Do	Examples
4.1	*Formulate* specific questions about the topic chosen under 3.5. Consider questions that pertain to all three research modes.	a) What is *simple?* What is *familiar?* Would a phenomenological approach toward the question be necessary prior to any further work?
		(b) What do we mean by "musical perception"? Can the term be defined clearly? Must an attempt be made philosophically? Empirically?
		(c) What comparisons between children would truly show differences in perception? What kind of tasks should be designed? How would one account for differences in socioeconomic background or other external factors?
		(d) How have music educators of the past dealt with questions like those in (a), (b), and (c)?
4.2	*Select* one of the questions stated under 4.1 and *speculate* about possible ways of researching it. *Formulate* one possible answer in the form of a purpose statement.	The purpose of the study is to investigate: (a) Constructs of familiar and simple in the context of perceptual tasks in music.
		(b) Children's long-term ability to identify melodic patterns in familiar and unfamiliar musical contexts.
		(c) The relationship of age and gender to the ability to identify pitch patterns in familiar and unfamiliar musical contexts.
		(d) Children's ability to recognize structures of pitch and rhythm patterns in familiar and unfamiliar melodic contexts.

77

Table 4.5 (*Continued*)

Step	What To Do	Examples
		(e) The influence of general learning theories on theories of learning in music.
		(f) The relationship of socioeconomic background and the execution of perceptual tasks in music.
4.3	*Reflect* on your intellectual, financial, and time resources; experiences; teaching skills and background in various research methods; availability of subjects, research literature, and equipment; and level of cooperation among individuals likely to be directly involved with the project.	How much will the project cost? Are there good research models to follow? Will you have access to all documents, other primary source materials, people, measurement tools, and equipment to investigate any of the research purposes? In which of the research methods are you best trained?
4.4	*Select* one purpose statement for your investigation.	
	Conduct a preliminary investigation (pilot study) to familiarize yourself with the specifics of the project.	(a) In philosophical research, establish premises, axioms, propositions, arguments.
		(b) In historical research, develop a series of specific questions and know content of all primary sources.
		(c) In empirical research, select, test, and establish the usefulness of major measurement tools and equipment and secure subjects for the investigation.
4.5	*Finalize* the purpose statement.	

Level 4: Formulating the Research Purpose (Table 4.5)

Developing a research purpose from one selected research topic requires less reading than is necessary at the first three levels. The process is, instead, guided mainly by one's ability to reflect about the research literature and by one's skill in giving those reflections the proper wording. The questions posed should include all possible avenues of inquiry. The questions given as examples for Step 4.1 make use of different modes of inquiry, suggesting that a research topic may be studied from various perspectives. Choosing the perspective most suitable for one's own purpose is the beginning of Level 4. Which of the questions are ultimately selected as the basis for a research purpose, depends, once again, on the researcher's insights into the extant research literature on all the questions. Some investigations reveal flaws in reasoning as well as design. Other studies suggest interesting ways of answering specific research purposes. The pros and cons of a variety of research methods, purposes, possible problems in the investigation of each of them, the isolation and control of variables, one's training in research, and knowledge about research methods are weighed against each other. And, again, personal, financial, and time resources necessary for the completion of a research project must be considered. A college student should also take into account the expertise and professional background of his or her primary academic advisor.

The best way to finalize a research purpose is by conducting a pilot investigation on the question that seems most appealing to a researcher. A pilot investigation differs from a full-fledged study in that the researcher is allowed to check out a variety of ideas while the study is being conducted. Research tools may be tested or developed and specific difficulties in researching particular questions may be determined. Based on insights gained from such preliminary investigative efforts, a question may be reexamined and, if necessary, reworded and more clearly delimited. From there, the final purpose statement is developed.

What Teacher X Did

As the result of wanting to study the nature of the constructs of musical perception of children, Mike had come up with five possible research topics. He had then selected the first topic for further delimitation: to provide proof for the reasoning that children's ability to perceive tonal elements isolated from each other developed later than their ability to perceive and identify melodic patterns. In attempting to prove the validity of this statement, decisions had now to be made about the mode by which the proof would best be established. Would a philosophical discourse provide the most convincing argument, or would the gathering of new empirical evidence be most appropriate? Which aspect of the proof should be looked at first? Was it important to study whether the isolation of tonal patterns into rhythmic and pitch patterns constituted a different task than the identification of melodic patterns, or was it important to show the difference between familiarity and simplicity from the viewpoint of the learner and the teacher/musician?

Mike knew that if he chose the avenue of philosophical inquiry he would have to develop a logical argumentation about the terms *simple* and *familiar* in their relationship to each other, *perception,* and modes of identifying such perceptions. If he wanted to provide new empirical evidence he would have to decide whether the study should be experimental or descriptive. Would he compare groups of children who received different musical instruction for the purpose of the investigation, or would he gather the evidence from a systematic description of children's musical responses in regular classroom music teaching? What age group should be involved, what would be the nature of the musical tasks, and what modes of response would the children be allowed to utilize? Would such descriptive evidence be sufficient for providing the desired proof? Or could he perhaps conduct a study in which evidence for his proof was gathered by interviewing a large number of music teachers about their thinking on the matter? Answers to these and similar questions caused Mike to formulate six different research purposes similar to those given as examples for Step 4.2. From that list of purposes, he chose to investigate the third purpose, and reworded it as the investigation of the relationship of gender and chronological age to the ability of children to identify pitch patterns in familiar and unfamiliar musical contexts.

4.4 Summary

The actual research purpose is chosen and decided upon by five equally important and interrelated considerations: (a) the initial, general question that originates from personal and professional experience; (b) an in-depth understanding of the body of knowledge of music education; (c) the place and significance of the research purpose in the context of already existing research studies; (d) one's personal experience in conducting research; and (e) financial and other resources available for investigating a given research purpose.

The reading of the literature should occur on levels of increasingly more clearly defined questions, and a cycle of reading, reflecting, and questioning should lead one through that process. A researcher should become thoroughly familiar with all aspects of those studies that pertain closely to the chosen research topic so that the purpose may develop from knowledge of what is and is not known in the field.

A person should be acquainted with each step reported in a study because a thorough familiarity with the methodologies of other investigations may determine the nature of one's own research. Thus, for each study read, one should know its precise purpose statement and its related questions, problems, and/or hypotheses; one should know the rationale—the reasoning—behind the choice for a particular purpose; and one should be familiar with all aspects of the methodological steps taken and know all major findings and conclusions. Finally, a researcher should be able to evaluate critically the weaknesses and strengths of any given study and understand how it relates and contributes to the proposed investigation. The more knowledgeable one is about all those aspects of extant research in the field, the easier it will be to find one's own purpose statement and place it into a framework that makes sense, not only to the research community in music education in particular but also to the music teaching profession at large.

Suggested Activities

1. Find an area of research interest.
2. List three topics in that area that could be the subject of a research investigation.
3. Ask questions about the chosen topics.
4. Turn the questions into purpose statements.
5. Identify major questions in historical, philosophical, and empirical research studies. List names of researchers who have used each of these techniques.

Topics for Discussion

1. Difficulties in finding research areas. The mind as the practice room.
2. The relationship between a research area and purpose of study.

Suggested Readings

Barnes, S. H. (Ed.) (1982). *A cross-section of research in music education.* Washington, D.C.: University Press of America.

Bloom, B. S. (1976). *Human characteristics and school learning.* New York: McGraw-Hill.

Bruner, J. S., Goodnow, J. J., & Austin, G. A. (1956). *A study of thinking.* New York: John Wiley.

Carroll, J. B. (1973). Basic and applied research in education: Definitions, distinctions, and implications. In H. S. Broudy, R. H. Ennis, and L. I. Krimerman (Eds.), *Philosophy of educational research* (pp. 108–121). New York: John Wiley.

Ebel, R. L. (1973). Some limitations of basic research in education. In H. S. Broudy, R. H. Ennis, and L. I. Krimerman (Eds.), *Philosophy of educational research* (pp. 122–130). New York: John Wiley.

Gordon, E. E. (1985). Research studies in audiation: I. *Council for Research in Music Education, 84* (Fall), 34–50.

Gordon, E. E. (1984). *Learning sequences in music: Skill, content, patterns*. Chicago: G.I.A.

Gordon, E. E. (Ed.) (1972). *Experimental research in the psychology of music: 8.* Iowa City: University of Iowa Press.

Gordon, E. E. (Ed.) (1970). *Experimental research in the psychology of music.* Iowa City: University of Iowa Press.

Hopkins, P. (1982). Aural thinking. In R. Falck and T. Rice (Eds.), *Cross-cultural perspectives on music* (pp. 143–161). Toronto: University of Toronto Press.

Howell, P., Cross, I., & West, R. (Eds.) (1985). *Musical structure and cognition.* Orlando, FL: Academic Press.

Lefrancois, G. R. (1982). *Psychological theories and human learning: Kongor's report* (2nd ed.). Monterey, CA: Brooks/Cole.

Petrie, H. G. (1973). Why has learning theory failed to teach us how to learn? In H. S. Broudy, R. H. Ennis, and L. I. Krimerman (Eds.), *Philosophy of educational research* (pp. 122–130). New York: John Wiley.

Petzold, R. G. (1963). The development of auditory perception of musical sounds by children in the first six grades. *Journal of Research in Music Education, 11* (1), 21–54.

Piaget, J. (1952). *The origin of intelligence in children.* New York: International Universities Press.

Radocy, R. E., & Boyle, J. D. (1979). *Psychological foundations of musical behavior.* Springfield, IL: Thomas.

Rasch, R. A., & Plomp, R. (1982). The perception of musical tones. In D. Deutsch (Ed.), *The psychology of music* (pp. 1–24). Orlando, FL: Academic Press.

Serafine, M. L., Crowder, R. G., & Repp, B. H. (1984). Integration of melody and text in memory for song. *Cognition, 16,* 235–303.

Wittrock, M. C. (Ed.) (1986). *Handbook of research on teaching.* (A project of the American Educational Research Association, 3rd ed.). New York: Macmillan.

Zimmerman, M. P. (1971). *Musical characteristics of children.* Reston, VA: Music Educators National Conference.

REFERENCES

Andress, B. (1986). Toward an integrated theory for early childhood music education. *Council for Research in Music Education, 86* (Winter), 10–17.

Atterbury, B. W. (1984). Children's singing voices: A review of selected research. *Council for Research in Music Education, 80* (Fall), 51–62.

Bash, L., & Kuzmich, J. (1985). A survey of jazz education research: Recommendations for future researchers. *Council for Research in Music Education,* 82 (Spring), 14–28.

Bennett, P. D. (1981). *An exploratory study of children's multi-sensory responses to symbolizing musical sound through speech rhythm patterns.* Unpublished doctoral dissertation, North Texas State University, Denton, TX.

Colwell, R. J. (1985). Program evaluation in music teacher education. *Council for Research in Music Education, 81* (Winter), 18–62.

Cooksey, J. (1974). An accountability report for music education. *Council for Research in Music Education, 36* (Spring), 6–64.

Deihl, N. C., & Partchey, K. C. (1973). Status of research: Educational technology in music education. *Council for Research in Music Education, 35* (Winter), 18–29.

Deutsch, D., & Roll, P. L. (1974). Error patterns in delayed pitch comparison as a function of relational context. *Journal of Experimental Psychology, 103,* 1027–1034.

Glenn, N. E. (1972). A review of recent research in high-school general music. *Council for Research in Music Education, 27* (Winter), 17–24.

Gonzo, C. (1973). Research in choral music: A perspective. *Council for Research in Music Education, 33* (Summer), 21–33.

Greenberg, M. (1976). Research in music in early childhood education: A survey with recommendations. *Council for Research in Music Education, 45* (Winter), 1–20.

Holt, D. M. (1974). Competency-based music teacher education: Is systematic accountability worth the effort? *Council for Research in Music Education, 40* (Winter), 1–6.

Katz, L. G. (1986). Current perspectives on child development. *Council for Research in Music Education, 86* (Winter), 1–9.

Klemish, G. (1973). A review of recent research in elementary music education. *Council for Research in Music Education, 34* (Fall), 23–40.

Lenz, S. M. (1978). A case study of the musical abilities of three- and four-year-old children (Doctoral dissertation, University of Illinois at Urbana-Champaign, 1978). *Dissertation Abstracts International, 39,* 2809A.

Leonhard, Ch., & Colwell, R. (1976). Research in music education. *Council for Research in Music Education, 49* (Winter), 1–30.

Ramsey, J. H. (1983). The effects of age, singing ability, and instrumental experiences on preschool children's melodic perception. *Journal of Research in Music Education, 31,* (2), 133–145.

Rimm, D. C. (1966). *The effect of context on tonal memory.* (Doctoral dissertation, Stanford University, 1965). *Dissertation Abstracts International, 26* (11), 6877.

Shatzkin, M. (1981). Interval and pitch recognition in and out of immediate context. *Journal of Research in Music Education, 26* (2), 111–124.

Sergeant, D., & Roche, S. (1973). Perceptual shifts in the auditory information processing of young children. *Psychology of Music, 1* (2), 39–48.

Simons, G. (1986). Early childhood musical development: A survey of selected research. *Council for Research in Music Education, 86* (Winter), 36–52.

Taylor, J. A. (1972). Perception of melodic intervals within melodic context (Doctoral dissertation, University of Washington, Seattle, WA, 1971). *Dissertation Abstracts International, 32* (11), 6481A.

Webster, P. R., & Zimmerman, M. P. (1981). Conservation of rhythmic and tonal patterns in second through sixth grade children. Paper presented at the Music Educators National Conference, Minneapolis, MN, April 22.

Zimmerman, M. P. (1986). Music development in middle childhood: A summary of selected research studies. *Council for Research in Music Education,* *86* (Winter), 18–35.

Chapter Five

Research Purpose, Rationale, and Problems

Definition of Terms and Other Delimitations

5.1 Introduction

In chapters 3 and 4 the researcher's efforts were described as centering around the library and other deposits of information. The investigator gathered and made value judgments on the work and writings of other people in various fields of knowledge. As a result of the orientation stage, a purpose for the project was found by way of personal observation and critical reading.

Following the orientation stage, a phase of planning begins. It, too, should be characterized primarily as a time of reflection and critical thinking. However, an important juncture has now been reached because the planning stage of a research project entails the determination of (a) the reason for and the purpose of the investigation, and (b) the data to be gathered in order to accomplish the purpose of the study. Such reflections are likely to change the researcher from a novice in the field to a knowledgeable expert. The actual activities of the planning stage are: (a) the development of a rationale for the study; (b) the specification of several research problems or questions that will be subjected to an in-depth investigation; (c) the delimitation of the scope of the study; and (d) the determination of the specific techniques associated with the selected mode of inquiry by which the problems, events, or questions are to be investigated.

Prior to carrying out all planned activities, the rationale, purpose of the study, and research problems/questions should be written down. This affords the researcher the opportunity to review the logic behind the reason for the study and to apply self-criticism to that logic. Writing down the research problems/questions also permits the researcher to determine: (a) if all necessary points of research interest are included; (b) if the mode of inquiry and the chosen investigative techniques are appropriate for obtaining all essential data; and (c) if the researcher needs to acquire additional skills or techniques to complete the planned investigation successfully.

Placing the rationale, purpose, and research problems/question in writing is an important step for both the novice as well as the experienced researcher. In addition to helping one tighten the logic of a proposed study, the written form of one's research plans becomes a necessary tool for delimiting a study to truly researchable proportions. Beyond that, it may be necessary to explain the nature of the study to others if financial assistance for a project is sought or if one wishes to consult with colleagues about the feasibility of a certain research design or measurement tool.

5.2 The Connection Between Research Rationale, Purpose, and Problems/Questions: Specific Examples

Research rationales, purpose statements, and problems should be found in all studies that are reported in respected research journals. Because of the limited space available in most journals, the length of the rationale may be considerably shorter than that used in a formal thesis or dissertation. Some researchers prefer to call the research purpose the problem. What we refer to as research problems would then become subproblems. Often, researchers elect to state those subproblems in the form of questions. Which term to use—problem, subproblem, or question—is ultimately a matter of individual preference. In the final analysis it is imperative to have well-formulated research objectives; it matters much less which term is attached to the objectives.

In the following, we present to the reader three studies, each of them in a different mode of inquiry. Inspite of their seemingly different formats, all three studies contain the elements of rationale, purpose, and problems in some explicit form. Two of the three studies have been published as research reports; one is available only in dissertation form. The sections on rationale, purpose, and research questions have been quoted as published by the respective researchers. The reader may also want to consult examples of research articles published in journals other than music education journals. Stylistic features tend to be handled differently from journal to journal and discipline to discipline, but in better research reports the reader should always be able to identify readily the three components we consider the heart of all research: rationale, purpose, and problems/questions.

Example of a Study Based upon Principles of Empirical Inquiry (Ramsey, 1983)[1]

Rationale

Aural perception is a crucial component of the music learning process, and a basic knowledge of the manner in which aural perception of musical sounds develops and functions during childhood is essential to music educators. Recent research (Michel, 1973) has indicated that significant musical development, particularly the development of vocal and auditory abilities, occurs during the preschool years. However, little information about the nature of the development of musical auditory perception of the preschool child is available.

Studies in other sensory modes, particularly visual perception (Piaget, 1970; Vernon, 1960) have disclosed that perceptual learning changes as children's cognitive structures change and develop. Some research (Carter, Ricker, & Corsini, 1972) has suggested that a similar phenomenon may also exist in auditory perception. Particularly in the area of melodic perception (De Gainza, 1970; McDonald & Ramsey, 1979; Sergeant & Roche, 1973), research has suggested that young children may focus on different aspects of melody and that their perceptual responses, consequently, may differ with age. The conflicting results in age differences in these studies, however, point to the need for further research in this area.

Furthermore, several studies (Buckton, 1977; Moore, 1973; Sergeant, 1969) have suggested that young children's melodic perception may be enhanced by experiences with pitched instruments during early childhood. No study, however, has explored specifically the effect of instrumental experience on preschool children's ability to perceive component aspects of melody. In addition, research (Lenz, 1978; Williams, 1932) has indicated that a singing response is a viable measure of young children's perception of musical stimuli, particularly perception of pitch and melody, if some index of the child's vocal control abilities is available before the onset of research procedures. Although singing has been used frequently as a mode of response for measurement of melodic perception among preschool children, no study has attempted to control singing as a variable or to investigate its effect on measurement of melodic perception. (pp. 133–134)

Purpose and Problems

The purpose of this study, therefore, was to investigate the effects of age, singing ability, and training with pitched instruments on preschool children's auditory perception of melody. The study investigated children's perception (as indicated by song vocalization) of five specific melodic components: absolute pitch level, melodic rhythm, melodic contour, tonal center, and melodic interval. Specific research questions, which the study sought to answer, included the following:

1. Are there significant interactions among the factors of age, singing ability level, and training treatments as reflected through the perceptual task mean scores of preschool children?
2. Are there significant differences across age groups in preschool children's auditory perception (as measured through song vocalization) of melodic components such as (a) absolute pitch level, (b) melodic rhythm, (c) melodic contour, (d) tonal center, and (e) melodic interval?
3. Is there a significant difference between the auditory perception of melodic components of preschool children classified as high-ability singers and that of preschool children classified as low-ability singers?
4. Is there a significant difference between the auditory perception of melodic components of preschool children whose training included experiences with pitched instruments and that of preschool children whose training did not include such experiences? (p. 134)

The rationale begins with a rather generalized view of the researcher's concerns in that the opening paragraph contains an idea most people in music education can accept as being true: Aural perception is important in the learning process, and a better understanding of the development of skills in aural perception may enable a teacher to guide the students' learning experiences much more effectively. In the next two paragraphs the concerns are delimited. The second paragraph cites studies supporting the idea that in visual perception a child's learning modes change with maturation. Ramsey adds that research tends to suggest that some auditory perceptual responses in music may differ with age, but that such research has produced conflicting results. The third paragraph further delineates the reason for conducting the research by citing investigations that suggest the study of instrumental music may enhance the melodic perception of children. According to the researcher, these ideas have not been fully investigated. Therefore, she proposed to conduct an investigation that would measure the relationship of young children's ability to sing and their ability to perceive a melody. The rationale in the first three paragraphs thus leads into the purpose of the study, which is stated as the first sentence of the fourth paragraph. This sentence narrows the study down to an even greater degree. The research questions then specify the research purpose by breaking the latter into specific investigative tasks that should, if pursued properly, provide a satisfactory resolution to the research purpose. The questions have become the guide (or road map) for the investigation.

Historical and philosophical studies frequently have a different format than the majority of empirical studies. The modes of inquiry dictate some of the differences. Aspects common to empirical, historical, and philosophical studies, however, are (a) the rationale—the "why" of the study; (b) the "what"—that is, what portion of an historical event will be investigated; (c) the perspective from which the investigator will view the data; and (d) the conclusions, the "so what" aspect of the study.

Example of a Study Based Upon Principles of Historical Inquiry (Barresi, 1981)[2]

Rationale

Throughout the centuries, governments of great nations, states, and cities have participated in promoting the arts for enrichment and edification of the lives of their citizens. These governing bodies believed, as did John F. Kennedy, that societies are ultimately judged by the quality of their cultural environment, and that nations are remembered, not for their victories or defeats in wars or politics, but for their contributions to the human spirit.

The above analysis implies that government support of the arts, both financial and advisory, is important to the development of a healthy cultural environment. Moreover, support of a nation's arts establishment and arts education programs should be of prime concern to any national government. Contrary to popular belief, American government involvement in the arts supports this contention.

This report outlines the role of the federal government in support of the arts and music education by examining historical precedent for arts support from 1790 to the establishment of the National Endowment for the Arts in the 1960s. It will also examine cooperative ventures of artists and arts educators that were, to some degree, influenced by government personnel, funds, and programs.

A chronological investigation of federal involvement may assist in the comprehension of those factors that have influenced past government arts intervention. By placing instances of past federal assistance into periods identified by the common thread of "necessity," a better understanding may be gained of factors influencing present-day funding procedures—as well as the likelihood of continued funding for the arts and music education. A policy of "practical necessity," followed during the nation's formative years, provides the setting for early federal support; that of "economic necessity" encompasses the financial crisis of the Great Depression period; while the period of "cultural necessity" provides a framework for considering government response to the social, financial, and artistic needs of Americans during the decades of the 1960s and 1970s. (pp. 245–246)

In the first two paragraphs, Barresi stated rather clearly why the study was justified. He noted that the idea of governmental support for the arts was normal in most nations, cities, and states, and had been so for centuries. Barresi also observed that the United States government has been actively involved in such support for an extensive period of time. The final sentence in the second paragraph represents the purpose of the study. The third paragraph describes Barresi's delimitations (1790–1960s) and those events within that time frame that the researcher had decided to examine. The final paragraph establishes the organizing principle of the study—the way the researcher had planned to look at the data. The first sentence supports the "why" of the study, whereas the remainder of the paragraph serves to guide the reader in the perspective from which the research should be viewed and interpreted.

Example of a Study Based Upon Principles of Philosophical Inquiry (Turley, 1976)[3]

Rationale

In the preceding pages we have discovered a strong lack of agreement among music texts in their approach to leading the novice to an understanding of music. The distinctions between appreciation, enjoyment, prerequisite skills (especially music notational reading), knowing, and understanding are not consistent. The precise skills involved, even among those who list them, vary in importance. Finally, the conditions for understanding music are, to say the least, questionable. That the concept of understanding in relationship to music is mired in a state of ambiguity is thus evident. (p. 10)

Problem Statement

There is not an agreement among musicians in general and music educators specifically, as to what is meant by understanding music. Therefore, the methods employed to arrive at any "understanding" are diverse and vary in accordance with whatever goal is contrived. This disparity affects the public school curriculum. In addition, it does not allow for the construction of an agreed-upon base leading to the music education of our youth. Until music education as a profession is presented with and accepts a uniform description of terminology, in this case "understanding," there will continue to be a lack of communication concerning the preparation and training of our progeny. (p. 11)

Purpose of Study

The present endeavor will first conduct a conceptual analysis of the concept *understanding*. Concurrently with the analysis, references will be made to some of the prominent epistemological literature which deals directly, or indirectly with *understanding*.

Second, will be a conceptual analysis of the concept *music*. Concurrently with this analysis, reference will be made to prominent literature which attempts to arrive at an effective description of *music*.

Third, application will be made, through discussion, of the results of the analysis concerning *understanding* and *music*, as the two concepts may qualify each other. This will result in establishing some parameters of *understanding music* as it relates to *music education*. The treatment of *music education* will be primarily through some of the activities of teaching music.

[3]Reprinted by permission of the author.

Concurrent with this, reference will be made to prominent literature which refers to music education and the activities of teaching.

Finally, a summary of the endeavor, which will include ramifications for curriculum in *music education.* (p. 12)

The introduction to the first chapter of Turley's dissertation contained a lengthy discussion of issues germaine to the investigation (pp. 9–16). Subsequently, Turley summarized that discussion in order to provide the rationale for the study—that is, the first paragraph in the quotation reprinted here. The rationale for the study rested on the conflicting statements found in music text books regarding the question of what constitutes *musical understanding.* Turley saw the roots for that basic conflict primarily in the unclear definition of the meaning of the term *understanding of music.*

The purpose of the study (paragraphs three to six) sets forth the areas to be discussed and the delimitations (parameters) of the study. Furthermore, the methodology to be employed in the investigation—epistemology—was mentioned. Turley also noted that he expected the results of the study to be of practical value for the development of a music education curriculum.

5.3 Steps in the Development of the Research Rationale and Problems/Questions

As just illustrated, the rationale, purpose, and research problems are a complete package in that one aspect should logically follow from the other. The reason why a study is being conducted should smoothly lead to the purpose statement which, in turn, should point to the research problems that specify precisely what is to be investigated. The difficulties in conceptualizing the research purpose and problems/questions are generally far greater than finding answers to the how-to-do-it aspects of the study—that is, the methodological questions about an investigation.

The Research Rationale

A rationale is a logical explanation of the fundamental reasons why something exists. In research, the rationale constitutes an abstract of the facts and points pertinent to the chosen purpose of study. It is thus a selected summary of the body of knowledge that is specific to the investigation, and serves as the justification for the purpose statement. Through the use of critical reasoning, the rationale also positions the research project into a specific theoretical framework within the body of knowledge. The rationale thus has a dual function: (a) For the researcher it provides the logical framework for the definition of the purpose of the investigation; and (b) for the reader it serves as the explanation for the purpose of the study, establishing the theoretical framework within which to place and interpret the results of the investigation.

The organization of the rationale follows a procedure similar to that outlined in Tables 4.2–4.5 in chapter 4: moving from the general to the specific. The literature that has been collected through the reading of dissertations, articles, and books serves as the resource material. From this extensive body of resource materials, those studies, articles, or statements are selected that seem to be the most salient in supporting the need for the study.

To illustrate this point, the reader is asked to refer back to the purpose statement Mike, the elementary music teacher, developed in Chapter 4: After he had observed the learning behavior of his children in the classroom and after he had read the pertinent literature about children's responses to music, he decided to investigate the relationship of gender and chronological age to the ability of children to identify pitch patterns in familiar and unfamiliar musical contexts. Such a study lies in the realm of empirical inquiry, and its rationale is therefore likely to utilize empirically based studies more than philosophical or historical investigations.

What Teacher X Did

Mike saw the purpose statement directly linked to the idea that the perception and identification of sound structures is an important factor in the development of musical literacy. Therefore, he searched for support of the notion that the perception of sound structures is vital in the development of hearing and the performing of musical patterns and phrases.He reviewed the notes taken during previous readings and looked for general statements in method books or articles that confirmed music listening and sound discrimination as important objectives of elementary general music. Appropriate statements to that effect were paraphrased and/or cited. He briefly referred to sources that suggest music educators are not satisfied with the progress they have made in the successful teaching of listening skills in music.

Next, Mike found support in the literature for the idea that there was a need for understanding the sequence in which children develop perceptual skills in music. He cited investigations that addressed such issues as children's ability to do certain perceptual and listening tasks in a variety of contexts. He described those studies and their findings, indicated possible contradictions in results among several studies, and documented those investigations that showed differences in children's abilities to perceive tonal elements in various musical contexts. He included studies in his argument that supported the notion of a marked difference between the perception of melodic patterns in familiar and unfamiliar musical material. He referred to studies that suggested the ability to do certain musical tasks may be related to gender and may vary with maturation. Because of that possibility and because the hearing of pitch patterns is considered important to overall listening abilities, Mike pointed out the need to investigate the relationship of chronological age to the perception of pitch patterns in familiar and unfamiliar melodic material.

In preparing to write a research rationale, first, all references are gathered. Then they are placed in order, from general to specific. Subsequently, an outline must be developed in which the findings of all studies are linked together in such a way that the need for a specific study becomes evident. The rationale thus becomes a logically organized narrative of personal comments, observations, and research studies that lead directly to the purpose statement. The rationale is not intended to be a detailed discussion of all that has been read. The related literature section of the proposal, thesis, dissertation, or research paper may provide such an in-depth approach. Conflicts in the finding and conclusions of various studies may be described, and the researcher considers what may have caused the conflicts and how one may find more definitive answers that would solve the conflicts. The rationale of a study may be viewed as an abstract of such a discussion.

When writing the narrative, excessive quotations should be avoided. Instead, a researcher's own words should be used to describe the statements and findings of other writers. Verbatim quotations should appear only if the full wording of a statement is essential to the logical development of an argument. All quotations as well as paraphrases should be kept as brief as possible and should, wherever possible, be cited from primary sources.

The length of a rationale varies. If it is to appear in a journal article or a scholarly paper, the rationale will have to be kept to a maximum of one to two typewritten, double-spaced pages. In most theses and dissertations, 6 to 10 pages may suffice; however, it is not unusual under those circumstances for the rationale to be longer than 10 pages. On the other hand, on rare occasions one page of writing has provided a perfectly acceptable justification for a research purpose.

The Relationship of Research Purpose to Research Problems/Questions

In order to utilize the stated purpose of a study as the compass for all subsequent research steps, the questions, problems, or subproblems become of importance because they specify precisely, step by step, what one wishes to investigate. As all research problems or questions are derived from the purpose statement, they should, if investigated in an adequate manner, provide the results that help satisfy the purpose of the study.

The procedure of breaking the research purpose into smaller, workable units is not unlike the procedure employed in the writing of a good term paper, good journal article, or a good written response to an essay question: All aspects referred to in the title (purpose) must be investigated if the topic is to be handled adequately. Consider, for example, the title of a philosophical dissertation conducted several years ago: "A philosophical study of qualitative movement: Implications for early childhood music programs" (Ball, 1982). At least three aspects are inherent in that title and should be identified by appropriate research problems/questions after all terms have been defined: the nature of qualitative movement, the essence of early childhood music programs as currently practiced, and the relationship of both aspects to each other.

93

The explicit presentation of questions relevant to those three areas serve as delineation, if not delimitation, of the research purpose. If such a delineation is lacking, the investigation may wander into territories not pertinent to the purpose of the study. That danger, however, is particularly evident in studies where the purpose statements are rather general in nature. Thus, when researching the essence of ideas and philosophical concepts, the statement of problems/questions provide the researcher with the parameters that determine, beyond the purpose statement, the major line of argumentation. A preconceived line of argumentation is essential if one wishes to avoid a thinking-while-you-work approach.

In research that is rooted in the historical mode of inquiry, the equivalent to specific research problems should consist of a series of questions about the times, events, or people studied. For example, if a research study is entitled "Musical aesthetics and social philosophy in France 1848–1879" (Fulcher, 1977), at least three problem areas emerge from which appropriate questions should be formulated. First, one would expect a variety of problems/questions regarding the concept of musical aesthetics in France during the designated time period; second, one assumes that the researcher would address questions relevant to an understanding of the social philosophy of the time and locale; and, third, the researcher would have to pose questions that refer to the relationship of the musical aesthetics of the time to its underlying social philosophy.

In research that is rooted in the empirical mode of inquiry, the problems/questions of the study are usually dictated by the number of variables—that is, observable units of behavior referred to in the purpose statement. Second, one determines whether the observable behavior can be manipulated or not. In the case of the earlier-cited purpose statement, "to investigate the relationship of gender and chronological age to the ability of children to identify pitch patterns in familiar and unfamiliar musical contexts," at least two variables can be manipulated and two variables cannot be manipulated: Pitch patterns in familiar as well as in unfamiliar music can be manipulated; chronological age and gender are variables that cannot be manipulated. Consequently, the following could be stated as the research problems of the study chosen by Teacher X:

1. To estimate the ability of boys in different chronological age groups to identify pitch patterns in familiar music.

2. To estimate the ability of boys in different chronological age groups to identify pitch patterns in unfamiliar music.

3. To estimate the ability of girls in different chronological age groups to identify pitch patterns in familiar music.

4. To estimate the ability of girls in different chronological age groups to identify pitch patterns in unfamiliar music.

5. To compare the results from these problems to determine the relative importance of gender and chronological age in identifying pitch patterns in varying musical contexts.

The research purpose could also have resulted in three rather than five problem statements if the following wording would have been chosen: (a) to estimate the ability of boys in different chronological age groups to identify pitch patterns in familiar and unfamiliar music; (b) to estimate the ability of girls in different chronological age groups. . . ; and (c) to compare the results between the investigated boys and girls. Another choice for the researcher would have been to formulate any of the problem statements as questions. For example, the first research question might have been: Does the ability of boys to identify pitch patterns . . . differ significantly from that of girls?—or—What is the ability of boys in different chronological age groups to identify pitch patterns. . . ?

Regardless of the form in which research problems are posed they should always express what variables the investigator intends to study. The problems should not reflect, however, how these variables are to be investigated. The development of a measurement tool, a test, a questionnaire, an observational system, interview questions, the review of literature, or the development of a philosophical argument should not be considered a part of the research problems. These items belong to the methodology section of an investigation because they refer to the procedures by which a question is resolved. The researcher may have difficulties in developing a measurement tool, in conducting interviews, or in finding an adequate number of primary sources, but the difficulties are not the problems of a study.

5.4 Definition of Terms and Other Delimitations of the Study

There is some conjecture in the research textbooks over whether or not delimitations other than purpose and problems should be spelled out in a specific section of a research report. The purpose of such delimitations would be to make explicit the boundaries of an investigation and to inform the reader of the limitations the researcher imposed on the investigation. One such delimitation lies in the researcher's effort to define clearly all terms that are crucial to an understanding of the study. The other kind of delimitation may arise from a variety of sources, such as the amount of time the researcher has available for the completion of the investigation; the availability of funding, resource materials, specific technological devices, or of measuring tools; and the researcher's own intellectual skills.

Definition of Terms

It almost goes without saying that the success of a research project lies undoubtedly in the clarity of all key terms, variables, and constructs of thought that make up the heart of an investigation. Thus, a researcher should never embark on a project without having defined ahead of time what certain key words mean in the context of the study. This step is a crucial part in the development of the research rationale in any mode of inquiry. (For specifics on the nature of and steps in developing good definitions, see chapter 7.)

Many theses and dissertations and some other types of research reports have specific sections in which the most important terms are alphabetically listed together with the definition chosen by the researcher. Other investigations do not have such a section. The question therefore arises: When does it become necessary to provide a detailed definition of terms? Unfortunately, there are no clear-cut answers to that question. Some suggestions seem in order on how to handle this uncertainty.

In our view, terms, words, and phrases generally used in the field of music education and commonly employed in research reports should not be formally listed unless the researcher uses them in an uncommon context. For example, statistical terms, such as *t*-test or analysis of variance; musical terms, such as quarter note, trumpet, key signature; or educational terms, such as preschool, elementary school, teacher, orchestra, choir need not be listed when they are used within a generally agreed upon context.

If terms possess a common definition that can be found in a standard reference dictionary, and if the writer or researcher employs the term in a manner consistent with that definition, then a formal, written definition is unnecessary. If the researcher is using "soft terms" or jargon-like terms, such as creative, aesthetic response, holistic experience, psychomotor domain, home environment, musical ability, or self-concept, it might be prudent for the writer/researcher to state precisely the meaning of those terms. A formal definition would be in order. (Again, see chapter 7 for some rules about the process of developing definitions.)

In many instances of music education research, the investigative tools overlap into other fields of study, such as physics, physiology, or social psychology. In those cases the researcher is obligated to understand and use the terminologies employed in the related fields. Since the researcher may be writing for two audiences—the music education audience and the audience outside of music—it may be necessary to provide more extensive definitions of the terms. For example, to clarify the aims of a study in the physiology of voice, the researcher may have to provide illustrations of where the muscles, nerves, and skeletal structures of the throat are located. While such information might not be necessary for the medical research audience, it would be essential for the musically trained reader.

The object of research is the communication of ideas. In most communication it is preferable to use commonly understood words and terms. But in the case of an operational definition—that is, a specific indication of how a term will be recognized in a particular investigation—that is not always possible. Researchers should exercise their best judgment in whether or not to provide a formal definition of a term.

When in doubt about the clarity of a term, locate a definition of the word in a reference dictionary. If that definition is consistent with the way you intend to use the term, refer to the dictionary (if possible, compare the definitions of several dictionaries and select the one that is the most clear). If the dictionary definition is unclear or differs from your usage of the word, find another word that has a clear and agreed upon meaning. If all this fails, then develop a precise meaning for the word and introduce it as your own definition. Above all, be consistent in the use of that definition throughout the research project and subsequent report.

Other Delimitations of the Study

Another section often included in a research report is that titled "Delimitations of the Study." In that section, a researcher lists all the factors that limited the study beyond those limitations implied by the research purpose and problems. Careful researchers, however, are aware of the limits of their own resources and abilities prior to finalizing their purpose statements and research problems/ questions. As we pointed out earlier in this chapter, the functions of a clear purpose and explicitly stated problems/questions lie precisely in the delimitation of an investigation. If delimitations have to be made, why not reduce the purpose and, consequently, the research problems to appropriate size and feasibility?

As much as the delimitations of a study begin with the delineation of the purpose of the study and its specific questions, novice researchers often select a research topic that is far too broad in scope and may, in fact, represent three or four projects, or even a life-long research endeavor. Also, even if a research purpose appears initially to be quite specific, the development of the research problems/questions may reveal the magnitude of a project much more clearly than the purpose by itself was able to do. To illustrate this point, we offer the following purpose statement to examine a hypothetical research purpose with regard to its implied problems/questions. We then discuss whether the purpose can be accomplished as stated or whether revisions/modifications of the purpose statement should be made in order to bring the study to manageable proportions—that is, delimit it more properly. From such a discussion we hope to show the nature of delimitations in research.

PURPOSE STATEMENT

The purpose of the study is to investigate the role of the offices of president and executive secretary in policy-making decision within the Music Educators National Conference during the years 1934–1984.

The intent of the study is clear. The researcher wishes to investigate two official positions within the organization of the Music Educators National Conference (MENC). The position of president is an elected one and the president may serve only one two-year term. The other position, that of the executive secretary, is an appointed position and may be held for an indeterminate period of time. Tenure in that position is at the pleasure of an executive board. The larger question behind the study addresses aspects of power and decision-making in the professional organization of music educators. Results of the study may help to shed light on the nature of that organization and on the image music educators have of themselves as a group of professionals. Beyond that, insights gained from the proposed study might contribute to the validation of theories in management and leadership structures.

In discussing the development of research problems pertinent to the purpose statement, the question format has been chosen because the study lies in the realm of historical inquiry. The questions refer to at least two aspects of study: the identification of the individuals who served as presidents and executive secretaries for MENC during the designated years, and the identification of policy decisions regarding MENC during the same years.

The first set of questions relates to the identification of the various individuals associated with MENC and pertinent to the purpose statement:

1. Who were the presidents of MENC during the years 1934–1984?

   (a) When did each of the presidents serve?

   (b) According to the Constitution of MENC, what was the stated role of the presidents during their period of tenure?

2. Who were the executive secretaries of MENC during the years 1934–1984?

   (a) When did each of these secretaries serve?

   (b) According to the Constitution of MENC, what was the stated role of the executive secretaries during their period of tenure?

The second set of questions relates to policy decisions during the years 1934–1984:

1. What policy decisions occurred during the years 1934–1984?

   (a) What policy was in effect in the year 1934?

   (b) What policy changes were made during the time frame under investigation?

   (c) According to MENC files and documents, who was most involved in initiating the policy change, the president or the executive secretary?

   (d) Did disagreements exist between the president and the executive secretary over the initiation of a policy change?

   (e) Did disagreements exist between the president and the executive secretary over the implementation of policy?

   (f) If disagreements between the two offices were found, what caused those disagreements?

   (g) If no disagreements were found, how did the president and the executive secretary involved coordinate their efforts?

   (h) Throughout the 50 years under study, what overriding picture emerges: agreement or disagreement between the president and the executive secretary?

It is not difficult to see that these questions are extremely broad since no attempt has been made to specify what kind of policy decisions the researcher should focus on in the investigation. A brief glance into the records in the archives may indicate that four major aspects of policy decisions have been of foremost importance to the organization of MENC. These are (a) constitutional changes; (b) programatic issues, such as official reports, position statements about the role of music in the schools and in society, the sponsorship of symposia, and other such issues; (c) budgetary decisions; and (d) the affiliation of professional societies and organizations with MENC. Taking these policy issues into consideration, the questions would be:

1. What *constitutional changes* took place during the years under investigation?

(a) According to MENC files and documents, who was most involved in initiating the change of constitution—the president or the executive secretary?

(b) Did disagreements exist between the president and the executive secretary over the initiation of a change of constitution?

(c) Did disagreements exist between the president and the executive secretary over the implementation of constitutional changes?

(d) If disagreements between the two offices were found, what caused those disagreements?

(e) If no disagreements were found, how did the president and the executive secretary involved coordinate their efforts?

(f) Throughout the 50 years under study, what overriding picture emerges: agreement or disagreement between the president and the executive secretary?

2. What *programatic issues,* such as reports, the role of music in the schools and in society, symposia, and so forth, took place during the years under investigation?

(a) According to MENC files and documents, who was most involved in initiating such issues as reports, position statements about the role of music in the schools and in society, symposia, and so forth?

(b) Did disagreements exist between the president and the executive secretary over the initiation of reports, position statements about the role of music in the schools and in society, symposia, and so forth?

(c) If disagreements between the two offices were found, what caused those disagreements?

(d) If no disagreements were found, how did the president and the executive secretary involved coordinate their efforts?

(e) Throughout the 50 years under study, what overriding picture emerges: agreement or disagreement between the president and the executive secretary?

3. What *budget decisions* were made during the years under investigation?

(a) According to MENC files and documents, who was most involved in budget decisions—the president or the executive secretary?

(b) Did disagreements exist between the president and the executive secretary over budget issues?

(c) If disagreements between the two offices were found, what caused those disagreements?

(d) If no disagreements were found, how did the president and the executive secretary coordinate budgetary decision making?

(e) Throughout the 50 years under study, what overriding picture emerges: agreement or disagreement between the president and the executive secretary?

4. What decisions about *publication policy* were made during the years under investigation?

(a) According to MENC files and documents, who was most involved in decisions on publication policy—the president or the executive secretary?

(b) Did disagreements exist between the president and the executive secretary over publication policy?

(c) If no disagreements were found, how did the president and the executive secretary coordinate decision making about publication policy?

(d) Throughout the 50 years under study, what overriding picture emerges: agreement or disagreement between the president and the executive secretary?

5. What *professional societies* and *organizations* became affiliated with MENC during the years under investigation?

(a) According to MENC files and documents, who was most involved in decisions on publication policy—the president or the executive secretary?

(b) Did disagreements exist between the president and the executive secretary over the affiliation of specific professional societies and organizations?

(c) If disagreements between the two offices were found, what caused those disagreements?

(d) If no disagreements were found, how did the president and the executive secretary coordinate efforts to affiliate with specific professional societies and organizations?

(e) Throughout the 50 years under study, what overriding picture emerges: Agreement or disagreement between the president and the executive secretary?

The actual number of questions one could pose for each of the five selected aspects of MENC policies exceeds those stated here. The topic is evidently very broad, and prospective researchers would be well advised to delimit the study by including in the title only those aspects they truly wish to investigate—for example, decisions on budgetary or constitutional policies.

It must be stressed that any modification of the purpose statement due to unwieldy research problems also leads to a revision of the rationale, because tampering with any one component in the rationale-purpose-problems package generally necessitates adjustments in the other two components. Such tampering, however, tends to result in research activities that resemble "fishing expeditions" more than serious attempts to contribute to theory testing in the area of music education. Therefore, all revisions within the rationale-purpose-problems package should always be made very cautiously.

Finally, to answer the question whether a section on delimitations should be included in a research report: The delimitations of a study begin with the formulation of research purpose, rationale, and problems/questions. Therefore, the success of all subsequent research stages hinges largely on the researcher's ability to narrow the parameters of a proposed study early in the orientation stage. Furthermore, a study is always delimited by the selected mode of inquiry and its related methodology. Historical, philosophical, and empirical research techniques have inherent rules, perspectives, and biases that serve to delimit the investigation. Ideally, the researcher should provide logical reasons for all delimitations because they serve to cast a research project in terms of what the researcher will and will not explore. Delimitations should not and do not serve as an excuse for avoiding work.

Suggested Activities

1. Write a rationale for a chosen purpose statement.
2. Select a purpose statement related to a historical topic and develop a list of questions necessary to resolve the purpose statement.
3. Select a number of purpose statements from literature related to philosophical inquiry and identify their appropriate subtopics.
4. Select a purpose statement related to an empirical topic and develop the appropriate research problems.
5. Read five research studies and critique rationale, purpose, and problem statements.

Topics for Discussion

1. The place of the rationale in the research project.
2. The relationship of research purpose to problems/questions.

Suggested Readings

The following sources may be found in H. S. Broudy, R. H. Ennis, and L. I. Krimerman (Eds.). *Philosophy of educational research*. New York: John Wiley, 1973.

Brodbeck, M., Logic, language, definition and concepts (pp. 614–623).
Ennis, R., Operational definitions (pp. 650–669).
Hempel, C., The vocabulary of science: Technical terms and observation terms (pp. 179–181).
Kerlinger, F. N., The mythology of educational research: The methods approach (pp. 102–107).
Skinner, B. F., The operational analysis of psychological terms (pp. 624–635).

REFERENCES

Ball, W. A. (1982). A philosophical study of qualitative movement: Implications for early childhood music programs (Doctoral dissertation, Case Western Reserve University). *Dissertation Abstracts International, 43* (6), 1870A.

Barresi, A. L. (1981). The role of the Federal Government in support of the arts and music education. *Journal of Research in Music Education, 29* (4), 245–256.

Fulcher, J. F. (1977). Musical aesthetics and social philosophy in France 1848–1879 (Doctoral Dissertation, Columbia University). *Dissertation Abstracts International, 37* (7), 3217A.

Ramsey, J. H. (1983). The effects of age, singing ability, and instrumental experiences on preschool children's melodic perception. *Journal of Research in Music Education, 31* (2), 133–145.

Turley, M. R. (1976). *A study of the concept of understanding as it may be applied to understanding music in music education* (Doctoral dissertation, The Ohio State University).

PART THREE

Modes of Inquiry: Approaches to Resolving the Research Purpose/Problems

Parts 1 and 2 of this book have centered on the conceptual aspects of research. This part focuses on some of the more technical aspects of the research activity, such as planning and conducting a study and gathering data for that purpose. The first three chapters in this part address the modes of inquiry that researchers employ. Because the investigative process tends to be different for each mode of inquiry, one chapter each is devoted to the description of historical inquiry (chapter 6), philosophical inquiry (chapter 7), and empirical inquiry (chapter 8).

The purpose of a study determines its mode of inquiry. But although different in specific methodological steps, each of the modes reflects principles of scientific inquiry: A purpose is clearly stated, specific questions are posed, testable questions/hypotheses are formulated, and evidence is gathered to test the hypotheses and to answer the questions. From the evidence, conclusions are drawn that help to resolve the stated purpose.

Each mode carries with it its own advantages and limitations. Therefore, and in order to strengthen an investigation, a researcher may utilize techniques drawn from several of the modes. It is this reasoning that places chapter 9 (The Development of Measurement Tools) and chapter 10 (The Use of Statistics in Quantitative Data Analysis) at the end of Part 3. Traditionally, these topics have been considered germane only to empirical research. We propose to view them as tools that, in certain situations, may be appropriate for data gathering and/or analysis in historical as well as philosophical inquiry.

Chapter 6 (Approaches to Historical Inquiry) discusses principles of data collection and verification as well as the development of researchable questions. Included is a description of historical approaches that scholars outside the field of music education have utilized: oral history, psychohistory, and quantitative history. Finally, there is a section on the interpretation of data. The chapter concludes with an example of planning the methodology for a specific study.

The philosophical mode of inquiry is addressed in chapter 7 (Approaches to Philosophical Inquiry). Music students seldom elect or have the opportunity to enroll in philosophy courses. As a result, philosophical inquiry may for many students be the least understood of the three modes of inquiry. The chapter centers around two aspects of philosophical discourse: definition of terms and the development of an argumentation. In the discussion of those two aspects, propositional and dialectic argumentation are stressed as two of the systems of logic that in our view may be most beneficial to researchers in music education. In addition to those systems, phenomenological and speculative systems of argumentation are briefly described.

Chapter 8 is a discussion of the empirical mode of inquiry. It begins with a description of its basic assumptions and logic. From there, the levels of empirical research are introduced—namely, description, correlation, experimentation. The nature of data, the design or planning of a study, and the drawing of conclusions from the data are the major points of discussion.

The empirical mode of inquiry does require the construction of data gathering tools and an understanding of statistical concepts. Chapters 9 and 10 address those points. Chapter 9 is devoted to a description of the development of measurement tools. Included are aspects of test construction, survey instruments, rating scales, and observation systems, as well as the techniques of content analysis.

Chapter 10 is the most technically oriented of the five chapters in Part 3. Various parametric and nonparametric statistical tests are discussed and step-by-step procedures for working basic statistical problems are described. The chapter contains a word of caution on the use of statistics in music education research.

A final word about this more technically oriented part of the book: The chapters presented in this part are summaries or simplifications of rather broad and complicated areas of study. Summarizing and simplifying carries the danger of displeasing the knowledgeable specialist. In simplifying, one tends to make mistakes that to the uninitiated reader may not be noticeable, whereas to the expert they are monumental and inexcusable. We acknowledge that such danger may occur as a result of the attempt to make complicated matters seem a bit easier to comprehend.

Chapter Six

Approaches to Historical Inquiry

6.1 Introduction

Barzun and Graff (1985, p. 46) have suggested calling history the story of past facts. Some individuals believe that knowledge of those facts will serve as a preventative from the mistakes of the past. Others have gone beyond that and suggest that historical knowledge may aid in predicting future events. Most historians do not share such notions, and propose that historical research should only be viewed as an effort toward understanding the past. They assert that understanding can be gained by obtaining insights into why things may have happened; who may have played a role in causing those things to happen; and what events, both natural and man made, may have influenced the course of human events.

History as an attempt to understand the past is not just a collection of facts and names, although facts and names do play a role in creating an understanding of the past. Instead, historians who engage in research pose questions about the past and assemble data to answer the questions. General knowledge of the time period under study is applied to interpret the findings of the questions and to draw conclusions from them. As careful scholars, historians are equally concerned with finding facts as well as with the development of theories of history.

Since the mid-point of this century, historians have considerably broadened the scope of their research techniques (Kammen, 1980). They have become more analytical and "have tried harder than ever before to theorize and generalize" (Kammen, p. 30). In addition, Kammen points out that in the field of history a revolution has occured regarding the utilization of a wide variety of research techniques (p. 31). Historians are presently incorporating research techniques from the social sciences as well as from the natural sciences in their quest for knowledge. Particularly after having adapted quantitative methods to the needs of analyzing the past, several distinctly new research divisions in history have emerged. In addition to the "traditional," chronological approach, there are such research dimensions as psychohistory, oral history, quantitative social-scientific history, and comparative history. Of these five research branches, four of them—the chronological approach, oral history, psychohistory, and quantitative history—offer, perhaps, the most direct application to research in music education.

There are, of course, arguments over which historical research branch is the most honorable or provides the "true" path to knowledge. These arguments are not unlike those generated among musicologists and ethnomusicologists as well as among music educator-historians and music educator-empiricists as to whose research method is the most valid approach toward the development of a body of knowledge in music education. The traditionalists always appear to claim supremacy because their techniques are, after all, much older and have a long-standing acceptance in society. One would have to say, however, that good and bad quality can be produced in all branches of research regardless of the technical approaches used or of how old or new the research techniques may be. Ideally, researchers should have a working knowledge of all available techniques in order to evaluate properly the contributions of their peers.

Whatever the dispute over specific techniques may be, certain methodological steps should remain the same for all branches of the historical method. These steps are (a) to ask a multitude of precise questions related to particular events or person(s) of the past; (b) to gather and verify facts (data) related to those questions; (c) to develop criteria for selecting the data most useful in answering the questions and for rejecting information that may be considered irrelevant within the context of the study; and (d) to interpret the data by answering all questions posed. In the following, each of these steps will be discussed in detail. Subsequent to that discussion, consideration will be given to those techniques that specifically pertain to each of the branches of historical inquiry referred to earlier.

6.2 The Development of a Multitude of Specific Questions

In chapter 4 the process of how to move from a general concern to a specific research purpose was described. Whereas that process was primarily guided by the in-depth, critical reading of the professional literature, the final wording of the research purpose should not be determined until a preliminary investigation has produced evidence that the researcher's envisioned purpose may be useful and feasible. This means that some data gathering must precede any final wording of a research purpose. The gathering of information prior to conducting the actual study should accomplish two goals: The researcher should identify and confirm the existence of a substantial amount of relevant primary sources; and the researcher should identify specific "holes of knowledge" about the event or person(s) under study.

When conducting an investigation on individuals or events that are believed to have had an impact on the development of music education, a certain number of preliminary questions should be answered prior to the continuation of a project. A few of those questions might be: "Under what political and socioeconomic conditions did the individual live or did a particular event take place?" "Who were the general policy makers and educational leaders at the time under study?" "Were they instrumental in the promotion of specific music educational concerns?" "Who were the people that considered a particular individual or event to be important?" "Why?" "Did the person make truly identifiable contributions?" "If so, according to whom?" "Is it likely that the individual under study had equally as many enemies as supporters?" "May one assume that the importance of a particular event for the development of music education as a discipline, profession, or field of study was exaggerated by one group and down-played by another?" "Were specific events indeed as important as existing literature or some people have purported them to be?" "What happened to a person's best students, weakest students?" "Who were they?" "How did they assess the person's influence on them?" "What exactly did the person contribute to the field?"

Questions like these should lead the researcher to the pilot investigation. During that phase of the project, some primary evidence should be located that is pertinent to the various questions posed. Key witnesses to and/or documents of the events investigated should also be identified. Or, in the case where one wishes to investigate the life of an important person in music education, friends, relatives, acquaintances, colleagues, and/or students of that person should be identified and contacted. Only after a certain number of sources have been located and inspected by the researcher, and only after the feasibility of the research topic has been ascertained, should the research purpose be stated in final form.

6.3 Principles of Data Gathering and Verification Procedures

There is always a good possibility that a researcher might find unexpected sources of evidence throughout the course of a research project. Nevertheless, the process of gathering data should never be haphazard. Instead, the gathering of data and their verification should be clearly guided by the stated research purpose and a hypothesis, or hunch, about what may be found. All modes of inquiry need such a conceptual framework, and historical inquiry is no exception. Second, decisions as to what data to collect and how to verify their accuracy should also be influenced by the researcher's knowledge of the social, political, and economic pressures surrounding the chosen research topic. Most historical developments are shaped by a combination of such pressures, and the researcher must consider those most relevant to the study when the data collected are being reported and interpreted.

To illustrate: If the situation under investigation existed in the period from 1880 to 1900, the researcher should become familiar with what transpired during that span of 20 years politically, economically, and culturally on a worldwide, national, and local basis (if the research purpose was concerned with local issues). Such knowledge could be obtained from first-hand sources and might come from reading of historical chronicles, newspapers, and periodicals of that period. In addition, the researcher must be able to compare that knowledge with the general educational and social issues of the time. Developments in music and music education seldom occur in a vacuum, and often may be influenced, if not caused, by any number of political, social, or general educational developments in the period under study. Knowledge of the social and cultural history of the time is therefore imperative for any good historian in music education. Such knowledge should of necessity include familiarity with the occurrence of those nonmusical events of the past that may be held responsible for having shaped the course of historical developments in the field of music education.

Sources of Data

Depending on the purpose of a study, primary historical data may be located in libraries; specific archives; national, regional, and local newspapers; periodicals and pamphlets; professional publications; dissertations; governmental documents; and other local, regional, and national public records. Personal letters, diaries, and documented interviews with witnesses of past events may also provide sources of evidence.

International, national, and *state* and *local newspapers* as well as *major government documents* are housed in the research libraries of most major universities. These libraries also have large collections of general periodicals and professional publications from many periods. All these sources are invaluable in providing the necessary background for an understanding of the research project. They can be located in most research libraries either in their original form or as microfilm or microfiche. These sources may also provide the primary data for the study and provide clues as to where to search for additional data. In some instances the researcher may have to visit public libraries to acquire newspapers or periodicals not located in university libraries or known archives.

Archives and *manuscript* files are often catalogued in a way that makes it difficult to locate specific sources. Unless one has clearly defined research problems/questions and knows precisely the type of data one is seeking, the reading of documents may be endless. Even if one has a clearly defined purpose, it is still easy to get side-tracked into the reading of issues remote from the topic at hand. Sometimes, getting side-tracked can be fun and can result in interesting—and unexpected—findings. Frequently, however, it tends to confuse rather than help the collection of data.

Heller and Wilson (1982) point out some of the problems in the use of archives, and reading their article is recommended to anyone who wishes to engage in historical research. The authors discuss several directories for historical archives as well as the archives of the Music Educators National Conference Historical Center, located in the library of the University of Maryland in College Park, Maryland. This archive is growing and should become a valuable source for historical research in the field of music education.

In archival as in library research it is important to keep accurate records of: (a) source of data, (b) attributed author of the data, (c) location of the source (call number, archive location), and (d) date of document or source. This information should be attached to each copy, paraphrase, or quote one accumulates. Whenever possible, it is wise to obtain permission to photocopy those documents that are deemed to be the most important evidence in one's research.

Interviews may serve as the source of historical data if witnesses to events are still alive and are alert enough to speak about those events. Oral history (see section 6.4 of this chapter) is one area that utilizes interview techniques for that purpose. As with archival research, the collection of data from interviews requires prior knowledge about the kind of specific information needed to answer the research questions. Unless one is conducting informal interviews for the purpose of studying the feasibility of a specific research purpose, the questions should follow a structured outline because there is a danger that the person interviewed will ramble or talk of humorous events or side issues not pertinent to the purpose of the study.

Types of Evidence

Historical evidence is categorized into primary and secondary types of evidence. Primary evidence is provided by sources closest to the original event or person under investigation. An eye-witness account, an original document or manuscript, a diary or personal letter, or governmental records, such as birth and death certificates, may be considered primary source material. Secondary evidence is derived from sources like written histories, reference books (encyclopedias, dictionaries), and biographies in which the occurrence of original events has been described. A good term paper relies generally on secondary data; good research relies basically on primary data. Both types of evidence, however, can play an important role in the gathering of evidence. Secondary sources help to initiate a research question since written histories, biographies, and references often provide clues for the need of a study. Secondary data may thus provide the rationale for obtaining the primary evidence. Furthermore, secondary sources may aid the researcher in locating primary evidence.

The Verification of Evidence.   Once data are gathered, the researcher must verify their truth. Two examples may illustrate that process: In 1981, Bozarth assessed the influence of a former Duke Ellington bassist, Jimmy Blanton, on his contemporaries and succeeding jazz bassists (Bozarth, 1981). The researcher

111

began his investigation by consulting secondary sources (standard jazz reference sources and published articles on Blanton, available in jazz periodicals). Various authors speculated that Blanton had been born "around 1920" (Balliett, 1976), "some say 1919, others say 1921" (Feather, 1955). An obvious discrepancy existed in the reporting of Blanton's birth date, and a resolution was needed. Bozarth contacted the State of Tennessee, where Blanton was born, and requested a copy of the birth certificate. The clerks in the records department initiated a search of the records and provided Bozarth with a copy of the requested certificate. The certificate, signed by the physician attending the birth, indicated that all the published references to Blanton's birth dates were incorrect. Blanton was born on October 5, 1918, in Chattanooga. The author of the encyclopedia article and the authors of other articles had failed to seek primary evidence to verify the date of birth. The primary source proved the secondary sources incorrect and provided eye-witness evidence for the correct date.

A more detailed example of data verification may be found in Charles Sollinger's dissertation, "The music men and the professors: A history of string class methods in the United States, 1800–1911" (Sollinger, 1971). Until Sollinger completed his research study, it was commonly believed that class string instruction in the United States originated in 1911. Charles Farnsworth and Albert Mitchell were credited with transporting the idea from England to the United States (Grover, 1960). Sollinger uncovered information that suggested that Mitchell and Farnsworth's actions were only the culmination of a long development of instrumental class instruction in the United States (Sollinger, 1971, pp. 8–9).

Sollinger's data suggested that there were many teachers of singing who sold their books and offered music instruction. The data also indicated that many of the singing masters taught instrumental music lessons and sold instruments to their students. To allow more students to be taught and more instruments to be sold, some teachers during the mid-1800s combined the class techniques of the singing schools with instrumental teaching, actions which then produced class instrumental instruction (p. 9). Sollinger reported that these teachers used the materials of popular instrumental music—dance and social music—in their lessons.

The Howell brothers of Cotton Plant, Arkansas, were used as examples of the music teacher-merchants who were involved with class instruction. The *Howell's New Class-Book* (Howell, 1859) was located in the Library of Congress, and Sollinger verified the existence of the Howell Brothers through regional records. He demonstrated his knowledge of U.S. copyright laws by tracing the whereabouts of the Howell book from its registration in an Arkansas District Court in 1859 to the Smithsonian Institution and, hence, to the Library of Congress.

In a similar manner, Sollinger documented the existence of mass instruction on string instruments by the Benjamin family in New York, Brooklyn, Philadelphia, Camden, Pittsburgh, and Chicago. The researcher verified his data through the use of newspaper reports and public records of city residence

(Sollinger, 1971, pp. 42–82). He supported his contention that class string instruction was conducted in two different ways: (a) a popular-music oriented approach by the Howells, Benjamins, et al., and (b) a European-influenced art music approach with class instruction given by European-trained conservatory professors. Sollinger documented conservatory class instruction through official records obtained from Cincinnati Conservatory, New England Conservatory, Boston Music School, Oberlin Conservatory, Peabody Conservatory, and the records of the Chicago music schools (pp. 120–148).

The process by which Sollinger verified his data may serve as an excellent model for all historical research utilizing documents to establish evidence. Not only were the data obtained from primary sources, but the documents were also cross-verified by corroboration with other sources. Complete documentation was provided, and Sollinger demonstrated his knowledge of the time frame within which his topic fell by reporting the copyright law and publishing laws extant in the mid-1800s. His research may be considered an excellent model, almost a textbook for data verification in the realm of published evidence.

In the case of data obtained from diaries, a researcher should be cognizant of the fact that diaries are generally written because an individual wishes to be remembered at a later date. Therefore, information gleaned from diaries, while often very accurate, may be biased in favor of the writer. Diarists do not generally write about the darker side of their thoughts or actions since they wish to be remembered for what they perceive to be good. A similar bias is frequently found in preserved letters or other personal communications and mementos. It is human nature to discard bad performance reviews, publication rejections, and letters that refer to late payments of debts. Good reviews and complimentary letters are generally preserved for posterity. A researcher should be aware of that side of human nature and use that knowledge in making discretionary decisions about the content of information obtained through private primary sources.

Reporting the processes of data verification is essential to all historical investigations because the quality of a piece of research is assessed by the skill and care the researcher employed in carrying out and describing all verification processes. If the verification of evidence has been conducted with vigor, the reader can have confidence in the researcher. If verification of data is lacking or if seemingly inadequate procedures are employed, confidence in the investigator's skills and integrity becomes weakened.

6.4 Oral History, Psychohistory, and Quantitative History

In recent years, some historians have begun to advocate the use of methods common to research in the social and behavioral sciences. Some of those methods have developed from survey development and interview techniques, others from psychological inference and measurement. The three methods we consider to be most fruitful for historical research in music education are oral history, psychohistory, and quantitative history. Oral history has already been used quite extensively by some music educators; psychohistory and quantitative history might prove important in the future.

Oral History

The advance in recording technology provided an impetus for the development of oral history as a research technique. The goal of the oral historian is to preserve the views and insights of people who either have proven to be important for the development of certain causes in history or who are likely to be important for the development of such causes. The technique of oral history focuses on data collection by means of interview. The interviewing techniques advocated by oral historians are similar to those used in sociological research (see, for example, Downs, Smeyak, & Martin, 1980). The procedures include formal interviewing of an individual, tape-recording of all interview sessions, transcription and interpretation of all tapes, and preservation of the tape-recorded and transcribed interviews for posterity.

Prior to undertaking an oral history project, the researcher must, as in all research, establish topical boundaries by defining the purpose of the study and its related problems/questions. The researcher establishes these boundaries "by reading files on newspapers, going through official reports, begging wives for old letters and diary notes and talking with associates" of the person to be interviewed (Nevins, as quoted by Hoover, 1980, p. 400). From these sources the researcher must extract a list of central questions to be explored with the interviewee. This effort is, according to Nevins, "much as the written drafts of a tentative table of contents for a book he or she is about to write" (Nevins, as quoted by Hoover, p. 400). The interview takes an immense amount of time to prepare in advance. A researcher should be well advised that good oral history is not something that can be "winged." It is, instead, the result of careful planning, a comprehensive knowledge of the subject in the study, and skill in the ability to conduct interviews (for a more detailed description of interview techniques, see chapter 9).

In oral history, all interviews must be sound-recorded and/or video-recorded, a practice that is also recommended for all other research based on interview data. Permission to tape record an interview must be obtained *in writing* from the interviewee prior to any official interview sessions. Following all sessions, typed transcripts of the recordings must be made. The subject should be afforded the opportunity to read the transcript and correct possible mistakes caused by slips in memory. As a part of the data file, the complete transcript must be identified by date and name of person interviewed. It is customary to obtain from the person a waiver of legal rights in the recorded interview. The tape is then normally kept in a locked case in the library and made available to scholars on request.

Interview transcripts become the data base of a study: What is reported in the interview must be verified using both the researcher's knowledge of the historical events and skills in acquiring external validity corroboration. The person transcribing the text should be a typist with skills demanded of a court reporter. Researchers should be cautioned and advised that the procedure is a costly one and that this approach should not be considered without adequate sources for funding (Hoover, 1980, p. 400).

Oral history has become a recognized branch within the general field of history, and its basic research skills seem to have been worked out. But, according to Hoover, oral history has not consistently produced quality scholarship as many articles in publications by the Oral History Association tend to read "like show-and-tell reports on individual projects." (Hoover, pp. 399–400). In spite of these shortcomings, oral history should be considered as a potentially useful technique for music education research.

Psychohistory

The area of psychohistory is one of the newest approaches in historical research (Loewenberg, 1980), and may also prove of interest to researchers in music education. Its objective is to expand the definitions of historical research by including procedures of the behavioral sciences. Thus, in order to create a more comprehensive view of the past, psychohistory uses historical analysis in combination with psychodynamic theories and clinical insights into human behavior.

Historical events and changes in the course of time have not always been accidental, nor have they always been caused by wars or famines. Instead, historical developments have often been instigated by specific individuals who either worked with social-political groups or alone. Psychohistorians assume that the sociopsychological make-up of the individual may serve as the source for explaining either continuity or change of events. It is assumed that human psychology is a science and that by applying the presently known insights of human psychology, one might better interpret and explain why certain events or changes occurred.

Data gathering and verification procedures are similar to previously described historical techniques. An event is investigated in the traditional sense (i.e., interpretation based on chronological reporting), but the individuals who influenced the events are studied in greater detail and from the perspective of their psychological make-up. Such data may be produced by the application of content analysis techniques to the individual's writings (see chapter 9 for details), or they may be derived through an analysis of descriptions about events provided by the individual's colleagues, friends, or opponents. From such information a psychological profile may then be developed.

While data gathering and verification procedures in psychohistory resemble those of all historical and social science research, psychohistory differs from the more traditional history in the interpretation of events. Psychohistorians use their knowledge of the present to understand the past. They assume that the social sciences may provide the researcher with a new under-

115

standing of past human behavior and with new tools to interpret such behavior. As the sciences accumulate more knowledge about human emotions and reactions to emotions, there is reason to believe that the actions and motivations of present-day humans may not be much different from individuals of preceding generations. Thus, past behavior may be explained by what contemporary society has learned about human behavior. The manner in which data are interpreted, and the causation by which either continuity or change may be explained, marks the boundaries of and determines the differences between psychohistory and the other approaches toward historical inquiry.

Although still in its infancy compared with other research techniques in historical inquiry (Loewenberg, 1980), psychohistory is undoubtedly an approach that provides the investigator with an added dimension for interpreting past events. As such, techniques of psychohistory may also prove to be a useful tool to music education historians who wish to develop in-depth profiles of specific individuals who affected the development of the field. Not only would those techniques be applicable to the investigation of certain music teachers, performers, and conductors, but they might also be useful in developing insights into the psychological make-up of school board members of past generations who supported or opposed music instruction in the schools. As the techniques of psychohistory are rather new, they should be well understood and employed with caution in music education research.

Quantitative History

In the United States, quantitative social science procedures invaded the field of history during the years 1957 to 1961 (Kousser, 1980). Lee Benson (1972), a historian schooled in sociology, published in 1957 a critique of the "impressionistic" treatment of the 19th-century elections in the United States. Benson urged historians to expand their definition of primary sources beyond newspapers and manuscripts to include quantifiable data. For example, he urged that attitudes of people be used rather than attitudes of newspaper editors or politicians. By 1970, according to Kousser (p. 435), the fight to prevent the use of quantitative procedures in historical data interpretation was over. Most historians now agree that knowledge of empirical data-gathering techniques may be an asset to the development of their own body of knowledge.

Whereas most historical data continue to be gathered and verified by the use of standard historical procedures of qualitative description and analysis, verification of evidence has also been based on mathematical devices by which to determine the reliability of data. Interview consistency, stability of attitudes and judgments, and voting behavior have been analyzed quantitatively. In the case of voting behavior, for example, the Guttman scaling technique is often used to study the factors influencing the voting trends in political organizations (Oppenheim, 1966, pp. 143–151). Braudel (1981–1982) used statistical analyses of populations, food, and commerce to breath life into his study *Civilization and Capitalism, 15th–18th Century*. As Breisach (1983) has noted: "Historians have overcome the purely political historiography and brought most aspects of life within range of the historian's scrutiny" (p. 407). In doing so, historians, like their colleagues in the social sciences, aim at the development of social theories of history (see Kousser, p. 446).

Music education researchers may find many useful ways to employ quantitative techniques in the quest to learn about and understand the past. Take, for example, an investigation to determine the social factors that may have influenced the voting of past school board members on issues relevant to music instruction. The investigator might utilize some quantification techniques in order to establish trends and patterns in past voting behavior. Similarly, the study of decisions made by various professional organizations with regard to advancing the causes of music education may be approached by quantitatively analyzing the membership's consistency in voting. Quantitative measures could also be used to assess the financial support for arts programs in selected schools and communities over a long period of time. Using constant dollar figures and corrections for population growth or decrease, it would be possible to estimate the relative backing of the arts at any given time.

6.5 Interpretation of Historical Data and the Drawing of Conclusions

The successful interpretation of historical data is, first, dependent on a clear format in which the data are organized and reported. Second, a good writing style is essential for putting the data in perspective and for determining possible cause-and-effect relationships between the events under study. Understanding the significance of the data depends on the researcher's knowledge of events during the period under study. Without such a knowledge, thorough data comparisons and evaluation of the findings become impossible.

Organizing Data

There are several ways in which historical data may be organized in the research report and presented to the reader: chronological order, topical order, or a combination of both. Barzun recommends the last of the three approaches, in which each section of the project deals with a topic or one of its subdivisions and the chronology moves forward with the topic (Barzun & Graff, 1985, p. 276ff.). Each topic should be dealt with in an exhaustive and complete manner.

All three approaches have been employed by historians. Sollinger reported chronologically within topics, while most biographies of specific music educators tend to be organized strictly on a chronological basis. In biographies the chapters are often based on the individual's teaching positions or professional leadership positions within musical organizations. If the data have been organized and categorized according to the research problems/questions posed at the outset of the investigation, the topic arrangements should become self-evident.

Interpreting Data

Interpretation of data and reaching conclusions about them are tasks frequently beyond many music educators who undertake historical investigations. Too often, their studies end up being mere stories of what happened, without providing any critical evaluation of the happenings. To interpret data properly and to reach conclusions regarding their cause and effect relationships, a researcher must be informed on how people lived during the period under investigation, what transpired prior to and after the event(s) under study, and whether what happened was part of the continuity of the past or whether it represented change.

If a study is involved with the development of musical life in a community during a specific time, the researcher must not only know that community but be equally knowledgeable about the nature of musical life in similar cities within other states or countries. There must be a basis for comparison if conclusions are to be drawn. Did an opera house in a small Western town around 1870 really produce grand opera, or was the "art" production in such opera houses relegated to vaudeville and burlesque?

In the case of a biography of a band director in which evaluative judgments about the person's contributions to music education must be made, the researcher should be informed about the contemporaries of the band director. How did his contributions measure up to those of his peers? Did he exert an important influence on others? Did the contributions result in noticeable changes of teaching materials and instructional practices or were the contributions negligible ones? The evaluation must be honest and based on all data gathered. If the contribution turns out to be insignificant in the larger scheme of things, then that is the verdict and it must be so concluded.

It is exciting to find information in archival files, letters, and diaries. But the reader will only share this excitement when the researcher makes a clear case regarding the significance of the findings. To determine that significance, one must go beyond the mere reporting of the collected data. Relationships among the data have to be pinpointed, synthezised, and interpreted as to possible cause-and-effect characteristics. Such interpretation is accomplished if the questions "So what?" and "What does it mean?" have been answered.

Historical data are, at best, only fragmentary remains of what was once a reality. The historians, unlike the empiricists, cannot check their interpretation of events or conclusions against a personally known and inspected reality; the interpretation can only be checked against the fragmentary remains. In working with the data, the historian must keep in mind that history is factual, not fictional, and the goal of history is to reconstruct the past, not to create it.

The end result of historical research is normally reported in narrative form. Ideally, it should resemble reasonably good literature. If, for a variety of reasons, a research report in history cannot measure up to the standards of good literature, it should at least be precise and present the reader with a clear conception of the purpose of the study, how the investigation was carried out, how the data supported the conclusions, and how the conclusions may affect existing knowledge in and about the field of music education.

6.6 An Illustration of the Application of Various Methodological Approaches to Historical Inquiry

Next to a good purpose statement, the quality of good historical investigations lies in the planning of a strong methodology. As much as the researcher should be open to unplanned discoveries and findings, the quality of most research rests on the degree to which one has looked ahead and planned all steps in the investigative sequence. Even in historical inquiry, much of the methodology can be anticipated if the researcher is sufficiently knowledgeable about the purpose of the study.

As in all good research, thoughtful planning is essential to the process. However, methodological approaches commonly utilized in the historical mode have not been clearly described and are not necessarily agreed upon by all historians. More than a decade ago, Hexter (1971, pp. 12–14) lamented the lack of textbooks that would state in black and white terms what methods a researcher should employ in a historical investigation. A review of current historical and musicological research books shows that Hexter's lamentation is appropriate even today. The books discuss how and where to find data and they allude to the process of data verification, but any specific instruction seems to stop "just when the actual process of writing history begins. . . . What history stands sorely in need of is a pedagogic equivalent of *The Joy of Cooking*" (Hexter, p. 14).

Historians have a virtually unlimited number of methods to employ in their search to reconstruct the past. Depending on the questions that serve as the basis of such a reconstruction, any or all methods utilized by each of the other research modes may also be applied to historical inquiry. The nature of the questions asked therefore determine the methodology appropriate for the investigation. With a modified version of the hypothetical research purpose introduced in chapter 5 we hope to demonstrate how the nature of the research questions may influence the methods employed in the gathering and analysis of data.

The purpose of the proposed study is: To investigate the role of the Executive Secretary in policy-making decisions in the Music Supervisors National Conference (MSNC) and the Music Educators National Conference (MENC) during the years 1930–1955.

From this purpose, an initial theoretical framework will be presented, along with a rationale for doing the investigation. The discussion will be limited to two aspects of policy: publication policy and policy connected with the biennial conventions of the organizations under investigation. In presenting the rationale and line of reasoning, it should be understood that in a "study proper" all statements in the theoretical framework would have to be documented. Such documentation would not only pertain to quotations, but also to specific facts, such as names and dates in MENC history. The citations would have to refer to primary sources.

Background and Rationale for the Study

The MENC was established in 1934. It evolved from an older organization, the MSNC. In 1930 the governing body of the MSNC announced that it was seeking an executive secretary to manage the day-to-day responsibilities of running the organization. The duties of the proposed position were defined as follows:

> . . . all business details of the Conference, including (1) the present duties of the President, (2) the handling, under bond, of all Conference funds now administered by the Treasurer, (3) the business management of the publications office, (4) the sale of convention exhibit space now administered by the offices of the Music Education Exhibitors Association and all other business responsibilities now existing in the Conference and developing from the very establishment of the Executive Secretaryship itself. (*Music Supervisors Journal*, Vol. 16, No. 4, March 1930, p. 5)

Mr. Clifford V. Buttelman assumed the office of executive secretary in the Fall of 1930 and also the role of managing editor of the *Music Supervisors Journal*. At the time Mr. Buttelman's appointment was announced, the president of the Conference, Mr. Russell Morgan, announced that he had appointed an editorial board whose duties were to be

> concerned with the policy and content of the Journal, as well as planning and preparation of other conference planning. (*Music Supervisors Journal*, Vol. 17, October 1930, p. 15)

The board consisted of eight members of the Conference, and they were to serve two-year terms. This was the first time that the *Music Supervisors Journal* had an official editorial board.

In 1934 the MSNC evolved into the MENC, an organization with a much larger potential for membership than the previous supervisors' Conference. Mr. Buttelman remained as executive secretary of the new organization as well as managing editor of the new journal, the *Music Educators Journal* (MEJ). He remained in these positions with the Conference until his retirement in 1955.

Line of Reasoning in Rationale

Political scientists have suggested that two basic power structures are present within any formal political organization: the appointed civil servants who run the bureaus, agencies, and departments, and the elected leaders and parliamentarians who represent the organization to the public. The appointed bureaucrats tend to remain in their positions for longer periods of time than the elected leaders. It is therefore likely that the bureaucrats represent the power that in reality runs or motivates a political organization, be it the government itself or specific agencies. For this reason, the focus of the proposed study rests on the investigation of the role of the executive secretary of the MSNC/MENC in decision-making processes within the organization.

Professional organizations become most visible and influential in their publications—journals, monographs, and books—and in their sponsorship of conventions and other professional gatherings. The hypothesis to be tested is that, because of Mr. Buttelman's long years of service as executive secretary, he was more influential in policy decisions regarding the nature and content of publications and convention programs than were the elected and appointed officials of the conference.

Prior to developing a series of questions to be used in the investigation of the stated purpose, a few assumptions need to be made regarding the work already behind us. Note that this is a hypothetical study and that the following assumptions have been made:

1. We have already returned from a preliminary visit to the library of the University of Maryland in College Park, Maryland. During that visit we spent several days in the MENC historical archives.

2. Rather complete office records concerning the executive secretary's career with the music organizations have been located.

3. The archives included official correspondence with both appointed and elected officials of the organization.

4. The archives held the minutes of most, if not all, official meetings.

5. A quantity of data regarding Mr. Buttelman's personal life has been located.

6. In our own university library, all the journals and other publications produced by MSNC and MENC in the years 1925–1955 have been studied. We are thus cognizant of the style and content of the journals, other publications, and topics of convention programs from five years prior to the arrival of the first executive secretary until his retirement.

7. As evidenced by his long tenure in office, we have concluded that Mr. Buttelman was successful in his position and pleased the constituency.

With this brief background and with the stated assumptions there are possibilities for many substantive questions and several methodologies by which such questions could be answered. For each of the two policy areas—publications and convention programs—we offer a series of questions from which we then suggest the methodology that might be most appropriate to resolve the purpose of the study.

Publications

Questions could be, but should not be limited to, the following:

1. What role did the executive secretary have in establishing a need for an editorial board for the journal?

(a) If it was initiated by the executive secretary, what reasons were given?

(b) If it was initiated by the president, what reasons were given?

2. Who determined the membership of the editorial board?

(a) Executive Secretary

(b) President

(c) Cooperative effort

3. Who determined the term of service to be two years? Why two years?

(a) Executive Secretary

(b) President

(c) Cooperative effort

4. Other than announcement articles, how were articles for the journal acquired? (This question should be answered for each year under study.)

(a) Unsolicited contributions from membership:

Number of unsolicited articles

If unsolicited, were they sent to the editorial board for review and recommendation regarding acceptance or rejection?

Was the decision to reject or accept left to the executive secretary as managing editor?

(b) Solicited articles from eminent personages, nonmembers:

Number of solicited articles

If solicited, were articles submitted to editorial board for review?

Did executive secretary make final decisions on editorial changes?

If solicited, did the idea for the topic originate from (a) the executive secretary, (b) the editorial board, or (c) other people?

Who suggested the actual topics?

(c) Solicited articles from the membership [Same questions as under (b)]

(d) How many articles were in each category each year? Determine total of solicited and unsolicited articles.

Answers to any of the questions listed would have to come from an inspection of documents in the archives. For example, the determination of who established the need for an editorial board would have to be based on the analysis of office memoranda or correspondence between the secretary and the president. Memos and letters may reveal the person responsible for the charge assigned to the editorial board. If the executive secretary initiated the charge, then one would conclude that a style of cooperation existed between both the president and the secretary because it was the president who formally announced the board's inception.

Regarding the acquisition of journal articles, written documents would again have to be studied. Letters acknowledging receipt of a manuscript, letters soliciting manuscripts, and records showing the mailing of manuscripts for board review would provide the needed evidence.

Quantitative measures could also be employed in the investigation of policy decisions regarding publications. In analyzing the nature of the solicited journal articles, for example, one could establish a ratio of journal articles solicited by the president, the executive secretary, or by members of the editorial board. A tabulation of that information by year and as a total could eventually lead to a statistical analysis (see chapter 10), from which a clear picture might emerge as to who was most involved in the solicitation of specific articles and, thus, in the shaping of programmatic issues for the profession at large. A similar analysis of the ratio of solicited and unsolicited articles would provide some insight into the degree to which the political leadership did or did not offer programmatic leadership.

Conference Conventions

In the investigation of policy decisions on conference conventions, one would begin the series of questions with the biennial national meetings, then proceed to the divisional meetings that were organized in alternate years. The executive secretary and the president, along with other individuals, played important roles in organizing the programs and in selecting the locations for the conventions. The following questions might thus be posed:

1. What were the convention themes from 1930 to 1954? (List each theme by year.)

  (a) Who determined the theme?

    Executive Secretary

    President

    Other

  (b) Who were the guest speakers? (List by year.)

    How were they selected? Who had the most influence on that selection: (a) the executive secretary, (b) the president, or (c) other members of the organization?

    What was the major focus of the content of the addresses/speeches each year?

    Is there a pattern of issues among the major addresses/speeches given?

2. What were the issues of discussion in the various societies and associations of the organization?

(a) Band, Choir, Orchestra

(b) Elementary, Secondary

(c) Research, and so forth

3. Did the executive secretary have any impact on decisions about content of membership groups?

4. What control over meeting times did the executive secretary exert over the membership groups?

5. Is there a pattern in the time frame under investigation for:

(a) Allotted meeting time for groups

(b) Issues being discussed

(c) Fear of losing music teaching positions in the public schools?

Answers to these questions would best be found by the study of convention and conference records, official correspondence, and memos. Quantitative measures might be less likely to yield results even though the counting of convention sites over the years might reveal some interesting pattern of decision making. Such a pattern might also provide some insight into leadership style within the earlier years of the MENC.

If the procedures mentioned did not provide a clear-cut delineation of the role of the executive secretary and the editorial board in determining publication policy, then a third method—personal interviews—should be employed. Only a small number of individuals who served on the editorial board during the years under investigation are still alive today, and they should be contacted by letter to determine if they would be willing to discuss their perceptions of Mr. Buttelman and the role they themselves played as members of the *MEJ* editorial board.

If any of the former board members responded favorably, a telephone call to that individual would be made and an interview date set. Three weeks prior to the scheduled interview, a letter would be sent to the person confirming the date and time of the interview and reminding the individual that the conversation would center on his or her role as a member of the editorial board of *MEJ*. A brief questionnaire would accompany the letter, seeking information about the amount of time the person devoted to board duties and about the person's perceptions of his or her role on the board. The questionnaire would be retrieved after the interview was conducted. The questionnaire would be expected to accomplish two purposes: (a) to get the former board member to begin to think about that period, (b) to provide some written, personal information that might not be available in existing records.

The complete interview would be tape-recorded and transcribed verbatim. A copy of the transcription would be forwarded to the interviewee for the purpose of assessing the accuracy of all statements as well as for suggesting editorial changes. The interview data would serve to corroborate the archive data and would provide in-depth knowledge about how a former editorial board member viewed his or her duties in MENC. Transcripts of the edited interview should be placed in the MENC Archives in the University of Maryland. The results from the interview would help to strengthen any conclusions regarding the decision-making power in the leadership of MENC during the years 1930–1955.

The investigation proposed here has as its theoretical foundation the role of the governing power of continuing bureaucracy versus the governing power of continued transient leadership within a professional organization with regard to decision making on programmatic issues and publication policy. The conclusions of the specific study should shed some light on the validity of that theory and should also relate to other investigations into leadership roles in professional organizations.

To conclude, the mode of historical inquiry has a wealth of research methodologies at its disposal. The choice of the appropriate methodology and related investigative techniques rests with the nature of the questions posed. The careful planning of the questions therefore becomes the necessary prerequisite to the planning of the specifics of the methodology. Both types of planning are desirable and possible, even in historical research.

Suggested Activities

1. Review three historical studies and identify
   (a) The rationale.
   (b) The purpose.
   (c) The questions.
   (d) The nature of the data (primary and secondary sources).
   (e) Methods of data collection and verification.
   (f) The conclusions.
   Could the purpose have been investigated by another mode of inquiry?
2. Select several purpose statements already researched by historians and develop questions you think would be needed to resolve the purposes. Compare your questions with those of the authors of the articles. Identify similarities and differences in the questions.

Topics for Discussion

1. The role of the historian in music education.
2. The place of chronology in historical reporting.
3. Methods of historical inquiry.

4. Strengths and weaknesses in historical methods.
5. Limitations of the historical mode of inquiry.

Suggested Reading

Barzun, J. (1974). *Clio and the doctors: Psychohistory, quanto-history, and history.* Chicago: University of Chicago Press.

REFERENCES

Balliett, W. (1976, November 22). Jazz, New York notes. *New Yorker, 52* (40).

Barzun, J., & Graff, H.F. (1985). *The modern researcher* (4th ed.). New York: Harcourt Brace Jovanovich.

Benson, L. (1972). *Toward the scientific study of history: Selected essays.* Philadelphia: University of Pennsylvania Press.

Bozarth, R. (1981). *An assessment of the role of James "Jimmy" Blanton in the development of jazz bass.* Problem in lieu of thesis, North Texas State University, Denton, TX.

Braudel, F. (1981–1982). *Civilization and capitalism, 15th–18th century.* (S. Reynolds, Trans., rev.). (Vol. I: The structures of everyday life: The limits of the possible. Vol. II: The wheels of commerce. Vol. III: The perspective of the world [(c) 1984].). New York, NY: Harper and Row.

Breisach, E. (1983). *Historiography—ancient, medieval and modern.* Chicago: University of Chicago Press.

Downs, C.W., Smeyak, G.P., & Martin, E. (1980). *Professional interviewing.* New York: Harper and Row.

Feather, L. (1955). *The encyclopedia of jazz.* New York: Horizon Press.

Grover, P.B. (1960). *The history of string class instruction in American schools and its relationship to the school orchestra.* Unpublished doctoral dissertation, University of Illinois, Urbana-Champaign.

Heller, G., & Wilson, B. (1982). Historical research in music education: A prolegomenon. *Council for Research in Music Education, 69,* 1–20.

Hexter, J.H. (1971). *Doing history.* Bloomington: Indiana University Press.

Hoover, H.T. (1980). Oral history. In M. Kammen (Ed.), *The past before us* (pp. 391–407). Ithaca, NY: Cornell University Press.

Howell, J.L. (1859). *Howell's new class-book.* Cotton Plant, AR: James Howell.

Kammen, M. (1980). (Ed.), *The past before us: Contemporary historical writing in the United States.* Ithaca, NY: Cornell University Press.

Kousser, J.M. (1980). Quantitative social-scientific history. In M. Kammen (Ed.), *The past before us* (pp. 433–456). Ithaca, NY: Cornell University Press.

Loewenberg, P. (1980). Psychohistory. In M. Kammen (Ed.), *The past before us* (pp. 408–432). Ithaca, NY: Cornell University Press.

Oppenheim, A.N. (1966). *Questionnaire design and attitude measurement.* New York: Basic Books.

Sollinger, Ch.E. (1971). *The music men and the profession: A history of string class methods in the United States, 1800–1911.* Unpublished doctoral dissertation, University of Michigan, Ann Arbor, MI.

Chapter Seven

Approaches to Philosophical Inquiry

7.1 Introduction

In its popular usage the term philosophy carries a wide range of meanings. At its best the term reflects a carefully thought-out, logically reasoned answer to a question; at its worst it points to a personal opinion or point of view, hastily developed on the spur of the moment. Such personal views have usually more to do with reacting to a given situation than with applying rules of logic to a line of argumentation. This diversity of meaning behind the term philosophy should be understood as emanating from a multifaceted discipline in which little agreement exists about the true purpose of good philosophical inquiry.

Ayer (1952) stresses that the purpose of philosophical discourse is the same as that of scientific inquiry: to contribute to the growth of human knowledge by means of formulating hypotheses, defining their meaning, and showing their logical base. Compare Ayer's notion with that of Alston and Brandt (1978), who reserve philosophical inquiry for questions that have not or cannot be treated by the methods of specific disciplines. Newell (1967) suggests that philosophers should be concerned with the verification of statements generated by the research efforts of scientists in various disciplines. This view seems to imply that the philosopher should take on the role of a "watchdog," by looking over the logic of the work of the scientists who have chosen to study specific questions about physical and mental characteristics of human beings and nature.

Angeles (1981, p. 211) suggests that philosophy has as many meanings as there are philosophers. Flew proposes that philosophy is whatever philosophers do. A perspective similar to that is taken by Mandelbaum (1984), who believes that philosophers do not share so much "a particular subject matter or a particular method" as they share "some underlying intention or aim . . . , regardless of the problems with which they deal and of the precise methods they actually employ" (p. 120). This aim, Mandelbaum suggests, lies in the philosopher's attempt "to overcome contradictions and incoherencies in widely accepted opinions" by means of analysis and argumentation (p. 122). This definition may be elucidated by calling philosophy a mode of inquiry by which contradictions, incoherencies, and inconsistencies in accepted opinions, actions, and thoughts may be overcome by means of analysis and logical argumentation.

No matter what definition is being utilized, philosophy should always be viewed both as a discipline with a body of knowledge and as an activity. As a discipline, philosophy is concerned with the study of human knowledge; as an activity, philosophy stands for methods of logically correct reasoning. This distinction is not unlike that in music: As much as music is an activity— that is, a performance—it is also a discipline with a defined body of knowledge. Mastery of that knowledge and advanced skills in performance combine into what is considered to be the accomplished musician. In philosophy, command over its knowledge and skills in the activity of "philosophizing" characterize the philosopher. This chapter describes both aspects of the discipline.

7.2 Philosophy as a Discipline

When studying the history of philosophy and its chronological development, one cannot help noticing commonalities in the views of philosophers who lived at different times. The study of such commonalities as well as differences in philosophical views may be called the systematic dimension of philosophy. Regardless of when certain ideas developed historically, philosophers have extracted from these ideas the concerns, concepts, constructs, theories, and methods of thinking that have either remained constant over time or that may have guided the development of new constructs of thought. There is an abundance of professional literature that focuses primarily on the description and analysis of various systems of thought and the exploration of ideas (e.g., Margolis, 1978; Morgenbesser, Suppes, & White, 1969; Russell, 1945, 1976; Sellars, 1968; Wiener, 1974; Wild, 1953).

The study of philosophy in chronological order may be called *historical philosophy*. The study of constructs of thought that remained constant over time may be referred to as *systematic philosophy*. Both dimensions—the historical and the systematic—have brought forth an enormous variety of belief systems and approaches to reasoning. The study of those belief systems has become the prerogative of several branches within the discipline of philosophy. For all practical purposes, the discipline can be divided into five different categories: logic, metaphysics, epistemology, phenomenology, and ethics.

Logic deals with questions of good or correct reasoning. *Epistemology* is the branch in which one reasons about the nature and origin of knowledge. *Metaphysics* investigates the nature of ultimate reality and is divided into ontology (the study of being) and cosmology (the study of the structure of the universe). The analysis of all forms of human experience is known as *phenomenology*. Inquiries into morals and human values are generally categorized as belonging to the branch called *ethics*, in which the study of artistic values, perception, and judgments is said to be the domain of aesthetics and the study of civil-social values the domain of politics. Some philosophers have preferred to call the branch that deals with questions of value, *axiology*, and have treated the areas of ethics, aesthetics, and politics as subbranches of axiology.

It is by no means a simple undertaking to delimit the purposes of the various philosophical branches in an unambiguous manner. Seemingly, most if not all branches are concerned about the relationship of knowledge to the perception of reality. For instance, phenomenology is generally defined as that method of inquiry in which the reality of a material object is not separated from the way it is viewed by the perceiver (see, for example, Angeles, 1981; Flew, 1984; Halverson, 1981). Metaphysics is defined as the branch of philosophy that studies the ultimate nature of reality. Aesthetics is generally defined as the philosophical study of art (Flew, 1984). However, in its Greek derivation and until the mid-18th century, aesthetics meant the study of sense experience. How else than through experience can reality or, for that matter, anything else be studied? Any of these questions addresses topics relevant to the study of what constitutes knowledge. That, however, is the domain of epistemology, which "enquire[s] about the nature and origin of knowledge" (*American Heritage Dictionary of the English Language* [AHDEL], 1970).

An individual untrained in philosophy is bound to be confused about the place of *reality* and *knowledge* in the definitions of all philosophical branches. Why do seemingly different areas of concern end up studying similar if not the same questions? There is no simple answer to that question. Suffice it to say that the methods by which answers to the questions are sought tend to differ for each of the philosophical branches. In phenomenological discourse, for example, a descriptive, introspective analysis of thoughts is assumed to lead toward the revelation of truth. References to subjective experiences and personal views of what may be true are considered important components of philosophical method. They are contrasted with formal systems of logic and mathematics and with the way empirical sciences approach the study of human knowledge.

Ethics and its related subbranches (including aesthetics) seek to understand the origin and nature of values. Values, however, are not necessarily based on principles of logic, but rather on what has traditionally been accepted by society to be good or bad, desirable or not desirable. Because the study of ethics should not be restricted to logic alone, other methods of philosophical discourse are necessary to reflect the nature of the subject under investigation. According to that reasoning, the focus of philosophical discourse in both ethics and aesthetics has been a combination of speculative analysis and personal description of insights developed by the writer/researcher through introspection and contemplation of what is and what should be.

Philosophical Schools of Thought: The "-isms"

The origin of any philosophical inquiry lies in the philosopher's basic convictions about something. Mandelbaum (1984, p. 124) has referred to those convictions as the motivation for all philosophical analysis and argumentation. It delineates the philosopher's basic assumptions about the world and may therefore also be referred to as the philosopher's primary belief. That belief shapes the way in which a philosopher approaches the verification of all given assertions, statements, theses, or propositions.

The systematization of primary beliefs according to their major premises has resulted in the identification of various philosophical perspectives, also known as schools of thought. In the vernacular of the college student, philosophical schools of thought are better known as the "-isms." Their number seems staggering. It is therefore not surprising if they tend to confuse the novice philosopher. In fact, a debate about their exact definitions may seem sterile and technical "gobbledygook" to the nonphilosopher. But knowledge about the different schools of thought can lead to self-criticism and an understanding that philosophical thoughts should be imbedded in a system of belief rather than be "a series of personal pronouncements" (Mandelbaum, p. 122).

Philosophical perspectives that have been of particular interest to music educators seem to be: absolutism, existentialism, formalism, idealism, naturalism, and pragmatism (Abeles, Hoffer, & Klotman, 1984; Phelps, 1986). Table 7.1 gives definitions for these terms as taken from three different sources. The purpose of the figure is two-fold: first, to illustrate the difficulty of delineating clearly the philosophical positions that separate one school of thought from the other, and second, to point out the ambiguous definitions a single term may be given in different reference sources. To illustrate: The term idealism when used in metaphysics, generally reflects the view that ideas, not things, are the fundamental reality. When used in ethics, idealism may also be defined as devotion to moral ideals. Phelps (1986) suggests that idealism in art and music may be "construed to mean that the realm of reality may be attained only in a person's imagination" (p. 114). A similar dilemma exists for the term formalism. In mathematical philosophy the term means reliance on the formal structure of mathematical proof; in the realm of aesthetics related to music it means adherence to the structural elements of the musical composition. The categorization of thought may be a good idea for the sake of organizing one's own thought; for all practical purposes, however, the boundaries are not clear-cut.

The music student wishing to understand differences of perspective and argumentation among philosophical schools of thought is reminded of the difficulty many untrained music listeners may encounter when attempting to understand the nature of musical style. As Mandelbaum (1984) suggested, musical style develops as composers modify or elaborate on existing musical tradition. New styles are set "by the intrusion of powerful influences as expressed in the work of one or more creative figures who themselves tend to establish a new tradition that others then follow" (p. 125). A thorough knowl-

Table 7.1 Comparison of Selected Schools of Thought and Paraphrased Definitions

Absolutism	Relativism
AHDEL	AHDEL
1. A political form of state in which all power is vested in the monarch and his advisers. 2. The political theory reflecting this form.	Truth is viewed to be relative to the individual and to the time or place in which he acts.
Angeles: 1. Truth (value, reality) is viewed to be objectively real, final, and eternal. 2. Only one unchanging and correct explanation of reality exists. 3. Political theory: Unquestionable allegiance to a ruler or ruling class in a political system.	Angeles: Re: value theory. Values differ from society to society, person to person, are not universally applicable at all times or in all places, are correct or incorrect only relative to their conformity with accepted norms or values; opposite to *absolutism*. (Re: protagorean). Relativity of knowledge and the *relativity of sense perception*. . . .
Flew: 1. Politically, exercise of unrestricted power. 2. Philosophically, juxtaposed to *relativism*.	Flew: Variety of meanings: 1. The social environment is considered important in the determination of beliefs of what is and what ought to be. 2. Because of the diversity of social environments, there are no universal standards of good and bad, right and wrong. 3. Relativism regarding factual knowledge: the belief that there is objective knowledge of realities independent of the knower.
Existentialism	Rationalism
AHDEL: "A body of ethical thought, current in the 19th and 20th centuries, centering around the uniqueness and isolation of individual experience in a universe indifferent or even hostile to man, regarding human existence as unexplainable, and emphasizing man's freedom of choice and responsibility for the consequences of his acts."	AHDEL: The exercise of reason, rather than the acceptance of empiricism, authority, or spiritual relevation, provides the basis for action or belief. Reason is the prime source of knowledge and of spiritual truth.
Angeles: As a modern philosophical view incepted by Soren Kirkegaard and Friedrich Nietzsche (historical roots of the view go back to the Greeks and medieval philosophy). Selected points: *existence* precedes *essence*. . . . Truth is subjectivity. The reality of individual existence cannot be communicated by abstractions. Individuals have complete freedom of the will and can become completely other than what they are. "The universe has no direction or scheme. It is meaningless and absurd."	Angeles: Reason is the primary source of knowledge and independent of sense perception. Some points: 1. By abstract reasoning (thinking), fundamental truths can be obtained. 2. Reality is knowable and knowledge is independent of observation and experience (empirical methods). 3. Some truths about reality are known prior to any experience. 4. The principal origin of knowledge is reason, and science is basically a result of that reasoning. 5. "Truth is not tested by sense-verification procedures, but by such

Table 7.1   *(Continued)*

criteria as logical consistency." 6. Rational method can be applied to any subject matter whatsoever and can provide adequate explanations. 7. "Absolute certainty about things is the ideal of knowledge." . . .

Flew:
Not a dogma or system of thought but a philosophical attitude. Its origins: Attributed to Kierkegaard. . . . View opposite to rationalism and empiricism. There are no natural laws that govern all beings. Reason is not necessarily the power that guides human activity. . . .

Flew:
1. The doctrines of philosophers like Descartes, Spinoza, and Leibnitz. Some characteristics: (a) Reason alone can provide a knowledge of what exists; (b) knowledge forms a single (deductive) system; and (c) everything can be brought under a single system of knowledge. 2. Term refers to those philosophers who accept only (b) and (c). 3. Religious belief is rejected as being without rational foundation. A commitment to reason means opposition to faith, prejudice, habit or any other source of conviction that is considered irrational.

Empiricism
AHDEL:
1. Experience, especially of the senses, is the only source of knowledge. 2. (a) The employment of empirical methods, as in an art or science. (b) An empirical conclusion. 3. The practice of medicine without scientific knowledge.

Angeles:
1. Ideas are abstractions formed by "compounding (combining, recombining) what is experienced (observed, immediately given in sensation)." 2. Experience is the sole source of knowledge. 3. Knowledge is dependent on sense data and directly derived or indirectly inferred from the sense data. . . . 4. Reason cannot be the sole source of knowledge of reality. Reference to sense experience and the use of the sense organs are necessary in the use of reason. . . .

Idealism
AHDEL:
"1. The action of envisioning things in an ideal form. 2. Pursuit of one's ideals. 3. An idealizing treatment of subject in literature or art. 4. The theory that the object of external perception, in itself or as perceived, consists of ideas. . ."

Angeles:
Also referred to as *mentalism* or *immaterialism*. 1. "The universe is an embodiment of a mind. 2. Reality is dependent for its existence upon a mind and its activities." 3. Reality is mental (spiritual, psychical) matter. . . . 4. Knowledge exists only in the form of mental states and processes. Reality expresses itself as ideas and thoughts. . . . The external world is not physical. (Angeles continues with a discussion of idealism in various forms: Berkeley, Plato, absolute, absolute—Hegel, critical—Kant, epistemological, metaphysical, pantheistic, personal, pluralistic, subjective, transcendental—Kant).

Flew:
All knowledge or "at least all knowledge of matters of fact as distinct from that of purely logical relations between concepts is based on experience." . . . Empiricism has taken several forms, "but one common feature has

Flew:
A group of philosophical theories with the common view that "the external world" is created by the mind. "Idealism does not quarrel with the plain man's view that material things exist; rather, it disagrees

133

Table 7.1 *(Continued)*

been the tendency to start from experimental sciences, as a kind of prototype or paradigm case of human knowledge." Should be contrasted to rationalism which assigned a similar role to mathematics. . .

with the analysis of a material thing that many philosophers have offered, according to which the material world is wholly independent of minds." Three principal types of idealism are acknowledged: *Berkeleian idealism, transcendental idealism,* and *objective idealism* (may also be called *absolute idealism*). . .

Formalism

AHDEL:

1. "Rigorous or excessive adherence to recognized forms. 2. The mathematical or logical structure of a scientific argument, especially as distinguished from its content."

Pragmatism

AHDEL:

1. *Philosophy.* "The theory, developed by Charles S. Peirce and William James, that the meaning of a proposition or course of action lies in its observable consequences, and that the sum of these consequences constitutes its meaning. 2. A method or tendency in the conduct of political affairs characterized by the rejection of theory and precedent, and by the use of practical means and expedients."

Angeles:

"Any system that stresses form (principles, rules, laws) as the significant or ultimate ground of explanation or evaluation."

Angeles:

1. "Knowledge is derived from experience, experimental methods, and practical efforts." . . . 2. "Knowledge must be used to solve the problems of everyday, practical affairs . . . and thinking must relate to practice and action." 3. The truth and meaning of ideas are asserted by their consequences. . . . 4. "Truth is that which has practical value in our experience of life." . . . 5. Truth changes and is tentative. . . .

Flew:

1. (mathematics). A view pioneered by D. Hilbert: the only foundation necessary for mathematics is its formalization and the proof that the system produced is consistent.

Flew:

"A label for a doctrine about meaning first made a philosophical term in 1878 by C. S. Peirce. . . ."

Naturalism

AHDEL:

"1. Conformity to nature; factual or realistic representation, especially in art and literature. 2. *Philosophy.* The system of thought holding that all phenomena can be explained in terms of natural causes and laws, without attributing moral, spiritual, or supernatural significance to them. 3. *Theology.* The doctrine that all religious truths are derived from nature and natural causes and not from revelation. 4. Conduct or thought prompted by natural desires or instincts."

Materialism

AHDEL:

1. The opinion "that physical matter in its movements and modifications is the only reality." Thought, feeling, mind, and will is explainable by physical law. . . . 2. Physical well-being and worldly possessions constitute the greatest good and highest value in life. 3. Undue regard for worldly concerns. . .

134

Table 7.1 *(Continued)*

Angeles:
1. *Monistic:* Nature is the only reality. . .
2. *Antisupernaturalistic:* "All phenomena can be explained in terms of the inherent interrelationships of natural events. . ."
3. *Proscientific:* (a) Natural phenomena can be explained by the methodology of the sciences, assuming the methodologies improve. . . 4. *Humanistic:* "Humans are one of the many (natural) manifestations of the universe. . ." [It follows naturalism (critical, ethical).]

Angeles:
1. Nothing but matter in motion exists. "Mind is caused by material changes . . . and is completely dependent upon matter" . . . 2. Purpose, awareness, intention, goals, meaning, direction, intelligence, willing, and striving are not characteristic of matter and the universe. 3. Nonmaterial entities such as spirits, ghosts, demons, angels do not exist. Consequently, there is no God or nothing supernatural in the universe. . . . 7. . . . "Matter can be neither created nor destroyed. 8. No life, no mind, is immortal. . . . 11. Values do not exist in the universe independently of the activities of humans." [This definition is followed by definitions for: materialism (dialectical—Marx, Engels, mechanistic, reductive)]

Flew:
1. What is studied by the non-human and human sciences is all there is. There is no need for finding explanations for things outside the Universe. . . . 2. (in philosophical ethics) Since G. E. Moore, the view . . . "that value words are definable in terms of neutral statements of fact. . ."

Flew:
What exists is "either matter or entirely dependent on matter for its existence. The precise meaning and status of this doctrine are, however, far from clear." . . .

Sources. The American Heritage Dictionary of the English Language, 1970; Angeles, P. A., Dictionary of Philosophy, 1981; Flew, A., A Dictionary of Philosophy (rev. 2nd ed.), 1984.

edge of musical traditions is necessary before stylistic changes may become evident to or may be appreciated by the listener.

So it is with the study of philosophical schools of thought and their categorization: The tradition of argumentation and philosophical debate must be understood clearly by the student before different positions in philosophical reasoning as well as changes in points of view may be fully appreciated.

Because of the large number of extant philosophical positions, it is unlikely that scholars will ever agree on any one system for the categorization of philosophical perspectives. Therefore, it is wise to be less concerned about the label one attaches to a set of beliefs and more concerned with describing the content of that set of beliefs. This is to say that a concise statement about a philosopher's general perspective may be more valuable than how that perspective is categorized and made to fit the existing labels of schools of thought.

7.3 Philosophy as an Activity

The activity of clear thinking is the key to any discussion on methodological issues in philosophical inquiry. Although there is little doubt among scholars that clear thinking is also a requisite of all other modes of inquiry, there is some disagreement as to the meaning of *clear* in philosophical discourse. Specifically, logicians raise the question of whether there is a particular logic applicable to the search of all knowledge or whether different issues mandate the use of different "logics" (Tragesser, 1977).

Particularly, some philosophers in music education may argue that "aesthetic sensibility in the arts, like in religion, transcends the limitations of man's ability to reason logically" (Schwadron, 1972, p. 36). Often, the belief is held that philosophical argumentation in matters of aesthetics and/or music and the arts will by definition transcend analytical ways of thinking. This position has its merits from the point of view that music—a nonverbal mode of communication—must be researched through the verbal mode of speech (Schwadron, 1972, p. 36). As in the translation of one language to another, important nuances of meaning may be lost in the process of transposing the meaning of one set of symbols to another set.

If it is difficult to translate one language into another without losing important information, how much more difficult must it be to describe music by means of a mode that is not its own? This is the point Schwadron and other philosophers have repeatedly made. In dealing with the arts in a nonartistic manner, important information may inevitably become distorted or lost. Does one do justice to the arts when researching them intellectually?

To answer these and related questions, it becomes paramount to understand the role logic plays in the pursuit of searching for knowledge. Many philosophers have addressed that issue (e.g., Abel, 1976; Armour, 1972; Ayer, 1952; Berlin, 1979; Bittle, 1945; Bobik, 1970; Copi, 1982; Girvetz, Geiger, Hantz, & Morris, 1966; Halverson, 1981; Leonard, 1957; Mandelbaum, 1984; Newell, 1967; Nozick, 1981; Reck, 1972; Tragesser, 1977; Wheelwright, 1962). The next section cannot be anything else but a brief summary of what has been said about the place of logic in philosophical discourse.

The Place of Logic in Philosophical Inquiry

In *Principles of Right Reason,* Leonard (1957, pp. 12–13) draws an analogy between the rules that exist in logic and rules that exist in sports. In all of sport there are two sets of rules. The first set defines the game itself—that is, football, baseball, tennis. The rules determine those most basic characteristics of the game that must not be tampered with if the game is to be called what it claims to be—football, baseball, or tennis. The second set of rules actually determines the outcome of each individual game. Those rules are decided on by the team, players, coach, or manager, and are developed in response to the specific situation of where and with whom the game takes place. Leonard refers to the first set of rules as logic and the second set as methodology. The methodology of each individual study must comply with the rules of logic in order to be called a valid argument (in sports, a good game; in research, a good study). Thus, a valid argument must adhere to established principles of logic, but may at the same time utilize additional methods of reasoning. These, while being compatible with the first set of rules, also respond to the special situation of the research question at hand.

Bittle (1945) refers to the same duality of rules in logical reasoning as described by Leonard, when she states that

> logic as a *science* consists of a comprehensive body of established principles and laws with their legitimate conclusions; logic as an *art* is the mastery of the technique embodied in these principles and laws. (p. 17)

It appears that some philosophers stress the art of reasoning over its scientific base; others only see the scientific base without considering the finer points of the art. Ideally, however, the truth may lie somewhere in the middle: The basic rules must be known before one can be free in developing an argumentation that is germane to the question posed. A similar situation prevails in music performance: The best improvisation rests on one's solid knowledge of the basic chord structures, scales, and other defined, structural limits of the music. Possessing this knowledge enables one to move freely in the exploration of deviations from the rules.

Applied to the description of logic, only the first set of rules can be described. They pertain to (a) the formal structure of a line of argumentation, and (b) the logistics of how to define terms. The second set of rules develops when a specific purpose statement challenges the researcher to resolve all research problems in the best possible way, but within the confines of the rules of logic. The confines, however, become the opportunity since the researcher can make judgments as to where to deviate from the rules, where to take liberties and risks, and where to insert skillful rhetoric in order to explore unknown ground.

Principles of Developing a Line of Argumentation. Any number of statements that lead to an explicit conclusion may be called an argument. A logical argument is a sequentially ordered series of sentences about people, things, events, and ideas from which the conclusions are expected to become self-evident. However, in ordinary conversation and in many written documents, a conclusion will often precede or be even intermittently woven into the evidence. For example:

> Ralph is a second-year choir director in Humana Junior High School, located in the downtown area of the city of Humana. He cannot vote in the upcoming school board election because he resides outside the city limits and only citizens of Humana are eligible to vote.

This statement becomes a formal argument if the order of the sentences follows the order of evidence by which the conclusion becomes factual. The conclusion, of course, is that Ralph cannot vote in the school board election. The order of the argument should be:

1. Humana Independent School District lies within the city limits of Humana.
2. Residents outside the limits cannot vote in school board elections.
3. Ralph resides outside the city limits.
4. (Therefore), Ralph cannot vote in the upcoming school board election.

When all arguments have been connected by the researcher in such a way that the conclusion of one argument becomes the beginning of the next argument, a line of argumentation has been developed. It should resolve the research questions at hand and lead to the conclusion of the purpose of the investigation.

Much of the content of a philosophical argumentation depends on which type and system of logic one subscribes to—formal or informal, propositional or dialectic logic. For each of these systems the methods differ as to how each argument in the line of reasoning is developed, its content justified, and the conclusions validated.

In *formal logic*, rules and symbols of mathematical logic are applied to the process of reasoning in such a way that all conclusions result clearly from defined and verified/verifiable axioms—that is, factual sentences or statements. Often, axiomatic reasoning is also referred to as propositional logic. Formal logicians would, however, insist there is a difference between the two as axiomatic reasoning requires command over a rather sophisticated system of symbols and rules of inference. Propositional logic allows the researcher more freedom in the way the propositions in an argumentation are logically strung together. Somewhat different from propositional logic is *dialectic logic*. In it, two statements, called thesis and antithesis, are juxtaposed to each other so that the researcher may draw from them a compromise statement—the synthesis.

Informal logic utilizes a combination of various methods of argumentation. One of its main tools is phenomenological analysis, the method of inquiry in which the reality of the object is not separated from the way the researcher sees and describes it. Informal logic may also utilize speculation and selective observation. This type of philosophical method is sometimes referred to as heuristic-hermeneutic (*heuriskein*, Greek, "to discover, find"; *hermeneutikos*, Greek, "by interpretation"). The kind of knowledge investigated by this method is neither asserted to be objectively true nor evaluated as necessarily being true. Instead, the truth of the conclusions lies in the degree to which the argumentation convinces at face value.

7.4 Basic Rules of Propositional and Dialectic Argumentation

Of all the lines of argumentation accepted among the various schools of philosophical thought, propositional and dialectic argumentation are in our view the most promising and scientifically sound techniques for philosophical discourse in music education. Two reasons may be given for this choice: first, the development of logically based arguments demands a thorough and exhaustive command of the body of knowledge in a given field; second, all the statements in the argument should be supported by evidence from that body of knowledge.

Propositional Argumentation

In this method of logic, all statements that make up the argument are referred to as propositions. A proposition is a statement that contains whatever it takes to describe a situation or state of affairs. That statement can be one sentence or a series of paragraphs, each of them containing several sentences. A proposition may be considered true when observations, experimentation, analysis and inference have corroborated their content as factual (see Leonard, 1957, pp. 58–63).

Any proposition that precedes a conclusion may be called a premise. An argument may consist of one premise and one conclusion (immediate inference), it may have two premises and a conclusion (syllogism), or it may contain three or more premises. In all cases, the line of argumentation is developed in such a way that the conclusion of the first argument becomes the first premise of the second argument, and so on, until the final conclusion has been reached. In the standard form of logical or mathematical proof, all statements may be numbered in consecutive order and the conclusion may be marked by a dotted triangle [∴], the symbol for "therefore" in a mathematical proof. Another way to separate the conclusion from the premises may be a horizontal line under the last premise.

In propositional reasoning, both the beginning and the end point of a line of argumentation has to be somewhat "mapped out" by the researcher. The propositions become the "proof" for the accuracy of one's final conclusion. Scientifically speaking, they become the data for one's research. The more data one can provide in support of one's final conclusion, the more trustworthy the conclusion becomes. This kind of inference may be called a linear line of argumentation.

Inductive and Deductive Reasoning.   There is an ongoing debate among philosophers and scientists as to whether the line of argumentation in propositional inference is deductive or inductive in nature. It is beyond the scope of this chapter to describe that debate in detail. A few points should be emphasized, however. In the past, deductive inference has been defined as the process in which one argues from a general premise to a specific conclusion (Bittle, 1945). For example:

> Every human responds to music.
> Mary is a human.
> Therefore Mary responds to music.

Inductive inference, as defined in the past, would move from a specific premise to a general conclusion and/or law (Bittle, 1945). For example:

> Mary responds to music.
> Mary is a human.
> All humans respond to music.

In many educational philosophy classes, the distinction between inductive and deductive reasoning is still explained in the same way as just exemplified. In more recent writings on the nature of propositional reasoning, however, one can often find the difference between induction and deduction in the degree of truth attached to the conclusion. Thus, an argument is called deductive if the conclusion follows by necessity from its premises, regardless of what other premises may be added to the argument (Copi, 1986). An inductive argument only provides some support for the truth of a conclusion. Consider the following argument:

> John and Mary play trombone in the college concert band.
> They graduated from the same high school.
> They plan to become band directors.
> They enjoy the same type of music.
> They are taking the same courses.
> John joined the choir.
> Therefore Mary will probably also join the choir.

If the premises in this argument were true, then the conclusion would likely be true as well. However, if the premise were added that Mary has a vocal disorder prohibiting her to sing, the conclusion would not necessarily follow logically from the premises. The argument would cease to be valid.

Inductive reasoning is considered a more open process of argumentation than that of deductive reasoning. Inductive reasoning allows for the revision of an argument if new evidence invalidates a previously inferred conclusion. Thus, a conclusion is never assumed to be more than probable. Probability of truth stands against the absolute of truth, corroboration of evidence against verification of evidence. (We would not be in the realm of philosophy if there were total agreement even on this issue. See, for example, Popper, 1959, 1968).

Valid and Invalid Arguments, True and False Propositions. As stated earlier, the validity of a propositional argument may be judged by (a) whether the premises are true or false, (b) whether the conclusion is true or false, and (c) whether the connection from the premises to the conclusion can formally (logically) be made. All three conditions must be met in a useful argument. To illustrate all three points, a series of propositional arguments are presented and analyzed according to their validity as well as to the truth and falsity of their propositions.

ARGUMENT 1   Professionals may be defined as people who get paid for their work.

A musician works by performing or composing music.

Therefore, a professional musician is defined as someone who gets paid for performing or composing music.

All propositions are true and the premises lead logically to the conclusion; therefore, the argument is valid and true.

ARGUMENT 2   Violins have six strings.

All Western six-stringed instruments have frets.

Therefore all violins have frets.

Although the first premise is false, the argument is valid because the line of reasoning is valid. However, the false premise leads to a false conclusion. Were the premise true, the conclusion would also be true. Thus, this argument is valid although it is false.

Argument 3 is an example in which the conclusion does not follow logically from the premises:

ARGUMENT 3   Professional musicians usually get paid for playing an instrument.

If I made my living by playing in the symphony, I would be a professional musician.

I do not make my living in the symphony.

Therefore I am not a professional musician.

Although all propositions (both the premises and the conclusion) may be true, the argument itself is invalid since it is possible that I could make my living as a studio musician. Thus, the conclusion is not a logical outcome from the premises. The argument is therefore invalid.

An example of a valid argument with one false premise and a true conclusion would be:

ARGUMENT 4   All instruments have keys.

All flutes are instruments.

Therefore all flutes have keys.

Argument 4 is typically found when a writer has a predetermined conclusion and begins the argument with a premise that makes it easy to get to the conclusion. Once the reader believes in the truth of the first premise, then everything else follows logically and convincingly.

An invalid argument with two false premises and a true conclusion might be:

ARGUMENT 5   All instruments have keys.

All violins have keys.

Therefore all violins are instruments.

This type of argument lends itself very well to the development of a justification. The beginning is convincing, the conclusion can be agreed upon as being true, but the step that it took to get to the conclusion is false. One could have stated the conclusion without the pretense of a logical argumentation. Postulative type of writings tend to make use of this kind of discourse.

Finally, an example of an invalid argument with false premises and a false conclusion:

ARGUMENT 6   All instruments have keys.

All violins have keys.

Therefore all instruments are violins.

Given that a writer has great command over rhetorical skills and can convince by virtue of possessing an elegant style of writing, Argument 6 can be very powerful. It is the tool of the dictator. Its purpose is not to promote knowledge but to manipulate it. The propositions need to contain much jargon and many unintelligible words to pass as true statements in a valid argument.

What does all of this mean? The examples demonstrate that a propositional argument may be valid (logically correct) yet untrue if any of the premises is false. Arguments with untrue conclusions are always invalid. But an argument may also be invalid even if all its propositions are true. The invalidity results from the fact that the propositions do not logically follow one from the other.

For anyone who wishes to employ propositional argumentation in philosophical discourse, the writing of and differentiation between valid and invalid arguments and true and false propositions must become second nature. The determination of whether an argument is valid or invalid appears to be easy as long as propositions contain the description of familiar everyday-life conditions or events. Once an argumentation deals with more complicated constructs of thought and ideas or with rather specialized knowledge, such a determination ceases to be easy.

The intellectual acceptability of the truth of a proposition may be asserted when three questions can be answered in the affirmative: (a) Are the premises true, and on what evidence and by what criteria can they be judged to be true? (b) Is the language in which the argument is couched free from ambiguity and shift? (c) Is the conclusion soundly applicable to the context in which the question was raised and in which the issue is being considered? (Wheelwright, 1962, p. 197).

Ideally, propositional reasoning utilizes controls in each step of the process during which evidence is provided for the drawing of conclusions. The steps should be clearly identified by the researcher so that the reader is afforded the opportunity to follow the reasoning in the same step-wise progression in which the researcher established the line of argumentation. In that sense, propositional logic is replicable and, thus, scientific. It underlies the laws of disciplined inquiry.

Dialectic Reasoning

While propositional argumentation may be considered linear in nature as it requires a beginning and an end point in the drawing of inferences, dialectic

142

reasoning draws inferences by taking into consideration propositional opposites. To illustrate:

The thesis is:
Music has been found to serve as a deterrent to criminal behavior.

The antithesis may be:
Several inmates of the state penitentiary are musicians.

From these two statements, the synthesis is found:
Music does not necessarily serve as a deterrent to criminal behavior.

In short, dialectic argumentation makes use of statements of truth, but utilizes a plurality of various truths. From the documented plurality, a unified view is developed that immediately becomes, again, one kind of truth against which another kind of truth must be juxtaposed. Unlike in propositional argumentation, the line of reasoning is a never-ending, "spiraling" process. There is no absolute ending point in the argumentation.

To continue the illustration, the first round of argumentation ended in the synthesis
Music does not necessarily serve as a deterrent to criminal behavior.

Being a synthesis, it now becomes the new thesis to which an antithesis must be found:
The percentage of musicians being incarcerated is much smaller than that of the nonmusicians.

The synthesis of these two statements may become:
Music has the potential of positively influencing social behavior.

The next antithesis may read:
Music has the potential of negatively influencing social behavior.

From this, the synthesis may become:
Music can influence social behavior.

In dialectic argumentation, truth is considered relative to the process by which it was derived. It is illusive yet present as long as the description of polarities creates tension out of which a synthesis (release) emerges. Paradoxical as it may seem, however, the release is the cause for new tension. In the relationship of release and tension lies the knowledge of truth. Never fully grasping it, one may get closer to truth as long as the process of dialectic argumentation is ongoing. This line of reasoning causes proponents of dialectic discourse, particularly those following in Hegel's footsteps, to view the dialectic method as the only truly scientific method of inquiry. The acceptance that agreed-upon constructs of truth may be wrong is incorporated into the method of argumentation, and the search for truth is acknowledged as being a never-ending process.

Various schools of dialectic reasoning have originated from the thoughts of such philosophers as Hegel (1929), Lukacs (1964), and Adorno (1973) (see also Armour, 1972; Lichtheim, 1970; Perelman, 1975). Specifically, the thoughts differ on the question as to what degree content and method of argumentation should be one and the same. In all cases, however, one point is certain: The act of dialectic thinking requires a tremendous amount of knowledge of the professional literature in fields that may pertain to a given question. Statements of truth in support of both the thesis and the antithesis must be found. The researcher must be willing and able to acknowledge the temporal relativity of each of the dialectic positions reflected in the discourse since no statement can ever claim to be the finite truth.

7.5 Basic Rules of Defining Terms

Regardless of the type of argumentation chosen, the success of ascertaining the validity of any logical reasoning rests with the definition of all terms used in all propositions. Consider, for instance, the following text:

> I am certain that Mary sings soprano in the choir because the teacher said the other day that Mary can sing up to an octave higher than Billy, and Billy told me that he sings alto in the choir.

As simple as the conclusion in the argument appears to be—that Mary must be a soprano—the logic becomes apparent most readily once the definitions for alto, soprano, and octave are known and if the context has been clarified in which the terms *high* and *low* are utilized in music. Because musicians are at ease with the meaning of the terms, the conclusion of the argument is convincing. However, if an argument pertains to a context familiar only to astrophysicists, philosophers, or physiologists, the meaning of its conclusions would likely be unclear to musicians. Consequently, the logical correctness of a conclusion becomes evident foremost by the use of *clear and unambiguous language.*

Clarity of language is achieved if the terms used are familiar to those to whom the reading is directed. Potentially unclear or unfamiliar terms must be defined by means of a careful description of the meaning the researcher has attached to them. However, the decision as to which terms need defining, and how and when to define them, is entirely in the hands of the researcher.

A term may be a single word or a composite of words that form a "distinguishable entity which carries meaning" (Wheelwright, 1962, p. 10). *Understanding music* would be one such meaningful entity. Other terms that are important to music education and that may be called distinguishable entities of meaning may be: music appreciation, aesthetic sensitivity, good music, harmonic progression, music ability, auditory perception, and the like.

Three Types of Definitions

If a term is a single word, composite expression, or a complete phrase, it is generally necessary to decide what type of definition may most appropriately draw the boundaries of the meaning of that term. The most often used types are *synonymous definitions, operational definitions,* and *definitions by genus and difference.* All three are important in the translation of technical terms regardless of the kind of research being conducted.

Synonymous Definitions.   There are many foreign language terms in music that tend to convey a meaning only to musicians, such as *forte*—loud, *piano*— soft, and *presto*—fast. In writing a philosophical treatise, these and other terms are regularly used. They should be defined/translated in a glossary at the end of one's research report. This is especially the case if a specific (technical) term has one meaning in music and another meaning either in ordinary life or within another discipline.

Operational Definitions.   If a term refers to nonvisible and abstract things such as ability, intelligence, musicality, effectiveness, and so forth, it becomes useful to define the term operationally. An operational definition indicates how the researcher intends to use a term in the specific context of an investigation. In that case the researcher must describe concrete behaviors, results of actions, or verbal statements that may be assumed to be linked to the term for which a definition is sought. For instance, intelligence may be defined as "the capacity to acquire and apply knowledge—the faculty of thought and reason" (*The American Heritage Dictionary of the English Language,* 1970). Instead of using that rather vague definition, the researcher may elect to define the term in an operational sense as the test score a person obtains in a particular intelligence test. That definition, while not necessarily any more valid than the theoretical definition from the dictionary, is more concrete—if one knows the content of the test. Likewise, musical ability may be defined in terms of specific tasks children should be able to complete if they are to be labeled *musically able.*

Definitions by Genus and Difference.   In the search for truth, researchers do not always agree on the validity of operational definitions because the theoretical constructs behind those definitions are frequently not clearly established. In such a case, definition by genus and difference becomes of importance to philosophical inquiry. This means that a definition should state (a) the class to which something belongs (reference to some characteristics common to all class members), and (b) the attribute that characterizes it as belonging to a particular subclass. The more specific the class, the more narrow the specific difference becomes. Compare, for example:

The violin is an instrument with strings

|_____| |_____|

    class   subclass

with

The violin is a bowed string instrument without frets.

|_____| |_____|

        class   subclass

The second definition is more narrow than the first, and in this case is also more precise. It may happen, however, that a definition becomes so narrow that it is inaccurate. For example, the definition "A painting is a picture drawn on canvas with a brush" excludes the possibility of paintings done in water-color, on wood, or on stone walls. The definition does not include collage techniques, mixed media, and so forth.

Approaches for Constructing Definitions

Denotative and Connotative Definitions. There are two ways in which a researcher can define a term. Either one can list all the things that fall under the term *(denotative definition)*, or one describes the characteristics common to all the things to which the term applies *(connotative definition)*. For example, the general term *symphony* is applicable to more than a single composition as it denotes all the symphonies that fall under it: The definition consists of all works intended to be, and thus labeled, symphony. The collection of items constitutes the meaning of the term. In the situation where the term symphony is to be defined connotatively, the researcher would have to list the attributes that are common to all musical compositions whose primary focus is sym-phonic in nature. The most informative and complete definition of a term would incorporate both the denotative and the connotative meaning of a term. However, not all terms have both types of meaning. As Copi illustrates (1982, p. 158), the unicorn can be defined connotatively (its characteristics can be listed) but not denotatively (the unicorn does not exist as a species).

Stipulative and Lexical Definitions. Sometimes a researcher considers it necessary to attach to a term a meaning heretofore unknown or uncommon. In addition, some researchers might want to coin a new term, as did Gordon with the term "audiation" (Gordon, 1984). Any of these kinds of definitions is called stipulative. It is neither true nor false since it merely suggests the boundaries of the meaning of a term. Sometimes, this type of definition is not unlike an operational definition. The difference lies in the degree to which the profession as a whole has agreed upon the definition.

When a researcher utilizes a definition whose meaning is agreed upon by convention and tradition of usage, the definition is lexical. Thus the def-inition of *pianoforte*—"a manual keyboard instrument whose wire strings are struck by felt-covered hammers via a mechanic action"—is true; it reports the meaning of the word as it has been traditionally used by English-speaking people. A definition like "the word *pianoforte* means a dynamic indication of medium loud" is false because, traditionally, the term has not been used that way, although it might make sense to some people.

Lexical definitions may be taken from standard dictionaries or accepted texts on a subject. It is advisable, however, to consult several dictionaries and more than one text in order to locate the best possible definition of a term. If a researcher finds existing definitions lacking in clarity, the most suitable and valid definition may be obtained by combining several sources and syn-thezising several standard definitions into one.

146

Selected, Formalized Rules for Defining Terms

In order to be exacting when terms need to be defined, philosophers distinguish between the two components of a definition—namely, the term that needs defining and that which defines it. In the technical language of the logicians, one must learn to differentiate between the *definiendum*—the term that needs defining—and the *definiens*—that part of the definition that actually does the defining. All rules regarding the definition of terms consider the relationship between the two parts of the definition.

Some of the rules stated here have already been discussed and may serve as a summary of what has been said before. Some other rules should be considered logical outcomes of those things already mentioned. To understand the rules, it is only necessary to remember that the definiens is always the part that does the defining.

First Rule.   The definiens should make use of terms that carry only one meaning and have been defined.

Wherever possible, the definiens should make use of words that may be assumed to be more familiar than the words used in the term that is to be defined.

Example. A diatonic scale is a sequence of eight tones, arranged in a stepwise progression of whole and half steps, and ranging from the tonic to the octave. In this case the definiens makes sense only if one is familiar with the terms whole and half step, tonic, and octave. For musically untrained persons the following definition might therefore be better: The diatonic scale is a step-by-step succession of eight musical tones, arranged in a prescribed order.

Second Rule.   The definiens should include the *essential* attributes of the thing to be defined.

The essential attributes include, if possible, the denotative and the connotative meaning of the term. (As an example, we used earlier the two ways in which one might define the term symphony.) In the case of a connotative definition, both the class and the subclass of the thing to be defined should be described. In the case of a denotative definition, as many items as possible should be listed; trivia or unimportant characteristics, however, should not be included in any definition.

Third Rule.   A definition should neither be too broad nor too narrow.

Example. Musical improvisation is a form of jazz performance in which a musician stands up and plays the chorus of "Tea for Two." It is obvious that here the definiens is too narrow as it does not account for all situations in which improvisation may be utilized in music. Compare this with: Musical improvisation is a form of performance during which the players do not read music. Here, the definiens leaves the definition wide open. The definition is broader than the term improvisation generally implies.

Fourth Rule.   The words used in the term that needs defining must not appear in the definiens.

Example. Musical ability refers to the abilities of a person in musical matters; or, *creativity* is what comes from a creative mind. Both definitions are circular in that both parts in each definition use the same term. Sometimes, operational definitions may be criticized for being circular—for example, when intelligence is defined as the mental trait measured by the scores of an intelligence test. The definiens (the intelligence test) and the definiendum (intelligence) are, for all practical purposes, the same. Circular definitions, however, tend to lead to circular argumentation.

Fifth Rule. The definiens and the term to be defined should have the same logical (and grammatically correct) structure. The definition "music is when people sing and play instruments" is grammatically incorrect in that the definiendum is a noun and the definiens a sentence. A grammatically better definition would be "music is organized sound" or "music is a combination of organized sound and silence." Whether that definition is adequate in its content remains subject to debate. At least it is grammatically correct!

Sixth Rule. The definiens should be positively stated.

Sometimes it seems easier to define a term by saying what it is not than by saying what it is. This rule is similar to the rule that states a teacher should give constructive rather than negative instructions to the students. Instead of saying "don't rush", the teacher should give instructions as to how to hold the playing tempo steady. In string class, for example, the statement "don't play with a poor hand position" should be reworded into "bring the wrist back so that your hand and arm form a straight line," or "remember the straight line."

7.6 Methodological Guidelines for Philosophical Inquiry in Music Education

The application of the scientific process to philosophical, investigative methods entails the following steps: A question/purpose is clearly stated and presented together with its problems (or specific questions); the evidence (constructs of thought, ideas) for answering the problems is gathered in the form of propositions; from that evidence an answer is formulated that resolves the purpose guiding the inquiry. The stronger the proof that the evidence is valid, the more trustworthy the conclusions become. The validity of that evidence is determined, however, by the validity of the line of argumentation employed in the discourse and by the precision with which all terms in the argumentation are being defined.

Philosophical inquiry is at its best if the researcher does not come to conclusions before all evidence has been weighed and evaluated. Too often, philosophical research suffers, as does research in other modes of inquiry, from the fact that the conclusions one wishes to obtain determine the research purpose. In such a situation the data tend to be gathered selectively and merely in support of one's hoped-for conclusions.

How a research purpose is worded and supported in philosophical inquiry depends largely on the researcher's belief system and view of the field of music education. Unlike historians or empiricists, philosophers should be expected to describe both their basic belief systems (i.e., to which "-isms," if any, they subscribe) and their view of what they believe music education to be. In our opinion, neither the belief system nor the view of the field have to be *justified*. However, they must be *described* as that description provides the framework within which the purpose is being developed and explained.

Once the purpose is stated, the problems inherent to studying the purpose should be identified as described in chapter 5. The equivalent of methodology in philosophical inquiry is, in our view, straightforward. First, the researcher should develop the argumentation by which the research purpose is to be resolved. Second, all terms important in the line of argumentation must be defined. Third, the researcher should gather all evidence that is relevant to each argument in the complete line of argumentation. The relevancy of evidence should be determined by the degree to which a thought/idea speaks to an issue, not whether it speaks favorably to the issue. The sources from which to draw the evidence should be varied. They should include empirically derived findings, common-sense experiences, historical information, and the like. In all cases, the researcher should evaluate critically whether the information is trustworthy.

In any mode of research, evidence collected may either strengthen or weaken one's initial line of argumentation. It is therefore the philosopher's task to assess whether the collected evidence supports or contradicts the conclusion in an argument. If only a small amount of evidence can be found in support of a conclusion or a thesis, then a revision of the line of argumentation would likely be in order. Otherwise, the researcher would have to acknowledge the speculative nature of the argument and continue the discourse with the realization that its conclusion is based on a greater degree of uncertainty than that with which it was initially proposed.

To summarize: The steps of philosophical research methodology outlined here suggest proceeding in the following way:

1. Describe your own belief system and view of the field of music education.
2. Develop a research purpose and rationale.
3. Identify aspects (research problems) inherent to the stated purpose.
4. Discuss the literature pertinent to the research purpose and rationale.
5. Develop the formal line of argumentation. In propositional reasoning, include premises and subsequent conclusions. In dialectic reasoning, include all theses, antitheses, and syntheses, and set guidelines as to when to terminate the process of argumentation.
6. Define all terms.
7. Collect evidence pertinent to each argument (use only primary sources).

8. Separate supportive evidence from the pool of all evidence.

9. Develop a final conclusion in light of the supportive evidence in each argument.

10. Identify new questions that emerged as a result of Step 9.

The format within which to present a research report based on philosophical inquiry depends generally on the purpose for which the research is being conducted (see chapter 11). Generally, however, it is advisable to combine Steps 1–4 into one thought process. Much of this decision hinges on the amount of literature needed to illuminate one's primary belief system and one's view of music education as a field of study. A second criterion would be the wealth of extant literature in support of the stated purpose and rationale.

Each argument in the line of argumentation is likely to make up its own unit (chapter of dissertation, section or paragraph in an article). All premises and conclusions in an argument are described in a narrative form. That narrative would include an abstraction and critical analysis of the evidence gathered in Step 7. All sources should be footnoted, and a clear distinction should be made between supportive and contradictory evidence. The final unit could be a summary of all steps taken, focusing the discussion on Steps 9 and 10 of the suggested methodology.

It should be emphasized that different purposes and different lines of argumentation chosen by the researcher may mandate somewhat different ways of handling the organization of the research project. Nevertheless, the format may provide the novice researcher with an initial framework within which to make the first successful strides in philosophical discourse. To be sure, a reader may neither agree with the researcher's primary belief system nor the chosen mode of inquiry. But even if there is disagreement on these two issues, readers of philosophical research should at least be able to follow clearly all subsequent steps in the argumentation, so that even the most critical reader cannot help but acknowledge the accuracy of the conclusions within the confines of the chosen philosophical perspective.

7.7 In Lieu of a Summary: Fallacies of Argumentation and the Place of Philosophical Inquiry in Music Education

Yarbrough (1984) conducted a content analysis of the modes of inquiry employed in the issues of the *Journal of Research in Music Education* (JRME) between 1953 and 1983. The results were reported by Yarbrough to the JRME Board at its biennial meeting in 1984. Of all articles published, 80% fell under empirical research, approximately 17% of the studies were historical, and the remainder of all articles (about 3%) could be labeled philosophical and speculative. If one examines the annual lists of "Doctoral Dissertation International in Progress," published in the *Council for Research in Music Education*, a similar distribution of types of projected dissertations can be detected: Of all studies in progress, a very small percentage (approximately 3–5%) can be labeled philosophical in nature.

As much as the proportional disparity among research modes is regrettable, it should not be surprising. Very few music students have ever been systematically introduced to and trained in methods of logical inference or rhetoric. For this reason it takes a great deal of courage for novice researchers to "stick out their necks" and develop in-depth discourses on topics relevant to the field of music education. The questions to be examined are complex and difficult, whereas the methodological guidelines of philosophical reasoning in music education tend to be vague and lacking in specificity.

In 1973 and 1984, Schwadron reviewed and described the status of American-based philosophical research in the field of music education (Schwadron, 1973; 1984). In those articles, he employed three different categories that he believed represented the types of philosophical research present in the American research literature. The categories were labeled theoretical, synthetic, and applicative.

Theoretical studies were those that described and analyzed philosophical positions and systems of thought, or that developed definitions of concepts and terms important to the understanding of aesthetics and music education. Synthetic studies were defined by Schwadron as those that addressed the impact of specific philosophical positions and systems of thought on music education. According to Schwadron, they often contained "judicious yet speculative interpretations" with regard to values in music education, curricular matters, and education reform (1984, p. 14). Applicative studies were those that served as "the testing ground" for the first two types of studies (Schwadron, 1973, p. 45). They were primarily directed toward the development of prescriptive measures for teaching music in the schools. Methodologically, the researchers tended to utilize description, speculative text interpretation, conjecture, and programmatic writing. Often making use of secondary sources, several of those studies lack in scholarship what they possess in enthusiasm for their subject.

Highly eclectic systems of reasoning carry with them the danger of appearing to be a "thinking-while-writing" approach. Rather prescriptive in nature, that kind of approach resembles the defense of a preconceived idea more than that of a logical argumentation in which propositions are stated and supported and conclusions are drawn. The ultimate result of both approaches may be the same in that they convince, but valid argumentation stands against the employment of fallacies of argumentation.

Fallacies of argumentation are those types of inquiry that render an argument invalid because of inherently faulty logic. Table 7.2 lists a series of those fallacies and their causes. These most commonly occur when the researcher fails to define rigorously all terms in an argument and when a stepwise reasoning is lacking. Fallacies of argumentation are the pitfalls of logically cohesive, philosophical discourse. They can be encountered both in the

Table 7.2 Informal Fallacies in Logical Argumentation

Type of Fallacy	Characteristic	Causes
1. Fallacies of relevance	Premises irrelevant to conclusion	Highly expressive language
a. Appeal to force	Use of intimidation when setting up the argument	Reference to people with power and influence
b. Abusive argument	Argument labeled untrustworthy as the person stating it is considered untrustworthy	Reference to who said something rather than what was said
c. Circumstantial argument	Argument assumed valid because alternative is equally weak	Arguing the opponent's position rather than one's own
d. Arguing from ignorance	Proposition held true since not proven false (or vice versa)	Persuasion by lack of evidence
e. Appeal to pity	Conclusion is to be accepted because of sympathy rather than true premises	Use of sentiment and emotion
f. Appeal to the public	Conclusion hoped to be convincing because of associations familiar and convincing to the majority of those making the judgment	Use of advertisement and propaganda
g. Appeal to authority	Conclusion argued to be correct because of reference to "big names." Differentiation must be made between expert knowledge and authoritarian decree. (See: "Sources of Truth" in chapter 1.)	Use of authority and inferiority complex
h. Hasty generalizations	Propositions refer to atypical rather than typical situations	Reference to the unusual
i. False cause	Coincidental and temporal relationships interpreted as causal	Wrong interpretation of facts
j. Begging the question	Premise of an argument becomes its conclusion	Circular argumentation[a]
2. Fallacies of ambiguity	Meanings shift within an argument	Persuasion by remaining vague
a. Equivocation	Term has different meanings in different contexts	Double meaning, relative terms (e.g., idealistic, romantic, classic, etc.)

Table 7.2   *(Continued)*

Type of Fallacy	Characteristic	Causes
b. Composition	Propositions relative to the *part* of something lead to a conclusion about the *whole*	Persuasion by "jumping" from parts to the whole
c. Division	Reverse of b	

[a]For example, "To provide every child with the opportunity to study music in school must be considered beneficial to society for it is highly desirable for a nation that music be a vital part of every child's learning experiences."

Source: Adapted from *Introduction to Logic,* 6th edition, by I. M. Copi (pp. 89–130).

professional literature and in everyday discourse. Music educators should be cognizant of those pitfalls if they wish to employ philosophical inquiry in the pursuit of knowledge.

In referring to "big names" or experts in support of a statement, appeal to force or authority is at work, not logic. In conversational arguments, an idea tends to be attacked more on the grounds of who the person is who holds an idea than what the idea entails (abusive argumentation). In a similar vein, if an argument lacks good reasons for being valid, there is the temptation to ridicule one's opponent's view rather than to give proof of the accuracy of one's own position. This kind of circumstantial argumentation may be as regularly encountered as argumentation by false cause.

Finally, begging the question is a fallacy of argumentation in which the strength of one's belief is cited as the evidence in support of that belief. This kind of fallacy may occur, for example, when music educators are asked to justify the place of music in the school curriculum. In that case it will not be enough to refer to the importance of music simply because of one's own belief in it. Instead, music teachers are expected to provide concrete evidence in support of their belief. That, however, is hard to do, and often causes music educators to find themselves at a loss for a well-founded line of argumentation that is based on documented evidence.

There are several studies in music education in which researchers have sought to develop either justifications or rationales for music as a school subject. Various approaches have emerged: (a) The field of music education has been described and analyzed according to selected general philosophical beliefs, or world views; (b) the field has been viewed from the explicitly described perspective of aesthetics; and/or (c) specific aspects of aesthetic theory have been studied in order to illuminate more clearly the place of aesthetic thought in music education. Such aspects have been: the nature of musical/aesthetic experience (see, e.g., Pike, 1953, 1967, 1972; Reimer, 1963; Schwadron, 1970a); the aesthetic sense (e.g., Benn, 1956; Dimondstein, 1967) and perception (Floyd, 1979; Sorenson, 1974); aesthetics and music of the 20th century (Demand, 1971); and meaning and value in aesthetics (Lessing, 1962). Some researchers have attempted to provide various frameworks within which to reason about the importance of music as a part of the school curriculum (e.g., Broudy, 1967, 1978; Reimer, 1970; Schwadron, 1967; Smith, 1964; Soellner,

1971). Based on the suggested frameworks, the researchers often included proposals outlining what should be the focus of a music curriculum. Mark (1982) has pointed out how such frameworks have changed over time from the "utilitarian view" to the "aesthetic view."

There have been some efforts to propose general theories by which the body of knowledge of music (and music education) could be explained. In most cases, however, researchers have chosen to investigate selected aspects about which to develop specific theories of thought. Such aspects have been the nature of music listening, the definition of culture, taste, music cognition, and the nature of musical understanding. The study of the works of potentially important educators and/or musicians has been another major area of philosophical inquiry and has included, among others, analyses of the works of Jerome Bruner, John Dewey, Edwin Gordon, Suzanne K. Langer, Abraham Maslow, Leonard Meyer, Jean Piaget, and Bennett Reimer.

In most of the research on the issues listed earlier, the particular point of view, or theoretical position, was described and critically analyzed. In some instances the researchers also speculated about the impact of those views/theories on music education. Efforts were made by some researchers to go a step further and demonstrate how the development of a theory of music education might be affected by those views.

When summing up the research efforts made by music educators in the realm of philosophical inquiry (for a selected bibliography, see Suggested Readings at the end of this chapter), it appears that the majority of studies have primarily addressed questions relating to aesthetic values in music, and music education as aesthetic education. That emphasis, however, should not allow one to conclude that the philosophical mode of inquiry in music education is solely restricted to research on questions on value judgments; on assessments of what constitutes the beautiful; or on speculations of what might define a meaningful, musical experience. After all, how and why individuals perceive and respond to musical stimuli is as much a philosophical question as an empirical question. Questions of perception and musical responsiveness should thus lead to the development of theories of musical behavior. The mode of philosophical inquiry is as suitable as any other research mode to move the profession into that direction.

The field needs knowledge about the nature of musical/artistic preferences and taste and their relationships to musical abilities and achievement. Characteristics of leisure behavior need to be investigated in relation to general principles of socialization. Such information might help to illuminate and define the term *music appreciation*, a crucial term in the music instructional process. Furthermore, clarification is needed on sociopsychological aspects of schooling in conjunction with those musical objectives that seek to foster creativity in the learner. Finally, the study of the nature of music as work versus the nature of music as a hobby may shed light on knowledge about the teacher-student relationship in the classroom. In fact, it seems that any aspect relevant to the triadic relationship of the learner, the teacher, and the subject of music can be important areas for philosophical inquiry. Models and theories of thought need to be developed and clarified for any of the issues discussed here because the profession needs a framework within which to place empirically and historically derived knowledge.

In summary, the application of disciplined inquiry to philosophical discourse in music education is a necessary and much-needed dimension of research. The results of such inquiry, however, can be of benefit to the field only if the truth of each statement in an argument is asserted before any conclusion is drawn. Also, the more the assertions are based on principles of verification/corroboration of evidence, the closer the researcher may come to finding valid answers to a given question.

Suggested Activities

1. Select three articles in the realm of philosophical inquiry. Identify their
   (a) Purposes and/or questions.
   (b) Lines of argumentation.
   (c) Definitions of terms.
   (d) References to pertinent literature (primary and secondary sources).
   (e) Conclusions.
2. Evaluate the studies according to the criteria described in this chapter.
3. Select several purpose statements of philosophically based studies and develop your own line of argumentation for each of them. Compare your ideas with those provided by the authors.
4. Select several terms relevant to literature in aesthetic education and define them according to synonymous and operational definitions, as well as definitions by genus and difference.
5. Develop examples that fit the fallacies of argumentation provided in this chapter.

Topics for Discussion

1. The role of the philosopher in music education.
2. A comparison of the various schools of thought described in Table 7.1.
3. Russell states that value and dogma should not be the subject of philosophical inquiry because their truth cannot be probed by methods of logical argumentation. Provide evidence for and against that assertion.
4. Differences in heuristic and propositional argumentation.
5. Differences in propositional and dialectic argumentation.

Suggested Readings

Belth, M. (1977). *The process of thinking.* New York: David McKay.

Brink, E. (1983). A look at E. Gordon's theories. *Council for Research in Music Education, 75* (Summer), 2–14.

Broudy, H.S. (1957). Does music education need a philosophy? *Music Educators Journal,* November-December, 28–30.

Cohen, M., & Nagel, E. (1934). *An introduction to logic and scientific method.* London: Routledge and Kegan Paul.

Dewey, J. (1934). *Art as experience.* (Copyright © renewed by Roberta Dewey, 1962.) New York: Putnam.

Durant, W. (1957). *The story of philosophy: The lives and opinions of the world's greatest philosophers.* New York: The Pocket Library.

Emmet, E.R. (1960). *Handbook of logic.* New York: Philosophical Library.

Foster, E.M. (1972). A phenomenological study of the foundations of music (Doctoral dissertation, Florida State University). Reviewed by A.A. Schwadron (1977). *Council for Research in Music Education, 53* (Winter), 37–42. With a rebuttal by author in same issue, p. 43–44.

Gates, J.T. (1974). A philosophy of music education based on writings of John Dewey (Doctoral dissertation, University of Illinois at Urbana-Champaign). *Dissertation Abstracts International, 35* (1), 238A. Reviewed by S. Wassum (1978). *Council for Research in Music Education, 55* (Summer), 45–49.

Heller, J., & Campbell, W. (1982). Music communication and cognition. *Council for Research in Music Education, 72* (Fall), 1–15.

Howard, V.A. (1972). Symbolism, art, and education. *Council for Research in Music Education, 30* (Fall), 1–10.

Intentionality, minds, and perception: Discussions on contemporary philosophy. A symposium (1967). (Compiled with an Introduction by Hector-Neri Castaneda). Detroit: Wayne State University Press.

Killiam, D.D. (1972). Aesthetic realization: Rationale and structure of a new approach to music education (Doctoral dissertation, Boston University). *Dissertation Abstracts International, 33* (11), 6390A. Reviewed by A.A. Schwadron (1975). *Council for Research in Music Education, 33* (Fall), 33–42.

Larson, R.L., & Boody, Ch.G. (1971). Some implications for music education in the work of Jean Piaget. *Journal of Research in Music Education, 19* (1), 35–50.

Lemon, D.C. (1977). Strategy in Bennett Reimer's *A Philosophy of Music Education. Council for Research in Music Education, 51* (Summer), 1–9.

Leonhard, C., & House, R. (1972). *Foundations and principles of music education* (2nd ed.). New York: McGraw-Hill.

Madeja, S.S., & Perkins, D. (1982). *A model for aesthetic response in the arts.* St. Louis, MO: CEMREL.

Mason, J. (1970). A conceptual analysis of an evolving theory in music education (Doctoral dissertation, Arizona State University). *Dissertation Ab-*

stracts International, 31 (6), 2960A. Reviewed by A.A. Schwadron (1972). *Council for Research in Music Education, 29* (Summer), 33–38.

Mauk, F.H. (1982). Aspiring to the condition of language: An examination of aesthetic considerations in the application of structural (semiological) principles of musical problems (Doctoral dissertation, Harvard University). *Dissertation Abstracts International, 43* (6), 1741A.

McKay, G. (1955). Toward cultural definition. *Journal of Research in Music Education, 3* (2), 92–100.

McMurray, F. (1956). A pragmatic approach to certain aspects of music education. *Journal of Research in Music Education, 4* (2), 103–112.

Meyer, L.B. (1956). *Emotion and meaning in music.* Chicago: University of Chicago Press.

Meyer, L.B. (1967). *Music, arts and ideas.* Chicago: University of Chicago Press.

Mueller, J.H. (1956). The social nature of musical taste. *Journal of Research in Music Education, 4* (2), 113–122.

Northrop, F.S.C. (1959). *The logic of the sciences and the humanities.* (Copyright © 1947 by the Macmillan Co.) Cleveland: World Publishing Co.

Phelan, C.M., Sr. (1972). The influence of Susanne K. Langer's symbolic theory on aesthetic education (Doctoral dissertation, Temple University). *Dissertation Abstracts International, 36* (6), 3480A. Reviewed by A.A. Schwadron (1978). *Council for Research in Music Education, 54* (Spring), 26–35.

Prince, W. (1972). A paradigm for research in music listening. *Journal of Research in Music Education, 20* (4), 445–455.

Reimer, B. (1962). Leonard Meyer's theory of value and greatness in music. *Journal of Research in Music Education, 10* (2), 87–99.

Reimer, B. (1965). Effects of music education: Implications from a review of research. *Journal of Research in Music Education, 13* (3), 147–158.

Research in the arts and aesthetic education: A directory of investigators and their fields of inquiry (1977). Project Coordinators R.A. Smith and C.M. Smith. Prepared for the National Institute of Education by the Research Program for the Study of the Arts and Aesthetic Education. St. Louis, MO: CEMREL.

Riedel, J. (1964). The function of sociability in the sociology of music and music education. *Journal of Research in Music Education, 12* (2), 149–158.

Ruchlis, H. (1962). *Clear thinking.* (Illustrated with photographs, cartoons and drawings.). New York and Evanston, IL: Harper and Row.

Rumbelow, A.S. (1969). *Music and social groups: An interactionist approach to the sociology of music.* Unpublished doctoral dissertation, University of Minnesota. Reviewed by R.R. Hornyak (1974). *Council for Research in Music Education, 40* (Winter), 11–17.

Schwadron, A.A. (1962). *An interpretation of philosophy and aesthetics for contemporary music education.* Unpublished doctoral dissertation, Boston University.

Schwadron, A.A. (1970b). Philosophy in music education: Pure or applied? *Council for Research in Music Education, 19* (Winter), 22–29.

Schwadron, A.A. (1975). Research directions in comparative music aesthetics and music education. *Journal of Aesthetics, 9* (1), 99–109.

Sexton, A.J. (1963). Music in general education (Doctoral dissertation, Michigan State University). *Dissertation Abstracts International, 25* (1), 204. Reviewed by P. Labach (1966). *Council for Research in Music Education, 8* (Fall), 84–87.

Sledge, L.J. (1971). The application of selected writings by Gagné, Bruner, and Ausubel to music therapy pedagogy (Doctoral dissertation, Florida State University). *Dissertation Abstracts International, 32* (11), 6481A.

Smith, F.V. (1970). Toward a phenomenology of musical aesthetics. In E. Straus & R.M. Griffith (Eds.), *Aisthesis and aesthetics* (pp. 197–228). Pittsburgh: Duquesne University Press.

Sudano, G.R. (1973). Aesthetic theory: Its uses in music education (Doctoral dissertation, University of Illinois at Urbana-Champaign). *Dissertation Abstracts International, 34* (2), 816A. Reviewed by A.A. Schwadron (1974). *Council for Research in Music Education, 39* (Fall), 21–27.

Wade, R.E. (1965). Suzanne K. Langer's musical aesthetics with implications for music education (Doctoral dissertation, Indiana University). *Dissertation Abstracts International, 26* (9), 5478. Reviewed by Ch. H. Ball (without a year). *Council for Research in Music Education, 16,* 22–23.

Whitehead, A.N. (1929). *The aims of education and other essays.* New York: Macmillan.

REFERENCES

Abel, R. (1976). *Man is the measure: A cordial invitation to the central problems of philosophy.* New York: Free Press; London: Collier Macmillan.

Abeles, H., Hoffer, Ch. R., & Klotman, R.H. (1984). *Foundations in music education.* New York: Schirmer; London: Collier Macmillan.

Adorno, T.W. (1973). *Ästhetische Theorie* (G. Adorno and R. Tiedemann, Eds.). Frankfurt: Suhrkamp.

Alston, W.P., & Brandt, R.B. (1978). *The problems of philosophy. Introductory reading* (3rd ed.). Boston: Allyn and Bacon.

The American Heritage Dictionary of the English Language (2nd ed.). (1970). New York: American Heritage Publishing Co.

Angeles, P.A. (1981). *A dictionary of philosophy.* New York: Barnes and Noble Books.

Armour, L. (1972). *Logic and reality. An investigation into the idea of a dialectical system.* Assen: Van Gorcum.

Ayer, A.J. (1952). *Language, truth and logic.* New York: Dover.

Benn, O.A. (1956). Esthetics for the music educator: The maturation of the esthetic sense. *Journal of Research in Music Education, 4* (2), 123–132.

Berlin, I. (1979). *Concepts and categories: Philosophical essays* (Henry Hardin, Ed., with an Introduction by Bernard Williams). New York: Viking.

Bittle, C. (1945). *The science of correct thinking* (rev. and enl. ed., 8th printing). Milwaukee: Bruce Publishing Company.

Bobik, J. (Ed.) (1970). *The nature of philosophical inquiry.* Notre Dame-London: University of Notre Dame Press.

Broudy, H.S. (1967). The case for aesthetic education. In R.A. Choate (Ed.), *Documentary Report of the Tanglewood Symposium* (pp. 9–13). Reston, VA: Music Educators National Conference.

Broudy, H.S. (1978). How basic is aesthetic education. Or, is "RT" the fourth R? *Council for Research in Music Education, 57* (Winter), 1–10.

Copi, I.M. (1986). *Introduction to logic* (7th ed.) New York: Macmillan; London: Collier Macmillan.

Demand, M.F. (1971). Aesthetics and twentieth century music in music education (Doctoral dissertation, University of Southern California). *Dissertation Abstracts International, 33* (8), 4452A.

Dimondstein, G. (1967). A conceptual model of the arts as sensuous expression in the education of young children (Doctoral dissertation, University of California, Los Angeles). *Dissertation Abstracts International, 28* (6), 2115A.

Flew, A. (1984). *A dictionary of philosophy* (rev. 2nd ed.). New York: St. Martin's Press.

Floyd, S.L. (1979). A phenomenological account of aesthetic perception and its implication for aesthetic theory (Doctoral dissertation, Vanderbilt University). *Dissertation Abstracts International, 40* (6), 3355A. Reviewed by: K.P. Thompson (1982). *Council for Research in Music Education, 72* (Fall), 67–70.

Girvetz, H., Geiger, G., Hantz, H., & Morris, B. (1966). *Science, folklore, and philosophy.* New York and London: Harper and Row.

Gordon, E.E. (1984). *Learning sequences in music: Skill, content, patterns.* Chicago: G.I.A.

Halverson, W.H. (1981). *A concise introduction to philosophy* (4th ed.). New York: Random House.

Hegel, G.W.F. (1929). *The science of logic.* (W.H. Johnston and L.G. Struthers, Trans.). London: George Allen and Unwin.

Leonard, H.S. (1957). *Principles of right reason.* New York: Henry Holt.

Lessing, A. (1962). Meaning and value in music: A study of the problem and theories of musical aesthetic (Doctoral dissertation, Yale University). *Dissertation Abstracts International, 28* (9), 3714A.

Lichtheim, G. (1970). *George Lukacs.* New York: Viking.

Lukacs, G. (1964). *Studies in European realism.* New York: Grosset and Dunlap.

Mandelbaum, M. (1984). The history of philosophy: Some methodological issues. In *Philosophy, history, and the sciences: Selected critical essays* (pp. 120–130). Baltimore: John Hopkins University Press.

Margolis, J. (Ed.) (1978). *Philosophy looks at the arts: Contemporary readings in aesthetics* (rev. ed.). Philadelphia: Temple University Press.

Mark, M. (1982). The evolution of music education philosophy from utilitarian to aesthetic. *Journal of Research in Music Education, 30* (1), 15–22.

Morgenbesser, S., Suppes, P., & White, M. (Eds.) (1969). *Philosophy, science, and method: Essays in honor of Ernest Nagel.* New York: St. Martin's Press.

Newell, R.W. (1967). *The concept of philosophy.* London: Methuen.

Nozick, R. (1981). *Philosophical explanations.* Cambridge, MA: The Belknap Press of Harvard University Press.

Perelman, C. (Ed.) (1975). *Dialectics.* (Internationaľ Institute of Philosophy, Entretiens in Varna, 15–22 September 1973). The Hague: Martinus Nijhoff.

Phelps, R.R. (1986). *A guide to research in music education* (3rd ed.) Metuchen, NJ: Scarecrow Press.

Pike, A. (1953). *A theology of music.* Unpublished doctoral dissertation, Philadelphia Conservatory of Music.

Pike, A. (1967). The phenomenological analysis and description of musical experience. *Journal of Research in Music Education, 15* (4), 316–319.

Pike, A. (1972). A phenomenological analysis of emotional experience in music. *Journal of Research in Music Education, 20* (2), 262–267.

Popper, K.R. (1959). *The logic of scientific discovery.* New York: Basic Books.

Popper, K.R. (1968). *Conjectures and refutations: The growth of scientific knowledge.* New York: Harper and Row.

Reck, A.J. (1972). *Speculative philosophy: A study of its nature, types and uses.* Albuquerque: University of New Mexico Press.

Reimer, B. (1963). The common dimensions of aesthetic and religious experience (Doctoral dissertation, University of Illinois). *Dissertation Abstracts International, 24* (12-1), 5455. Reviewed by M. Kaplan (1964). *Council for Research in Music Education, 2* (Winter), 41–43.

Reimer, B. (1970). *A philosophy of music education.* Englewood Cliffs, NJ: Prentice-Hall.

Russell, B. (1945). *A history of Western philosophy* (14th paperback printing). New York: Simon and Schuster.

Russell, B. (1976). *Human knowledge: Its scope and limits.* New York: Simon and Schuster.

Schwadron, A.A. (1965). On relativism and music education. *Journal of Research in Music Education, 13* (3), 131–135.

Schwadron, A.A. (1967). *Aesthetics: Dimensions for music education.* Washington, D.C.: Music Educators National Conference. [See also: Schwadron, A.A. (1982). *Aesthetics: Dimensions for music education* (2nd ed.). Wakefield, NH: Longwood Press.

Schwadron, A.A. (1970a). On religion, music, and education. *Journal of Research in Music Education, 18* (2), 157–166.

Schwadron, A.A. (1973). Philosophy in music education: State of research. *Council for Research in Music Education, 34* (Fall), 41–53.

Schwadron, A.A. (1984). Philosophy and aesthetics in music education: A critique of the research. *Council for Research in Music Education, 79* (Summer), 11–32.

Sellars, W. (1963, 1966, 1968). *Science, perception and reality.* London: Routledge and Kegan Paul; New York: Humanities Press.

Smith, R. (1964). Esthetic theory and the appraisal of practices in music education (Doctoral dissertation, University of Illinois). *Dissertation Abstracts International, 25* (8), 4745.

Soellner, G.E. (1971). Formalism as an aesthetic theory for music education (Doctoral dissertation, Boston University). *Dissertation Abstracts International, 32* (4), 2123–2124A.

Sorenson, J.E. (1974). Modalities of musical attention and perception.: A phenomenological view of aesthetics and style (Doctoral dissertation, Washington University). *Dissertation Abstracts International, 35* (8), 5454A. Reviewed by A.A. Schwadron (1976). *Council for Research in Music Education, 47* (Summer), 41–50.

Tragesser, R.S. (1977). *Phenomenology and logic.* Ithaca and London: Cornell University Press.

Wheelwright, P. (1962). *Valid thinking: An introduction to logic.* New York: Odyssey Press.

Wiener, P.P. (Ed. in chief) (1974). *Dictionary of the history of ideas. Studies of selected pivotal ideas.* New York: Scribner.

Wild, J.D. (1953). (Ed.), *The return to reason: Essays in realistic philosophy.* Chicago: Henry Regnery.

Yarbrough, C. (1984). A content analysis of the *Journal of Research in Music Education,* 1953–1983. *Journal of Research in Music Education, 32* (4), 213–222.

Chapter Eight

Approaches to Empirical Inquiry

8.1 Introduction

At the heart of empirical inquiry is the assumption that human knowledge derives from sense perceptions: the acts of seeing, hearing, touching, tasting, feeling, and smelling. Under certain conditions, these sense perceptions may be called observations. When planned, they become the source of data from which the empiricist reasons, makes inferences, and draws conclusions about specific events, human behavior, emotions, and affects.

To put the diverse observations into some perspective, each observation must be placed into one of a number of mutually exclusive classes. The classes, once they are precisely defined, are called variables. Empiricists assume that a variable can be expressed in the form of a numerical value that may be mathematically manipulated. That manipulation is believed to provide one with better insights into the relationship of observations than could be obtained by a purely qualitative analysis.

To many individuals the idea of quantifying human behavior seems questionable. Any attempt to attach numerical values to artistic thought and musical behavior seems even more horrifying. However, a distinction should be made between numbers by which things are counted and numbers that are used to represent observations or constructs of thought. Modern societies make use of both types of numbers to represent many of the basic concepts by which current life is structured. A day is artifically divided into 24 hours, the hour has been given 60 minutes, and a minute has been defined as 60 seconds. Mechanical devices such as watches and clocks are needed to make the numerically derived construct of time concrete and useful. Indeed, it seems safe to say that modern life would not be what it is were it not for the introduction of the construct of measured time. Similarly, temperature, speed, and distance are constructs of measurement that depend on agreed-upon sets of numerical values.

Governments employ numbers to describe the relative health of the economy. Such indices as Gross National Product (GNP), balance of trade, Dow-Jones industrial average, or the index of inflation are examples of expressing various economic conditions in numerical form. Sporting events rely equally on statistical-numerical evaluation. The batting ability of a baseball player, the shooting accuracy of a basketball player, and the passing efficiency of a football quarterback are expressed in percentages of successful attempts, which may then be used by the well-informed fan to infer an athlete's relative effectiveness.

Most individuals are familiar with and understand the numerical symbols of time, temperature, economic health, or sports success. They understand the meaning of the numbers and make inferential use of them. Because these numbers are useful and carry an agreed-upon meaning, they can become nonthreatening. Familiarity with the meaning behind a symbol thus alleviates intimidation. We suggest that the same may happen in the case of statistical symbols employed in empirical inquiry and employed to represent and measure musical behavior. Numbers may become meaningful when one feels comfortable and familiar with them.

A Brief Discourse on the Role of Numbers in Empirical Research

Numbers are generally used either for enumerating (counting) things or for measuring things. Counting yields frequencies; measuring something means comparing that which is to be measured against an existing set of numerical values to which a meaning has been attached. Observations expressed in frequencies may be called discrete data. Observations expressed as measurements are referred to as continuous data. An example of discrete data may be that of the teacher who has been observed to say ok 20 times during an instructional period of 15 minutes. The oks were counted one after the other. Compare that with the observation that Johnny has an IQ of 120 or that Teacher X has spent 45 minutes rehearsing the same piece. The latter observations report continuous data as the behaviors are each compared against preestablished measures of intelligence and time.

Regardless of whether continuous or discrete data are gathered, many researchers consider that measurement has occurred in some form whenever *numbers are assigned to any unit or variable as a way of representing that property* (e.g., Guilford & Fruchter, 1973, p. 19; Moore, 1985, p. 112). The important thing to remember is that discrete data are less precise than continuous data, and that in all cases the classification of a measurement ultimately determines the selection of the tools by which the measurements are analyzed.

Discrete Data.   In the terminology of the empiricist, discrete data may either be *nominal* or *ordinal*. Nominal data are those that represent a name, a class, or a category, such as trumpets, girls, or apples. Each label by itself carries very little information; together, the information gained from the labeling is that there is a total of three separate categories. The information can be increased somewhat if the frequencies of the items in each category are counted (e.g., 10 trumpets, 30 girls, or 18 apples). The numbers indicate the quantity of items in each category; they do not, however, carry any qualitative information about the items.

Qualitative information about the items could be obtained if one ranked the items within each category according to some given criteria. Using discrete data, the 18 apples and 30 girls could, for example, be ranked according to physical size. Each apple and girl would be assigned a number that corresponded to their relative size within the group—the largest being 1, the next largest 2, and so on, until the last number was assigned to the smallest apple or girl. The ranking process has attached to the integers the additional characteristic of ordinal numbers.

By ranking phenomena according to a given criterion, one obtains an estimate of comparative quality among the phenomena under study. But there is still a lack of precision regarding the exact difference between each ranked item. For example, Girl 1 may be very tall, whereas Girls 2–30 are all much smaller. The difference between 1 and 2 may not be the same as the difference between 2 and 3. How much all girls differ in size from each other can be indicated only by measurements on an evenly proportioned continuum.

Continuous Data. Continuous data have all of the properties of both nominal and ordinal data in that they can be used for the purpose of labeling as well as ranking. In addition, continuous data provide information about the qualitative difference among objects or individuals because the numbers used to portray such differences are taken from known interval measurement scales.

An interval scale can employ both integers and fractions in a sequential order in which each number is a standard unit apart from the next number. Thus, the rank order of the apples and girls could be specified according to exact size measured in inches, age measured in days or months, or weight expressed in ounces. In music, a measure on a continuum might be an octave with 1,200 cents, the distance between each half-step being 100 cents, or it could be expressed as a score on a musical aptitude test.

Continuous data are based on interval scales and ratio scales. Interval scales assume equality of units in which "the same numerical distance is associated with the same empirical distance on some real continuum" (Guilford and Fruchter, 1973, p. 21). A score of zero usually indicates that no measurement has been taken; it does not mean that a person or property being measured did not have any trace of that which was measured (Guilford & Fruchter, p. 22). Ratio scale numbers are composite measures of two factors in relationship to each other—for example, a test to determine which sound appears to be twice as loud as a stimulus sound. Such scales usually begin with an absolute zero point (i.e., the point where the sound did not exist) as an integral part of the measurement. For all practical purposes, most measurements in empirical research in music education are primarily based on interval scales.

8.2 Some Assumptions Underlying Empirical Measurement

Several assumptions underlie the idea of attaching numerical values to the observation of human behavior. A few of these assumptions need to be introduced prior to a discussion of the various methodologies that may be employed in empirical research. The following discussion focuses on the nature of a normal curve, the concept of probability, and the difference between population and sample. All three concepts are important for an understanding of the various levels of empirical research, the testing of hypotheses, the development of research designs, and the testing of theory. Some aspects of the concepts introduced in this chapter will be described in greater detail in the next two chapters.

A Normal Curve

An introduction to the concept of a normal curve should not begin without a brief introduction to Francis Galton (1822–1911), one of the first modern researchers to urge the application of the logical principles of mathematics to the observation of human behavior. He must be credited with the introduction of principles of measurement theory to the behavioral sciences (Mueller, 1973).

In the late 1860s, Galton became aware of the work of the German mathematician Carl Friedrich Gauss and his theory described as the law of errors. The law of errors was a visual represention of errors in measurement that had occurred during the gathering of a large number of physical measurements. Gauss reported about those error measurements by representing them in the form of a polygon, a closed figure bound by straight lines or arcs. Galton reasoned that this polygon might also be used as a means of expressing how individual measurements of physical traits might deviate from the average of a large number of measured human traits.

During the 1870s and 1880s, Galton set out to test this assumption by collecting a vast amount of data on human measurements (height, weight, arm span, etc.) and making measurements of plants and seeds (size and weight) (see Kevles, 1984). He plotted the frequency distributions for each of these groups of measurements and found that the shape of the distribution supported the Gaussian curve of error measurements. Galton thus concluded that the Gaussian curve was an appropriate and useful model for explaining the distribution of both human and plant measurements. For all practical purposes, this distribution is now commonly referred to as the standard normal or bell-shaped curve.

The normal curve serves as a mathematical model that describes how repeated independent measurements of an infinite number of characteristics of objects may be distributed over a continuum. The following assumptions are made: If a population of properties, such as all male children born in 1985, were measured on a specific characteristic—for example, weight—and if these measurements were plotted as a histograph with the weight on the horizontal base line in ounces and the frequency (number of humans) on the vertical line, the distribution of these various measurements would resemble a standard normal curve model. That model would represent how the individual measurements of an infinite number of people would be distributed around the value of their average.

While it is impossible to measure all individuals in order to test the accuracy of an assumption, large groups of people, closely resembling and representative of the characteristics of all people, can be obtained. And so it is that many independent measures of large samples of observations of individuals have supported the normal curve model with regard to most physical traits, such as height, weight, suit size, blood pressure, and length of life. A similar distribution of measures has been shown to exist for other characteristics of objects of the natural-physical world as well. The model has stood "the test of extensive checks against the real world" (Blommers & Lindquist, 1960, p. 4). For a visual representation of that model, see Figure 8.1.

All statistical information about the nature of a normal curve is presented in chapter 10. At this point it may suffice to describe a normal curve as the representation of a frequency distribution in which all measures of a group of people are plotted out in relation to the average measure for that group of people. That average measure is called the mean. It is determined from the

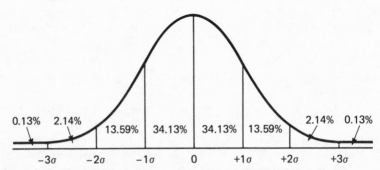

Note: In this figure, 0 is the symbol to represent the mean or center of the population. The numbers on the base line represent a standard deviation. The percentage figures under the curve represent those portions of the population that would normally be found in the areas away from the mean.

Figure 8.1 Model of the Standard Normal Curve Distribution

sum of all measures, divided by the total number of measurements. A normal curve is a graphic representation of where individual measures fall on a continuum in relation to the mean. The numbers on the base line indicate a standard unit of measurement (for details, see chapter 10 on standard deviation). The figures under the curve reflect the percentage of the population that would normally be expected to rest in the various areas to the left and right of the mean. Note that the percentages become less as the sections move farther away from the center. Therefore, the occurrence of an unusual measure is accounted for by the normal curve to the same degree that more "normal" measures are.

The Concept of Probability

Generally, empiricists attach numerical values to their observations in order to determine where along the normal curve a particular measurement may fall. Questions are posed regarding the measurement: Does it come close to the average of all measurements or does it deviate greatly from that average? If a particular measurement falls repeatedly far away from the average, why does it do so? If a measurement repeatedly resembles the average, is there some reason for that? Because of these and similar questions, empiricists place great importance on making repeated measures of same observations. In fact, formal statistical reasoning is based on the question of what would happen regarding the measurements if they were made repeatedly by means of observation and experimentation.

However, "real world" experiences can never be fully repeated. Two experiences may be very much alike, but they cannot be the same. The passing of time causes all experiences to be unique even if they closely resemble each other. In addition, new knowledge gained by an individual during an interim period of time, as well as changes caused by natural or man-made events, are likely to produce conditions that effect all moments of life and, therefore, all experiences. Knowledge must be considered as probable knowledge rather than exact, or absolute, knowledge. Under certain circumstances it may be true, but it may not remain true under all possible conditions.

The concept of the relativity of knowledge has important ramifications for the repeated observation of human traits and behaviors. Empiricists assume, first, that the truth or falseness of any knowledge can never be verified but only *corroborated* against repeated, similar sense experiences. A distinction between corroboration and verification is crucial because verification means "a proof of the truth through the presentation of evidence or testimony," whereas corroboration "strengthens or supports other evidence" (*The American Heritage Dictionary of the English Language*, 1970). Thus, corroboration can only support the probability of something being accurate; it does not support the observed event as being true.

The construct of corroboration of evidence also affects the nature of measurement in empirical research. As we stated earlier, measurements may be assumed to be symbolic representations of observed experiences. When repeatedly measuring such experiences, the truth or falseness of the measurement can only be assumed to be probable, not absolute. Thus, empiricists never conclude that measured observations are true; rather, they report the degree of probability to which the measured observations are assumed to be true. Beyond that, empiricists assert the degree of probability to which measurements may fall within the model of the normal curve.

Probability is a concern of all research. Philosophers account for it in the process of inductive argumentation, in which arguments only corroborate the validity of the conclusion. In historical research, the probable truth of evidence is established by procedures of verification. External confirmation of the data is sought by consulting public records, documents, or manuscripts. When a researcher corroborates the data against other sources, both the researcher and the reader gain confidence in the accuracy of the data. A certain degree of assurance exists that the data are accurate. There remains, however, a possibility that the data can be wrong.

How does one determine how much trust or confidence to place in data? In historical research, the trust depends on the degree to which the researcher describes all efforts to verify the data. The reader's own knowledge of the subject and the reader's perception of the researcher's integrity are additional factors that may instill confidence in the accuracy of data. In empirical research, the confidence a researcher has in the accuracy of data is expressed in mathematical terms as probabilites of chance that the data may be in error.

Probabilities of Chance

Assume you toss a coin to see whether it comes down heads or tails. If the coin is evenly shaped and without a major flaw (i.e., if it is unbiased), the chance that you get a head is 1:2 or 50%. The same, of course, is true for the chance to get a tail. The probability remains the same for each time the coin is tossed in the air. Now assume there is a box with a small slot on one side. The box contains 10 disks. Each disk is of equal size and weight and each disk has been numbered from 1 to 10. You shake the box and let one disk fall through the slot. You repeat that procedure until all 10 disks have come out of the box.

If all disks were indeed the same size and all of them had an equal chance of falling out of the box, the probability that any particular one of the 10 disks would come out on the first draw is one out of ten (1:10); the probability of its coming out on the second draw is one out of nine (1:9), and so on, until the second to the last of the disks has a chance of 1:2 to be drawn.

Next assume that there is a need to obtain a selection of 5 disks (a sample) from the total of 10 disks (the population). You want the disks numbered 4, 5, 6, 9, and 10 to appear. To determine the probability that the sample will contain the specified set of 5 disks, you need to know (a) the probability by which every possible set of 5 disks arranged in every possible order would be drawn; and (b) the probability by which 5 disks arranged in no specific order would be drawn. Again, if all disks were the same and your method of shaking the box consistent, then on each draw each of the disks in the box would have an equal probability (i.e., the same chance) of being selected. Thus, the fifth disk drawn would have the probability of one out of six (1:6). Multiplying all five probabilities by each other, you obtain:

$$\frac{1}{10} \times \frac{1}{9} \times \frac{1}{8} \times \frac{1}{7} \times \frac{1}{6} = \frac{1}{30,240}. \tag{1}$$

It is highly probable that you would not obtain the specified set of 5 disks on the first draw.

If you were not concerned about the order in which any 5 disks appeared out of the total of 10 disks, then the probabilities of drawing each of 5 disks would be much greater, namely:

$$\frac{1}{5} \times \frac{1}{4} \times \frac{1}{3} \times \frac{1}{2} = \frac{1}{120}. \tag{2}$$

To find out in how many ways the previously specified 5 disks can be selected from a total of 10 disks, divide 30,240 by 120: There are 252 ways in which 5 disks can be selected from a total of 10, provided the order in which the disks are drawn is unimportant. This means that a comparatively large number of trials may be necessary in order to obtain 5 specified disks from the rather small total of 10 disks.

Now assume that each disk represents an observation. Given that all observations have the same chance of occuring and that they are made without a bias, the basic assumptions underlying the constructs of probability of chance are: When selecting a sample of observations from a total of all possible observations, (a) every possible sample of a given number of observations must have the same probability of occuring, and (b) every observation in the total of all observation must have the same probability of being part of the sample. Thus, the probability of chance means that a large number of observations have to be made before one can be confident that the mathematical odds favor the drawing of a specific conclusion.

From this example it follows that in planning the methodology of a study, the researcher must make considerable efforts to create a situation in which all possible observations have an equal chance of occurring. Empiricists call this effort the elimination of bias. The more one's observations are free of bias, the better is the chance for the findings to be accurate. It is not always possible to eliminate all bias from the design of a study. In that case, one must be aware of the fact that the chances for the findings to be in error may be rather great. The smaller the chance of error, the more a measurement may be considered a probable representation of the behavior under investigation. It is relatively easy to describe, and even to measure, a large number of observations. It is much more difficult to assure that the selected observations are also accurate representations of the total of all possible observations.

The Relationship of a Population to Its Sample

In the technical language of the empiricist, the words population and sample carry precise meaning. Population is defined as "the entire group of objects about which information is desired" (Moore, 1985, p. 3). A sample is defined as "a part of a subset of the population used to gain information about the whole" (Moore, p.3).

In the example of the 10 disks in the box, the total of 10 disks represents a population of disks. In conducting research, a population needs to be precisely defined in terms of the information the researcher seeks to obtain. For instance, if information is to be gained on the singing ability of children attending public school in the United States in 1985, the researcher would eliminate from the population all children enrolled in private schools.

In the example of the box with 10 disks in it, there was a subset of 5 disks to be drawn from the total of the population of disks. That subset represented a sample of the population. In the example, 5 disks were drawn from the population in such a manner that each disk had an equal chance of being selected. When each object in a population has an equal opportunity of being selected as part of the sample, that sample is considered to be a randomized sample.

Randomization. Randomization is the preferred way of assuring that bias is eliminated from the selection of a sample. Many research designs make use of randomization procedures, and a standard randomization process is generally followed. In empirical research, random does not mean without planning or haphazard. Instead, it means a procedure by which all objects in a population have an equal chance of being part of a sample.

One way of randomizing a sample is as follows: Assume you wish to study the vocal range of fourth-grade female students. That population consists of 100 students. You do not have the time to test all the students. Therefore you decide to select a sample of 20 students from that population at random. The following steps could be employed:

Step 1.   Place the names of all 100 subjects in some order on a sheet of paper.

Step 2.   Assign to the first subject the number 00, to the second subject 01, to the third 02, until the final subject is labeled 99.

Step 3.   Locate the table of random numbers in a statistics textbook and follow the instructions given there.

Table 8.1 is a partial table of random numbers. In statistics books these tables may cover several pages. One way of selecting the numbers by which

Table 8.1   Partial Table of Random Numbers

Column	1	2	3	4	5	6
Row 1	99116	51089[a]	41995[b]	05540	80609	10909
		∨ ∨	∨ ∨			
2	15696	98215	86211	54076	89755	93643
3	97720	02132	22281	86413	44464	58103
4	11666	84342	15496	48472	03134	51459
.	......	......	......	......	......	......
.	......	......	......	......	......	......
.	......	......	......	......	......	......

[a]∨: Reading from right to left.

[b] ‾ : Reading from bottom to top.

Note. All numbers were randomly generated by computer.

to randomize a sample is to close your eyes and put your finger on any place in the table. From that point, read up or down, left or right, or on the diagonal. For example, if you entered Table 8.1 at the second column and went from left to right, the first four 2-digit numbers selected would be 51, 08, 94, and 19. If you entered the table at the bottom of the third column and read the numbers in an upward direction, the first four 2-digit numbers would be 96, 81, 11, and 95. The students to whom you had assigned these numbers would thus become part of your randomly selected sample.

8.3 The Testing of Hypotheses

The testing of hypotheses in empirical investigations is another important step in assuring that all aspects inherent in the research purpose are properly addressed. A *hypothesis* is an educated guess about the outcome of each of the research problems or their specific subquestions. This educated guess takes on the characteristic of an assertion subject to corroboration. The researcher seeks to confirm or refute the accuracy of that assertion by the evidence gathered.

Empiricists have set rather clear guidelines for when to accept or reject an assertion. These guidelines are based upon principles of statistical concepts and measurements and it is for his reason that a hypothesis is frequently referred to as a statistical hypothesis.

The Concept of Statistical Hypothesis

To illustrate, let us refer to a fictitious research investigation. The purpose of the study is "to investigate the relative effectiveness of two procedures for teaching 6th-grade students to sing music at sight." Two samples, Group A and Group B, are each selected at random from a larger population of sixth graders in a metropolitan school district. Each group contains 65 students (N_A = 65, N_B = 65). Group A is taught using Method Y; Group B is taught using Method Z. The teaching content and the teacher are the same for both methods. Prior to instruction (in technical terms: treatment), the students in both groups are tested for their ability in sight singing. Both groups have similar scores. The relative effectiveness of the two methods is expected to show up in differences in sight singing scores obtained after the completion of the treatment. Those differences will be tested by a comparison of the means of the two sets of scores. Following an equal time of instruction, each group is administered the same sight singing test again to assess any additional amount of learning that may have taken place under each teaching method.

The problems of the study are to determine the learning outcomes for each of the methods and to compare their relative effectiveness. Statistical tests are to be utilized to estimate the effect of the two treatments. Three outcomes are possible: (a) There will be no difference in the relative effectiveness of the two methods; (b) Method Z will be more effective than Method Y; and (c) Method Y will be more effective than Method Z. Each of the three options is an assertion of a possible outcome of the study. The researcher hopes to find support for one of the three possibilities.

Statistical hypotheses may be stated in terms of direction of outcome or in terms of no outcome. For example, the statement that Method Y will be more effective than Method Z reflects a direction of an expected outcome; the statement that there will be no difference between Method Y and Z does not anticipate a particular direction. The latter is called a *null hypothesis*. It assumes that there will be no significant differences between the two groups or no significant effect on the performance of the groups due to the treatments.

The null hypothesis is symbolized by H_0. In the illustrated example, the null hypothesis would be stated as H_0: $A = B$. This formula is used to assess the strength of the evidence *against* H_0. The strength of that evidence is stated in terms of probability. The question being answered is: "Can the differences that exist between the treatment groups be attributed to a chance occurrence?" If the differences are small and within the realm of chance as defined by the research community, the answer to the question is no. In that case, the researcher concludes that the evidence does not permit one to reject the null hypothesis. In the terms of the statistician, the differences are not significant. If the null hypothesis is maintained (i.e., not rejected), no further statistical testing is appropriate.

In the event that the differences between the scores of two or more groups are so great they must be considered beyond a chance occurrence, the null hypothesis would be rejected and the alternative hypothesis (H_1) would be accepted. The differences were significant. The alternative hypothesis would state, for example, H_1: $A > B$. (or, the mean scores of Group A are significantly greater than those of Group B). In the case of the illustrated example, this would mean that Method Y was more effective than Method Z. Rejecting the null hypothesis and accepting the alternative hypothesis permits the researcher to do additional testing into the various relationships of the data.

Empiricists and statisticians tend to be cautious people, and their language, while precise, is often couched in double negatives. Rather than assuming differences between treatments, statisticians prefer to assume at the outset that there are no significant differences between the treatment groups. The null hypothesis states that position. If the null hypothesis *cannot* be rejected, statistical tests are not warranted and any further statistical testing becomes unnecessary. Further testing takes place only when the null hypothesis *is rejected*.

Level of Significance.   In calculating the differences between the scores of two groups, one seldom sees a situation in which both groups are identical. They differ from each other on a continuum from very little to very much. The question to be resolved is whether such observed differences are likely to have been caused by a bias due to a specific treatment or by the probabilities of chance. If differences are determined to lie within the range of chance, the null hypothesis is not rejected. If the differences are large enough to exceed the range of chance, the alternative hypothesis—the treatment caused a systematic difference—is tested.

In general, a researcher rejects a statistical hypothesis if the probability of its occurrence is so low that it may be considered due to chance. Thus, the result of testing a statistical hypothesis does not afford irreversible proof for the acceptance or rejection of the hypothesis; it merely provides a probability of acceptance or rejection within set and restricted limits. The researcher has control over these limits of accepted probability levels. These levels are called levels of significance.

The level of significance is usually stated in terms of small probability values, such as .05, .01, or even .001. In selecting the .05 level of significance, the researcher acknowledges that a hypothesis may be rejected even when it has a chance of being true 5 times (or less) out of 100 (the .05 level of significance). The researcher is saying, "I reject the null hypothesis if the odds are greater than 5 times in 100 that the observed results occurred by chance alone." Stated positively, the researcher accepts a hypothesis with a 95% chance of being correct. In selecting the .01 level of significance, the odds are greater than 1 time in 100 that the results have been obtained by chance alone. Worded differently, the chance of making an error in judgment is set at 1%. Normally, the researcher sets the desired levels of significance prior to conducting the investigation. Research findings are reported as being significant when they fall above the stated limits of a level of significance. (See chapter 10 for a description of basic procedures to determine the significance of findings.)

In summary, the following steps should be taken when testing empirical data for significance:

1. Choose the null hypothesis H_0 and the alternative hypothesis H_1.

2. Choose the level of significance—that is, the amount of evidence needed to reject H_0.

3. Choose the test statistic to measure H_0 (for specifics, see chapter 10).

4. Find the probability value *(p)* for the data. If the *p* value is less than or equal to the level of significance chosen, the test was statistically significant at the stated level (Moore, 1985, p. 315).

8.4 *Purpose of Data Collection and Levels of Empirical Inquiry*

In the last five decades, research textbooks in music, music education, education, and psychology have frequently organized the categories of research by the tools the researcher employed in the data gathering process. For instance, if a questionnaire were used as the tool to obtain data, the study itself was frequently classified as a descriptive survey study: Investigations in which the researchers utilized observation systems as their primary data gathering devices were often called analytical surveys, or observational studies. Only projects that required the use of tests seemed to fulfill many music educators expectations of truly empirical research.

There are several reasons why the categorization of studies according to the use of their data gathering devices has created confusion and has clouded the vision of the ultimate purpose of research. First, a casual glance at the research journals indicates that many investigators tend to employ more than one data gathering technique in a single study. Second, most data gathering techniques can appropriately be employed in more than one category of research or mode of inquiry. Third, tests are a specific form of observing behavior, just as are surveys, rating scales, and systematic observation. It is the researcher's task to decide which tool(s) will serve best in gathering the needed data.

The ultimate goal of all research is to predict behavior and to explain the observed behavior within the framework of a theory. Given this overriding purpose of research, it may be more logical to classify empirical investigations according to the function and purpose they assume within the framework of developing a theory. Within that framework three levels can be identified: Level 1 comprises those studies whose purpose is the description of behavior through the use of specific variables. That level may be called *descriptive research*. Level 2 subsumes studies whose purpose is the determination of (a) relationships among specific variables, and (b) the association of an observed behavior to an external event. Both purposes fall under the label of *correlational research*. Level 3 represents those studies whose purpose is to estimate the effect one specific variable may have in causing changes in another variable. This kind of study requires the manipulation of certain behaviors/variables. Controlled manipulation of variables, however, is the essence of *experimental research*.

All three levels of empirical research—the descriptive, the correlational, and the experimental—are of equal importance in music education. One level should become the prerequisite to the other, and at all levels the gathering of data by means of various tools is necessary.

Descriptive Research

The description of things is the starting point of all empirical work. The researcher answers the questions, "What kind of characteristics are common to the group(s) of people observed?"; "How do the characteristics differ from those of other group(s) of people?"; "What variables of observation and analysis seem to hold the most promise in comparing teaching effectiveness, student learning, or the development of musical growth?" Descriptive research may pertain to observation and measurement of teacher and student characteristics in the classroom; the responses of children to specific musical tasks; teacher ratings of student learning and musical development; and skills in teaching, characteristics of musical ability, and achievement. Clues regarding a large variety of variables may thus be provided. From such an assessment of "what is," those variables that seem to hold the most promise for further studies may then be identified.

Descriptive research does, however, have its limitations. Each study is an end product. It is a description of an event that has already taken place. While the description may be systematic and conducted with care, a single observation will neither permit the making of inferences and generalizations nor the drawing of conclusions beyond the studied sample. Many repetitions of the same or similar event are needed to corroborate the results of descriptive investigations. As long as corroboration exists, the description of an event cannot be deemed false. Thus, a repetition of studies is essential to the accurate description of variables.

Correlational Research

Investigations at the second of the three levels of empirical research are generally based on data acquired through a number of descriptive studies. The intent of correlational research is to extract from the pool of descriptive studies those variables that may show some relationship to other variables. The objective of the correlation is to gain an insight into how certain variables may interact with each other and, possibly, influence behavior. Such interactions are not to be construed to indicate cause-and-effect relationships among the variables. Correlations merely indicate degrees of simultaneous occurrence of two or more behavioral traits, without saying anything about the existence of one trait as causing the existence of the other trait.

To illustrate: A small city succeeded in passing an ordinance allowing the sale of alcoholic beverages within city limits. During the following year, citizens who originally opposed the sale of alcoholic beverages mounted a campaign to overturn the ordinance. The primary reason presented in support of that campaign was that a 75% increase in crime occurred during the year such sales were allowed. A positive correlation did exist between crime and the sale of alcoholic beverages. One group blamed the alcohol as the culprit—the assumption was made that the sale of alcoholic beverages caused the increase in crime. Proponents of the existing ordinance noted that during the same year there was also a 50% increase in the construction of new churches. They thus pointed to the positive correlation that existed between the building of churches and crime, saying the building of churches caused the increase in crime rate. In fact, a third positive correlation could also be established between the sale of alcoholic beverages and the increase in the number of churches in town. Issues of cause and effect were thoroughly confused with the correlational relationships.

Correlational studies often seek to establish a close relationship among variables in order to provide a description of a pattern of behavior. Such description may also be accomplished by "summing up" previous studies that have described or correlated variables. By taking a number of investigations that utilized identical variables, it may be possible, through inference, to gain an insight into possible cause-effect relationships. Bloom (1964) provided one of the most thorough summing-up type of studies, in which he brought together several independent investigations on the relationship of the stability and change over time of several human characteristics—namely, physical characteristics, intelligence, achievement, interests, attitudes, and personality. Many of the articles in the *Council for Research in Music Education* have the purpose of showing patterns of variables as they emerge from many isolated, primarily correlational-type studies.

Experimental Studies

In experimental studies the researcher wishes not only to determine whether two or more variables correlate with each other but also whether one causes the other(s). This is done by hypothesizing which variable might be the reason for the occurrence and/or change of other variables. A research design is then planned in which that variable is either present or absent when a sample of subjects is observed. This deliberate manipulation of a variable for the purpose of determining its effect on other variables is considered a treatment. The variable that is manipulated is called the treatment variable. If a markedly changed behavior can be observed between the groups of individuals who received the treatment and those that did not, the researcher may conclude that the changed behavior was due to the treatment variable.

Empiricists call all treatment variables the independent variables because of the fact that they can be manipulated. The behaviors that are assumed to be contingent on the presence of the independent variables are referred to as dependent variable(s). Researchers thus seek to determine a cause-and-effect relationship among variables by looking at the relative effect of the independent variable on changes in the dependent variable.

For an experiment to be of much value, the subjects included in the experiment should be selected randomly from a population and also be randomly assigned to either the control group or the experimental group. In the experimental group(s) the researcher interferes with the "natural" process by introducing the treatment, while the control group receives no such treatment. There are many different ways (i.e., research designs) in which the number of control and treatment groups in a study can be varied (see Campbell & Stanley, 1967). As a rule, a large number of repetitions of the study is desirable if one wishes to suggest that a particular variable is the cause for the presence of other variables.

Experimental research is the ultimate tool for testing theory. In the area of science, theory becomes subjected to repeated experiments in an attempt to disprove or falsify the accuracy of a theory. True experimentation, however, is not possible under all circumstances. In astronomy, for example, and many other scientific disciplines, experiments cannot be conducted. Instead, some knowledge must be gained primarily by observation and inferential logic only. In areas of human behavior, true experimentation may also be impractical, if not impossible, because researchers may rarely obtain true randomization of subjects. Furthermore, it is difficult to control fully either the variables that are to be manipulated or some intervening variables, such as school environment, testing environment, and the like. Experimental research requires careful control and systematic and advanced planning if it is to provide useful information. Before a theory merits serious support, the results of a number of rigorous investigations must repeatedly corroborate the constructs of the theory.

8.5 The Process of Designing Empirical Studies

The design of an empirical investigation includes all the procedures that must be undertaken to fulfill the stated purpose of the study and to answer all stated research problems, questions, or hypotheses. The initial step in planning an empirical study is to review the purpose of the study and to determine where the study fits within the levels of descriptive, correlational, or experimental research designs. Once that determination has been made, the planning of the design of an investigation may become more focused and specific.

The second step in planning the study consists of the development of a complete list of all methodological steps to be taken in the investigation of each research problem/question. Four broad areas should be considered: (a) subjects to be investigated; (b) special physical conditions for conducting the study; (c) type of data to be gathered; and (d) selection of data analysis and statistical test and design. In many instances, not all four areas will be applicable to each research problem/question. We therefore recommend considering each research problem or question as a separate entity.

Planning the Study

The following outline can be used as a checklist to help the researcher in the planning and organization of a proposed project.

I. Subjects for the study
  A. Classification of type of subjects
     1. Intact classroom population
     2. Random sample(s) from defined population
     3. Volunteers
     4. Other
  B. Necessary criteria for subjects
     1. Age
     2. Grade level
     3. Gender
     4. Specific experience, expertise, skills
     5. Other
  C. Optimal number of subjects, groups, or classes
     1. Ideal number (use inflated estimate to anticipate dropouts)
     2. Plan to replace subjects or groups in case of emergency or unanticipated problems
  D. Administrative procedures related to obtaining subjects
     1. Letters to school officials
     2. Letters to leaders of professional organizations
     3. Letters to solicit prospective volunteers
     4. Clearance to use human subjects in study (obtain permission in writing)
     5. Prepare form to obtain consent agreement of subjects
     6. Prepare letter to inform subjects of their rights to withdraw from study
     7. Other
  E. Estimated cost for obtaining subjects
     1. Rewards for participating $ _____
     2. Reimbursement for transportation $ _____
     3. Costs for telephone $ _____
     4. Costs for forms, letters and mailing $ _____
                     Estimated total costs $ _____

The researcher may not always enjoy complete control over the selection of the subjects. It is therefore often difficult, if not impossible, to obtain a true random sample from a school district population. More often than not, access will be granted to intact classrooms if the researcher can establish a good working relationship with the local school administrators and teachers. If the population is a volunteer population or sample, it would be wise to overestimate the number of subjects needed. Volunteers do have an interest in participating in a study, but they do not like to let a study infringe upon their free time. It is therefore wise to anticipate dropouts and include in the study more than the minimum number of required subjects.

Most universities and schools require a researcher to submit to a committee detailed plans of how the subjects will be used in the study. The researcher must show that an involvement in the investigation will not cause physical or psychological harm to any of the subjects, and that each person is free to withdraw from the study at anytime. Failure by the researcher to gain that clearance may result in unfortunate legal consequences.

II. Physical conditions
   A. Use of intact classrooms
      1. Inspect facilities (space, lighting, chairs, and so forth)
      2. Obtain official access to facilities on specific date(s) and time(s)
      3. Assure full cooperation in the use of facilities
      4. Other
   B. Laboratory facilities
      1. Inspect facilities (electrical outlets, lighting, tables, and so forth)
      2. Obtain assured access on specific date(s) and time(s)
      3. Arrange for technical assistance in using facility
      4. Other
   C. Availability of needed special equipment (video camera, phono system)
      1. Obtain written assurance that all equipment will be available
      2. Inspect condition of all equipment: Repair or replace if necessary
      3. Learn to operate all equipment
      4. Develop emergency plans for equipment breakdown (new test dates, backup equipment)
      5. Other
   D. Specific time frame for use of facilities
      1. Estimate total time needed for rooms, equipment, and so forth
      2. Estimate total time per subject, group, and so forth
      3. Consider scheduling time, for example after breakfast or after lunch
      4. Consider special holidays in developing scheduled use of facilities
   E. Estimate of costs
      1. Rental or purchase fees for equipment $ _____
      2. Fees for other materials $ _____
      3. Cost for self-constructed materials $ _____

Data Collection

The following is a partial checklist for use in considering the selection of data gathering tools.

A. Type(s) of Data Needed
 1. Frequency of occurrences—list categories in which counting occurs
 2. Rank-order occurrences—state criterion for ranking
 3. Measurement of occurrences according to some standard measure—list measures

B. Type of Data Collection Tool Needed
 1. Survey instruments (questionnaire, attitude or preference scale, etc.)
  (a) Readily available, published, and standardized
  (b) Available from other researcher(s) (nonstandardized)
  (c) Existing instrument(s) requiring modification [for items to be considered see 1(d)]
  (d) Researcher-constructed instrument(s)
   Things to consider:
    i. Time needed for construction
    ii. Time needed for administration and collection of replies
    iii. Plan for obtaining maximum return
    iv. Estimate of cost for development, distribution and collection
 2. Tools for expert ranking
  (a) Determination of criterion for ranking
  (b) Development of ranking form
    i. Commercially available
    ii. Self-constructed (time, cost)
  (c) Special instruction or training for experts
    i. Time needed
    ii. Determination of ranking reliability
  (d) Selection of experts—qualifications needed
    i. Estimated cost (reimbursement of travel, food, etc.)
  (e) Special equipment (T.V., tape recorder, video equipment, etc.)
 3. Observation tools
  (a) Used and/or developed by other researchers
  (b) Modified by researcher [for items to be considered see 3(c)]
  (c) Constructed by researcher
    i. List variables to be observed
    ii. Determine type of observation (i.e., tally, ranking, rating; frequency of occurrence or measure of time)

       iii. Time needed for construction
       iv. Time needed for establishing observer reliability
    (d) Establishment of criteria for usefulness
  4. Test
    (a) Types of test
       i. Group testing
       ii. Individual testing
    (b) Standardized
       i. Type of validity needed
       ii. Reliability
       iii. Norms
       iv. Cost
       v. Length of testing time
    (c) Researcher-developed test
       i. Content of test
       ii. Validation of test
       iii. Time needed for test construction
       iv. Determination of reliability level
       v. Consideration of testing fatigue
       vi. Development of test manual

C. Estimated Total Time for Data Collection
  1. Time needed for administration of measurement tools and collection of data
  2. Determination of best time(s) during which to administer measurement tools

D. Administration of Multiple Data-Gathering Tools
  1. Number of tools to be administered
  2. Time frame in which to administer all tools (provision of "breathing space" between the administration of the various measurement devices)
  3. Plan for replacement of missing data because of illness, absence, failure to return measurement device (in the case of questionnaire or other "take-home" devices)

E. Special Equipment Necessary for Data Collection
  1. Recording equipment (video, audio)
  2. Microphones, monitors
  3. Testing materials, manuals, observation forms, etc.
                Estimated cost of data tools $ _____

When undertaking empirical investigations the researcher depends on various instruments to gather data. Some of the instruments, and especially tests, are commercially available, whereas other instruments, such as questionnaires, observation tools, and some achievement measures will have to be constructed by the researcher as the need arises. The construction and evaluation of questionnaires, achievement tests, and observation instruments are described in detail in chapter 9. Some of the technical aspects of test development, however, are discussed in this chapter in order to provide some guidance to the investigator who needs to evaluate and select suitable tests from the vast array of standardized and currently available tests.

What to Look for in Standardized Measurement Devices

Standardization implies a uniform procedure in the administration and scoring of a measurement device, be that device a test, a psychological profile, or an attitudinal inventory. When standardizing a measurement tool of any kind, specific information must be provided for those who wish to utilize the tool. In the case of a standardized test, for example, the test constructor will provide detailed directions regarding the administration of the test, sample exercises, ways of handling questions asked by the person tested, time limits for taking the test(s), and other details related to the testing situation. In addition, the test must have a precise and uniform scoring system as well as appropriate test norms. The latter are important because they provide a comparative scale against which the scores obtained may be measured (for evaluation of standardized tests, see Buros, 1978).

All measurement or data gathering devices, be they standardized or not, must have a certain degree of reliability and validity in order to be useful for the purpose for which they have been selected by the researcher. Details of these aspects of measurement are discussed in chapter 9; here we give a brief overview.

Reliability. The term reliability in data gathering instruments is concerned with how consistent an instrument is in producing similar results when that instrument is employed under highly similar circumstances. In psychological testing, reliability refers to a consistency of scores obtained by the same person when that person has been retested with the identical or an equivalent form of the test.

The manuals of most standardized tests contain information on their reliability in the form of reported correlation coefficients. The test constructors also tend to report the manner in which that coefficient was obtained—for example, test-retest, split-half, or through checks of internal consistency (for a description of these techniques, see chapter 10). In many of the commercially published tests, reliabilities are reported for the entire test as well as for the various subsections of the test.

The reliability of a test often depends on the length of a test battery. Generally, the known reliability coefficient for the whole test is higher than the reliability coefficients for each of the individual subtests in the battery. Knowledge of such subscores will provide one with a measure of consistency even if only selected subtests are utilized in a study. If not all individual subtest reliabilities in a test battery have been reported, new subtest measures of consistency need to be established prior to any efforts to apply certain subtests to the measurement of specific traits or abilities.

How high must a reliability coefficient be in order to be of value in the measurement of specific traits? Anastasi (1976, p. 106) suggests that reliabilities *(r)* in the .80s or .90s allow one to conclude that a measurement instrument is reliable. It is not unusual, however, to find researchers who employ measuring tools with a reliability in the .60s or lower. The final decision is left to the researcher. The lower the reliability, the greater the inconsistency and, thus, the probability of substantial measurement error. The researcher would be wise to accept Anastasi's recommendation.

Validity.   The validity of a data gathering instrument is concerned with what the instrument measures and how well it does it. The validity of an instrument is determined by its specific use, under specific conditions. Validity can only be determined by a thorough examination of the contents of the instrument and by an examination of how that reported validity was empirically established. *Standards for Educational and Psychological Tests,* published by the American Psychological Association (1974), classifies validity under three categories: content, predictive and concurrent, and construct validity.

Content validity is determined by an analysis of the content of the test. The question to be answered is whether that content covers a representative sample of what needs to be measured. This type of validation is important in selecting achievement tests. If a test claims to be assessing pitch perception, and the test includes pitch items, the test could be considered valid. If the test was to determine knowledge of Renaissance music and several items related to Verdi and Mahler, the validity of the test may be questioned. In checking content validity it is important to assess if the distribution of items covers all necessary areas in a proportional manner.

Predictive and concurrent validities are determined empirically. Predictive validity infers that an assessment given today will successfully predict a future outcome. Gordon (1965, 1979) obtained a measure of predictive validity for the *Music Aptitude Profile* (MAP). This was done by administering the MAP test to a group of young children prior to providing them with organized instrumental instruction. Following several years of musical instruction, a correlation was made between the original MAP score and an evaluation of the children's music performance ability. Very few music tests have attempted to demonstrate predictive validity empirically.

Unlike predictive validity, concurrent validity is relevant to an assessment in which a researcher wishes to make a diagnosis of current events or behaviors. For example, the question at hand is whether George is musical. He and his fellow students take a test on music ability. To determine the concurrent validity of the test, George's music teacher is asked to rank all students in order of what she perceives to be their musical ability. George's score on the test is then compared with the rank order score assigned by the teacher by establishing the degree of correlation between the two measures. If the two scores account for each other to a very high degree, one might say that the teacher's judgment is as valid a measure of musical ability as the test, which tends to be lengthy, more tedious to administer, and more expensive to purchase. As one measure serves as the correlate of another one, concurrent validity may enable a researcher to obtain a "simpler, quicker, or less expensive substitute for the criterion data" (Anastasi, 1976, p. 141).

Construct validity refers to the theory behind a test. Music ability, for example, has been the subject of testing and evaluation since Seashore's first standardized test battery in 1922. Initially, the Seashore test had separate measurements that were assumed or hypothesized to be related to musical ability. The subtests—pitch, memory, rhythm, and so forth—represented the theoretical constructs of music ability. Such constructs need empirical validation if the measuring instrument is to have a known construct validity. The issue is whether the idea of musical ability is accurately measured by the variables represented by the subtests. Instruments that attempt to describe an individual's personal or intellectual functioning are other examples of measures needing verification of their construct validity. The measures may be highly reliable, but the question remains whether the measures adequately describe that theoretical trait.

In selecting or developing measurement devices, the researcher must be cognizant of the technical aspects of test evaluation. Most test manuals provide this information to varying degrees, and a researcher must be knowledgeable in selecting an appropriate measuring instrument with care. The researcher must study and know the test. Just because a test has been published, one cannot assume that it is a worthwhile measurement instrument or that it is an appropriate data gathering tool for all instances. Most tests are specific in what they purport to measure, and a researcher must honor the stated limitations.

Administering Data Gathering Devices

In using a data gathering instrument, it is advisable for the researcher to personally oversee the process from beginning to end. If this is not practical, training must be provided for those individuals who will administer the tool. Care must be taken that all procedures be appropriate for the task at hand. A researcher should avoid rooms and testing areas where there are disturbances like traffic noise, intercom messages, or overly noisy fans or air conditioners. Unnatural disturbances may invalidate data, and the researcher must see that such events do not occur. If they do occur, the researcher should be prepared to discard the tainted data and obtain additional data at a later time.

In all data gathering situations, the researcher must anticipate some unforeseen circumstances. Bad weather may cause the closing of school and thus cancel an observation or testing appointment; volunteers may not keep an appointment; or the phonograph used to administer a test may not work. Whenever possible, the audiovisual equipment should be tested in advance. The unusual must be anticipated because it will most likely occur.

Analysis of Data

This phase in the planning stage is critical to the final analysis of the data and the drawing of inferences and conclusions regarding the data. This stage of planning one's research should not be done without some reasonable degree of knowledge of statistics. Without such knowledge the appropriate statistical tests cannot be intelligently selected. For this reason the following checklist for the planning of the data analysis will be appropriate for readers who have acquired some basic knowledge in statistical procedures.

A. The Nature of Data and Appropriate Statistical Tests
1. Nonparametric tests—nominal and ordinal data
   (a) Chi square (χ^2)
   (b) Mann-Whitney U
   (c) Kruskal-Wallis
   (d) Spearman rho
2. Parametric tests—interval data
   (a) t test
   (b) ANOVA and related tests
   (c) Correlation and related tests
   (d) Factor Analysis and related tests
   (e) Profile Analysis

B. Statistical Assumptions
1. Size of N
2. Randomized or nonrandomized sample
3. In the case of survey data, percentage of return

C. Specialized Technology for Data Evaluation (acoustical, neurological, and other measurement devices)
1. Availability
2. Availability of trained technician
3. Procedure of technical data analyis (time frame, familiarity with technical language)

D. Access to Computer for Data Analysis
1. Determination of appropriate statistical packages
2. Determination of data entry and exit protocol
3. Estimation of computer time needed

E. Speculation on Data Result Options
 1. No statistical significance obtained—what it might mean
 2. In ANOVA and related tests:
    (a) Statistical interaction—what it might mean
    (b) Main effects obtained—what it might mean
 3. In correlational test: significant but "low" correlation—what it might mean
 4. In factor analytical tests:
    (a) Low *eigenvalue*—what it might mean
    (b) The labeling of factors—what they might represent

In determining the statistical design of a study, the researcher must not hesitate to seek the counsel of others. Even the most experienced person should at this point consult with those who are experts in the field of psychometrics. To obtain adequate advice, the researcher should be prepared to describe the nature of the study as well as the data gathered. Consultation with others, the exchange of ideas, and listening to well-intended criticism is an important part of the investigative process. Good scholars are aware of the limitations of their own knowledge.

Application of Checklists in Two Empirical Investigations

Two different studies have been selected to illustrate the use of the checklists in the previous sections. The first study is a longitudinal investigation that required advance planning; the second involved a cooperative (exploratory) investigation between a music education researcher and an assisting team of medical researchers.

Study 1.   A Final Report on a 3-Year Investigation of the Rhythmic Abilities of Preschool-Aged Children (Rainbow, 1981).
    The purpose of the study was "to investigate the role of maturation on the ability of preschool-aged children to learn specific rhythmic tasks." The research problems were:

1. To estimate the ability of 3-year-old children to learn successfully selected rhythmic tasks during one school year.
2. To estimate the ability of 4-year-old children to learn successfully rhythmic tasks during the course of one school year.
3. To compare the ability of 3- and 4-year-old children to learn selected rhythmic tasks.
4. To estimate the learning difficulty rate for each rhythmic task for each age level.
5. To estimate the effect of training on the ability of preschool-aged children to learn selected rhythmic tasks.

Subjects for the Study

Step 1: Sample of Subjects.   The first decision to be made was on subject selection. Ideally, a random selection of students would have resulted in a stronger study; however, the logistics of obtaining a randomly selected sample within a large metropolitan area posed insurmountable travel and time problems. The decision was made to use intact classrooms.

Step 2: The Determination of Age Requirements.   The problems to be investigated specified the age groups. Therefore, the population of 3-year-old children would include all subjects who were between 2.5 and 3.4 years of age on the first day of class (September 1) and who attended a specific school. The same procedure was applied to the selection of the population of 4-year-old children. Their ages had to range from 3.5 to 4.4 years of age on the first day of school. Both the 3-year-old children and the 4-year-old children would be attending the same school.

Step 3: Experience of Subjects.   The researchers decided to accept both musically trained and musically untrained children. It seemed highly unlikely that children of either age group would have undertaken intense musical training.

Step 4: Population.   The decision was made to use all intact classes of 3- and 4-year-old children within one school. The reasoning was that classes for very young children are small in size (usually less than 15), and in using all the classes within each age group the total number of subjects in each class should be greater than 20.

Step 5: Availability.   Because of the previous decisions, considerations about sampling procedures ceased to be relevant. Availability of subjects became the next concern: Several private preschools were contacted to determine if they would permit the researchers to observe their students. A favorable response was received from one of the schools that had more than an adequate enrollment of students in each desired age level. Additionally, it was a well-established school with a good reputation. Permission to observe the children was granted on condition that the researchers provide a trained music teacher. To fulfill this condition it became necessary to seek a 3-year grant to support financially the teacher of the children. The teacher/coresearcher was essential to the study, and a 3-year support grant was obtained. If the grant had been denied, the study would have ended at this point.

Step 6: Administrative Procedures to Obtain Subjects.   Letters to the administration of the preschool were sent by the researchers, notifying the administration that the music teacher would be provided and asking for written permission to conduct the study. Written permission was obtained.

Step 7: Permission to Use Human Subjects.   A letter was written to the University Committee on the Use of Human Subjects in Research. The letter described how the students would be treated, that the subjects were not required to participate in any activity, and that they could withdraw from the study at any time. Permission to conduct the study was granted by the Committee in writing.

Step 8: Consideration of Missing Subjects. Past school records indicated that only a very small number of students withdrew from school during any given school year. Thus, the desired minimum number of subjects would not be jeopardized. Absence due to illness was not deemed a serious problem because appropriate assessments could be made at a later time when a child was no longer ill.

Step 9: Cost for Subjects. There would be no direct costs for the subjects; however, there was a hidden cost for the part-time music teacher. That cost was accounted for; it amounted to approximately $6,000 for each year of the study.

Physical Requirements

Step 1: Intact Classrooms. The availability of intact classrooms on a regular, scheduled basis was assured by the school administration. Music classes were presented two or three times per week and alternated with an art class. A classroom for the exclusive use of music instruction was provided.

Step 2: Availability of Special Equipment. The school administration provided a piano, preschool instruments, and a phonograph. Other equipment would be provided as needed.

Step 3: Time Frame of Study. Five one-half days every 2 weeks were assured and scheduled by the school administration.

Step 4: Cost for Facilities. No specific costs involved.

Data Collection

Step 1: Types of Data Needed. It was determined to use a criterion-referenced ranking procedure for the collection of data. The ranking would be a 5-point scale—5 meaning successful completion of the criterion of the observed task, 1 meaning complete failure to meet the set criterion.

Step 2: Type of Data Collection Tool Needed.
   Criterion. Videotapes were made for Criterion categories 5, 3, and 1 for each evaluated rhythmic task. A ranking form was developed and experts were trained in using the form.
   Ranking Form. The form was self-constructed. It cost approximately $75 and it took 3 weeks to develop the training videotape. *Ranking reliability* was established after rater training. It took 4 weeks of 2 hours work per week. The training ended when the interjudge reliability was a consistent $r = .90$ or better, and the overall reliability coefficient reached the same level.
   Selection of Experts. Experienced teachers at no cost.
   Special Equipment. T.V. monitor and videotape recorder and tapes (funds to purchase the equipment had been obtained through a grant).

Step 3: Observation Tools. Developed by the researcher. The activities in the classroom were videotaped, and each child was regularly and frequently observed in a group situation while all children attempted to complete a specific task. The tasks were developed on the basis of similar activities suggested by the literature. The tasks were subjected to a 3-month pilot study and modified. The videotapes of the children's class activities were evaluated by the trained raters.

Step 4: Total Time for Data Collection.   Three and one-half years, including a pilot study.

Data Analysis.   Problems 3 to 5 of the study provided the framework for all data analysis. Problem 3 compared the ability of the two groups of children to learn selected rhythmic tasks.

Step 1:   Analysis of Variance for Repeated Measures was used to determine if significant differences existed among each age group for each task and between both age groups for each task.

Problem 4 estimated the learning difficulty rate for each rhythmic task for each age level.

Step 1.   The problem was investigated by developing a rank order of item difficulty for each of the observed tasks. The item difficulty noted the percentage of task completion (ranking of 5) and percentage of noncompletion (ranking of 1) as the index of difficulty.

Problem 5 estimated the effect of training on the ability of preschool-aged children to learn the selected rhythmic tasks.

Step 1.   It was determined that a comparison would be made between children who entered the music class at the 4-year-old level without having experienced the previous year of music instruction. The logic was that if these nontrained children were successful in reaching the level of the previously trained children within 2 months of class instruction, it could be assumed that while training could prove important, maturation was probably the explanation for the rapid acceleration in learning musical skills.

Step 2: Access to Computer Data Analysis.   SPSS-X program was used for the analysis of all data pertinent to all problems.

The total time to complete the study was as follows:

1. One-half year to plan the pilot study and to write the grant request.
2. One-half year for the pilot investigation in which the tasks were screened and the data gathering techniques developed.
3. Three years for the main study.
4. Four months for data analysis.
5. Three months for writing the report.

The total time was thus 4 years, 7 months.

Study 2.   An Investigation of Extrinsic Laryngeal Muscle Response to Auditory Stimulation (Wallace, 1985).

The purpose of the study was to provide some empirical evidence to support or reject the assumption that auditory stimulation by discrete pitches would elicit consistent muscle reponses in the extrinsic laryngeal muscles. The problems of the study were:

1. To investigate the relationship of specific pitch stimuli to specific extrinsic larnygeal muscle responses in males.

2. To investigate the relationship of specific pitch stimuli to specific extrinsic muscle responses in females.

3. To determine if consistencies in responses to stimuli exist among subjects.

Two hypotheses were tested. The first stated that the perception of a specific pitch (F—349 Hz for the males, 698 Hz for the females) would result in the observation of a measurable response in the elevator muscle; no strong measurable response would be observed in the depressor muscle. (Note: Unless the individual is dead, there is always some measurable muscle activity. Strong response infers a sudden surge, or peak, in the activity.) The second hypothesis stated that the perception of a low pitch (D—138.5 Hz for males, 273 Hz for females) would result in the observation of a strong measurable response in the depressor muscle; no strong measurable response would be observed for the elevator muscle.

Because of its very nature, the study required the aid of medical researchers and medical research equipment. It also mandated that the researcher follow the rules of two areas of research; medicine (neurology and neuroanatomy) and various areas within music.

Subjects for the Study

Step 1: Sample. The study utilized 18 to 30-year-old adults. The sample included musically trained as well as musically untrained subjects. The sample made use of nonrandomized volunteers. The sample size was 21—10 males and 11 females.

Step 2: Availability of Subjects. The subjects were junior college students who could be available at unusual hours; the use of medical equipment and the involvement of medical experts mandated flexible scheduling during times when the equipment was not used by the medical staff.

Step 3: Use of Human Subjects. As in the previous example, clearance was given.

Step 4: Replacement of Subjects. Drop-outs did not occur; no advance provisions were made.

Step 5: Cost for Subjects. The researcher provided all transportation for the subjects. The subjects did not get paid.

The sample size was rather small, but by standards of medical research, as attested to by the related literature and the medical experts themselves, it was still larger in size than many medical studies that measure reactions to consistent stimuli.

Physical Requirements

Step 1: Access to Equipment.   Access on weekends or late evenings. The laboratory equipment was located in a major hospital in the Dallas-Ft. Worth Metroplex.

Step 2: Testing Time.   Five hours of total testing per individual at times when the subject was not fatigued.

Step 3: Estimate of Cost.   Clinic and staff donated services and equipment because they were interested in the possibility of new knowledge and the application of that knowledge to speech pathology.

Data Collection

Step 1: Measurement.   Muscle responses measured in millivolts (mV).

Step 2: Collection Tool.   Electrodes placed on muscles.

Step 3: Special Equipment.   Nicolet Analyzer with electromyographic plots.

This data gathering tool was able to control the stimulus presentation and in real time register latency between stimulus and registration of muscle reaction, then muscle reaction in mV. It was a very "high-tech" unit and, as one might suspect, subject to unanticipated break downs.

Step 4: Reliability of Measurement.   Based on repeated measurements.

Analysis of Data

Step 1: Selection of Appropriate Statistics.   The hypotheses to be tested had yes or no answers. The muscle either reacted to a pitch or it did not. It was therefore decided to report the data as a percentage of responses to stimuli.

Step 2: Sample Size. N (males) $= 10$; N (females) $= 11$.

Step 3: Specialized Technology.   A trained technician was on duty to help until the researcher was sufficiently trained in the handling of the equipment. Training time: approximately 6 months.

Step 4: Data Analysis Tool.   Computer analysis was built into the Nicolet Analyzer.

The research project took 4 years from inception to completion. Because the study was unusual, 1 year was required for the development, through trial and error, of a testing protocol. This was not anticipated. In addition, there were unanticipated breakdowns in equipment. Because emergency medical treatments required the use of the equipment, the total time for collecting the data became unusually long. While the delays could not be fully anticipated, the researcher allowed 3 years for completion. That mark was missed as the acquisition of appropriate medical knowledge took longer than the researcher had anticipated. The study also needed the support and good-will of the medical staff, whose availability was subject to frequent changes.

The cooperative effort described here supplied the medical community with new information and also provided music educators with information basic to their knowledge of the pitch discrimination processes. The results regarding the speed of hearing were unexpected, whereas the physical reaction to sound was anticipated. There was an immediate application of the find-ings—a speech pathologist alerted his deaf clients to the muscle movements as a means of speaking in a register close to that used by persons with normal hearing ability.

In demonstrating the use of the checklists for planning research studies, it should be noted that not all research problems are applicable to all parts of the checklists. We recommend that the researcher attempt to apply all re-search problems to all items in the lists to ensure that nothing is overlooked. The lists cannot be all-inclusive, but they may serve as a guideline for organ-izing the planning stage of a research project. The reader should also be aware that the studies described here were completed investigations and that they described events that had already taken place. In the planning of studies, factors of time, cost, and availability of equipment often mandate revisions of research designs and operations.

The completion time of the two studies described may discourage the novice researcher. In the first study, however, several things must be noted: (a) The 3-year length of the planned study obviously made it longitudinal; (b) the researcher had chosen to do a pilot investigation in order to eliminate some of the "bugs" in the main study. Pilot studies are mini-investigations that involve the planning and the doing of actual research. Whenever possible, we recommend a pilot study preceding any main investigation.

The second study was a doctoral dissertation. The length of time for com-pleting the investigation was unusual because the protocol for gathering the data had to be determined by trial and error. The researcher could not rely on evidence produced by either the music or the medical fields because neither field had previously addressed the topic. The researcher had to participate in human anatomy classes to gain basic skills in dissection in order to learn to identify muscles in the human body.

Careful planning is essential in the successful completion of an empirical study. Therefore a researcher should set a projected timetable for conducting the study. The discipline of setting schedules and attempting to meet them is an important aspect of the research process. As in musical performance, if you do not schedule your practice time and plan what to practice, little gets accomplished. So it is in conducting research: Lack of planning and scheduling produces a lack of accomplishment.

In conclusion, although these outlines for research planning and analysis are likely to be incomplete, they contain those aspects of planning that are most important in all empirical investigations. The four areas to which the planning should primarily pertain are subjects, physical facilities, data gath-ering devices, and data analysis devices. The planning should be precise because a lack of precision generally results in confusion and haphazard decision making. The purpose of research should be to sort out and place in order what seems to be in a state of confusion. That purpose, however, can only be accomplished if the researcher exhibits a sense of *disciplined* inquiry. The lists will not alleviate all pitfalls and difficulties, but the difficulties may be made easier and the pitfalls less painful. Some plan is infinitely better than no plan at all.

8.6 Drawing Conclusions and Inferences

As important as the planning of research methodology is, empirical research requires equally careful attention to the interpretation of all reported research results. Conclusions need to be drawn. They are generally based on three factors: (a) the data that have been gathered, (b) the data that were reported by other researchers (the related research), and (3) the researcher's own intuition and knowledge of human behavior.

The initial step in drawing conclusions and inferences lies in the organization of the data according to the stated research problems or questions. If the researcher has used a computer to aid in the analysis, the data are probably already presented in table form and may also be in graphic form. Most computer programs have the capability of presenting data in this manner.

The next step is to inspect the summary tables and determine if statistically significant differences occur among measures. The researcher should always keep in mind that significance merely serves as a guide to where to begin the data analysis process. Finding significance does not necessarily mean that what is being found is also important. As researchers examine the various relationships among variables, they must also consider the data with reference to error measurement and the reliability of the measurement tools. The data should be compared with those reported in the related research. The interpretation of one's data should in all cases be accompanied by one's personal experience and insights into the subject matter under study. The conclusions should be guided by the evidence presented as well as by the logical process that led the researcher to the research purpose in the first place. Finally, all conclusions should be assembled and enumerated in order to clarify for the reader how the study answered or failed to answer the purpose of study.

It is normal procedure, following the statement of conclusions, that the researcher present some cautious generalizations regarding the findings. Some speculations about the nature of the outcome of the study are usually permissible if they are identified as speculations. Frequently, suggestions for future research endeavors can be of great value because the researcher—an expert at this point—has more insight into the topic of the investigation than most other researchers. As such, knowledgeable suggestions for further research can provide valuable guidance for the next generations of scholars.

Suggested Activities

1. Review three empirical studies and identify
   (a) The rationale.
   (b) The purpose statement.
   (c) The research problems/questions.
   (d) The subjects studied.
   (e) The nature of the data.
   (f) The results of the study.
   (g) The conclusions.
   Critique each study and determine whether it could have been investigated by one of the other modes of inquiry.

2. Select a study and use its purpose and problems to develop a (hypothetical) methodology. Compare your methodology with that actually described in the study.

Topics for Discussion

1. The role of the empiricist in music education.
2. The logic behind empirical inquiry.
3. The relationship between descriptive, correlational, and experimental research.
4. The role of hypotheses in empirical research. When should they be stated?
5. Limitations of empirical inquiry.
6. Empirical versus historical versus philosophical inquiry: A debate.

Suggested Readings

Anastasi, A. (1982). *Psychological testing* (5th ed.). New York: Macmillan; London: Collier Macmillan.

Brislin, R. W., Lonner, W. J., & Thorndike, R. M. (1973). *Cross-cultural research methods.* New York: John Wiley.

Bulmer, M. (Ed.) (1977). *Sociological research methods: An introduction.* London: Macmillan Press.

Colwell, R. (1970). *The evaluation of music teaching and learning.* Englewood Cliffs, NJ: Prentice-Hall.

Colwell, R. (1967). *Elementary music achievement tests.* Chicago: Follett.

Durkheim, E. (1982). *The rules of sociological method.* (Ed. with an introduction by S. Lukes. W. D. Halls, Trans.). New York: Free Press.

Ebel, R. L. (1979). *Essentials of education measurement* (3rd ed.). Englewood Cliffs, NJ: Prentice-Hall.

Goldstein, M., & Goldstein, I. (1984). *The experience of science: An interdisciplinary approach.* New York and London: Plenum Press.

Guilford, J. P., & Fruchter, B. (1977). *Fundamental statistics in psychology and education* (6th ed.). New York: McGraw-Hill.

Huck, S. W., Cormier, W. H., & Bounds, W. G., Jr. (1974). *Reading statistics and research.* New York: Harper and Row.

Madsen, C. K., & Madsen, C. H., Jr. (1978). *Experimental research in music.* Raleigh, NC: Contemporary Publishing Company.

Nitko, A. J. (1983). *Educational test and measurement. An introduction.* New York: Harcourt Brace Jovanovich.

Popper, K. R. (1959). *The logic of scientific discovery.* New York: Basic Books.

REFERENCES

Anastasi, A. (1976). *Psychological testing* (4th ed.). New York: Macmillan; London: Collier Macmillan.

Blommers, P., & Lindquist, E. F. (1960). Elementary statistical methods in psychology and education. Cambridge, MA: The Riverside Press.

Bloom, B. S. (1964). *Stability and change in human characteristics.* New York: John Wiley.

Buros, O. K. (1978). *The Eighth Mental Measurements Yearbook.* (2 vols.). Highland Park, NJ: Gryphon Press.

Campbell, D. T., & Stanley, J. C. (1967). *Experimental and quasi-experimental designs for research.* Chicago: Rand McNally.

Gordon, E. E. (1965). *Music aptitude profile.* Chicago: G.I.A. Publications.

Gordon, E. E. (1979). *Primary measures of music audiation.* Chicago: G.I.A. Publications.

Guilford, J. P., & Fruchter, B. (1973). *Fundamental statistics in psychology and education* (5th ed.). New York: McGraw-Hill.

Kevles, D. J. (1984, October 8). Annals of eugenics, Part 1. *The New Yorker.*

Moore, D. S. (1985). *Statistics. Concepts and controversies* (2nd ed.). New York: W. H. Freeman.

Mueller, F. L. (1973). Psychological schools in European thought. In P. P. Wiener (Chief Ed.), *Dictionary of the History of Ideas: Vol. IV. Psychological Ideas in Antiquity to Zeitgeist.* (pp. 10–16). New York, NY: Scribner.

Rainbow, E. L. (1981). A final report on a three-year investigation of the rhythmic abilities of pre-school aged children. *Council for Research in Music Education,* 66–67 (Spring-Summer), pp. 69–73.

Standards for educational and psychological tests. (1974). Washington, D.C.: American Psychological Association.

Wallace, J. (1985). *An investigation of extrinsic laryngeal muscle response to auditory stimulation.* Unpublished doctoral dissertation, North Texas State University, Denton, TX.

Chapter Nine

The Development of Measurement Tools

9.1 Introduction

The types of data a researcher wishes to gather determine the choice of the measurement tools. They may be selected from a wide variety of instruments including questionnaires, surveys, interviews, tests, rating forms, categorical systems for the observation of behavior or for the content analysis of printed materials, attitude and preference scales, and various systems for the linguistic analysis of teacher-student communication in the classroom. Many of these tools are available from commercial publishers; others are in the public domain and may be modified as the researcher sees fit. Unfortunately, many researchers frequently find that the commercial and public domain measuring tools do not fit the precise needs of a study. By necessity, new instruments must be developed.

The purpose of this chapter is to discuss a variety of measurement tools and describe the technical aspects of their development and use. While the variety of devices is enormous, principles of their construction are not as varied as the novice researcher may assume. To illustrate that point, we describe some basic guidelines for: (a) developing a variety of measurement and analysis tools—namely, survey instruments, rating scales, tests, observation systems, and content analytical systems; (b) establishing the validity and reliability of the tools; and (c) analyzing the data gathered by such tools. The reader should be aware that the principles of measurement construction as described here may apply equally to the development of most other measuring devices.

9.2 The Development of Survey Instruments

It is probably safe to assert that anyone with a mailing address will in a given calendar year receive at least one unsolicited communication seeking an opinion about or attitude toward a specific political issue. During the 1984 political campaigns, the two major political parties swamped the electorate with pseudosurvey instruments that sought the recipient's opinion on campaign issues. At the end of each short survey, the respondent was requested to return the survey and include with it a minimum contribution of $25. That contribution was ostensibly to be employed in making one's answers to the questionnaire become a reality through the election of "our" candidate.

Was the real purpose of the survey instrument the gathering of a citizen's opinion and attitude toward political issues or was the intent to gather campaign funds? The real purpose was not entirely clear; perhaps it was a bit of both. Obviously, however, a monetary contribution was warmly welcomed and the answers to the questions had a predetermined political bias.

Political parties are not the only groups to take advantage of the fact that individuals enjoy the opportunity to express opinions and offer advice. Telephone sales people frequently use the ruse of conducting a survey or seeking public opinion when they are in fact trying to sell the public a variety of items ranging from frozen food to cemetery plots. This form of solicitation through the distribution of surveys and questionnaires has been misused by unscrupulous individuals from all walks of life, with the result that a potentially valuable tool has been turned into one of the most disliked and mistrusted of data gathering devices.

Why is this the case? One probable explanation is the fact that many recipients of the kind of questionnaires described are likely to be smarter than the people who send the surveys. It does not take too long to conclude from the bulk postage fee on the envelope that the questionnaire has been mass-mailed to several million other individuals.

Such questions as "Do you favor higher taxes? Yes or No," "Are you in favor of huge budget deficits? Yes or No," "Do you want America to be strong? Yes or No" are rhetorical. No one favors higher taxes unless there is a good reason for having them. No one really wants a huge budget deficit and everyone would like someone else to pay for reducing it. Naturally, we want a strong country but how strong is strong enough? All the questions posed have predetermined responses. If one felt that the information gathered from political surveys would be organized to draw conclusions, and if those conclusions would then be acted on in a way to produce visible change in policy, perhaps most of us would be more generous in responding to the questions posed.

A contrasting example of survey research occurred while this chapter was being written. One evening shortly after 7:30 p.m. a caller telephoned and identified himself as an employee of the U.S. Department of Transportation. He stated that the National Highway Traffic Safety Administration had randomly selected the household and requested us to provide information during the next 4 months on any automobile accident we might have that involved a bumper collision. A few, very brief questions were asked and the caller then informed us that a questionnaire would be sent along with instructions for responding. We were also informed that another contact by telephone would be made in approximately 4 months.

The questionnaire from the National Highway Safety Administration (U.S. Department of Transportation, 1985) arrived approximately 2 weeks after the telephone conversation. The letter confirmed the telephone call and reiterated that the household was not only one of 22,000 households randomly selected nationwide, but that we could expect another telephone communication in approximately 4 months.

The survey instrument was a single focus tool assessing damage to the automobile through

> incidents in which: Your front or rear bumper unintentionally contacted or was contacted by another vehicle at a very low speed, your bumper made contact with a tree, signpost, or other stationary object, or your automobile was involved in any other kind of bumper collision. (cover letter.)

The instrument was concise and could be completed with a minimum of effort. It began with a filter question asking if any of the respondents' cars had been involved in a bumper collision at any time during the last 4 months. If the response was no, that was the end of the questioning. If the answer was yes, a checklist of possible parts damage, fenders, cooling systems, and so forth was to be completed, as well as the cost of the repairs. The responses to the questionnaire would indeed provide the Highway Safety Administration with data not available to them by any other means.

Why do some questionnaires evoke an antagonistic response while others are looked on with favor? An unannounced mailing is impersonal; a telephone call is personal because it gives you the feeling that the calling party is interested in your opinion about something and that the information you have is important. In the case of the survey by the Department of Transportation, the caller introduced himself, asked for help, and requested specific information not normally available to him through public records or other such sources of information. All communications were brief, to the point, and cordial. The letter prefacing the survey instrument and signed by the chief officer of the department of transportation was courteous, addressed the purpose of the study, and confirmed the information the caller had presented.

The survey instrument was clear and easy to complete. The questions did not require any interpretation or guesswork on the part of the respondent. The purpose was clear and the fact that a follow-up telephone call was announced indicated to the respondents the urgency of their reply. These personal contacts were inserted to assure a reasonably high percentage of returned questionnaires.

In contrast to the questionnaire distributed by the Department of Transportation, the questionnaires sent out by the political parties did not provide the feeling that the recipient would be able to supply privileged information. The cover letter did not relate to the questionnaire, and there was a lack of personal interest in the individual receiving the questionnaire.

The Use of Survey Instruments

The meaning of the term *questionnaire* is rather broad as it implies many things to many people. The word has been applied to data gathering tools that seek factual information as well as attitudes, beliefs, and opinions. Factual information to be sought in music education research ranges from such items as the number of music teachers employed in a district, state, or region, to salaries of the teachers or number of hours attributed to the teaching of music in various school districts, states, regions, or the nation. Attitudes, opinions, and perceptions sought might be considered along with the quality of music programs, selected goals, and objectives in the school curriculum or in specific teacher training curricula. Questions that seek opinions rather than factual information may be used to study job satisfaction and expectations about one's professional training.

Oppenheim (1966, p. 9) categorizes surveys according to their purposes in the data collection process. In doing so, two categories seem to emerge: The first represents all those questionnaires that seek descriptive, enumerative, and census-type information; the second contains those survey tools that are analytic and relational in nature. The purpose of the data gathering in the first category is to count and to find facts; the purpose of the data gathering in the second category is to answer the question "why." That question leads to the examination of group similarities and differences, the exploration of relationships between variables, and the investigation of specific hypotheses. Thus, it is erroneous to assume that survey tools are only used for descriptive studies as the techniques can be equally valuable in all modes of inquiry.

Well-designed survey instruments have several potential advantages applicable to all modes of research. A survey can, with a modest amount of financial expense, reach many individuals or groups of individuals in diverse geographical areas. Data can be collected that are not contained in normal public records, and their results may be generalized to a population if the respondents to the questionnaire are selected on a random basis.

Designing a Survey Instrument

Many survey instruments take the form of a questionnaire in which either facts or opinions are sought. Opinion-seeking questionnaires are sometimes also referred to as opinionnaires. Such a label seems unnecessary, if not incorrect, since a questionnaire simply indicates the format by which data are gathered. It does not say anything about the type of information sought. In all cases, however, and regardless of the type of information sought, several important preparatory steps must be undertaken in the development of the survey instrument.

Consistent with all research design, the initial step in designing a questionnaire lies in the purpose of the study and the specific research problems or questions. The questionnaire may be appropriate for accumulating all the data in a study or for gathering only those data that are essential for but a small aspect of the investigation. The researcher must decide what role the questionnaire will play in the total scope of the projected study.

In considering the design of a survey instrument, Oppenheim (1966, p. 3) suggests that researchers should reflect for a moment on the end result of their investigations and consider the conclusions they wish to draw. By reflecting on the final product of the research, it is possible to arrive at a rather precise understanding of the nature of the required population or sample and of the types of data that will be necessary for resolving the purpose of the study. Knowing this information, it should then be possible to infer the categories of questions that should be asked and the way in which the responses can be quantified.

The second step in the process is to define and list all independent variables that should be measured. For each of the variables listed the scales or measuring instruments should be determined. Some may be readily available; others will have to be built or adapted. During this portion of the planning stage it is also wise to reflect on the type of data to be collected (nominal, ordinal, interval). This time of reflection will help the researcher in the final determination of the data analysis.

To determine if one should use a sample or an entire population, it is necessary to decide on the actual size of the target population. If that defined population contains 300 or fewer subjects, the most satisfactory approach may be to survey the entire population. If the population is greater than 1,000, then sampling techniques should be considered. Many external factors, such as cost for mailing, telephone, travel, employing interviewers, and so forth, will influence one's answers to these questions. The answers may also cause the researcher to scale down the scope of the original project. However, the precision of a sample measurement is related to sample size. The smaller the sample, the greater the possibility of a wider margin of error in the data (Moore, 1985, p. 306).

Prior to writing the first question, several decisions must be made regarding (a) data collection, (b) the way the respondent will be approached, (c) the sequence in which the variables will be addressed, (d) the order of questions for each variable; and (e) the use of open-ended questions or forced-choice answers (Oppenheim, 1966, p. 25). Conducting a pilot investigation is the best way to make decisions on each of those areas as the pilot study gives researchers a feel for what they are about to do.

Formulating Questions.   Formulating the questions for a survey is best approached if one first conducts informal or unstructured interviews with people who have characteristics similar to those of the target population/sample. By discussing their views on specific issues and by learning about the perceptions they harbor regarding the aspects that are to be investigated, other, hidden aspects of importance to the purpose of the study may become apparent and new, unanticipated variables may emerge. Indeed, a hierarchy of concerns that should be utilized by the researcher in the questionnaire design may become apparent. In addition, preliminary interviews give the researcher a better insight into the language and vocabulary that could best be used in constructing the questionnaire. When formulating the questions for the questionnaire, consideration must be given as to how the information gathered will be converted to numbers.

Following the interview stage it is appropriate to develop questions for each variable at hand. The questions may be in open form or multiple choice. They should also be pilot-tested with people who are similar to those of the desired target population/sample. Oppenheim (p. 26) warns that eight or more pilot revisions of a questionnaire with several hundred subjects should be considered common practice in survey research.

When developing and pilot-testing items for the questionnaire, the researcher should decide for each question why it should be included in the measurement tool and what can be done with that information. If a researcher cannot justify the use of data obtained from a particular question, the question should be eliminated. If a question provides too wide a dispersion of answers or results in too narrow a range of answers, it might have been worded poorly and needs either to be eliminated, revised, or pilot tested again.

In constructing questions, the motto should be "keep them short," preferably not longer than 20 words. Ambiguous questions, rhetorical questions, negative questions and questions that contain either-or options must be avoided. Likewise, the researcher must eliminate any leading questions that have "loaded" words. As much as possible, the questionnaire should be written from the respondent's point of view. After all, a questionnaire should be a communicative tool between the researcher and the population/sample of the study. The respondents should be at ease with the issues addressed and should understand the questions without having to guess their meaning. The style of language in which all questions are worded should therefore be that of the respondents. Some technical terms known to the researcher might have to be "translated" into words that make sense to the respondents.

In the process of piloting the questionnaire, it is also wise to pilot the cover letter that will accompany the mailed survey instrument. Generally, a well thought-out cover letter enhances the return rate during the main study. The letter should contain a clear explanation of the purpose of the questionnaire and should mention the official sponsor of the project, be it a professional organization, a school district, or a university. Where an investigation is in fulfillment of a doctoral degree, candidates should not mention that they are working on a degree (Leedy, 1985, p. 138–139). Instead, the respondents should be informed how they came to be selected and why their information is essential to the research project. Detailed instructions must be included regarding how to answer the survey and where to send it after completion. The researcher should offer to share the results of the study with the respondents.

Building a Sequence of Questions. It is important for clarity that all questions appear in a logical order. Consider, for example, the various types of questions that could be employed in the survey tool. It is possible to have a combination of open-ended questions, multiple choice questions, census-type or factual questions, and checklist items. Therefore, questions of similar type ought to be placed together. All checklist items, for instance, should be set apart from the multiple choice items or from the fact-seeking questions.

For each area to be addressed, the questions should be ordered in a sequence that goes from broad questions to very specific ones. Oppenheim (p. 38) labels this the "funnel" approach; others have called it "branching." This approach can be employed along with filter questions that are used to exclude a respondent from a question sequence if the items addressed by that sequence are not relevant to the respondent. An example of a filter question is:

Have you purchased a musical instrument within the last 12 months? Yes____, No____.

If yes, please continue with the following questions.

If no, go to Section B, page 3.

The Use and Evaluation of Open-Ended Questions. Open-ended questions are easy to ask and difficult to evaluate. If the intention is to quantify the responses to open-ended questions, the following procedure may be of value. From a pilot study, approximately 50–75 responses are selected at random from the pool of returned questionnaires. The answers are evaluated in a rank order according to levels of internal agreement, ranging from strongly agree, agree, undecided, disagree, to strongly disagree. Then a numerical value may be assigned to each category (5 = strongly agree, 1 = strongly disagree). All responses to the open-ended questions should be coded in a similar fashion.

When assigning scores to open-ended questions, the researcher must decide if 5 or 1 is the highest score. It is advisable to be consistent with other measuring tools that, along with the questionnaire, are being used in an investigation. For example, if 10 represents a high ranking in a checklist, it should also be used to represent the highest score in the scale for quantifying the open-ended questions.

Distributing the Survey Instrument

The success of a survey study depends on the return of a substantial majority of the instruments. The researcher is thus at the mercy of the subjects to fill out the questionnaires and return them. Careful planning of how to assure such return is crucial to the overall completion of the research project.

If the survey instrument is to be administered by the researcher or a group of assistants, overseeing the distribution of the instrument and retrieving the completed questionnaires may not be a major problem. Unfortunately, however, the personal touch cannot always be practical for many surveys because the instruments must be distributed and collected by the impersonal means of the postal service. The format and content of the cover letter therefore is of utmost importance. If the cover letter is appealing to the respondent and if the researcher encloses a stamped, self-addressed envelope, there is a reasonable chance that the questionnaire will be completed and promptly returned to the researcher.

To identify those who responded and those who failed to respond, each questionnaire that is distributed must be coded. This can be done by placing an identification number on each questionnaire or on the (stamped) return envelope. By keeping records of those who returned the surveys, those individuals who have not yet responded can be identified. Approximately 3 weeks after the initial distribution of the survey a follow-up mailing must be sent to those subjects tardy in returning their questionnaires. That mailing must contain a new cover letter, a second copy of the questionnaire, and another self-addressed, stamped return envelope. An I.D. code must be put on the questionnaire and the respondents should be reminded of the importance of the information they can provide.

In our experience, the second mailing will result in a total return of 70% or better. To reach what we would consider a respectable minimum return of 80%, an additional mailing or a personal telephone call may be necessary. The figure of an 80%-minimum final return of a mailed survey is arbitrary. There is, however, good reason why a researcher should strive for a return this large or larger. The questionnaires returned represent the final sample size; the precision of the questionnaire data is directly dependent on that sample size (see Moore, 1985, pp. 20–21).

In some instances, confidential information may have to be gathered. Under such circumstances, the following procedure may be considered: (a) The mailing is coded as before, but the coding placed on the self-addressed, stamped envelope; (b) an additional unmarked envelope is included in the package and the respondent is instructed to enclose the completed survey in the unmarked envelope, seal it, and place the sealed envelope into the self-addressed, stamped envelope. Furthermore, the respondent must be assured that all information will be confidential, that the individual's responses will not be made public, and that none of the respondents will be acknowledged as participants of the study.

A further consideration in the distribution of survey instruments is the time frame within which a researcher expects the return of the completed instruments. The opening and closing of schools and holidays and vacation periods must be viewed as poor times for a respondent to receive and fill out a questionnaire. Again, based on our research experience, if a questionnaire is delivered at a normal time in the year and if it carries with it a well-conceived cover letter, an initial return of 40–50% may be anticipated within a 3-week period. However, it is always a good idea to anticipate a rather low initial return and to have a contingency plan for recovering the remainder of the survey instruments. Particularly if the information sought is worth the researcher's effort, all possible avenues should be taken to obtain the ideal return of 100%.

Data Analysis

The data gathered by means of a questionnaire may be analyzed by statistical procedures that are consistent with the type of data gathered and appropriate for the purpose of the study. For this reason, the consideration of levels of measurement is of utmost importance while the questionnaire is being constructed.

Any analysis of questionnaire data should distinguish between quantitative and qualitative data (Oppenheim, 1966, pp. 254–255). Quantitative survey data include such things as music budgets, salaries for music teachers, amount of rehearsal time, or number of students enrolled in organizations. These data could be analyzed by statistical tests using t tests, analysis of variance, or correlational procedures. Qualitative data could be analyzed through techniques that evaluate percentages, chi-square tests, or other nonparametric statistical tests. In most surveys the data collected tend to be in the qualitative class and are thus most often presented in percentages.

9.3 The Development of Rating Scales

In the previous section, reference was made to the development of a ranking scale by which to quantify the answers to open-ended questions in a survey instrument. That suggested scale was modeled after the attitude scale developed by R. Likert (1932). Another kind of rating scale is the criterion-referenced scale, in which each ranking is defined according to specific criteria. Both types of scales are frequently employed in music education research and are therefore described in the following pages.

The Likert-Type Scale

The Likert Scale has become a standard measure for categorical rating. The scale as devised and reported by Likert (1932) had five response categories: "strongly approve," "approve," "undecided," "disapprove," and "strongly disapprove." Attitude statements were evaluated on the basis of responses to categories in that Likert used scale values as weights for the responses. For example, "strongly approve" was scaled as a 5, "approve" as a 4, "undecided" as a 3, and so on (for an example, see Table 9.1). This procedure allows the researcher to obtain summated, attitudinal ratings of a specific event, musical performance, or behavioral trait of a person.

The direction of the weighting of the values (from 1 to 5) is determined by the content of the items to be rated. The respondent's score is established by summing the values over all items. It is therefore wise not to mix positive and negative items in the same scale. A "strongly approve" or "strongly agree" item would be assumed to be positive toward the issue, whereas "strongly disagree" or "strongly disapprove" would suggest an unfavorable view toward

Table 9.1 A Likert-Type Attitude Response Scale

	Strongly Agree 5	Agree 4	Uncertain 3	Disagree 2	Strongly Disagree 1
Marching band should be the most important activity in school	5	4	3	2	1
It is fun going to marching band contest	5	4	3	2	1
The music played in marching band is excellent	5	4	3	2	1

an issue. The "approve" or "agree" answers and "disapprove" and "disagree" responses would represent moderate responses.

In practice, the scored responses are summed up and treated as having equal interval properties, a practice that may not be wholly accurate but is supported by research (e.g., Spector, 1976). Ghiselli, Campbell, & Zedeck (1981, p. 414) have recommended that all Likert Scales should be tested for item reliability through item analysis. In the final scale it is advisable to have "high item-total correlations, which would indicate that the items are measuring the same dimension" (p. 414).

The Criterion-Referenced Rating Scale

Whereas the Likert Scale is often employed to gather opinions on how groups of individuals perceive or react to an event, the criterion-referenced ranking scale is used for judging the absence or presence of specific phenomena according to predetermined, agreed-upon criteria. Whatever is determined as meeting the highest ranked criterion level must also meet the criterion specified in each of the lower levels. This type of ranking scale was alluded to in chapter 8 in which we described the use of a five-point criterion-referenced scale to evaluate the ability of preschool children to do certain rhythmic tasks. The criterion consisted of the task of marching to a recorded steady beat. The recorded musical excerpt was eight measures in length, with four metric beats in each measure.

The criterion ranking for 5, the highest rating, was defined as the children's ability to coordinate their marching in such a way that eight or more consecutive steps coincided precisely with the metric beat. A ranking of 4 was given to a student who was able to coordinate six to seven consecutive steps with the beat; a ranking of 3 represented four to five consecutive steps to the beat; a ranking of 2 to 3 indicated a child's ability to coordinate two consecutive steps; and a ranking of 1 meant that a child was unable to coordinate more than one step to the recorded metric beat. As in the case of the Likert-type Scale, the data from criterion-referenced scales are also evaluated by summing up the ratings in order to obtain a composite score for the rated phenomenon.

Consistency of Ranking.   The success or failure of obtaining reliable ranking scores for the children in the described study rested with the ability of the observers/judges to apply the criterion measure to the ranking on a consistent basis. Videotapes of each child doing the tasks were therefore assembled. Examples of various criterion rankings for each task were collected on one master tape. The judges viewed the tape and learned to differentiate between the various rankings. The judges were then given several different recorded examples of the children walking to the beat of the music and were asked to rank each example according to the established criterion of judgment. The internal consistency of the judges' rankings was established by correlating their consistency in ranking the same tape on two different occasions. A correlation of the rankings of all three judges provided the score that represented interjudge reliability. When that score had reached a value of $r = .90$ or better, the interjudge reliability was deemed satisfactory. The judges had received sufficient training to judge the children's ability to perform the tasks.

The training of the judges becomes an important aspect in obtaining a consistently high inter- and intrajudge reliability. Whenever ratings scales are employed in the course of research or teaching, establishing clear evaluation criteria and training for those who will employ the criteria must not be overlooked. Music competitions, for instance, often suffer because the judges are not provided with criterion examples of what the terms excellent, very good, good, fair, and poor mean. Without a specific criterion for each label, each judge establishes his or her own criterion. A comparison of the judgments becomes pointless.

One of the reasons the judging in music contests is often so inconsistent is the lack of training of the judges. The issue is not what an individual judge's criteria of evaluation are, but what the profession has agreed to be the criteria and whether or not all judges abide by them. Reliability in judgmental decisions can occur only if the criteria are clearly defined and spelled out and if the judges have been systematically trained to employ specific criteria in evaluating the performance.

9.4 The Construction of Tests

All music educators should have a degree of familiarity with the techniques of test construction because such knowledge is essential to both the evaluation and the development of measurement tools. The words testing and teaching bear a strong correlation; the weekly achievement tests in high school, the end of the semester tests at the university, and the entrance examinations for admission to graduate school affirm the importance of the testing process in teaching.

There are two basic types of written examinations: essay tests and objective item tests. Essay tests are preferred by many instructors because essays permit the students to respond to a question by organizing the information learned in a particular way and by presenting that information in an appropriate style. Essay tests work best in small classes because the problem of scoring or grading does not exceed the time the teacher has available for the process. Essay tests do, however, have several drawbacks: (a) The students seldom have time for proper contemplation and therefore cannot draft a good essay; (b) grading tends to be subjective because the reader of the question will seldom give the same grade to two papers that provide somewhat identical responses. The subjectivity of scoring/grading can be alleviated to a degree if the test writer provides a list of the points to be covered by the answer and an estimation of the credit to be assigned to each of those points of discussion.

Objective test forms include formats of true-false answers, multiple-choice answers, completion of sentences, matching items of information, and arranging given information in an appropriate order. Of these types of test forms, the multiple-choice test items have been most commonly used. They are suitable for large group testing because the items are easy to score and the presence of several alternative answers reduces the chance of guessing the correct response.

Anastasi (1976, p. 413) divides the development of tests into three parts: (a) planning the test, (b) item writing, and (c) item analysis. We follow Anastasi's divisions of test writing and devote the remainder of this section to a description of test item analysis and the item discrimination index, an area important to all types of tests. The achievement test is the most frequently employed examination, but the information should also be applicable to activities in the writing and evaluation of other tests.

Planning the Test

The test developer who rushes headlong into the writing of test items without having developed a well thought-out plan is courting disaster. Without some plan, certain areas of instruction may be overrepresented, while other areas may be virtually ignored. It is essential to realize also that it is easier to prepare test items that require the recall of facts than those that call for a transfer of facts to the explanation of new situations or to a critical assessment and evaluation of related facts. Tests constructed without a plan are often overweighted with factual or trivia items and are less likely to assess the critical skills of reasoning. Examples of improperly balanced tests can commonly be found in the homemade examination given by music schools and departments to incoming graduate students in an attempt to assess past achievement and assumed deficiencies.

To avoid some of the common mistakes in assembling test items, the author should devise a list of test specifications. In the case of an achievement

Table 9.2 Two-Way Specification Table for 60-Item Music Test on Selected Musical Elements (Adapted from Anastasi, 1976)

Content areas	Knows basic terms	Identifies same-different	Compares concepts	Applies concepts to the analysis of compositions	Total
Pitch					
Notation	3		3		6
Melodic patterns		3	3	3	9
Intervals		3			3
Rhythm					
Rhythmic quality			3	2	5
Rhythmic patterns		3		2	5
Note values	3				3
Tone color					
Instruments	3	2	2	2	9
Voices	2		2	2	6
Harmony					
Polyphony	2	2	2	2	8
Homophony		2	2	2	6
Total	13	15	17	15	60

measure, these specifications should be based on the objectives of a specific learning situation as well as a particular course content or the content presented during a unit of instruction. The specifications should thus cover the acquisition of knowledge as well as the development of certain intellectual skills.

Table 9.2 is a two-way specification table for a 60-item examination in an undergraduate music class for education majors who possess few music skills. The purpose of the course is to train music teaching skills. The test covers one unit of instruction. Across the top of the table are the categories of instructional objectives or types of learning to be tested. In the left-hand column, there is a listing of the content areas to be covered. The numbers in the cells state the projected number of questions for each area, assuming the test is limited to 60 items. The relative number of questions in each category relates to the importance of each topic. When a specific subject is not deemed appropriate to evaluate, the cell is left blank. The columns at the bottom of the table represent the relative importance of each instructional objective, and the total on the right-hand side of the table represents the relative weight attached to each of the content areas. While this is not the only way to plan the development of an examination or a test, it is a suggested way of balancing the objectives and instructional content areas to be covered in a test.

Writing the Items

Many excellent sources on the writing of test items are available. Among those sources, we recommend Nunnally (1972), Adkins (1974), and Gronlund (1976). These and other writers on test development agree that any test constructor should always determine the most efficient form in which to present all test items. In the instance of the teaching unit described earlier, the test may include multiple-choice items in the form of written and recorded music as well as short open answers or true-false answers. It is up to the test constructor to make those decisions.

There are a few general points to observe in test-item writing. Because items must be brief, a misunderstanding of the intention of a question can arise. To avoid that problem, the writer should strive for clarity in statements and avoid ambiguous or double meaning phrases. Either-or questions must be eliminated and all items have to be stated in correct grammar. In the case of a multiple-choice format, all response possibilities must not only be grammatically correct but also grammatically consistent and of approximately the same length. Test constructors tend to spend a greater time in phrasing the correct answer than in phrasing the wrong options. This often results in a longer item that, in turn, may suggest to the person taking the test that the correct response is in the longer test item. Similarly, the test constructor may concentrate on making the correct answer to a question grammatically correct, while less care is taken with the other choices. Thus, a response in poor grammar may serve as a clue to an incorrect response.

Item Analysis

When a sufficient number of test-items have been developed (there should be about 50% more items than are planned for each category), it will be necessary to administer the test to a small group of subjects to determine which items best evaluate that knowledge. This process of evaluating the test items is called item analysis. It consists of the administration of the test to a group of subjects with characteristics similar to the eventual target group. At this phase of the test construction, the author studies how a group of subjects responds to the test. The item analysis procedure is used to discover the scoring distribution of the various items, the deficiencies in the test, and the difficulty level of the various items. Item analysis also aids the researcher in improving the reliability coefficient of the final form of the test, it reveals questions that may have more than one correct response, and it points out poorly worded questions.

An Index of Difficulty helps to produce a balanced test because it indicates the percentage of individuals who answer a question correctly. If 90% of the subjects answer a question correctly, the item is considered easy; if 50% respond to a question correctly, the item is of average difficulty; an item is considered difficult if fewer than 10% of the subjects answer it correctly. In measuring achievement, the most preferable items are those that have a 50% correct response rate (Anastasi, p. 213).

A standard practice in item analysis is to compare the proportion of individuals who pass an item in widely differing groups. It has been common to compare the scores of the upper and lower 27% of the test distribution. That percentage is not an absolute figure, and it ranges from 50%, if the test sample is less than 20 subjects, to 27% if the sample contains 40 subjects or more. Anastasi suggests that any convenient figure between 25% and 33% may be satisfactory. By comparing the percentage of the upper (U) students who successfully answered a question with the percentage of lower (L) students who successfully answered the same question, an index of item validity or discrimination can be established. This can easily be done by hand if one has a smaller test sample and relatively few test items (see Tables 9.3, 9.4, and 9.5). The steps are as follows:

Step 1. Make a tally sheet listing test items by number from top to bottom on the left, and rank-order subjects according to their total scores from the left to right (see Table 9.3).

Step 2. Using 1 = right and 0 = wrong, note each subject's response to Items 1 through 10.

Step 3. Select an appropriate percentage to represent the upper group (U) and lower group (L)—in the case of Table 9.3: 30%.

Step 4. For each question, list the total in the U group that obtained the correct answer and the total in the L group that obtained the correct answer (Table 9.4).

Step 5. Convert the totals of Step 4 into percentages by dividing the number of correct responses in each group (U and L) by the number of people in that group and multiply by 100. This figure becomes the index of discrimination (see Table 9.5).

Table 9.3 Item Analysis of 10-Item Test

Items	1	2	3	4	5	6	7	8	9	10	Index of Difficulty
1	1	1	1	1	1	0	0	0	0	0	.50
2	1	1	0	0	1	0	1	1	0	0	.50
3	1	0	1	1	1	0	1	0	0	0	.50
4	0	1	0	1	0	1	0	1	1	1	.60
5	1	0	1	0	1	1	0	1	0	0	.50
6	1	1	1	0	0	0	1	0	0	0	.40
7	1	1	1	1	1	1	0	0	1	0	.70
8	1	1	1	0	0	1	1	0	0	0	.50
9	1	1	1	1	1	1	1	1	1	1	1.00
10	1	1	0	1	0	1	1	1	1	0	.70
$N_{Correct}$	9	8	7	6	6	6	6	5	4	2	

___ U ___   ___ L ___

Table 9.4 Number of Persons Giving Correct Responses in U and L
Groups

Items	Upper 30%	Lower 30%	U-L
1	3	0	3
2	2	1	1
3	2	0	2
4	1	3	-2
5	2	1	1
6	3	0	3
7	3	1	2
8	3	0	3
9	3	3	0
10	2	1	1

Step 6. The index of difficulty of a question is determined by the percentage of the entire sample that answered that question correctly (see Table 9.3.).

Determining item difficulty and discrimination indices is one way to improve the quality of a test, and the procedure described aids the researcher in the decision as to which questions to eliminate. Many institutions have computer programs capable of running a biserial correlation of all data in order to determine item discrimination and item index of difficulty. Many of these programs also provide a tally of the option responses for each question. Using the option tally response, the test maker can determine if weaknesses exist in the way item responses are displayed. If certain item responses are never selected, it could indicate a rather poorly structured question.

Table 9.5 Computation of Index of Discrimination

Item	Percentage Passing		Difference is Index of Discrimination
	Upper group	Lower group	
1	100	0	100
2	66	33	33
3	66	0	66
4	33	100	-67
5	66	33	33
6	100	0	100
7	100	33	67
8	100	0	100
9	100	100	0
10	66	33	33

Note. Data from Tables 9.3 and 9.4.

9.5 Measurement Tools for Direct Observation

Direct observation is a research tool utilized in many disciplines. In education it has been primarily applied to research on teaching in natural settings, specifically, of course, classroom settings (Evertson & Green, 1986; Medley & Mitzel, 1963; Rosenshine & Furst, 1973). This section is therefore limited to the description of observational techniques commonly considered suitable for classroom research.

Often also referred to as systematic observation, direct observation implies that activities are observed while they are ongoing. Therefore, even the analysis of audio- or videotaped behaviors belongs to the research technique of direct observation. Excluded are any observation approaches in which the analysis of observed events occurs in retrospect. For example, describing one's impressions about observed behaviors and events after they actually took place does not qualify as systematic observation. Similarly, rating the effectiveness of a teacher and tallying recollected events are generally not considered integral techniques of direct observation.

In "live" systematic observation situations, trained observers are placed into a classroom and record specific activities as they transpire during a lesson. Systematic observation by means of recording equipment generally implies that there are no observers in the classroom because the audiotaped and/or videotaped lessons are analyzed at a later time. The goals of both approaches are directed toward the description of specific events that can be observed within a "normal" instructional setting. Differences exist in the two approaches with regard to the methods they employ, in the assessment of the observations, and with regard to the focus of the research purpose.

Observational techniques in the classroom have usually been directed to the analysis of teacher behavior, student behavior, and the interaction between the two. Investigations have covered such issues as style of teaching and its effect on student response. In music education, researchers have studied the effect of rehearsal strategies in the instruction of vocal and instrumental ensembles on student performance or the relationship of a teacher's conducting skills and style to an overall index of rehearsal effectiveness. The observation of video- or audio-recorded lessons has frequently focused either on the teacher or the students alone; teacher-student interactions have seldom been assessed.

Observations conducted directly in the classroom have a limitation in that the events are recorded in real time and while classroom activities are proceeding. If an event is not noticed at the moment it occurs it is lost for all time. The observation of recorded lessons has the advantage that events can be reviewed and studied repeatedly. As a result, the degree of observer reliability may be higher than that of observers who are stationed in the classroom. The disadvantage of observing recorded lessons lies in the fact that the positioning of the camera in the classroom dictates to some degree what the observer may study. This is particularly the case when large classes or performance groups are to be investigated.

Both types of direct observation carry with them a certain degree of intrusion into the regular teaching process, and may be viewed by the teacher and the students as an interruption of a normal school day. Whether observers are stationed in the classroom or whether the recording of lessons requires electronic equipment (and, frequently, a recording technician) in the classroom, it is mandatory for any researcher who wishes to make use of observational techniques to minimize these instrusions by allowing both the teachers and the students to get accustomed to the recording equipment and/or the observers. Thus, at least the first two observation or recording sessions should serve only that purpose. We suggest utilizing the data obtained from those sessions only for the purpose of determining observer reliability.

Observational tools that seek to investigate teacher-student interactions are generally two-dimensional in that they account for antecedent and consequent events in a classroom. If a researcher wishes to observe the teacher or (selected) students only, one-dimensional observational tools should be developed. For example, the assessment of performance capabilities, instrumental and vocal skills, the ratings of such skills, or the rating of a teacher's classroom management behavior would demand observational tools that deal exclusively with a single dimension.

Two-dimensional observation tools and those used for direct observation of classroom settings are usually more complicated to develop than one-dimensional tools. More observer training is also needed in order to reach a respectable level of observer consistency. Thus, researchers must not only be concerned with the development of measurement tools that are valid and reliable; they must also consider the development of methods for the training of skilled observers. This is an important aspect in the use of all observational techniques. The observers are the collectors of data. The degree to which these individuals agree on what they see determines the precision of the measurement. The accuracy of the data thus hinges on the consistency and stability of those judgments.

Classroom observation has been an area of educational research for nearly six decades, and many different observational systems exist. Among the many that are available, the most commonly used systems seek to assess the verbal interaction style between a teacher and the students. One of the foremost contributors to that kind of research has been Flanders (1970), who analyzed various styles of teaching according to variables that reflected a continuum of teacher-centered instructional style to student-centered instructional style. The styles were investigated by an assessment of the quality and quantity of verbal communication that took place between teacher and students in the normal course of teaching. To illustrate the development of observational systems, we begin with a description of interaction analysis procedures. Following that description, we will introduce the reader to a few alternative observational techniques that have been utilized by researchers in music education.

Observational Tools for Interaction Analysis

To study the interactive style of teacher-student communication in the classroom, Flanders employed 10 different observational categories that according to him typified the kind of talk teachers utilize in the instructional process. As with any category construction, an observational category is a unit of analysis that ought to be derived from a single classification principle and be informative, precise, and independent from other chosen unit of analysis. The single classification principle that Flanders followed was that of describing teacher-centered versus child-centered learning. Each category therefore represents a particular meaning that a teacher's verbal statements seem to convey to the students. The categories, as paraphrased from the actual categories (Flanders, 1970, p. 34), are:

1. Statements that accept student feeling(s).
2. Statements that praise or encourage a student.
3. Statements that accept or make use of ideas of students.
4. Questions.
5. Statements that are intended as lecturing.
6. Statements that give directions.
7. Statements that criticize students or justify the teacher's authority.
8. Student talk as a response to teacher statements.
9. Student-initiated talk.
10. Silence or confusion in the classroom.

   The following procedures are used to code the observations according to the 10 categories. Every 3 seconds the observers tally on a prepared sheet the category that seems to describe best the meaning of a verbally made statement. A teacher-centered classroom climate exists if most of the tallies fall into Categories 5, 6, and 7. A student-centered classroom climate exists if the tallies center around Categories 1 to 3. An index can be developed from such codings in which the ratio of teacher-centered versus student-centered categories is used to report the overall interaction style. This coding technique enables the investigator to describe the form of communication that seems to be characteristic for particular teachers in their classrooms. Often, such communicative styles are also referred to as indicators of classroom climates.

   Many researchers have adopted and modified Flanders' categories for their own use, maintaining, however, the concept of teacher and student-centered interaction styles and also preserving the procedure of observing in 3-second intervals. Several observation systems have been designed for specific use in the subject areas of science, mathematics, and social sciences. In music, one of the first interaction analysis systems was developed by Erbes (1972). His study should be considered an excellent model for the development of an observational instrument. Care was taken by the researcher to construct a useful, reliable, and valid measurement tool for the observation of teacher-student interaction.

   Erbes' objective was to develop and assess an observational system that would report and describe the verbal interaction of teachers and students during the rehearsal of large musical organizations. He initiated his research by conducting several pilot investigations of observational systems that already existed. He determined whether any of the already existing systems would be adequate for the analysis of rehearsal situations, whether a system might need revision, or whether he needed to develop an entirely new system.

Erbes elected to try the Flanders system and a system developed by Snapp (1967). Both systems were employed in the observation of several live rehearsals, and the researcher concluded that the systems were not adequate for the purpose of his study. He specifically noted that the typical teacher would often attempt to speak to the students while they were performing. Likewise, a teacher would spend time in singing a phrase or in beating time while the group performed. Both types of teaching activities are crucial to and typical of music instruction, but were not accounted for by Flanders' or Snapp's system. Erbes also concluded that certain categories contained in the existing category systems were not relevant to a description of musical rehearsal situations.

The researcher made the decision to develop a new system that would be adequate for reporting teacher-pupil interaction within rehearsals. To accomplish this, approximately 15 hours of instrumental rehearsals in various schools were tape recorded. These tapes were transcribed into verbatim manuscripts and analyzed by content analysis techniques. All verbal communications were placed into a series of categories relevant to rehearsal activities, and the categories formed the bases of a new system that was pilot tested in several live rehearsals. The categories were then combined into groups according to who was initiating the communication, what was intended by the communication, what the affective quality of the communication conveyed (feeling, tone), and how often that particular type of communication had occurred.

Erbes found a total of 11 categories useful for a further analysis of reliability and validity. The categories, as paraphrased from the original categories (Erbes, 1972, pp. 101–102), were:

1. The teacher *uses* student ideas, musical phrasings, actions.
2. The teacher *encourages* student ideas, musical phrasings, actions.
3. The teacher *questions* with the aim of having the students answer.
4. The teacher *informs*, lectures, explains.
5. The teacher *demonstrates* how something is to be carried out.
6. The teacher *directs* by giving instructions and expects the directions to be followed.
7. The teacher *criticizes* student ideas, musical phrasings, actions.
8. The teacher *corrects* student ideas, musical phrasings, actions.
9. The student(s) *respond(s)* to teacher-initiated communication.
10. The student(s) *initiate(s)* interaction with the teacher.
11. Silence or confusion in the rehearsal hall.

Categories 1–3 reflect student-supportive behavior, whereas Categories 5–8 are considered student-nonsupportive behavior. In all technical aspects of coding and tallying procedures, Erbes closely followed those of Flanders (Erbes, 1972, pp. 108–116).

In order to ensure the criterion-related or *concurrent validity* of the tool, the codings of nine rehearsals were compared with the corresponding codings of the transcripts of the same rehearsals using the Withall Climate Index (Withall, 1949). A correlation of $r = .94$ was reported between the two instruments. The reliability among trained observers was established as $r = .83$. For relatively untrained observers, Erbes reported a reliability coefficient of $r = .61$, thus suggesting that the categories are quite easy to use even when only a brief time of training can be provided.

Observation Systems in Music Education Other than Interaction Analysis Categories

Erbes' category system is but one of the many observational tools currently available for use in music education research. As research questions develop, so do observational categories; and as a question changes, so does the tool by which the evidence is gathered in answer to the question. Therefore, what observational categories one chooses, what tallying procedures one employs, which techniques are used for data analyses, and which format one selects for the purpose of observing teaching behavior will depend on the purpose of the study and its related problems.

A researcher is well advised to find existing measurement tools for the gathering of any kind of data. The same advice holds true for observational research. If an already developed observation system fits one's research purpose, the researcher would be foolish to construct a new one. However, the use of an existing tool is advisable only if the rationale behind the structure of its categories is compatible with the rationale of the research purpose to be resolved. Unfortunately, it is not always easy to discern the rationale behind the categories of an already existing observational form. Not all theories of thought have been as clear as that of Flanders and other proponents of the analysis of interaction and teaching style.

Observational tools in music education reflect various rationales about the nature of the learning-teaching process. We suggest dividing them into three groups. The first group encompasses those developed by the "behaviorists" in music education, represented primarily by the work done in Florida State University (see Madsen, Greer, & Madsen, 1975; and Yarbrough & Price, 1981). The second group includes researchers who were most concerned about observing the learning-teaching process from the aspect of the role of the teacher as conductor (e.g., Daellenbach, 1970; Ervin, 1975; Roshong, 1978; Simon, 1984; Yarbrough, Wapnick, & Kelley, 1979). The third group consists of researchers who might be labeled generalists. For the most part, their work has been descriptive-correlational in that they attempted to identify those variables in the teaching of general music that correlated significantly with variables of teaching effectiveness (e.g., Moore, 1976; Froehlich, 1981, 1984; Taebel, 1980; Taebel & Coker, 1980).

Group 1: Behavior Modification. Madsen and Yarbrough (1980) and Madsen and Madsen (1981) have described in detail several categorical systems for the observation of student behavior modification. Those systems have provided the data base for analyzing positive and negative reinforcement patterns in the classroom in their relationship to learning behavior.

The systems utilized by this group of *behaviorists* are based upon the observation of behavior at 10-second intervals. The content of the observation focuses on the assessment whether students display "on-task" or "off-task" behavior. Both categories inform about the degree to which students seem to appear involved in the instructional activities. To answer that question, the observers take into consideration how the teacher tends to view a particular behavior. Thus, the criterion for both on-task and off-task depends on the attitude of the teacher toward discipline in the classroom. Observer training depends upon knowledge of that attitude. Observer reliability is determined by the quotient of all agreements between the observers divided by the sum of total agreements and total disagreements (Madsen & Madsen, 1981, p. 240). Using that formula, observer reliability measures ranging from less than .70 to .90 have been reported.

Group 2: The Teacher as Conductor. The most frequently employed descriptors of conductor behavior in the school environment have been specific conductor gestures, such as cueing, phrasing, the giving of cut-offs, the beating of time, inflection of voice, and facial expressions. Verbal-nonverbal communication has been assessed primarily when a conductor corrected the performance of the students by demonstrating or by explaining the correct approach. Negative and positive reinforcement, the degree of eye contact with the performers, and the relationship of individual coaching to sectional work and to work with the whole group were also frequently included in the list of observational categories.

Observation procedures differed from study to study. In some cases the researchers utilized a combination of categorical variables and rating scales. Other researchers maintained the previously described observation intervals of 3–10 seconds. Observer training was at times extensive, at times non-existent. The reported observer reliabilities ranged from .53 to .90.

Group 3: The "Generalists." Most of the researchers that may be placed into this category seem to have been primarily concerned with identifying those variables that either reflect the entirety of all ongoing activities in the teaching of general music or that relate significantly to selected constructs of teaching effectiveness. It is the latter concern that caused Froehlich to conduct her series of studies on the teaching of elementary general music. Specifically, she wished to see if clearly identifiable classroom activities were related to selected aspects of student performance. If such a relationship existed, it could lead to the identification of some valid constructs of effective music instruction.

The observational categories utilized in all studies were not developed from a particular, already existing observational system but from the informal observation of a large number of music lessons typical of elementary general music instruction. From the qualitative analysis of the observations, an initial set of a total of approximately 140 categories and subcategories were identified. These were organized into the areas to which they related the most: curriculum, subject matter, method, and materials. This categorical system, along with its coding procedure, was adopted from Brophy and Good (1969, 1973).

Brophy and Good's system of categorization is organized according to the time a teacher actually spends on an activity. Thus, the beginning time for each observed activity is noted. From those time entries, the elapsed time for each activity was calculated in seconds. (A complete description of the procedure is provided by Froehlich, 1976.)

The observational form underwent several revisions and refinements in the course of several pilot studies. Many categories had to be deleted and the coding procedures simplified. The form itself had to be arranged in such a way that a complete lesson could be observed on a one-page sheet of paper. That sheet had to contain the categories, their description, and the time roster into which to enter the categories. In the final version the observational form had 37 variables, divided into the aspects of teaching activities, teacher behavior, student behavior, and materials.

The next step in the development of the observational instrument was the writing of the manual in which the meaning of each variable was explained and the use of the form described and demonstrated. The manual was necessary for the training of the observers. The training took place during a period of approximately 6 weeks. The activities included the memorization of the variables and their meaning and the coding of videotaped teaching sessions. Interobserver reliability (consistency) was established prior to the time during which the data were gathered. Observer stability (consistency over time) was calculated based on the actual observation data. Both reliability coefficients were determined separately for all variables. For each reliably observed variable its criterion (or concurrent) validity was determined.

Determining the reliability and validity separately for all variables in an observation form seems advisable, especially for newly devised systems. Because the variables tend to be exploratory and descriptive in nature, the number of variables generally exceeds that of experimental studies. After all, the purpose of descriptive research is primarily the identification of those variables that seem to hold promise for further study.

The brief description of the initial steps Froehlich undertook in order to develop her measurement tool reiterates what might have become apparent in the description of Erbes' study: The development of observational tools is time-consuming and must be planned very carefully. If the purpose of a study seems to call for the development of more than one measurement instrument, the researcher should be prepared to devote a great deal of time to the project. Even if a researcher is able to make use of a category system already in existence, observer reliability and certain types of validities have to be determined each time a measurement tool is used as a data gathering device.

9.6 Content Analysis

Content analytical procedures have been widely used in many of the social sciences, but seldom in music education. There is no question, however, that there are many instances where these techniques could also be profitably employed in our field (see, e.g., Hooper, 1970; Kavanaugh, 1983).

Holsti (1969) defines content analysis as "any technique for making inferences by objectively and systematically identifying specified characteristics of messages" (p. 14). The messages are examined for the purpose of answering questions like, "Who was the author of a given document?"—that is, the person behind the name, and "What are the meanings, associations, values, motives, or intentions of the communication that can be inferred from the messages?"

The procedures of content analysis are not unlike those typical of interaction analysis or techniques of systematic observation in general: Highly complex interactive and communicative structures are broken down into mutually exclusive categories. From that process the researcher seeks to gain insights into the "architecture" of the structures, how they might have developed, and/or why they are what they are.

The Technique

Content analytic procedures may be applied to the investigation of any documentary evidence. That evidence may be the content of newspaper and journal articles, books, speeches, conference reports, minutes of professional associations, letters, and diaries. Techniques of content analysis may also be utilized in the analysis of creative writing, be it poetry or words put to music. Stated more abstractly, content analysis may be considered useful for all research in which written signs and symbols are employed by a sender (Source A) in order to communicate a meaning to the recipient (Source B). The signs and symbols in a communication are studied with regard to who produced and who received the communication.

According to Holsti (1969), the measurement tools of content analysis are categorical systems and rating systems by which the researcher assesses

WHO said WHAT to WHOM by WHAT MEANS, WHY, and TO WHAT EFFECT.
(p. 25)

Any one of these communicative characteristics of a message may be analyzed both quantitatively and qualitatively.

The criteria according to which documentary evidence is analyzed depend entirely on the purpose of a study. Traditionally, however, three investigative areas have emerged that may also prove useful for research in music education: (a) Values, attitudes and beliefs of specific individuals or groups of individuals have been studied in order to assess their impact on development in society, in a profession, or in a field of study. (b) The language of a person is studied in order to determine the communicative patterns among various groups of

Table 9.6 Areas and Questions Suitable for Content Analysis in Music Education Research

Area	Applied to music education
What	
To describe trends in communication content	Changes in instructional goals and objectives over time; changes in rationales and justifications over time. "To what extent have thoughts of the Bostonians in the 19th century affected the content of the 'Magna Carta' of Music Education in 1838?"
To relate known characteristics of sources to messages they produce	Consistency of positions of professionals on issues (e.g., Mursell-Seashore debate)
To audit communication content against standards	Comparisons of instructional goals and objectives to accepted standards set by the profession (e.g., theory of instruction)
How	
To analyze techniques of persuasion	Comparison of various justifications
To analyze style	Comparison of various approaches toward defining music education
To whom	
To relate known attributes of the audience to messages produced for them	To study target groups for justifying music education
To describe patterns of communication	To study structures of social groups involved in music education; to define the profession.
Why	
To analyze psychological traits of individuals	Motivations and reasons for specific music educators to promote various theories, rationales, justifications, and instructional methods.
To infer aspects of culture and cultural change	The impact of change in federal and state policies for the arts on rationales, goals, and objectives in music education. "What cultural differences are reflected in the songs/music of various nations?"
With what effect	
To measure readability (style vs. comprehension)	Comparison of the readability of a research article with the specific structure of sentence length, use of technical terms, and statistical information.
To analyze the flow of information	Comparison of the language of the band director and the general music teacher/ choral director/orchestra director in letters to parents; analysis of contest evaluations and comparison to judge's stand on purpose of music instruction.
To assess responses to communication	Investigation of parental reaction to communications from music teachers.

people. (c) Documents are studied in order to determine similarities and differences in the approaches of various people to solve problems and concerns of a profession.

Table 9.6 illustrates the specific research areas and questions that may be subjected to techniques of content analysis. The examples for the field of music education are hypothetical research questions and would have to be refined more thoroughly if one wanted to investigate them properly.

The Coding of Content Data

Methodologically, a researcher must address three questions in order to develop category systems by which the content of messages may be analyzed (Holsti, 1969, p. 94): (a) How is the research problem defined in terms of *categories?* (b) What *unit* of content is to be classified? (c) What system of *enumeration* will be used?

The categories determine whether and what attitudes, values, beliefs, or psychological positions are to be examined. Each category contains specific indicators—the variables—that define more specifically what it is being studied. Recording units are the items by which the nature of each variable in a category is assessed. Such units may be words, sentences, paragraphs, themes, or an overall topic. The more specific a unit is, the more difficult it is to establish the reliability of the measurement; the broader the unit, the more difficult it is to establish its validity. Systems of enumeration are frequency counts of recording units, space attributed to such units, or intensity of chosen terms to make a point. In the case of measuring the intensity with which something is being said, rating scales must be developed. For all procedures used, coders must be trained in order to establish the measurement reliability. It is generally reported as a composite coefficient that reads (Holsti, p. 137):

$$r_{agreement} = \frac{N \text{ (average interjudge agreement)}}{1 + [(N-1) \text{ (average interjudge agreement)}]} .$$

To illustrate the analytic process just described: Assume that the purpose of a study is to investigate changes over time in aesthetic versus utilitarian justifications for music education from 1950 to 1980. The problems might be (a) to identify utilitarian justifications for music education during the period under investigation; (b) to identify aesthetic justifications for music education for the same period; (c) to compare the relationship of the contents of the justifications to their chronological occurrence. Two themes are chosen as the categories of the content analysis tool:

Category 1. Music aids in the development of reading skills/other subjects/ physical health;

Category 2. Music exists in its own right and should aid in the development of aesthetic sensitivity only.

The chosen recording units are terms and sentences in selected journal articles from 1950 to 1980. The selection would be based on a random sample

Table 9.7 Format of Documenting Frequency of Themes by Frequency of Reference

Theme	Journal A (N = 10 issues)		Journal B (N = 10 issues)	
	Number of times the themes are referred to in			
	Terms	Sentences	Terms	Sentences
Music aids in the development of reading and other nonmusical skills				
Music must be taught for aesthetic purposes only				

Note. Table format adapted from Holsti (1969).

of 10 issues of two randomly selected journals. Key statements and words representing each of the two themes would have to be identified in the text, then categorized as frequency of themes and presence of themes. For frequency of themes, the frequency of explicit references to the themes is counted. For presence of themes, the number of articles in which the themes are addressed is counted. Tables 9.7 and 9.8 are examples of contingency tables into which the frequency counts would be entered.

In addition to counting the frequency of themes and presence of themes, the terms and sentences may also be rated according to the emotional/intellectual intensity with which they appear to have been expressed by the writers and seem to convince the reader. Depending on the researcher's rationale for the study, the rating scale could either be a Likert-type scale or a criterion-referenced scale. Both the ratings of the terms and the frequency counts should be done for each year for the period under investigation. Following that, a

Table 9.8 Format of Documenting Frequency of Themes by Presence of Themes

Theme	Journal A (N = 10 issues)	Journal B (N = 10 issues)
	Number of articles in which the themes are addressed	
Music aids in the development of reading and other nonmusical skills		
Music must be taught for aesthetic purposes only		

Note. Table format adapted from Holsti (1969).

comparison of frequency, presence, and intensity for both themes is made for each year. That comparison should reveal whether a major thematic change in justifying music in the schools took place in the course of the 30 years studied; whether the themes coexisted side by side; whether both themes were actually concerned with justifying music in the schools; or whether the aesthetic education theme actually addressed the development of a rationale more so than that of a justification.

It is with good reason that the research purpose chosen for illustrating the technique of content analysis is a historical topic. Rooted in the empirical mode of inquiry the potential of content analysis for historical research cannot and should not be denied. Since the analysis of historical data would become a two-fold activity, one would first describe what is in the document; second, one would interpret it. The same may also be said for the analysis of written evidence in both the philosophical and empirical modes of inquiry. Whenever and wherever the interpretation of existing communications become crucial to the understanding of a research question, content analysis may be considered a viable way of validating one's own interpretation of the message that may be contained in the communication.

Suggested Activities

1. Design a short (approximately 25-item) achievement test on factual knowledge.
2. Design three essay questions to assess some conceptual knowledge (list criteria for scoring).
3. Develop a rating scale to evaluate a particular teaching situation.
4. Design a questionnaire to assess how nonmusic students view music students regarding
   (a) Attitudes toward the rest of the university.
   (b) Attitudes toward social position within the university.
   (c) Abilities in nonmusic subject matters.
5. Obtain a videotape of a teaching situation and observe it by means of Erbes' categories. Develop your own observation criteria.

Topics for Discussion

1. Strengths and weaknesses of commercially available measurement tools.
2. Logic behind tool development.
3. Dangers of testing.
4. The role of data in empirical research or, "What do you do with the data?"

Suggested Readings

Baird, J.C., & Noma, E. (1978). *Fundamentals of scaling and psycho-physics.* New York: Wiley.

Bateson, N. (1984). *Data construction in social surveys.* London: George Allen & Unwin.

Berk, R.A. (Ed.) (1984). *A guide to criterion-referenced test construction.* Baltimore, MD: John Hopkins University Press.

Boyle, J.D., & Radocy, R.E. (in press). *Measurement and evaluation of musical behaviors.* New York: Schirmer.

Budd, R.W., Thorp, R.K., & Donohew, L. (1967). *Content analysis of communications.* New York: Macmillan; London: Collier Macmillan.

Buros, O.K. (Ed.) (1978). *The eighth mental measurements yearbook.* (2 vols.). Highland Park, NJ: Gryphon Press.

Chase, C.I., & Ludlow, H.G. (Eds.) (1966). *Readings in educational and psychological measurement.* Boston: Houghton Mifflin.

Colwell, R. (1970). *The evaluation of music teaching and learning.* Englewood Cliffs, NJ: Prentice-Hall.

Colwell, R. (1984). *Music teacher education: Program evaluation.* Paper presented at the meeting of the Music Educators National Conference, Chicago, March 1984.

Downs, C.W., Smeyak, G.P., & Martin, E. (1980). *Professional interviewing.* New York: Harper and Row.

Dunn-Rankin, P. (1983). *Scaling methods.* Hillsdale, NJ: Lawrence Erlbaum.

Dwyer, C.A. (1982). Achievement testing. In H.E. Mitzel (Ed.), *Encyclopedia of educational research* (5th ed.) (Vol.1, pp. 12–22). New York: Free Press.

Ebel, R.L. (1979). *Essentials for education measurement* (3rd ed.). Englewood Cliffs, NJ: Prentice-Hall.

Hogarth, R.M. (1982). *Question framing and response consistency.* (D.W. Fiske, Ed. in Chief, *New directions for methodology of social and behavioral science*, Vol. 11). *San Francisco: Josey-Bass, Inc.*

Hollander, P. (1982). Legal context of educational testing. In A.K. Wigdor and W.R. Garner (Eds.), *Ability testing: Uses, consequences, and controversies* (Part II, pp. 195–231). Washington, D.C.: National Academy Press.

Moore, R.P., Chromy, J.R., & Rogers, W.T. (1974). *The national assessment approach to sampling.* (A project of the Education Commission of the States.) Denver: National Assessment of Educational Progress.

Nitko, A.J. (1983). *Educational test and measurement: An introduction.* New York: Harcourt Brace Jovanovich.

Payne, D.A. (1982). Measurement in education. In H.E. Mitzel (Ed.), *Encyclopedia of educational research* (5th ed.) (Vol. 3, pp. 1182–1190). New York: Free Press.

Sax, G. (1980). *Principles of education and psychological measurement and evaluation* (2nd ed.). Belmont, CA: Wadsworth.

Wigdor, A.K., & Garner, W.R. (Eds.) (1982). *Ability testing: Uses, consequences, and controversies.* (2 vols.). Washington, D.C.: National Academy Press.

REFERENCES

Adkins, D.C. (1974). *Test construction: Development and interpretation of achievement tests* (2nd ed.). Columbus, OH: Merrill.

Anastasi, A. (1976). *Psychological testing* (4th ed.). New York: Macmillan; London: Collier Macmillan. [See also 5th ed., 1982.]

Brophy, J.E., & Good, T.L. (1969). Teacher-child dyadic interaction: A manual for coding classroom behavior. (Report Series No. 27). Austin, TX: The Research and Development Center for Teacher Education, University of Texas at Austin.

Brophy, J.E., & Good, T.L. (1973). Stability and teacher effectiveness. *American Education Research Journal, 10,* 245–252.

Daellenbach, C.C. (1970). *Identification and classification of overt musical performance learning behaviors using videotape recording techniques.* Unpublished dissertation, University of Rochester, NY.

Erbes, R.L. (1972). *The development of an observational system for the analysis of interaction in the rehearsal of musical organizations.* Unpublished dissertation, University of Illinois at Urbana-Champaign. Reviewed by E.L. Rainbow (1974) in the *Council for Research in Music Education, 40* (Winter), pp. 52–55.

Ervin, C.L. (1975). *Systematic observation and evaluation of conductor effectiveness.* Unpublished doctoral dissertation, West Virginia University.

Evertson, C.M., & Green, J.L. (1986). Observation and inquiry and method. In M.C. Wittrock (Ed.), *Handbook of research on teaching* (3rd ed.). (A project of the American Educational Research Association, pp. 162–213). New York: Macmillan; London: Collier Macmillan.

Flanders, N.A. (1970). *Analyzing teaching behavior.* Reading, MA: Addison-Wesley.

Froehlich, H.C. (1976). *An investigation of the relationship of selected observational variables to the teaching of singing.* Unpublished doctoral dissertation, University of Texas at Austin.

Froehlich, H.C. (1981). The use of systematic classroom observation in research on elementary general music teaching. *Council for Research in Music Education, 66–67* (Summer), 15–19.

Froehlich-Rainbow, H.C. (1984). *Systematische Beobachtung als Methode musikpädagogischer Unterrichtsforschung. Eine Darstellung anhand amerikanischer Materialien.* [Systematic observation as a research technique in music education research. A description of American studies.] (Vol. 21 of the series: *Musikpädagogik. Forschung und Lehre.* [Music education: Research and teaching.] S. Abel-Struth, Ed. Mainz, Tokyo: Schott.

Ghiselli, E.E., Campbell, J.P., & Zedeck, S. (1981). *Measurement theory for the behavioral sciences.* San Francisco: Freeman.

Gronlund, N.E. (1976). *Measurement and evaluation in teaching* (3rd ed.). New York: McMullen.

Holsti, O.R. (1969). *Content analysis for the social sciences and humanities.* Reading, MA: Addison-Wesley.

Hooper, M.D. (1970). Major concerns of music education: Content analysis of the *Music Educators Journal* (Doctoral dissertation, University of Southern California, 1969). *Dissertation Abstracts International, 30* (10), 4479–4480A.

Kavanaugh, J.M. (1983). The development of vocal concepts in children: The methodologies recommended in designated elementary music series (Doctoral dissertation, North Texas State University, 1982). *Dissertation Abstracts International, 43* (7), 2270A.

Leedy, P.D. (1985). *Practical research: Planning and design* (3rd ed.). New York: Macmillan; London: Collier Macmillan.

Likert, R. (1932). A technique for the measurement of attitudes. *Archives of Psychology*, No 140. New York, Columbia University.

Madsen, C.K., Greer, R.D., & Madsen, C.H. Jr. (Eds.) (1975). *Research in music behavior: Modifying music behavior in the classroom.* New York: Teachers College Press.

Madsen, C.K., & Yarbrough, C. (1980). *Competency-based music education.* Englewood Cliffs, NJ: Prentice-Hall.

Madsen, C.K. and Madsen, C.H. Jr. (1981). *Teaching discipline: A positive approach for educational development* (3rd ed.). Boston-Toronto: Allyn and Bacon.

Medley, D.M., & Mitzel, H.E. (1963). Measuring classroom behavior by systematic observation. In N.L. Gage (Ed.), *Handbook for research on teaching* (pp. 247–328). New York: Rand McNally.

Moore, D.S. (1985). *Statistics: Concepts and controversies* (2nd ed.). New York: W.H. Freeman.

Moore, R.S. (1976). Effect of differential teaching techniques on achievement, attitude, and teaching skills. *Journal of Research in Music Education, 24* (3), 129–141.

Nunnally, J.C. (1972). *Educational measurement and evaluation* (2nd ed.). New York: McGraw-Hill.

Oppenheim, A.N. (1966). *Questionnaire design and attitude measurement.* New York: Basic Books.

Rosenshine, B., & Furst, N. (1973). The use of direct observation to study teaching. In R.M.W. Travers (Ed.), *Second handbook of research on teaching* (pp. 122–183). Chicago: Rand McNally.

Roshong, J.C. (1978). *An exploratory study of nonverbal communication behaviors of instrumental music conductors.* Unpublished doctoral dissertation, Ohio State University.

Simon, S.P. (1984). *An investigation of the relationship of self-concept to selected communication skills of choral conductors.* Unpublished doctoral dissertation, North Texas State University, Denton, TX.

Snapp, D. (1967). *A study of the accumulative musical and verbal behavior of teachers and students in fifth grade.* Unpublished master's thesis, Ohio State University.

Spector, P.E. (1976). Choosing response categories for summated rating scales. *Journal of Applied Psychology, 61*, 374–375.

Taebel, D.K. (1980). Public school music teachers' perception of the effect of certain competencies on pupil learning. *Journal of Research in Music Education, 28* (3), 185–197.

Taebel, D.K., & Coker, J.G. (1980). Teacher effectiveness in elementary classroom music: Relationships among competency measures, pupil product measures, and certain attribute variables. *Journal of Research in Music Education, 28* (4), 250–264.

U.S. Department of Transportation (1985). National highway traffic safety administration survey. (Government printing office: 1985-525-395/30123). Washington, D.C.: Audits and Surveys, Inc.

Withall, J. (1949). The development of a technique for the measurement of socio-emotional climate in the classrooms. *Journal of Experimental Education, 17,* 347–361.

Yarbrough, C., Wapnick, J., & Kelley, R. (1979). Effect of videotape feedback techniques on performance, verbalization, and attitude of beginning conductors. *Journal of Research in Music Education, 27* (2), 103–112.

Yarbrough, C., & Price, H.E. (1981). Prediction of performer attentiveness based on rehearsal activity and teacher behavior. *Journal of Research in Music Education, 29* (3), 209–217.

Chapter Ten

The Use of Statistics in Quantitative Data Analysis

10.1 Introduction

Techniques employed in empirical research have been derived from concepts related to the quantitative analysis and manipulation of data. Such concepts belong to the field of statistics. Being commonly defined as "the mathematics of the collection, organization, and interpretation of numerical data . . ." (*The American Heritage Dictionary of the English Language*), all statistical concepts are in essence derived from the same mathematical-logical thought processes that form the basis of all disciplined and scientific inquiry and that govern philosophical discourse in its most structured and analytical form. A high degree of training in mathematics is needed to understand fully all mathematical constructs that have led to the development of statistical techniques. It is, however, possible to understand the basic concepts, applications, and interpretation of statistical techniques without thoroughly studying their mathematical base. Thus, this chapter provides an introduction to the terms and techniques commonly used in statistical data analysis that are relevant to research in music education.

The chapter is directed to those readers who wish to gain a rudimentary knowledge of the use of statistics or who feel a need to review some of the main constructs useful in quantitative data analysis. With the help of a pocket calculator and some practice, most students should be able to gain an understanding of the concepts discussed here. The mathematical manipulations are those normally taught at the elementary and junior high-school level. We hope that the chapter may also aid the novice researcher in the reading and evaluation of research articles. The chapter is not intended to equip the reader with a fully operational command of statistical techniques. For those wishing to utilize statistics in the context of an empirical investigation, a more thorough preparation will be necessary. It should entail the auditing of or enrollment in at least two formal statistics courses. If a university does not have a formal psychometric department, a music educator may find the courses in the departments of psychology or education.

10.2 Types and Classification of Statistics

One of the numerous tools employed in research is statistics. Its function is to take the data from many diverse observations or measurements and, through quantification, describe them in a common language—the language of mathematics. The conversion of observations/measurements to numerical values allows the researcher to use the logic of the mathematician as a vehicle for acquiring an insight into the observed data. The insight to be gained, however, is entirely dependent on the purpose for which the observations are made. The pure description of behavior calls for different statistics than if a researcher wished to explore relationships between data, or if the effect of one set of measurements on another set of behaviors is to be assessed.

To analyze quantified data, researchers apply mathematical formulae to them. Statisticians refer to these formulae as statistical tests. The tests can be parametric or nonparametric. Parametric statistical tests are employed when researchers believe that the population, sample or objects under study are "normal"—that is, representative of a universe of people. Parametric statistical tests also assume that there is a sameness of characteristics in the various samples under study. That sameness of sample characteristics is called homogeneity of variance. Nonparametric statistical tests do not make the assumption that samples are derived from a normal population, nor do they assume that there is homogeneity of variance in the population from which the samples were selected. In essence, it is assumed that the normal, bell-shaped curve is not an appropriate model for all observations. Male and female, black and white, yes and no tend to be sharp oppositions and not a smooth blending of one point to another.

Additional differences among parametric and nonparametric statistics do exist. They are best explained by referring the reader back to the discussion in chapter 8 on the nature of numbers. Nominal and ordinal data are frequently analyzed by nonparametric statistics. Parametric statistics are preferred when the data are intervallic in nature (i.e., if the data are based on equal units of measurement). The choice of the appropriate statistical tests for use in data analysis is thus related to the nature of the data as well as to the assumptions regarding the normality of the sample(s) of subjects.

Most researchers prefer to use parametric tests whenever possible because there is a greater variety of tests and because the tests are better able to discern small differences between samples of subjects. The ability to assess small differences within a sample or between several samples mandates parametric statistical tests because they are more likely to lead the researcher to reject the null hypothesis when, indeed, it *should* be rejected. Parametric tests are also able to assess larger samples and "to squeeze" more information out of the data.

Statistics may be applied to the analysis of data for three different purposes: (a) to describe what is; (b) to infer from what has been revealed in a smaller representative group to a larger population; and (c) to establish some relationship between what is and what might be in the future (Blommers and Lindquist, 1960, p. 4). The statistics employed for these three purposes are therefore called descriptive statistics, inferential or sampling statistics, and predictive statistics.

Descriptive Statistics

Descriptive statistics are useful and necessary tools in all empirical research because a description of what is should precede all further data analysis. Averages, indices of dispersion, and correlations are some of the most basic descriptive statistics. The average is reported either as the arithmetic mean, median, or mode, all of which serve as indicators of the central tendency of the data. Each of these averages tell the researcher (and the reader) how groups of people or things can be compared with one another. Indices of dispersion tell one how much variability or diffusion exists within a group. The primary indication of such dispersion (scattering) within a group is a statistic called the standard deviation. To describe the degree of closeness of relationships between two groups of people or measurements from these groups, a statistic called the coefficient of correlation may be employed. One often wishes to know what things go with what and to what degree things are different from each other. The correlation helps one to arrive at an answer to that question by describing "the extent to which scores on one variable go hand in hand with scores on another" (Ghiselli, Campbell, and Zedeck, 1981, p. 77).

Inferential or Sampling Statistics

Researchers often desire information regarding the characteristics of a population; for example, the attitude of 17-year-old North Americans toward symphonic music. The very nature of this defined population poses numerous difficulties for the researcher. The population is extremely large and scattered over a vast territory. To gather data on the entire population would be too costly in both time and money. To obtain the information wanted, researchers often use a procedure called sampling. From a defined population a smaller group is selected and examined. The results of that examination are then used to infer similar results for the total population from which the sample was drawn.

Prediction or Regression Statistics

These statistics are used to foretell (predict) events and to infer from known to unknown situations. The effectiveness of such predictions are determined by future outcomes. The scores of music aptitude tests by which students are selected for instrumental instruction, scores of the Scholastic Aptitude Test, or scores of the Graduate Record Examination imply that the tests predict some future success. All predictions represent an element of chance. Empirically generated evidence is needed to support the use of a measure designed to predict future events. It is improper to make decisions affecting the lives of others if the accuracy of the prediction cannot be determined.

10.3 Basic Concepts of Parametric Statistics

This section provides a description of such basic concepts in parametric statistics as measures of central tendencies, standard deviation, and normal curve. Additionally, the concepts of probability, statistical significance, and hypothesis testing are described. Step-by-step procedures for t test and analysis of variance are also included.

Measures of Central Tendencies

Most statistical tests are concerned with three different aspects of an observed event: (a) the number of people or objects or the number of groups of people or objects involved in the study; (b) the central tendency of the people or objects—that is, the usual or average behavior observed; and (c) how alike or different from each other these people or objects may be. The number of people or objects or the number of groups of people or objects is easy to determine as one only has to count them and record the final tally. Statistically, that tally is symbolized by N. For example, $N = 18$ would mean 18 people or 18 objects were studied.

The central tendency of a sample may also be called the average. The average behavior or characteristics of a group of people or objects may be indicated in several ways. The most frequently used indicators are the mode, the median, and the arithmetic mean. The procedures for computing the central tendencies of a sample will be limited to these three types of averages.

The Mode. In many large collections of data, certain measurement scores tend to occur with greater frequency than others. This often holds true with scores on classroom achievement tests. Assume, for example, that an instructor uses a 25-item test to evaluate how well students have learned the fingering system of the clarinet. The class contains 49 students. After correcting the tests, the instructor wishes to study the distribution of the scores and assign grades. The instructor observes that the scores range from a high of 21 correct answers to a low of 4 correct answers.

The initial step would be to develop an interval-frequency table (see Table 10.1). Such a table lists all scores in equal intervals. A tally is then made of the number of scores falling into each interval. Using the table, the instructor

**Table 10.1   Distribution of Class
Scores on a 25-Item Clarinet Fingering
Test (N = 49)**

X (score)	f (frequency)	fX
21	1	21
20	0	0
19	0	0
18	3	54
17	5	85
16	2	32
15	0	0
14	4	56
13	6	78
12	3	36
11	1	11
10	9	90
9	7	63
8	3	24
7	2	14
6	1	6
5	1	5
4	1	4
Total	49	579

plots a histograph. The graph permits a visual representation of the distribution of all scores (Figure 10.1). The left-hand side of the graph is the cumulative indicator for the number of students scoring in each score category, and the baseline numbers relate to the scores made on the test. The maximum number of students making the same score was 9; in several instances only one student each scored in several of the possible categories.

The point or points where the scores tend to group themselves or "pile up" in a histograph is called a mode. There are three modes in this example: the first around the 9-score point, the second on the 13-score point, and the third group on the 17-score point. In this instance, the histograph is multimodal. If only two modes were present, the histograph would be bimodal and, of course, with only one mode present, the frequency distribution would be unimodal. In each case, a mode shows tendencies for groupings. In the example given, the groupings tend to lean toward the lower end of the scoring range. The scores would then be considered *positively skewed*. If the scores "bunched up" at the other end of the scoring range, they would be *negatively skewed*. Under the circumstances of this distribution, the instructor may question, among other things: (a) the quality of the students, (b) the quality of the instruction, or (c) the test itself. The mode, in addition to helping with the analysis of test scores, may also be useful in the analysis of such groupings as salary distributions, work-load assignments, or publication records.

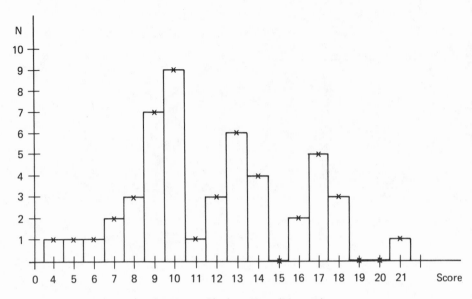

Figure 10.1 Histograph of 25-Item Clarinet Test (N = 49).

The Median. Information provided by the median can be important if one wishes to identify the typical student score, the typical salary within a unit of employment, the typical family in a community, or the typical attitude toward the arts in a community. This indicator of central tendency is defined as the point on a scale below which one-half or 50% of the scores fall. It represents the mid-point of the number of scores, and does not depend on a summation of all scores. It is a useful tool for ascertaining what is "typical." According to Table 10.1, the median, or typical score, on the clarinet examination would be 11. That value is found simply by counting the frequencies from the bottom of the scale to the point where there are as many *individuals* scoring above as below a point. In the case of the clarinet test, that point rests at the individual score of 11, which is the 25th score from the bottom (as one counts 24 individuals below that score: 4, 5, 6, 7, 7, 8, 8, 8, 9, 9, 9, 9, 9, 9, 9, 10, 10, 10, 10, 10, 10, 10, 10, 10, (11); and 24 individuals above the score: 12, 12, 12, 13, 13, 13, 13, 13, 13, 14, 14, 14, 14, 16, 16, 17, 17, 17, 17, 17, 18, 18, 18, 21).

If there is an even number of scores, the median rests at the mid-point between the middle scores. In the case of a large set of numbers, the following procedure can be used to find the location of the median: If there are N observations in all, arrange the observations from smallest to largest. Count the observations and apply the formula $(N+1)/2$. This will give you the location of the median. In the example of the clarinet fingering test, there are 49 observations. Applying the formula leads to $(49+1)/2 = 25$. The 25th observation from the bottom is the median score—that is, 11. If there are 526 observations, the formula would lead the researcher to a median of $(526+1)/2 = 263.5$.

Therefore, the median point would rest one-half the distance between the 263th and 264th observation.

The Arithmetic Mean. There are several types of means—the arithmetic, the harmonic, and the geometric. The arithmetic mean is the one used most often. The geometric mean is utilized at times for the measurement of pitch frequencies in hertz because that scale follows geometric rather than arithmetic principles. This discussion focuses exclusively on the arithmetic mean, which is the point on the scale of scores that corresponds to the sum of scores divided by the total of scores. Per capita income figures are means; a baseball team's batting average is expressed as a mean score; and when government statistics refer to the average wage of workers, it is generally reported as the mean statistic. This statistic is the only central tendency measure that is dependent on the exact value of each and every score in the entire distribution.

The symbol used by statisticians to represent a score is X. The symbol that commonly signifies the mean is $\overline{X}$. To find the mean score $(\overline{X})$ of any frequency distribution, (a) add all the individual scores to determine their sum (Σ); and (b) divide the sum (the total of all individual scores) by the total number of scores (N). This may be expressed mathematically as

$$\overline{X} = \frac{\Sigma X_i}{N},$$

where Σ is the symbol for the sum of, X_i stands for each ith score, or each score, and N is the total number of scores.

To apply this formula to the example of the clarinet test, consult Table 10.1. The total of all scores is obtained by multiplying the score (X) by the number of individuals (f) who obtained that score, then adding the products (fX). The fX column in Table 10.1 shows the frequency times interval score. The sum of the products equals 579. Because there is a total of 49 scores, we employ the formula

$$\overline{X} = \frac{\Sigma X_i}{N}$$

and obtain

$$\overline{X} = \frac{579}{49} = 11.8.$$

The mean score is 11.8 $(\overline{X} = 11.8)$. The median score of this distribution was reported as 11. The difference is small, but differences between median and mode may be influenced by extremes of high and low scores in a distribution. The arithmetic mean score is the central tendency score employed in almost all statistical procedures. It is the measuring point from which nearly all score variations are estimated.

Standard Deviation

The standard deviation (SD, or σ, the Greek letter *sigma*) is an important statistical measure because it is used to describe how a group of scores may disperse or vary from each other. In calculating the mean score, one merely adds each of the scores and divides the sum by the number of scores. The mean provides new information because it tells the researcher where to find the center point of the scores. Knowledge of the location of the mean does not, however, tell the researcher how all scores are dispersed around the mean score. It is of value to know if the scores are similar and have very little dispersion or variability from the mean, or if the scores are quite dissimilar and have a rather great variability. Many statistical tests are concerned with finding answers to just these questions and seek to determine the relationship between the central tendency (mean score) of measurements and the dispersion (variability) of the individual scores from the central tendency.

Gaining an insight into the dispersion of scores from the mean requires a mathematical computation that is a bit more difficult than the previous calculations. The variability of the scores, called *variance*, must be calculated by finding out how much each score deviates from the mean. The variance is the difference between the squared mean score ($\overline{X}^2$) and the sum of all squared scores (ΣX^2), divided by the number of scores (N). The symbol for variance is (s^2). Expressed mathematically, the formula for variance is

$$s^2 = \frac{\Sigma X_i^2}{N} - \overline{X}^2.$$

There are other formulae for the variance of a sample. In all cases, however, the formulae make use of information about the mean of the distribution, each score, and the sample size.

The square root of the variance is called the standard deviation. Thus, based on the definition of variance as provided here, the standard deviation of a sample is

$$SD = \sqrt{\frac{\Sigma X_i^2}{N} - \overline{X}^2},$$

where SD is the standard deviation, ΣX_i^2 is the sum of each score squared, N is the number of scores, and $\overline{X}^2 = $ the mean score squared.
To find the standard deviation of a sample,

1. Add each score to determine the total.
2. Divide the total by the number (N) of scores to determine $\overline{X}$.
3. Square $\overline{X}$ to obtain $\overline{X}^2$.
4. Square each score.
5. Determine ΣX_i^2 by adding all squared scores.
6. Divide ΣX_i^2 by N.

7. Subtract $\overline{X}^2$ from the result of Step 6.

8. Determine the square root of the result obtained in Step 7. A short computational example is given in Appendix B.

The formulae for various statistical tests and their symbolic representation can be confusing. For example, the symbols given below look different from each other although all of them of them represent a standard deviation. Ghiselli et al. (1981) utilize the Greek symbolization, Moore uses the lower case letter *s*, and in this book the capital letters *SD* have been chosen. All three symbols can be found in various books on statistics and research. The formulae, too, are represented differently even though they refer to the same statistical construct:

Ghiselli, et al. 1981, p. 45: $\quad \sigma_x = \sqrt{\dfrac{\Sigma x^2}{n}}$.

Moore, 1985, p. 116: $\quad s = \sqrt{s^2}$.

In this book: $\quad SD = \sqrt{\dfrac{\Sigma X_i^2}{N} - \overline{X}^2}$.

The solution to this confusing situation lies in being consistent. Find a good statistical source and become thoroughly familiar with the symbolization it uses. From there on, stay with that system and become comfortable with it.

Calculating the mean and standard deviation of a set of scores is central to most parametric statistical procedures because the mean represents the measure of central tendency and the standard deviation describes the dispersion of all scores relative to the central tendency. Both measures are also crucial in the explanation of the normal curve and the explanation of the construct of probabilities. The following discussion illustrates the role of the concept of standard deviation as it relates to the characteristics of a normal curve.

The Standard Normal Curve

In chapter 9 the standard normal curve was described as a model for the distribution of a large number of measurements. That distribution, when visually represented, resembled that of a bell-shaped (symmetrical) curve, where the mean resided at the center of the curve. Any distribution of measurements that resembles a bell-shaped, symmetrical curve whose mean, median, and mode lie in the center of the curve may be called a normal curve. The curve presented in chapter 9 was therefore only one within the large family of normal curves, and it is somewhat misleading to refer to that curve as *the* normal curve (Moore, 1985, p. 189). Normal curves become distinct by the standard deviation of their measurement distribution.

The normal curve employed in the following discussion is based on a population of infinite numbers. Thus, μ (mu) will be used to represent the mean, while the σ (sigma) stands for the theoretical standard deviation units that emanate from the mean point. The purpose of the discussion is to illustrate how the standard normal curve is employed in the reasoning process of statistical data analysis.

The standard normal curve is a visual representation of a frequency measurement distribution, where the space under the curve contains the area under which scoring frequencies of some measurement may be expected to fall. The standard deviation is a measuring point on the base line of the curve that indicates the dispersion of all measurements. Figure 10.2 is such a standard normal curve. Along the base line, the markings for the standard deviations from the mean are given: −3, −2, −1, 0 (i.e., the mean), +1, +2, and +3. The positive numbers represent the areas under the curve to the right of the mean point, and would contain all measurements equal to or greater than the mean. The negative numbers represent the area equal to or less than the mean. The numbers 1, 2, and 3 each represent one standard deviation of measurement from the mean.

The standard normal curve is that measurement distribution where (a) 99.7% of the observations fall within three standard deviations to both sides of the mean; (b) approximately 95% of the observations fall within two standard deviations to both sides of the mean; and (c) approximately 68% of the observations fall within one standard deviation to both sides of the mean, to be exact: 34.13% + 34.13%. The remaining observations lie in the tails or fringe areas to the left and right sides beyond the third standard deviations (positive and negative).

The area under the third standard deviation represents the unusual values or scores. For example, in a measurement of heights of individuals, the tallest 2.5% would be represented by the shaded area of the tail of the curve on the right side, and the shortest 2.5% by the shaded area of the left-hand tail of the curve. The exceptionally tall and short are unusual, but they can be expected to appear in a normal population.

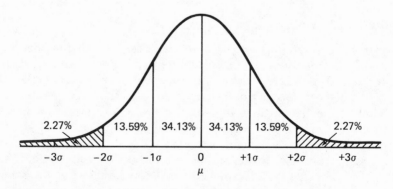

Figure 10.2   The Standard Normal Curve Distribution (the Bell-Shaped Curve).

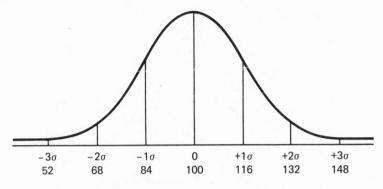

-3σ	-2σ	-1σ	0	$+1\sigma$	$+2\sigma$	$+3\sigma$
52	68	84	100	116	132	148

Figure 10.3   Distribution of Intelligence Scores With Means of 100 and Standard Deviation of 16.

To demonstrate the use of a normal curve and the standard deviation measure, assume a test of intelligence (IQ test) is administered to a large sample of the total population. Assume further that the mean score on this test is 100 and the standard deviation is 16 (see Figure 10.3). From these measures one could expect a little more than 2% of the population to obtain scores on the IQ test of 132 or better. If the sample consisted of 2,000 randomly selected individuals, approximately 40 subjects would be expected to receive an IQ score of 132 or better. However, if that sample included 100 individuals with IQ scores of 132 or better, serious questions might be raised regarding the sample. One would question if the sample were truly representative of the population at large. A sample with 100 persons possessing IQ scores above 132 would represent 5% of the total sample, while the normal curve suggests that only slightly more than 2% of the population will possess such an IQ score. Knowledge about the frequency distribution under the normal curve should alert one to question if the sample were a true representation of the population.

Testing a Statistical Hypothesis For Significance

Several statistical tests, such as the *t* test of means or the *F* test can be used to determine whether the null hypothesis should be rejected. The results of such statistical tests can be interpreted through the use of the normal curve and the areas encompassed within the critical area of significance (see Figure 10.4).

The critical area of significance is that portion of the normal curve under which the researcher has decided not to reject the null hypothesis, thus assuming that any differences in measurement are too small to be called statistically significant. Should the obtained value of a statistical test lie beyond the critical area, either to the positive or the negative side, the null hypothesis may be rejected. In that case, the researcher suggests that any differences

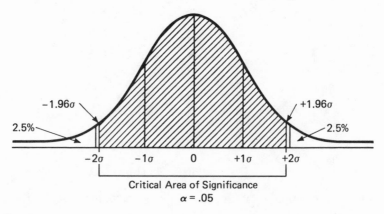

Figure 10.4 Critical Area of Significance in a Normal Curve Distribution.

between measurements are large enough to be considered beyond chance. In the language of the researcher, such a finding would be called significant at or beyond a specified level of chance. The researcher states that if the obtained value of a statistical test lies in the extreme areas beyond the critical area specified, the null hypothesis may be rejected.

The critical area is selected and specified by the researcher prior to any statistical testing. If, for example, a level of significance of .05 is selected, the critical region would include the area from -1.96 to $+1.96$ SD under the normal curve, an area representing approximately 95% of the total distribution. The remaining 5% of the distribution is divided equally into 2.5% on both the negative and positive side of the curve. The t values or F values would then have to exceed 1.96 SD if the null hypothesis were to be rejected. In the case of selecting a significance level of .01, the observed value of t or F would have to be larger than 2.36 (a difference in score magnitude of nearly 2.5 SD) before the null hypothesis could be rejected in favor of the alternative hypothesis.

The statistical tests that can be employed in the testing of significant differences between two or more groups are varied. The most commonly encountered statistical tests in music education research are the t test and the F test. For both tests there are specific tables from which the obtained score is translated into a figure that reflects the extremeties of the critical area, beyond which differences of values may be considered statistically significant. If the obtained score lies beyond the critical area indicated in the table, the null hypothesis is rejected.

Degrees of Freedom. In many statistical tables the letters *df* appear; these stand for *degrees of freedom*. The mathematical logic behind the concept itself and as it applies to a statistic is difficult to explain. Although purists in statistics may complain, suffice it to say that degrees of freedom are used to make the statistical procedures more "conservative"—that is, the researcher is less likely to reject the null hypothesis when it is true.

All statistical calculations make use of the number (N) of persons or groups of persons in a sample. When using a small sample statistic or samples with unequal numbers, a correction factor of $N-1$ is introduced. Thus, many statistical formulae show a denominator of $N-1$. In that case, if the sample size is 15, the degrees of freedom would be $15-1 = 14$.

A Statistic to Test the Hypothesis of Differences Between the Means of Two Samples: The t Test

The t statistic is commonly used in research where knowledge regarding the effect of a treatment is desired and where possible differences among sample means are to be tested. To show real differences between samples, larger numbers of subjects than those in the following example are generally required. *For illustration only and to facilitate easier computations, the following example deals with smaller groups of people than is normally deemed appropriate.*

Assume that you wish to determine the effectiveness of two instrumental instructional procedures. From a population of band students, you draw a random sample of 14 students. You assign the students at random to one of two groups, designated Group A and B. Each group receives musical instruction according to one particular method: Method X given to Group A represents a new approach, whereas an older approach, Method Y, is given to Group B. During the study, two students of Group A become ill and the number of subjects in that group decreases to five. After 6 weeks of music instruction, a music achievement test is administered in order to compare the learning achievement of the two groups of students with each other.

The test scores for the students are as follows:

Group A		Group B	
Subject Ss	Score X	Subject Ss	Score X
1	26	1	20
2	31	2	17
3	23	3	10
4	35	4	25
5	20	5	24
		6	22
		7	15

The null hypothesis will be tested (there will be no significant difference between the means). The selected level of significance will be .05—that is, there is a 20% chance that if a learning difference does exist between the two groups, it may have been caused by accident rather than by the treatment. (The critical area is represented in the shaded area of Figure 10.4).

One formula for the *t* test is

$$t \ (df = N_A + N_B - 2) = \frac{\overline{X}_A - \overline{X}_B}{\sqrt{\left(\dfrac{N_A s_A^2 + N_B s_B^2}{N_A + N_B - 2}\right)\left(\dfrac{1}{N_A} + \dfrac{1}{N_B}\right)}} \ ,$$

where

$$s_A^2 = \frac{\Sigma X_A^2}{N_A} - \overline{X}_A^2 \text{ (variance of Group A)}$$

and

$$s_B^2 = \frac{\Sigma X_B^2}{N_B} - \overline{X}_B^2 \text{ (variance of Group B)}.$$

A step-by-step calculation of the *t* ratio for the purpose of determining the difference between the mean scores on musical achievement of two groups of students is given in Appendix C.

The result of the calculation of the *t* ratio is 2.43. In a *t* ratio test, the computation results in a number that is an expression of standard deviation units from the mean. The level of significance was set at .05. Thus, the critical areas for failing to reject the null hypothesis is from −1.96 to 1.96 (see Figure 10.4). To determine if the *t* ratio (2.43) is a probable occurrence, it becomes necessary to consult a table of a so-called *t* distribution for critical values. When using the table, the researcher needs to enter it at *df* = 10 and for a two-tailed probability, at the .05 level. Because N_B = 7 and N_A = 5, the degrees of freedom for each group is 6 and 4; consequently the total degrees of freedom is 10. The null hypothesis assumes possible results in both directions of the normal curve. Therefore, the two-tailed probability has been chosen. The critical value for *df* = 10, two-tailed probability, is 1.96. Because the value 2.43 is greater than 1.96, the null hypothesis is rejected. You accept the alternative hypothesis (H_1) that the mean scores of Group A are significantly greater than the mean scores of Group B.

If the researcher had consulted the raw data shown in Appendix C, it would have become evident that Subjects 2 and 4 of Group A had exceptionally large scores compared with the scores of the subjects in Group B. This fact probably influenced the size of the variance in the scores of Group A. Thus, while Group A scored significantly higher (at the .05 level) than Group B, a researcher may wish to be cautious in declaring one of the two methods superior to the other. Consultation of the raw data is always a wise move once the *t* value of a set of data has been established. It is the raw data that may offer clues to the reasons for differences in the results of statistical tests, and they may warrant a change in the interpretation of the results.

Correlation (r)

Correlations indicate a degree of relationship between two or more variables, conditions, or observations. The relationship is always expressed as a decimal that ranges from -1.00, a perfect, negative correlation, to $+1.00$, a perfect, positive correlation. The concept of correlation is based on the use of a scattergram to plot the scores of the variables. If high scores of one variable lie on a straight line with high scores of a second variable, then a high positive correlation exists. If low scores on one variable are associated with the high scores of another, then a high negative correlation would exist. A zero correlation indicates little or no relationship between the two variables. (For the computation of a correlation, see Appendix D.)

Determining Degrees of Relationships Between Pairs of Variables. The relationships between pairs of variables are not always clear. Therefore, the *correlation coefficient* is used as the means of expressing a numerical value for these relationships. While there are several statistical procedures for obtaining correlations, the symbol r, used in the Pearson *product-moment correlation coefficient*, is usually employed in identifying the degree of relationship. In research reports, correlations are expressed in equation form, such as $r = .82$ or $r = -.23$. The interpretation of the meaning of such numbers must be approached with a word of caution because a correlational statistic merely indicates a degree of relationship; it says nothing about the cause of that relationship.

In the past it was common to classify r values as high, moderate, or low. An r of less than ($<$) .30 was considered a low correlation; an r ranging between .30 and .70 was considered a moderate correlation; while an r between .70 and .90 was called a high correlation. Many statisticians consider that labeling process to be a mistake because such classification can be misleading. A consistent $r = .25$ on a correlation between scores of music ability and intelligence (reported by many researchers who have investigated the phenomenon) could be important because it would suggest that intelligence might play some related role in musical ability. On the other hand, an $r = .60$ might be considered very low on tests of musical ability that purport to measure the same trait. The terms high and low describe comparative values; the researcher must therefore know the relativity within which these descriptive terms are employed.

Correlations have many uses in empirical investigations. They are frequently employed to check the reliability of observers or judges, or the consistency and stability of answers in tests or questionnaires. For example, in an observational study a researcher may videotape a classroom and use an observation tool to record specific student responses. At a later date, the researcher may look at the same videotape again and record observations. By correlating the two observation scores of the same event, the researcher obtains an index of the consistency between the two sets of observations. Correlations are also used as indicators of test reliability as well as of test validity—that is, they are used to tell if the measures are consistent and whether a test is accurately assessing a specific ability.

The test-retest and the split-half method are two correlational procedures by which test reliability can be determined. The test-retest method is based on the logic of using the same testing procedure twice. Both scores obtained for the same individual or sample are then correlated, usually by means of the Pearson product-moment correlation coefficient. A high, positive correlation coefficient for the two test scores would suggest that the scores may be considered reliable.

The split-half method requires the administration of a test only once. After the test is scored, two scores for each person are obtained by dividing the test into comparable halves. The scores for each half are then correlated, using a Pearson product-moment correlation or the Spearman-Brown formula. These fòrmulae are found in all statistics books and are also included in many computerized statistical packages.

Both of the correlational methods to determine test reliability have some limitations. The test-retest method has logical flaws in that the person who has been tested may remember some of the test items when the test is administered the second time. The limitation of the split-half method lies in the rather arbitrary division of the test into two equal parts. It is not always practical or logically feasible for a test to contain two exactly equal parts. The correlation formulas for both methods do, however, have some corrective "power" in that they tend to underestimate the relationship between both scores and provide a conservative estimate of the reliability of the test.

The correlation coefficient is utilized not only in the analysis of data but also in their interpretation. When squaring the correlation coefficient, the researcher obtains a measure of the strength of the relationship between those variables that are correlated with each other. The r^2 can be used as "a measure of the proportion of variance in one variable explained by the other" (Blommers & Lindquist, 1960, p. 403).

To illustrate the use of r^2, assume that a researcher is comparing the relationships of two groups of judges who evaluated a musical performance. The correlation of the two sets of ratings has been determined to be $r = .80$. By squaring .80 we find that $r^2 = .64$. The true known variance—the percentage of agreement between the two groups of judges—is 64%. By subtracting .64 from 1 we obtain an index of *disagreement*, expressed in percentages. Applied to the case of the two groups of judges, they were observed to disagree with each other 36% of the time. Thus, while an r of .80 appears to be rather large, the index of disagreement indicates that one-third of the ratings as measured were not in agreement with each other. This information can be of great importance when reporting all findings of a study. Therefore, both indices—those of agreement and disagreement—should be determined. Also, when interpreting correlational numbers the reader should be reminded that such numbers have an algebraic relationship much like hertz or decibels. 200 Hz is not a pitch twice as high as a pitch of 100 Hz; an r of .80 is not twice as great as $r = .40$.

As much as averages and correlations are valuable tools in many investigations, it is unfortunate that correlations can also become the tools of anyone who misuses them by inferring cause-and-effect relationships when, in fact, there exists only a common variance between two observations. The example of the sale of alcoholic beverages versus the building of churches (chapter 8) may be recalled here. Variance obtained by means of correlating two or more measures may result from a cause that is not even included in the variables measured. A researcher who employs correlational procedures must therefore know the limitations of correlational procedures and must exercise caution in drawing conclusions from such data.

Testing the Significance of *r*. If the researcher is willing to restrict conclusions only to the sample under study, the reporting of correlations will suffice. In many instances, however, the researcher may wish to extrapolate conclusions drawn from the sample to the population and make inferences about the population. In that case, an *r* is tested for statistical significance, and two assumptions must be made: (a) the sample studied must have been obtained by a random sampling procedure, and (b) the sample must have characteristics of normal distribution.

Testing for significance is relatively easy because most statistics books have a table for that purpose in their appendices; computerized statistical packages usually provide the level of significance as a part of their programs. In the case where the significance of a correlation is determined "by hand," the following procedure is used: Enter the appropriate table at either the 5% or 1% level of confidence and enter the degrees of freedom ($N-2$, pairs of scores). If the *r* value is greater than the table number, the *r* is considered significant at the chosen level. The null hypothesis would be rejected.

In the case where statistically significant correlations have been obtained, the researcher must be cognizant of the fact that large sample sizes will result in rather low yet statistically significant correlations. While such a significance may be reported as a finding, it may not be very important in a practical sense. The researcher will have to make a judicious decision as to how such findings may be interpreted.

Multiple Regression Analysis

Multiple regression analysis is often employed in research problems that seek the prediction of an event or the determination of the relationship of a number of independent variables to a criterion measure. A researcher may wish to predict success in a university-level music program based on variables such as SAT scores, high-school grade point, musical ability, hearing acuity, and past training. The criterion variable could be the students' college grade-point average. The grade-point average would be correlated with the scores of all independent variables. The results of the multiple correlation would produce an overall R as well as an R^2. (R is the multiple correlation; R^2 the amount of variance that can be explained by the independent variables and the standard error coefficient.)

Rainbow's investigation on constructs of musical aptitude may be utilized to illustrate the use of multiple regression (Rainbow, 1965). One aspect of the study was to determine the relationship of 14 variables to musical aptitude, and to determine how these variables contributed to the criterion measure, musical aptitude. Tables 10.2 and 10.3 contain statistical information provided by a regression analysis.

Table 10.2 reports a Multiple R of .727 and an R^2 of .529. The R is often called the coefficient of determination because it indicates that approximately 53% of the variation in musical ability can be explained by the 14 variables operating jointly. The unknown variance would be $1 - .53$—that is, approximately 47%. The standard error of estimates—.463—indicates that, on the average, predicted aptitude scores based on the variables in Table 10.2 would range $+.463$ or $-.463$ from the score obtained using the total of 14 variables. The F column indicates whether or not the relationship of the variable to music ability was statistically significant; df (degrees of freedom) is in this case 97 because 98 subjects were in the population ($df = N-1$).

Table 10.3 presents the beta weights for each variable. Beta weights are standardized coefficients that can be employed when two or more independent variables are measured using dissimilar units of measure, such as age and IQ. Beta weights "provide a way to compare the relative effect on the dependent variable for each individual variable," and they are used when two or more varying measures are employed in an investigation (Kim & Kohout, 1975, p. 325). The formulae for obtaining these weights are included in most statistical packages available for computer calculations. Beta weights and their test of significance (F column) tend to indicate which variables provide the best clues for the factors that have contributed to the individual differences on the criterion measure. By ignoring variables with nonsignificant beta weights, the investigator essentially removes from consideration those variables that may *largely overlap* others and are measuring identical or similar traits. The algebraic sign $(+, -)$ of beta weights is not of fundamental importance; only the numerical magnitude and statistical significance are crucial to their interpretation.

In the example given, one cannot infer that such musical tasks as pitch perception, tonal memory, and so forth are not important to the trait of musical aptitude. What can be inferred is that the variables found to be significant—

Table 10.2 Selected Statistics from Multiple Regression (Rainbow, 1965)

Source	Multiple R	R^2	Standard error of estimate	F	df
Junior High	.727	.529	.463	7.765*	95

*Significant at the .05 level.

Table 10.3   Multiple Regression Analysis for Junior High
School Students

Variable	beta	F
1. Pitch discrimination	.104	1.344
2. Tonal memory	.023	0.060
3. Rhythm	.069	0.674
4. Musical memory	−.104	1.107
5. Academic intelligence	.206	4.063*
6. School achievement	.028	0.049
7. Gender	−.141	3.197
8. Chronological age	.021	0.072
9. Musical achievement	.349	7.326
10. Musical training	.012	0.024
11. Home environment	.076	0.794
12. Interest in music	.068	0.549
13. Relatives in music	.191	4.765*
14. Socioeconomic background	.065	0.572

*Significant at the .05 level.

academic intelligence, gender, musical achievement, and relatives in music—
would be, in this instance and for this population, the best combination of
measures by which to predict music aptitude.

Multiple regression analysis is common in the investigation of constructs
of various abilities and mental traits, and it is used in the prediction of future
events based on presently known measurements. Its primary function is to
account for the known portion of a measured trait; that information is provided
by R^2. In the study by Rainbow (1965), the variables employed accounted for
a little more than 50% of the variance. Multiple regression analysis also serves
the purpose of informing one about the unknown portion of a measured trait.
The coefficient of nondetermination, represented by $1 - R^2$, conveys that information. It suggests that approximately 48% of the variance cannot be accounted for.

Analysis of Variance (ANOVA)

ANOVA is a statistical test employed in research designs that compare two
or more groups with each other. The test is used to evaluate mean scores of
groups and the variability of the group scores from the mean. The ratio of
variability among groups and within groups provides the basis for the statistical
evaluation and the determination of the F ratio, a ratio of the sum of squares
between groups and the sum of squares within groups.

ANOVA is a powerful statistical test and is capable of making several
comparisons among various groups at one time; a t test cannot make such
simultaneous, multiple comparisons. ANOVA can also evaluate samples that
contain unequal Ns, and it can assess nonexperimental variables, such as gender, religion, and race, as well as experimental variables. Primarily, ANOVA

seeks to determine how a single dependent, or criterion, variable will react or relate to independent variables or factors.

To illustrate: A class of 20 seventh-grade students are assigned randomly to four different groups, each group to be taught using a differing method. After a period of instruction, a test containing a common set of questions will be administered to all students. The criterion or dependent variable is the trait under investigation that cannot be manipulated. The independent variables, or factors that can be manipulated, are the methods of instruction. The one-way ANOVA would be an appropriate means of evaluating the differences in the scores between the varying methods of teaching. Appendix E presents an illustration of the calculation and tabulation of one-way ANOVA data.

One of the many useful statistical designs that employ ANOVA is the two-dimensional factorial design proposed by E.F. Lindquist (1953). This design may be referred to in other statistical manuals as a double classification ANOVA. It can be modified for various numbers of classifications and treatments.

Assume you wish to investigate the relative ability of children of differing ages and differing musical aptitude to acquire the ability to sing in tune. You decide to investigate children in fourth and sixth grade and you wish to see how a sample drawn from each music aptitude level, as determined by an earlier administered aptitude test, would compare with regard to singing accuracy by grade level and aptitude level. The design of the study could be illustrated as in Figure 10.5.

On the left-hand side of the illustration, each of the grade levels are represented by a row of three boxes running from left to right. The aptitude levels are represented by the columns. The statistical test to be employed would assess the ratio of the mean squares for all of the sources of variability— the mean square of each group, the mean square of each ability level, the mean square for the interaction of grade level and aptitude level, and the mean square of the total group. The step-by-step calculations and formulae are given in Appendix F for those who wish to follow the calculation procedure. Fortunately for most people, the computer programs will readily pro-

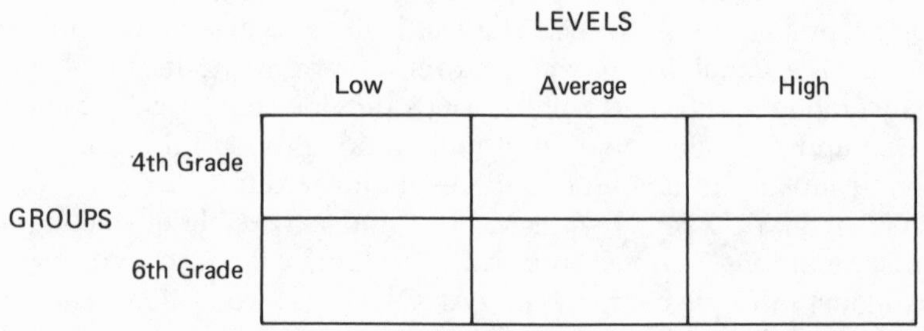

Figure 10.5 Two-Dimensional Factorial Design.

vide the final figures. Tables 10.4 and 10.5 give the results of the singing test for each grade level and for each aptitude level.

The mean scores given in Table 10.5 suggest that for each grade the scores increase from low ability to high ability, and that the mean singing scores for the sixth-grade children are higher for each ability level than those of the fourth graders. The statistical analysis will indicate if the differences can be expected to have occurred by chance, or whether age and ability may have a significant influence on the final mean scores. In effect, this design tests three statistical hypotheses:

1. There will be no difference in singing ability due to age factors.

2. There will be no difference in singing ability due to musical aptitude.

3. There will be no interaction between age and aptitude and the ability to sing in tune.

The mathematical computation assesses the association of (a) the scores in the rows to the total; (b) the scores in the columns to the total; and (c) the row cells to the column cells. The result of this computation is presented in Table 10.6. This summary format is used in many of the statistical packages currently available.

In Table 10.6, ability level (A) presents a sum of squares of 163.47; the degrees of freedom are 2 (remember there are three ability levels and $df = N - 1 = 2$); the mean square for A is the quotient of SS divided by the degrees of freedom (163.47 divided by 2 = 81.74). For grade level (B), the sum of squares is 158.70; the degree of freedom equals 1 because $N - 1$ is in this case $2 - 1$. The mean square for grade level (B) is 158.70 divided by 1—that is, 158.70. The interaction and Within Groups mean squares are found in a similar manner. The degree of freedom for the interaction is 2 because $2 \times 1 = 2$ (the degrees of freedom of A and B are multiplied by each other). The degrees of freedom for Within Group are determined by the sum of $N - 1$ for each of the six cells of students. With each cell having had five scores, $N - 1 = 4$: the degree of freedom for Within Group is 24. The total number of degrees of freedom is 29—that is, total sample size minus 1.

The F score is determined by the ratio of each source of variation—ability

Table 10.4   Data for ANOVA, 3 × 2 Design

4th Grade			6th Grade		
Low X	Average X	High X	Low X	Average X	High X
13	21	24	16	22	32
19	14	15	14	19	27
21	16	22	21	16	25
16	21	19	19	20	27
11	13	17	23	29	21

Table 10.5   The Mean Scores for Each Group by Grade Level

		Low	Average	High
	Fourth Grade	16	17	19.4
Groups				
	Sixth Grade	18.6	21.2	26.4

level (A), grade level (B), and interaction (A × B)—to the mean square of Within Groups. Thus,

$$F \text{ for level A} = \frac{81.74}{16.27} = 5.02,$$

$$F \text{ for level B} = \frac{158.70}{16.27} = 9.76,$$

$$F \text{ for A} \times \text{B} = \frac{12.40}{16.27} = .76.$$

To evaluate the F ratio, enter an F table (to be found in any good statistics book) at the intersection of the df value: for level A, enter at the crosspoint of 2 and 24: a value of 3.40 or greater is required for statistical significance at the 5% level and 5.61 or greater at the 1% level. The F value for the B level is 9.76: enter the table at df 1, 24. An $F > 7.82$ is required at the 1% level to be statistically significant. For the interaction level (A × B), the F value is .76. Enter the table at 2 and 24: the value is not statistically significant. In most cases, a researcher will seldom need to look up critical values in statistics books. This information is provided automatically in computerized statistical packages.

What does all this mean? How can one attempt to interpret the data? In an ANOVA table, the first step is to evaluate the interaction of the various rows and columns. In the example given, the A × B interaction is not significant. In Table 10.5, the mean scores for each grade and ability level were given. The table indicated that scores for the sixth grade students were greater at each ability level than the mean scores for the fourth grade students. Ad-

Table 10.6   Summary of Analysis of Variance for Singing Accuracy of Fourth and Sixth Grade Children as Related to Levels of Musical Aptitude

Source of Variation	SS	df	MS	F	P
Ability level (A)	163.47	2	81.74	5.02	<.05
Grade level (B)	158.70	1	158.70	9.76	<.01
Interaction (A × B)	24.80	2	12.40	.76	>.05
Within Groups	390.40	24	16.27		
Total	737.37	29			

ditionally, the mean scores progressed similarly for each ability level. There was no interaction between grade and ability levels.

If in the illustration the mean scores of the two groups of average ability students had been reversed (the average fourth-grade students scored 21.2 and the average sixth-grade students scored 17), a significant interaction would have occurred. To explain this phenomenon, the graphs presented in Figure 10.6 may be helpful. Graph A repeats the scores given in Table 10.5. Graph B shows the reversed average ability scores. The lines across the ability levels in each grade are nearly parallel, whereas those in Graph B show a sudden surge in the scores for the fourth-grade average ability group. Scores that result in nearly parallel lines produce no interaction; nonparallel lines, produced by unusual fluctuation, tend to create interaction.

In the example as initially set up, the data did not suggest the existence of an interaction between grade and ability level. The next step should therefore be to investigate more closely the nature of the two variables A (ability) and B (grade level). In statistical terms, one should look at the main effects.

The main effect of ability (A) is statistically significant. Because the mean scores for each group are greater as the ability level increases, we may assume that, for this sample, those students classified as having greater musical ability

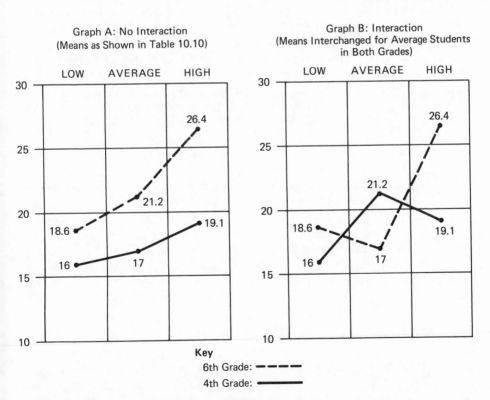

Figure 10.6   Graphs Illustrating Main Effects (Graph A) and Interaction (Graph B).

were, as a group, more accurate singers. The main effect of grade level (B) is also statistically significant. Because the magnitude of the effects of the age variable was the same as the magnitude of the effects for the aptitude level, it may be concluded that both school grade (or age) and aptitude (ability) are related to the criterion variable of learning to sing in tune.

If the interaction between main effects is significant, the first step is to determine where the interaction takes place and if and how it can be explained. For that purpose, cell means are frequently analyzed by means of the t test or other appropriate statistical tests. The analysis of main effects may then assume lesser importance. If the interaction turns out not to be significant, the data analyses will center on the main effects and, depending on the purpose of the study, a variety of statistical tests may be employed to analyze the cell differences.

The Computer as an Aid in Parametric Data Analysis

Most of the parametric procedures discussed here or those found in statistics books can be calculated by using a standard statistical package such as the *Statistical Package for the Social Sciences* (SPSS-X, 1983), or by other statistical packages designed for the quantitative analysis of empirical data in the behavioral and social sciences. Mathematical manipulations that once required several weeks of computation can now be calculated and printed in minutes or seconds by the computers found in many homes and in most colleges and universities. Nevertheless, some hand calculation is still advised because errors can be made in entering the data into the computer or in entering appropriate processing commands. It is wise, for example, to compute by hand some of the mean scores of the data in order to verify the accuracy of the computer-generated results. If substantial differences exist between the two sets of mean scores, mistakes in the entry of data into the computer may be assumed.

The computer has become a valuable tool for researchers who employ statistical data analysis in their work. In fact, the computer has become an aid to such a great extent that a danger now exists of trusting the "computer's knowledge" of statistics more than one's own. Researchers tend to become impressed with sophisticated data manipulations and devote lesser attention to the much more difficult question of whether such manipulations are necessary. Statistics are a useful component of empirical research, but the interpretation of the meaning behind a statistic rests on the knowledge, intellect, and integrity of the researcher.

10.4 Basic Concepts of Nonparametric Statistics

Often referred to as distribution-free statistical procedures, nonparametric statistics are employed when nothing is known about the shape of the frequency distribution under which a sample of people or a set of observations may fall. This is largely the case when a sample has not been drawn according to accepted randomization procedures; when the sample is very small; or when one has reason to assume that its distribution may be heavily skewed—that is, when the researcher knows that it might be biased beyond chance toward one side of the normal curve. There is a disagreement among statisticians at what point the shape of a frequency distribution does not allow one to use parametric statistics for data analysis. As long as that disagreement exists, music educators are advised to become familiar with both procedures.

When conducting research in the setting of the music classroom, samples tend to be relatively small. In this kind of research, nonparametric statistics may be called for because the samples are often too small for the researcher to make any assumption about their distribution. The use of nonparametric statistical procedures may also be proper in investigations on musical judgments, taste, and preferences in which the researcher operates with measurements employing other than interval scores, such as nominal and ordinal data. Nonparametric statistics should not be used with interval data because parametric tests are more powerful in assessing the information contained in those data.

One of the advantages of most nonparametric tests is their ease of calculation. Although the help of a computer is often not really a necessity, most nonparametric tests are to be found in commercially available statistical packages. These tests include measures of rank correlation and concordance, analysis of variance, and measures for analyzing the relationship of two or more independent samples. Table 10.7 lists some of the most common parametric tests and the corresponding nonparametric tests that provide similar data analyses. Chi-square, listed under both parametric and nonparametric statistical tests, is a measure that compares an actual set of scores with a theoretical (expected) distribution of scores. While many statisticans consider the chi-square test to be nonparametric, other statisticians disagree. Regardless with which camp one sides, chi-square statistical procedures provide a useful analytical tool for data in the social and behavioral sciences. (For an in-depth description of nonparametric statistics, see Kraft & Van Eden, 1968; Leach, 1979; Siegel, 1956). The following brief discussion of selected nonparametric techniques is primarily based upon these studies.

Table 10.7 Selected Parametric Tests and Corresponding Nonparametric Tests

Parametric	Nonparametric
Pearson product-moment correlation coefficient (r)	Spearman rank-order correlation coefficient (r_s)
t test, independent sample	Mann-Whitney U test
One-way ANOVA	Kruskal Wallis ANOVA of ranks
Chi-square (χ^2)	Chi-square (χ^2)

Correlational Measures

Spearman rank correlations along with the Kendall tau test (τ) produce measures of relationships similar to those known in parametric test as the Pearson r (Pearson product-moment correlation). The difference between the two measures lies in the type of raw data used. Whereas the Pearson r is calculated from continuous data on two measures, the Spearman r_s and Kendall τ are obtained by comparing the rankings of groups of individuals on two measures.

Calculating a Spearman r_s is a rather simple task by comparison with the procedure for calculating the Pearson r. Assume that two tests have been given to a sample of 12 fifth-grade students. The first test is a measure of general intelligence, the second a measure of musical achievement. The research purpose is to estimate the relationship between general intelligence and musical achievement. The nonparametric test is being used because of the small sample size and because the dissimilar scores on the two measures allow only a rank ordering of the students.

Assume you have collected the data (test scores) on intelligence and musical achievement for each of the 12 students. The first step in solving the problem is to rank each student's scores in two series of general intelligence and musical achievement. The ranking moves from 1 as the highest score to 12 as the lowest. Table 10.8 shows the rank order for each student on each measure, the difference that exists in the rankings, the square of that difference, and the sum of the squares of the difference. The numerical values for the data have been adapted from Siegel (1956, pp. 205–207).

The formula for calculating the Spearman rho (r_s) is:

$$r_s = 1 - \frac{6 \Sigma_i \overset{N}{d_i^2}}{N^3 - N} .$$

Table 10.8   Rank Order on General Intelligence and Musical Achievement

Student	Rank		d	d^2
	Intelligence	Achievement		
A	2	3	−1	1
B	6	4	2	4
C	5	2	3	9
D	1	1	0	0
E	10	8	2	4
F	9	11	−2	4
G	8	10	−2	4
H	3	6	−3	9
I	4	7	−3	9
J	12	12	0	0
K	7	5	2	4
			Total d^2 =	48

To find the Spearman r_s for the example given, five computation steps are necessary.

Step 1.   Multiply the sum of the squared d scores by 6.

Step 2.   Cube the number of ranked scores (in this case 11).

Step 3.   Subtract from the cubed N the number of ranked scores.

Step 4.   Divide the result of Step 1 by the result of Step 3.

Step 5.   Subtract the result of Step 4 from 1 in order to arrive at the decimal r_s correlation estimate.

Applying these steps to the data in Table 10.8, we obtain:

$$r_s = 1 - \frac{6\,(48)}{(11)^3 - 11}$$

$$= 1 - \frac{288}{1331 - 11}$$

$$= 1 - \frac{288}{1320}$$

$$= 1 - .218$$

$$= .78$$

The correlation between general intelligence and musical achievement for the students measured is estimated to be $r_s = .78$.

For larger samples, a researcher could anticipate a number of tied observations. Siegel (1956, pp. 205–207) explains the procedure under such condition. He also describes the Kendall τ measure, which is somewhat similar in nature and computational procedure (pp. 213–228).

Measures for Differences of Means

The Mann-Whitney U Test is the nonparametric counterpart of the parametric t test and measures the differences in central tendencies of two populations. A thorough discussion and calculation of the test is offered by Siegel (pp. 116–127 and pp. 156–158). Corresponding nonparametric tests in the area of analysis of variance are the Kruskal-Wallis One-Way ANOVA (Siegel, pp. 184–193) and the Freedman Two-Way ANOVA (Siegel, pp. 166–172). Probability tables associated with the various tests are found in the Appendix of Siegel's book. As with parametric statistics, the null hypothesis is normally tested at the .05 or .01 level of confidence.

10.5 The Relationship of Parametric and Nonparametric Statistics to Data Analysis

If nonparametric statistics are simple to compute and parametric test statistics are more time-consuming and difficult to calculate, why do most researchers prefer the employment of parametric tests? The answer lies in the degree of information the two approaches yield from the same set of data. In addition, parametric statistics are more powerful than nonparametric tests.

Powerful in statistical terms means that a test discriminates between two sets of data in such a way that the null hypothesis may be rejected even if the differences in scores are relatively small. Thus, testing two or more samples for significance of differences by way of parametric techniques requires smaller score differences to be judged significant than would be the case if nonparametric statistics were employed. Because researchers are concerned about minimizing the probability that a null hypothesis is maintained when it is in fact false, the more powerful statistic should be given preference.

When presented with the choice of using parametric versus nonparametric tests in a research situation, if there is no rush for data analysis and if the data meet the underlying assumptions of parametric measurement, parametric tests should be employed. The number of available statistical tests is greater, more sophisticated research designs can be used, and a maximum of information can be "squeezed" from the data.

10.6 A Word of Caution About the Use of Statistics

The purpose of this chapter was to introduce the reader to some of the statistical tests that have become the basis of data analysis in empirical research and have led to the making of inferences and the assessment of the probability of truth from quantified data. Many individuals express great distrust and fear of statistical tests and their use; much of the fear and distrust can be justified. It is true that one can lie with statistics, but it is also true that one can lie with philosophical argument or historical reporting. When someone states that "history tells us . . .," run, put your hand over your wallet, and lock the door. Lies and liars can be found traveling on all the avenues of truth.

Individuals reading empirical studies that employ virtuoso statistical tests should not feel ignorant or threatened. Statistical testing is important to empirical research, but it is not the heart of the matter. The essence of a research study resides in the purpose of the research and its related problems. All the fancy "number crunching" of the most powerful and sophisticated computer cannot take the place of a good idea. Statistical tests are a means to an end, not an end in itself.

Statistics generally do not prove anything; they simply suggest to the researcher a way of organizing and explaining observed phenomena. The results of all such tests must be interpreted by the researcher, who is expected to possess knowledge about how the statistical data relate to previous studies and events and what the data do or do not indicate. In such reports, statistical language is often accused of being jargon laden. In some instances, the accusation is warranted; however, most statistical terms have been defined rather precisely.

Take, for example, the term *significance*. It has one meaning in normal conversation and another in statistics. In normal conversation, significant is used to indicate importance; in statistics terms it refers to a value beyond the critical area under the normal curve. Statistical significance indicates that to a specified degree of probability one may assume true differences between two or more samples. The term does not imply that these differences are also meaningful. Everything that is statistically significant is not necessarily of practical importance to the finding of a study. On the contrary, a significance value greater than the .01 level may indicate a rather improbable, unusual, or even unimportant tidbit of information. The researcher must decide which option is most likely true for the data at hand.

Because the results of a statistical test only reflect a probable truth, there is always a need to verify the results by conducting the same investigation several times. The more a study is repeated and the more frequently similar results are obtained, the more likely the results of observations made can be generalized to a larger population. Beyond the need of repeating studies, there is also a need in the field of music education to summate the results of studies on similar issues, and to improve on previously conducted studies by using larger samples and better controlled research methodologies.

Suggested Activities

1. Use a computer terminal and enter data into a program, using ANOVA and two other appropriate statistical tests. Work your way through the printout and extract the most pertinent information.
2. Take any of the computational examples in Appendixes B, C, D, E, and F and substitute the raw data with a new set of data. Provide step-by-step calculations for the new data. Interpret the findings.

Topics for Discussion

1. The relationship of parametric to nonparametric statistical procedures.
2. The meaning of correlations.
3. Drawing inferences—assumptions and conditions.

4. The misuse of statistics
   (a) in research,
   (b) in everyday life.

Suggested Readings

Aldenderfer, M. S., & Blashfield, R. K. (1984). *Cluster analysis.* (Sage University Papers. Series: Quantitative Applications in the Social Sciences. Series editors: J. L. Sullivan and R. G. Niemi). Beverly Hills: Sage Publications.

Bennett, S., & Bowers, D. (1976). *An introduction to multivariate techniques for social and behavioral sciences.* London: Macmillan Press.

Bruning, J. L., & Kintz, B. L. (1977). *Computational handbook of statistics* (2nd ed.). Glenview, IL: Scott, Foresman.

Hildebrand, D. K., Laing, J. D., & Rosenthal, H. (1977). *Analysis of ordinal data.* (Sage University Papers. Series: Quantitative Applications in the Social Sciences. Series editors: J. L. Sullivan and R. G. Niemi). Beverly Hills: Sage Publications.

Newmark, J. (1983). *Statistics and probability in modern life* (3rd ed.). San Francisco: Rinehart Press/Holt, Rinehart and Winston.

Reynolds, H. T. (1984). *Analysis of nominal data* (2nd ed.). (Sage University Papers. Series: Quantitative Applications in the Social Sciences. Series editors: J. L. Sullivan and R. G. Niemi). Beverly Hills: Sage Publications.

Sax, G. (1979). *Foundations of educational research* (2nd ed. of book formerly titled: Empirical foundations of educational research). Englewood Cliffs, NJ: Prentice-Hall.

Thompson, B. (1984). *Canonical correlation analysis: Uses and interpretation.* (A Sage University Paper. Series: Quantitative Applications in the Social Sciences. Series editors: J. L. Sullivan and R. G. Niemi). Beverly Hills: Sage Publications.

REFERENCES

Blommers, P., & Lindquist, E. F. (1960). *Elementary statistical methods in psychological education.* Cambridge, MA: Riverside Press.

Ghiselli, E. E., Campbell, J. H., & Zedeck, S. (1981). *Measurement theory for the behavioral sciences.* San Francisco: W. H. Freeman.

Kim, J., & Kohout, F. J. (1975). Special topics in general linear models. In Nie et al. (Eds.). *SPSS* (2nd ed., pp. 320–367). New York: McGraw-Hill.

Kraft, C. H., & Van Eden, C. (1968). *A nonparametric introduction to statistics.* New York: Macmillan.

Leach, C. (1979). *Introduction to statistics: A nonparametric approach for the social sciences.* New York: John Wiley.

Lindquist, E. F. (1953). *Design and analysis of experiments in psychology and education.* Boston: Houghton Mifflin.

Moore, D. S. (1985). *Statistics. Concepts and controversies* (2nd ed.) New York: W. H. Freeman.

Rainbow, E. L. (1965). A pilot study to investigate constructs of musical aptitude. *Journal of Research in Music Education, 13* (1), 3–14.

Siegel, S. (1956). *Nonparametric statistics for the behavioral sciences.* New York: McGraw-Hill.

SPSS-X User's Guide: A complete guide to SPSS-X language and operations (1983). New York: McGraw-Hill.

PART FOUR

The Research Report: From the Proposal to the Published Article

In chapter 4 the point was made that researchers should begin to put their ideas in writing long before they actually involve themselves in the methodological activities of the research process. The need was emphasized to articulate clearly and in writing the specific investigative purpose and questions that would guide all subsequent steps of a particular study. Thus, as much as the specifics in the methodologies of any mode of inquiry may be activity-oriented, skills of writing permeate all steps—from the inception of the project (the proposal) to its completion (the written report). Generally, the relationship of research proposal to research report is a close one. This is illustrated in the first part of Chapter 11 for research projects in all three modes of inquiry.

Chapter 11 contains the description of three purposes for which a research report may be written: the writing of a thesis or dissertation; the writing of reports to fund-granting agencies, institutions, and foundations; and the writing of an article to be published in a professional journal or magazine. Two mundane yet important considerations should guide the writing of any research report: the style of writing one chooses in order to match the purpose for which the report is being written, and the code of ethics that all writers are expected to abide by when seeking to publish their work.

When researchers publish their findings they are assuming a risk: The work may be accepted by their peers, or it may be rejected. This is the same risk assumed by musicians who perform in public. Their efforts can either be accepted or rejected. Without taking that risk, the professional musician has no right to be called professional. Similarly, researchers cannot claim to have the status of professionals if they refuse or fail to submit their research results for publication.

Chapter Eleven

The Writing Task in Doctoral Research: Proposal, Dissertation, Journal Article; Code of Ethics

11.1 Introduction

When doctoral candidates embark on their dissertation projects, aside from actually conducting the investigation, two major hurdles have to be overcome: A formal proposal has to be written and the dissertation has to be written. The relationship of the proposal to any research report—be that report a thesis or dissertation, research paper, or research article—is a close one. Ideally, portions of the proposal should be easily adaptable to the content of the report. Therefore, the stronger the proposal, the better the final report tends to be. Attention to detail in the first part of the research project will reduce much frustration and anxiety in the last part.

The relationship between a finished research project and a subsequent research article, too, is a close one, although the task of condensing the complexity of a research project into a relatively brief journal article is formidable. Good writing skills must be coupled with a sensitivity toward the audience being addressed. Beyond that, the "ins and outs" of procedures common to the workings of editorial boards should be taken into consideration, and accepted standards of ethical conduct must be followed if novice researchers wish to gain the respect of their colleagues in the field.

11.2 The Dissertation or Thesis Proposal: Suggestions for Its Preparation

A thesis or dissertation proposal is a written document that indicates to the university faculty the topic a doctoral candidate wishes to research and the methodology that will be followed. The nature of that written document varies greatly from institution to institution. Some universities require the candidate to submit the topic or title of the proposed study along with a one-paragraph summary of how the student intends to pursue the investigation. Other universities demand the submission of a much longer and more formal document, and combine the submission of that document with an oral defense of the proposal.

The written proposal serves several useful functions for both the degree candidate and the faculty member(s) who will ultimately guide the investigation. For the candidate, the proposal is, first, a vehicle to demonstrate a broad knowledge of the field within which a specific research topic will be investigated. Second, the proposal provides the candidate with an opportunity to present a plan of action for the systematic study of a given question. Third, the candidate is afforded the chance to practice the writing skills that are so sorely needed. For the graduate faculty committee members, the proposal is an opportunity to probe the knowledge of the candidate in general and to provide assistance in detecting loopholes of logic or technique in the investigative plan. It is also a chance for the faculty to assess a candidate's ability in expressing thoughts in writing.

The proposal stage of writing a dissertation or thesis is a time when the faculty or institution can provide some quality control over the scholarly documents being produced. A poorly conceived or articulated proposal may mean that the candidate is improperly prepared to do an independent investigation. An inferior presentation of a proposal may result in the rejection of the entire plan, or it may result in the faculty committee's request to rethink the project and submit a modified proposal.

In all research, the proposal is much like a recipe one follows to achieve a finished product that is representative of one's best intellectual efforts. If the recipe is flawed, one may anticipate the final product to be equally flawed. Thus, the proposal stage is a crucial step in any research process; in the specific case of a dissertation or thesis, a more lengthy written document seems most desirable. It should consist of approximately 50 typewritten, double-spaced pages, describing clearly and comprehensively (a) why the study should be conducted, (b) how the purpose has been derived from and/or relates to the literature in the field, and (c) how the study is to be organized and executed.

Some Specific Guidelines

The procedures for developing a proposal vary depending on the mode of inquiry to be employed in the investigation. However, at the risk of repeating what has been stressed throughout this book, several components should be consistently present in all good research even if the way in which they are addressed may differ.

Research Proposal in the Empirical Mode of Inquiry. The proposal should be divided into three sections or chapters. The first section serves as the theoretical framework for the study and usually contains rationale, purpose, and the research problems (see chapter 5). At the end of that section, delimitations not addressed by the purpose and problems should be acknowledged. In addition, terms that need clarification must be defined. The first section, as described, should take up to 20 pages and may become, with minor revisions, a major portion of the first chapter of the eventual dissertation or thesis.

The second section consists of a *critical* (see chapter 3) discussion of the related literature. The discussion should contain a review of the most pertinent studies, along with a qualitative assessment of each of the studies. This section may with some expansion also become chapter 2—the related research section of the dissertation.

The third section in an empirically based proposal describes how the data will be gathered and analyzed. This section is the actual "recipe" of the proposal. If the recipe is clear and well thought out so that no ingredient is missing, the results dished up should be palatable! In this section, any pilot studies already conducted should be reported. A selected bibliography of materials that the researcher has actually read should conclude the proposal, along with any Appendices pertinent to the proposed investigation (measurement tools, cover letters, etc.).

The structure of a proposal as just described would look like this:

Section I
  A. Rationale
  B. Purpose of the Study
  C. Research Problems/Questions
  D. Delimitations of Study (if necessary)
  E. Definition of Terms (if necessary)
Section II: Critical Discussion of Related Literature
Section III: Discussion of Research Techniques
  A. Selection of Subjects
  B. Complete Plans for Data Gathering (measurement devices, sequence of events, etc.)
  C. Complete Plan for Data Analysis (statistical design)
Appendix
Working Bibliography

Proposal in the Historical Mode of Inquiry.   The first section or chapter in a proposal using historical inquiry should contain the rationale and purpose for the study, along with a substantial number of very detailed questions that need to be answered. It is not sufficient to ask whether someone contributed to music education. Instead, one must ask about the type of contributions that person may have made by encouraging new literature, developing new teaching techniques, establishing a leadership direction, and so forth. A detailed list of questions ought to address all of these and other points. Each question should be so specific that it reflects clearly the kind of data that need to be gathered in order to answer it. The rationale should contain references to most if not all pertinent literature on the subject under investigation. If the research questions are not specific enough to delimit clearly the scope of the study, then at the end of the first section any additional delimitations should be given. The second section/chapter of a proposal in historical research should be devoted to a description of how the data will be located, gathered, verified, and evaluated.

In outline form, a proposal in historical research would look like this:

Section I
    A. Rationale for the Study (reference to related literature)
    B. Purpose of the Study
    C. Research Questions
    D. Delimitations (if necessary)
    E. Definition of Terms (if necessary)
Section II
    A. A Listing of Sources for Data to be Gathered and Location of Sources
    B. A Listing of the Nature of the Data
    C. A Description of Some of the Most Pertinent Materials
    D. A Plan for the Interpretation of the Data and for Their Organization in the Final Report
Appendix (if applicable)
Working Bibliography

Proposal in the Philosophical Mode of Inquiry. A philosophical research proposal is normally presented in two sections. The first section would include the rationale and purpose of the investigation. We wish to emphasize that any of the literature that is discussed in the rationale should only pertain to the reason for conducting the study; it should not include the materials used in the line of argumentation. Following the purpose statement, the major line of argumentation and its most important premises would be sketched out and key terms in each argument would have to be defined and explicated.

The second section of the proposal would include a discussion of each argument with reference to selected literature pertinent to the documentation of all propositions (or theses) in an argumentation. This section is important to the success of the research project because philosophical argumentation rests on the collection of evidence as provided by the logical thought processes of other researchers, as well as those provided by one's own thoughts on the issue. Supportive evidence from many fields of knowledge and modes of inquiry should be included, and plans should be outlined in the proposal on how much additional evidence the candidate envisions utilizing in the argumentation. This is, of course, in contrast to the more speculative type of discourse that often brands philosophical inquiry as intellectually sloppy.

The format of a philosophically based proposal might look like this:

Section I
  A. Rationale (includes "world view" or basic perspective; reference to materials pertinent to the purpose only)
  B. Purpose
  C. Major Line of Argumentation and Definition of All Terms (reference to supporting evidence)
Section II
  A. Development of Broad Line of Argumentation
  B. Critical Description of Selected Literature Pertinent to the Argumentation
  C. Sample Section of Line of Argumention
Appendix (if appropriate)
Working Bibliography

These outlines suggest a particular way of how to put together a proposal for a dissertation or thesis. There are, of course, other ways and formats to present all planned research steps in an orderly fashion. The important point is that all critical steps must be clearly delineated. There are always surprises in research, even when it is planned well. However, the surprises should not occur as a result of wandering into the research process blindly.

11.3 The Research Report: Thesis/Dissertation, Journal Article, Research Paper

Conducting an investigation—be it for the purpose of writing a dissertation or be it guided by an experienced researcher—can take a lot of time. The process, however, does not end until the project is finally put in writing and the results of the investigation disseminated to colleagues within the research community. The manner in which the results are communicated, the length and detail of the communication, and its distribution are governed, in part, by the factors that generated the original research activity.

One or more of the following factors generally motivate an individual's research activity: (a) the wish to seek a graduate degree; (b) the need to obtain financial support for research through institutional grants; (c) personal inquisitiveness and desire to investigate problems; and (d) personal desire for professional visibility and advancement. These generating factors, when pursued to the completion of a study, result in theses and dissertations, summary reports of research activities to funding agencies, articles in professional journals, and the presentation of papers at professional meetings.

Each type of report mentioned differs in length, the style of the reporting, the content of the report, the details included in the description of all methodological-technical aspects of the project, the audience that will eventually read the report, and the procedures by which the report will be disseminated. The various avenues of reporting all seek to provide their audience with the maximum amount of information within the confines of the medium of publication. This is achieved if the writer/researcher strives for a clear line of description and argumentation in a jargon-free style. Logically clear writing thus becomes the requisite ingredient in all good research reports, no matter for what specific purpose they are written.

Logically Clear Writing

In chapter 2, section 2.4, some aspects of elements in a clear writing style were addressed. In addition, many of the issues described in chapter 7 (Approaches to Philosophical Inquiry) apply to the development of writing that seeks to be logically cohesive. This kind of thinking manifests itself if all sentences are sequentially connected with each other in such a way that (a) one statement results from a previous statement, and (b) the sequence leads smoothly into a conclusion that is derived from the chain of statements themselves rather than from thoughts the researcher assumed would be inferred by the reader.

To illustrate: A frequent mistake in the writing of research reports lies in the author's assumption that a reader will draw the same conclusions from given statements as the author did when writing the statements. For example, two sentences are given:

Sentence 1	"It is raining"	(p)
Sentence 2	"The street is wet"	(q)

According to a general experience, the street gets wet (q) when it is raining (p). Therefore, the order from p to q is logical and can be easily followed. Now assume the reader is presented only with sentence q: "The street is wet." Although the writer knows that rain is the cause for that condition, that sentence is omitted because it appears to be so obvious. The writer simply assumes that the reader will fill in the argument and draw the same conclusion as the writer: $p \rightarrow q$. The author is being unjust to the reader. Logically, a wet street does not necessarily mean it is raining. There could be other factors responsible for the wet street, such as someone having poured water on the street or the water main having broken. Unless the writer explicitly excluded other sources but rain as the cause for the wet street, p would not necessarily have followed from q. Thus, in the case where $p \rightarrow q$, the reader will easily agree with the writer's logic. In the case where $q \rightarrow p$, the reader could view the sentences merely as unrelated statements unless the author had inserted additional information that would make such a view illogical.

This illustration points to the fact that the same number of sentences, if put into different order, can lead to different conclusions. This knowledge is important for the writing of good research reports because it frequently happens that for every one sentence a writer puts down on paper, one to three connecting sentences are omitted. Such omission results in logical gaps of reasoning. These gaps will frequently occur when a writer is very knowledgeable in an area and falsely assumes that the readers are equally as knowledgeable or have had experiences similar to those of the writer.

Researchers should never assume that all readers will be exposed to like experiences or possess an equal depth of knowledge about a given topic. Thus, to avoid gaps in reasoning, great care should be taken by the researcher/writer to critically review all written evidence presented in an investigation. Undoubtedly, the skill of good writing rests in a writer's ability to detect, or be sensitive to, gaps of reasoning and to make the chain of logical argumentation as cohesive and explicit as possible.

Reporting Research in the Form of Theses and Dissertations

The difference between a thesis and dissertation is a moot point. A thesis is generally a research project associated with the requirements of a master's degree, whereas a dissertation is primarily a requirement for the granting of a doctoral degree. A thesis is usually a shorter and less comprehensive research report, whereas a dissertation is longer and requires the doctoral candidate to demonstrate the mastery of a body of knowledge as well as the ability to resolve independently a specific question or research problem. The dissertation/thesis distinction is not always clear cut because some degree-granting institutions label the doctoral-level research document a thesis submitted in partial fulfillment of the doctoral degree.

Of all the forms of reporting, the thesis/dissertation report is normally the most complete of all research forms. The length of the report is not restricted by an editorial board; thus, all aspects of the study may undergo thorough analysis and discussion. The dissertation is basically a document for the university audience and is written to serve as a scholarly and academic discourse. (Unfortunately, the style of writing in such documents tends to be somewhat less enjoyable than that used by a good novelist!) As a document that is presented to the university community, a dissertation or thesis should be considered a contribution to the academic field of study and should exhibit promising traces of scholarship and academic stature.

The actual organization of theses and dissertations and the accepted writing style may vary from institution to institution, and at times even within an institution. Thus, individuals preparing to write one of these documents must consult the graduate office within their university to make sure they follow an approved style manual. The manual describes how the bibliography is to be handled, how tables and figures are to be presented, and how other technical aspects related to the formal printing of the document are to be approached. All these problems must be addressed on an institutional basis.

Regardless of the number of chapters in a dissertation or thesis, a minimum of five areas should be covered: (a) the rationale for having conducted the investigation; (b) the purpose itself and, if applicable, all related questions; (c) a discussion of research relevant to the rationale and purpose of the study; (d) a description of how the researcher actually went about the research; and (e) all results and conclusions relative to the stated purpose. Some subsequent speculation about the subject may prove appropriate in the context of developing new questions that deserve further study.

In the case of empirical investigations, the actual written report may be organized so that each chapter covers one of the broad areas just mentioned: Chapter 1—Rationale, Purpose, and Problems; Chapter 2—Related Literature; Chapter 3—Methodology; Chapter 4—Results of Study; Chapter 5—Summary and Conclusions.

Following the chapters, the researcher should include as appendices all measurement instruments, all raw data (including, if applicable, complete interview transcripts or responses to questionnaires), and, depending on the chosen style of reporting, either a reference list or a complete bibliography of all pertinent publications read in preparation of the study. At the beginning of the work, there should be a title page, table of contents, lists of tables, figures, and illustrations—all with appropriate page references. Acknowledgments as well as an abstract of the report precede everything else.

In dissertation and theses that utilize historical or philosophical modes of inquiry, research procedures and verification methods are often discussed as a narrative within the text. All data (primary source evidence) relevant to the documentation of a thought process or logical argumentation should be described either in narrative footnotes or in the text itself. The latter is recommended as the comments are an important means to support or refute an event or a point of view. In philosophically based theses and dissertations, the chapters often represent major divisions in the argumentation; in historically based dissertations, the chapters tend to be organized according to the chronology reported, or according to significant events in the life of a person or in the course of a specific time period or event. Both in historical and philosophical dissertations, the chapters should stand by themselves as the development of a complete idea and coherent train of thought. The chapters should logically succeed each other, leading to a final summation and concluding chapter.

Most universities file all completed dissertations in their libraries and also deposit a copy with Xerox University Microfilm. *Dissertation Abstracts International* is the official reference to the holdings of dissertations by Xerox University Microfilm. Most master's theses are filed in the home universities' libraries. Their copies are not deposited with Xerox Microfilm.

Reports of Research Subsidized by Grants from Institutions and Foundations

Reports of research funded by grants from foundations, companies, or other extra-university funding agencies are often as complete and detailed as a dissertation report. The one aspect that is generally missing in the grant report is a detailed discussion of the related research. Funded research will normally be conducted by experienced researchers who apply for research funding on a competitive basis. Grants awarded by foundations and the federal government frequently have a predetermined bias for the type of study that is eligible for funding. Thus, researchers may not always exercise complete freedom in what they desire to investigate. It is not at all unusual to have foundations or government agencies fund research that attempts to support a desired or projected result.

Reports of funded research may be made available through the funding institution or, in the case of the federal government, by the Supervisor of Government Documents. The content of the report generally includes a description of the complete methodology, results, and conclusions. The audience for the report is primarily the grant-giving foundation or agency. These reports often find their way into the research community at large by being published as books, monographs, or articles in journals.

Submitting Research Reports to Professional Research Journals

Professional research journals serve as an important avenue in all fields of knowledge. The journals serve two basic audiences—those who are actively conducting research and those who wish to keep themselves informed about current investigative activities and new research findings. The journals publish not only reports of finished research projects but also critical reviews of research and literature pertinent to the field. They provide additional services for the readership by informing them about forthcoming meetings and by announcing calls for papers to be presented at regional, national, and international meetings and conferences.

Financial support for the journals is obtained in a variety of ways. Frequently, a portion of the dues paid to an organization will be used to support in part or fully one or more journals. In the case of partial support, the balance of the costs of publications will be generated through subscription fees. A few professional journals are partially supported by university or foundation grants, again the balance of the costs of publication being generated through individual and library subscriptions. Currently, the continuing increase in the cost of printing and mailing have placed some journals in serious financial jeopardy.

Publication schedules of professional research journals vary. Most journals attempt to circulate a new issue once every three months. Others do not follow a regular schedule but publish whenever funds are available or whenever a suitable number of manuscripts are ready for press. Research journals also vary in the number of pages that are made available for the reporting of research. Some journals have only a total of 24 pages, whereas others may provide more than 120 pages. For example, the *Journal of Research in Music Education (JRME)* provides about 60 pages per issue for reports of research. The limited number of pages available for reporting research studies thus limits the number of reports that can be published and places a constraint on the number of manuscript pages a researcher is allowed to submit.

Each journal generally focuses on specific research areas. Those areas are usually identified within each journal on a page that solicits contributions and describes the format to be followed in the preparation of a manuscript. *JRME* seeks research reports that clearly contribute to music education. (For information about a recent change (April 1986) in the instructions to contributors, see the most current issue of JRME for the exact wording.) *Update* states "All articles must be research-based. They may take the form of a 'review of literature' or may report findings of a single research study. . . ." (Instructions to Contributors). The main purpose of *Update* is to provide information to the reader who may not be a researcher, whereas *JRME* is primarily intended for the reader who is also an active researcher. The *Bulletin of the Council for Research in Music Education* publishes critiques of completed dissertations, "feature articles" and "articles of interest." These articles are geared toward the description and summary of research on a selected topic and speak primarily to the community of scholars.

The *Music Educators Journal* accepts articles that are comparatively short, in a non-academic style of writing, and that speak directly to issues encountered by music teachers in the field. The articles are not necessarily based on principles of scientific inquiry but express the personal view of the writer on timely issues.

Persons who wish to publish must be cognizant of the focus and primary function of the various journals and magazines available to a profession. Lack of such awareness will lead to the submission of articles whose contents lie outside the boundaries delineated in the journal. The prompt rejection of the manuscript is certain.

The Process of Having an Article Accepted for Publication

Most journals have a page on which contributions are solicited. On that page, one commonly finds a brief section outlining the steps a prospective contributor should follow in preparing an article for publication. The instructions normally include the suggested maximum length of the article, specific manuscript style, placement of bibliography, graphs, tables, and figures, and the number of copies of the manuscript that should be forwarded to the editor. On the same page, one also finds the name and address of the person to whom the manuscript should be sent.

There are two types of professional journals—refereed and nonrefereed.

A refereed journal has an editorial advisory board consisting of individuals who have been selected on the basis of their research or scholarly contributions to the field. That panel of experts is responsible for maintaining a certain degree of quality control for the journal by reviewing the manuscripts that have been submitted for publication. The reviewers (referees) make decisions on whether or not the manuscript should be published, revised and then reconsidered, or rejected for publication. In nonrefereed journals, the editor bears the sole responsibility for deciding whether or not a manuscript is accepted for publication. In academic circles, having an article published in a refereed journal is considered more prestigious than having an article appear in a nonrefereed journal.

Once an author has completed a manuscript and forwarded it to the editorial office of a refereed journal, the manuscript enters a rather methodical review process. On receipt of the manuscript, the journal editor reviews the article and decides if it meets the overall specifications as stated on the journal solicitation page. If the editor decides the manuscript does not meet the minimum criteria for publication, the article does not enter the peer review process and is immediately returned to the sender.

Based on statistics on manuscripts received by the editorial office of *JRME* during the years 1982–1986, the editor reported at the *JRME* Editorial Board meeting (April 8, 1986) that 30–40% of all submitted manuscripts were rejected at the outset. The most common reasons were failure to meet the mission or focus of the journal, faulty research techniques and design, improper writing style, and manuscripts too long for publication.

The manuscripts that do survive the initial screening are then submitted to members of the editorial board for evaluation. Normally, and in the case of the *JRME* review procedures, three or more members of the board review each manuscript. The reviewers are generally instructed to return their evaluations to the editor within 2 weeks and recommend to the editor whether the manuscript should be (a) accepted and published as received; (b) returned to the author for revision and corrections, with the opportunity to resubmit the manuscript to the review board; or (c) rejected as not suitable within the accepted journal standards, and perhaps recommended for submission to a more appropriate publication organ. Of the articles that were sent to members of the editorial committee for review, approximately 40% were accepted for publication (Taylor, 1986).

Most journals have a standard rating form for the referees to use in evaluating a manuscript. The form includes such items as quality of writing style (use of appropriate grammar, correct spelling, interpunctuation, etc.) and clarity of writing style. Other items are: the presence of a rationale and research purpose; defined research questions and/or problems; appropriate methodology for the mode of inquiry chosen; and conclusions based on the findings of the inquiry. If all of these points are found to be present and clearly described, the manuscript is usually accepted without change or with minor revisions.

It is a common procedure for reviewers to offer suggestions to the author.

These suggestions may result in a major revision of the manuscript or may be quite minor in nature. The author is free to accept or reject these suggestions, and may incorporate the suggestions in a revision of the manuscript or explain to the editor why the suggested changes should not be made. The editor generally reserves the right to serve as the final arbitor in any dispute over a manuscript, and is ultimately responsible for the final decision to publish or reject a submitted research report.

The article review process takes approximately 2 months to complete. If the manuscript is accepted without revision, it may be an additional 6 months or more before the article is actually published. Most journals publish on a regular basis, and will have two or more future issues in a ready state for distribution. Thus, a time lag of 9 months or more from submission of a manuscript to final publication is not unusual.

When a manuscript has been typeset, the editor normally sends the author a galley proof of the manuscript in type. At this point, minor changes may be made, errors and omissions are corrected, and final approval for publishing the article is given. This review process is admittedly slow and tedious. It is, however, followed by most prestigious journals, regardless of the academic discipline.

Just because the procedure described is followed by most journals does not mean that it is a good one. Without a doubt, there are times when both the editor and the members of the reviewing boards make mistakes and reject manuscripts that are worthy of publication. The peer evaluation process is, in a way, like the democratic process: It is slow and cumbersome, but preferred by many when one considers the alternative—an editorial authoritarian.

Preparing a Manuscript for Journal Publication. The first article music educators generally develop is usually based on their thesis or dissertation research. In fact, about 42% of all articles published in *JRME* from 1953 to 1983 were based on dissertation or thesis research (Yarbrough, 1984). The problem facing an author is how to condense a lengthy dissertation into approximately 20 typewritten pages without destroying or compromising the original study. In some instances it is an impossible task.

To solve that problem, some dissertations using historical inquiry may abstract the content of discrete chapters and produce more than one article suitable for publication. For example, in a music education study it may be possible to develop an article based on an individual's contributions to an educational institution, and to produce another article discussing the same individual's influence on setting directions for goals of a professional organization, such as the Music Educators National Conference. In some instances, excellent studies of a lengthy nature may be published in serial form in a journal if an editor considers them of outstanding worth. Exceptions in editorial policy can be made if the quality of the research is deemed to be of great value to the profession.

In all research articles, regardless of the mode of inquiry employed and regardless of space limitations, it is important to include a clear rationale for the study and some indication of references to other research. This is generally preceded by a brief discussion of the purpose of the study and what the author wishes to investigate. From there on, the formats of articles in the various modes of inquiry may differ. In empirical research, the methodology for the gathering of data must be described in detail and the results of the data should be presented in tabular form, followed by a section titled Conclusions.

If the study is historical in nature, the major primary sources for the investigation of all questions need to be listed. If applicable, procedures for their verification should be described. Because of the restricted space available in a journal, it is likely that the findings will have to be limited to a description of answers pertinent to a small number of all the questions investigated. The process of arriving at the answers should be described in detail with reference to all primary evidence collected.

In philosophical inquiry, a description of the writer's primary beliefs should precede a discussion of the form of argumentation the discourse follows. Subsequently, the most important points in the argumentation should be summarized and adequately documented. As is the case with all other research articles, philosophical writings should make room for a brief conclusion section in which the points made are consistent with the purpose and specific questions of the study.

Research Papers

Presenting papers at professional meetings is an important activity for any scholar. Such meetings frequently attract those individuals who are most active in research. The meetings also provide an excellent opportunity for those present to meet colleagues from all parts of the world and discuss matters of mutual concern. Most professional societies sponsor paper reading sessions whenever the society has a formal meeting. Notices of the meetings and the call for research papers are generally announced in the appropriate professional journals.

In announcing a call for papers, the association will usually state the topic for the meeting and the specifications for the paper. These include the conference language(s) if it is an international meeting, maximum length of the paper, number of copies to be submitted, number of accepted tables or graphs, curriculum vitae of the author, and due date for submitting the paper(s). Most of the time, papers are forwarded to the chairperson of the organization, who then distributes the applicant's paper on an anonymous basis for review to researchers in the field. The reviewers serve as referees and recommend to the chairperson those papers that seem most appropriate for the meeting. It should be noted that the procedures described are those normally found in the United States and Canada. The same procedures are not always adhered to in other countries.

The researchers whose papers are deemed most worthy of presentation are invited to read the paper to the attending membership. Following the reading, it is normal practice for the members to question the researcher and to offer critical comments. The papers are often published in proceedings of the society or association, or in the organization's journals.

Research papers generally tend to be brief compared with research submitted as dissertations or as journal articles. For example, the calls for papers by the Early Childhood Commission of the International Society of Music Education (ISME) and the ISME Research Commission state that papers should not exceed 2,000 words, about 10 double-spaced pages. The ISME Commission on Music Therapy and Music in Special Education requests a limit of 3,000 words (15 pages). The Society for Research in Music Education asks for "results of excellent research projects" to be presented in abstract form of 600 words. These reports are often presented in poster sessions—not publicly read to the profession—and the author may distribute a longer and more complete paper to interested colleagues if they so desire. These papers are not necessarily published in a magazine or journal.

Economy of words is essential. As in most investigative reporting, even a brief report should contain a rationale for the study along with some related research references. This should be followed by the purpose and problems/ questions of the study. If the paper has a maximum length of 10 pages, these should not take up more than 1½ pages. The bulk of the paper, if it is empirical, should describe how the study was completed. In a historical study, the bulk of the report should be devoted to a description of the process of data verification. Reports of philosophical studies should focus on the presentation of the sequence of arguments in the complete line of argumentation. Only a very brief portion of the report should be devoted to generalizations or speculations.

The reading of papers at professional conferences is an important avenue of communication among experienced researchers. While short reports are not always complete, most investigators in music education are aware that they obtain additional information and clarification from the author. Most scholars welcome questions about, constructive criticism of, and general interest in their work.

11.4 The Code of Ethics

When preparing or submitting articles for publication, all scholars in music education are asked to adhere to a certain ethical conduct when they (a) submit an article to several journals, (b) publish an article that has already been published elsewhere, (c) identify the authorship of a publication, (d) publish an article in several parts, (e) consider copyrights, and (f) present papers at professional conferences. The rules describing that conduct have been formalized in a code of ethics, developed and agreed upon by the Music Education Research Council in 1984. The Code is presented here as it appears in each issue of *JRME*. As stated, the code is based on materials of the American Psychological Association (1974) and the *American Psychologist* (1981).

The following code[1] has been approved by the Executive Committee of the Music Education Research Council, Music Educators National Conference, and the National Research Committee of the National Association for Music Therapy.

Research Publication/Presentation Code of Ethics

1. *Multiple submissions*—An author must not submit the same manuscript for simultaneous consideration by two or more journals. If a manuscript is rejected by one journal, an author may then submit it to another journal.

2. *Duplicate publication*—An author must not submit a manuscript published in whole or in substantial part in another journal or published work. Exceptions may be made for previous publication (a) in a periodical with limited circulation or availability (e.g., a government agency report) or (b) in a summarized form (e.g., a *Convention Proceedings*). In either case, an author must inform the editor of the previous publication.

3. *Authorship*—Authorship is reserved to those who make major scientific contributions to the research. Credit is assigned to those who have contributed to a publication in proportion to their professional contributions. Major contributions of a professional character made by several persons to a common project are recognized by joint authorship, with the individual who made the principal contribution listed first. Minor contributions of a professional character and extensive clerical or similar nonprofessional assistance may be acknowledged in footnotes or in an introductory statement. Acknowledgment through specific citations is made for unpublished as well as published material that has directly influenced the research or writing. Persons who compile and edit material of others for publication publish the material in the name of the originating group, if appropriate, with their own name appearing as chairperson or editor. All contributors are to be acknowledged and named.

4. *Piecemeal publication*—Investigators who engage in systematic programs of research report their results from time to time as significant portions of their programs are completed. This is both legitimate and inevitable in research programs of several years' duration. In contrast to this kind of publication, articles are received in which a single investigation has been broken up into several manuscripts submitted seriatim. When this kind of piecemeal publication comes to editorial attention, the policy is to defer any decision on any item in the series, returning such submission(s) to the author with the suggestion that a single comprehensive paper would be more appropriate.

5. *Copyright*—Once an article is accepted, an author transfers literary rights on the published article to the publishing organization (e.g., MENC, NAMT) so that the author and the association are protected from misuse of copyrighted material. An article will not be published until the author's signed copyright transfer has been received by the national office of the publishing organization. Contributors are responsible for obtaining copyright clearance on illustrations, figures, or lengthy quotes used in their manuscripts that have been published elsewhere.

6. *Conference presentation*—Papers submitted for presentation via any format (i.e.,

posters, paper-reading sessions, etc.) should not have been presented at another major conference. If the data have been presented in whole or in substantive part in any forum, in print, or at previous research sessions, a statement specifying particulars of the above must be included with the submission.

The code of ethics originated in response to a growing trend in academic circles to pad one's publication record by publishing the same article in more than one journal. In the past, there have been several instances in music education where duplicate publication has taken place. The habit of submitting the same manuscript to several publishers in order to get two publications out of one, may be the result of the so-called "publish-or-perish" syndrome in universities that expect their faculty to be productive scholars. In some institutions this pressure has been so great that the length of a publication list sometimes counts more than the quality of the research that underpins the writing. As much as a lengthy list of publications may, indeed, be required for someone to get ahead in academia, there are several reasons why the code of ethics should be taken seriously by anyone who wishes to be viewed as a serious scholar.

1. Many journals have lengthy backlogs of articles that are accepted for publication. It is not unusual for such backlogs to result in a waiting time of 1 year or more prior to the time the article appears in published form. There are only so many publications that can make up the content of one journal issue, and there is only so much space to print the articles. Individuals who duplicate publications deprive their colleagues of access to space in the journal. The same, of course, is also true for the presentation of papers at professional meetings and conferences.

2. The primary purpose of research journals and paper-reading sessions at professional conferences is to provide a forum for the exchange of ideas and the reporting of insights into the body of knowledge of a field. Attempts to obtain duplicate publications/papers out of one research effort violate the basic purpose for which research journals or conferences exist.

3. It is often difficult for editors, editorial boards, and panels of judges to recognize the recycling of material. Having an accepted code of ethics, however, reminds individuals of their obligations toward their profession. Serious violations of the code could result in a restriction of a person's publishing efforts and could mean denial of appearance at professional meetings.

Most researchers honored the sentiment of the code of ethics long before it was put into writing and long before it was endorsed by the various professional organizations. For most writers, the code of ethics is a matter of course and serves only as a reminder of proper conduct regarding the publication of manuscripts. Aspects that the code does not cover are those of plagiarism and the submission of false data. These instances are not frequent, but they do occur. In one case, a former president of a large state university was found guilty of having plagiarized his dissertation in history (from his wife's master's thesis). His degree was eventually revoked by the degree-granting university.

An example of knowingly submitting false data is that of the late psychologist Cyril Burt, who fabricated data to provide support for his conclusions about the relationship of genetic conditions and environmental influences.

The profession must have an agreement among its members that both plagiarism and fabrication of data are serious violations of all standards of ethical conduct in research. At the heart of accepting or rejecting the findings of a study is trust in the person who conducted the investigation. If that trust is broken, the basis of disciplined inquiry has been destroyed. The profession should beware of such destruction. Outrage would not be enough; instead, sanctions should be imposed against those who commit these offenses.

Suggested Activities

1. Find three articles that are based on dissertation research. Compare the dissertations to the articles and determine:

    (a) If the articles accurately describe the full-length report.

    (b) What information is missing.

    (c) Different means the author could have used to reduce the dissertation into a research article.

2. Develop a plan for writing a thesis or dissertation.

Suggested Readings

Campbell, W. G., Ballou, S. V., & Slade, C. (1982). *Form and style: Theses, reports, term papers* (6th ed.). Boston: Houghton Mifflin.

Davis, G. B. & Parker, C. A. (1979). *Writing the doctoral dissertation: A systematic approach.* Woodbury, NY: Barron's Educational Series.

DeBakey, L., & DeBakey, S. (1978). The art of persuasion: Logic and language in proposal writing. *Grants Magazine, 1,* 43–60.

Gorn, J. L. (1973). *Style guide for writers of term papers, master's theses, and doctoral dissertations.* New York: Simon and Schuster.

Gorn, J. L. (1984). *The writer's handbook.* New York: Monarch Press.

Lindvall, C. M. (1959). The review of related literature. *Phi Delta Kappan, 40,* 180.

Woodford, F. P. (1968). Writing a research project proposal. In F. P. Woodford (Ed.), *Scientific writing for graduate students.* New York: Rockefeller University Press.

REFERENCES

American Psychological Association (1974). *Publications Manual* (2nd ed.). Washington, D. C.

Ethical principles of psychologists. (1981). *American Psychologist, 36* (6), 633–438.

Taylor, J. (1986). Unpublished report to members of the *JRME* editorial board, Anaheim, Ca., April 8, 1986.

Yarbrough, C. (1984). A content analysis of the *Journal of Research in Music Education*, 1953–1983. *Journal of Research in Music Education, 32* (4), 213–222.

Coda

The process of disciplined inquiry is characterized both by an attitude of curiosity about knowledge in general and by the mastery of technical skills in a variety of modes of inquiry, so that the curiosity can be turned into the activity of actually doing research. Many musician-music educators do possess a curiosity about things; yet, they find the process of acquiring technical research skills threatening and foreign to their way of thinking. Too easily, the image arises of bespectacled scholars searching through archival dustbins of data, of developing complicated definitions for seemingly simple terms, and of manipulating numbers and statistics for the goal of writing an article that only a few can understand.

This image, whatever its degree of truth, only reflects one side of what research is all about. The mastery of seemingly cut-and-dried technical skills are the tools of the research trade, just as technical skills on a musical instrument are the tools of the musical trade. One cannot be considered a professional without the mastery of the skills and techniques that have been declared the hallmarks of that trade or profession.

In musical performance, the mastery of musical skills alone does not adequately describe the successful performer. There is the hidden spark, the enthusiasm toward performing music, that separates a good technical performance from a really memorable musical experience. In music, the memorable experiences are not as common as one might wish. So it is with research: Technical ability must be combined with that spark of enthusiasm toward asking questions, toward being inquisitive, before research transcends the dull stage of "command" performance. An exciting new piece of information, an intellectual spark, memorable research finding(s) are both personal and infrequent.

Not all persons should be expected to become professional researchers anymore than all music students should be expected to become professional musicians. The study of music is assumed to create in an individual an appreciation for music and an ability to evaluate a musical performance as being good or poor, stylistically correct or incorrect, and emotionally pleasing or cold. In a similar way, the study of the research process can lead the student to an understanding and appreciation of the process of disciplined inquiry. Knowledge about that process should enable the student to evaluate the quality of formal research projects as well as to appreciate the thought processes that are employed to complete a successful professional research performance.

There is some hidden benefit for all who undertake the study of music. Likewise, there is hidden benefit for all who study the research process. This benefit begins with the discovery of skepticism as a positive force in the search for truth. That skepticism, if applied to one's own work, leads to self-criticism, an important ingredient in the search for quality. Finally, skepticism and self-criticism can also cause one to seek solutions to some of the problems observed in one's work and environment. Although such an attitude is the essence of research, it must not be confined to those who actually conduct research. Instead, that attitude should be applied to musical performance, the writing of music, or the teaching of music to learners of any age group. To conclude, and at the risk of being repetitive: Being inquisitive, self-critical, and seeking solutions to perceived problems are traits needed in all music educators who search for quality in their work as musician-performers, teachers, and researchers.

Appendixes

A p p e n d i x A

List of Selected Research Journals Closely Related to Music Education[1]

Title	Business and Editorial Office	Editor	Issues per year
Bulletin of the Council for Research in Music Education	School of Music, University of Illinois, Urbana, IL	R. Colwell	4
The GALPIN Society	38 Eastfield Western Park, Leicester LE3 LFE, England	E. Hunt, Chairman	1
Historical Research in Music Education	Dept. of Art and Music Education and Music Therapy, University of Kansas, Lawrence, Kansas 66045	G. Heller	Irregular
International Review of the Aesthetics and Sociology of Music	Berislaviceva POB 25, YU-41001 Zagreb, Yugoslavia	I. Supicic	2
Journal of Band Research	American Band Masters Association, Troy State University Press, Troy, Alabama 36082	J. R. Piersol	2
Journal of Music Therapy	National Association for Music Therapy, Inc., 1133 15th St., NW, Suite 1000, Washington, DC 20005	R. M. Graham	4
Journal of Research in Music Education	School of Music, Florida State University, Tallahassee, FL 32306	J. Taylor	4
Journal of Research in Singing	Dept. of Music, Texas Christian University, Ft. Worth, TX 76109	J. Large	2

Title	Business and Editorial Office	Editor	Issues per year
Music Perception	University of California Press, Berkeley, CA 94720	D. Deutsch	4
Psychology of Music	Society for Research in Psychology of Music and Music Education, Dept. of Psychology, University of Keele, Keele, Staffordshire ST5 5BG, England	J. Sloboda	4
Psycho-Musicology	Psychomusicology Society, Dept. of Music, Illinois State University, Normal, IL 61761	D. Williams (Ed.)	Irregular
Update	School of Music, University of South Carolina, Columbia, SC 29208	C. Elliott	3·

[1]See also: *Bulletin of Research in Music Education* (Pennsylvania); *Contributions to Music Education* (Ohio); *Research and Applications in Music Education*, (New York State School Association).

A p p e n d i x   B

Calculation of Standard Deviation
of Scores on a Test of Musical Memory

Subject (Ss)	Score (X)	Score squared (X^2)
1	41	1681
2	38	1444
3	31	961
4	27	729
5	25	625
6	23	529
7	20	400
8	16	256
9	9	81

The formula is

$$SD = \sqrt{\frac{\Sigma X_i^2}{N} - \overline{X}^2}\,.$$

Step 1. Determine N of scores ($N = 9$).

Step 2. Determine sum of scores (ΣX):

$$\Sigma X = 41 + 38 + \ldots + 9 = 230.$$

Step 3. Determine mean of scores ($\overline{X}$):

$$\overline{X} = \frac{\Sigma X_i}{N} = \frac{230}{9} = 25.56.$$

Step 4. Square each score (see X^2 column).

Step 5. Determine sum of squared scores (ΣX_i^2):

$$\Sigma X_i^2 = 1681 + 1444 + 962 + \ldots + 81 = 6706.$$

Step 6. Determine mean of

$$\Sigma X_i^2 = \left(\frac{\Sigma X_i^2}{N}\right) = \frac{6706}{9} = 745.11.$$

Step 7. Square the mean score $(\overline{X}^2) = 25.56^2 = 653.31$.

Step 8. To determine the variance s^2, subtract the result of Step 7 from Step 6—that is, subtract the mean score squared $(\overline{X}^2)$ from $\frac{\Sigma X_i^2}{N}$. Thus,

$$s^2 = \frac{\Sigma X_i^2}{N} - \overline{X}^2 = 745.11 - 653.31 = 91.80.$$

The variance of the scores on the test of musical memory is 91.80.

Step 9. To obtain the standard deviation, determine the square root of the variance:

$$SD = \sqrt{s^2} = \sqrt{91.80} = 9.58.$$

The standard deviation of the scores on the test of musical memory is 9.58.

A p p e n d i x   C

Step-By-Step Calculations of a t Ratio Test for Differences Between Two Means

Raw data: Group A—26, 31, 23, 35, 20
Group B—20, 17, 10, 25, 24, 22, 15

t-test formula:

$$t = \frac{\overline{X}_A - \overline{X}_B}{\sqrt{\left(\dfrac{N_A s_A^2 + N_B s_B^2}{N_A + N_B - 2}\right)\left(\dfrac{1}{N_A} + \dfrac{1}{N_B}\right)}} \, ,$$

where

$$s_A^2 = \frac{\Sigma X_{iA}^2}{N_A} - \overline{X}_{iA}^2$$

and

$$s_B^2 = \frac{\Sigma X_{iB}^2}{N_B} - \overline{X}_{iB}^2 \, .$$

Step 1. Develop a table that reflects the scores for each individual in each group and the square for each score (calculate X and X^2; square each individual score).

Group A			Group B		
Subject (Ss)	*Score (X)*	*Score squared (X²)*	*Subject (Ss)*	*Score (X)*	*Score squared (X²)*
1	26	676	1	20	400
2	31	961	2	17	289
3	23	529	3	10	100
4	35	1225	4	25	625
5	20	400	5	24	576
			6	22	484
			7	15	225
Total	135	3791	Total	133	2699

Step 2. Σ squares of scores for each group (see scores for Group A and Group B).

Step 3. Calculate $\overline{X}$ for each group:

$$\overline{X} = \frac{\Sigma X_i}{N} = \overline{X}_A = \frac{135}{5} = 27; \ \overline{X}_B = \frac{133}{7} = 19.$$

Step 4. Calculate $\overline{X}^2$ for each group:

$$\overline{X}_A^2 = (27)^2 = 729; \ \overline{X}_B^2 = (19)^2 = 361.$$

Step 5. Calculate $\dfrac{\Sigma X_i^2}{N}$ for each group:

$$\frac{\Sigma X_{iA}^2}{N} = \frac{3791}{5} = 758.20.$$

$$\frac{\Sigma X_{iB}^2}{N} = \frac{2699}{7} = 385.57.$$

Step 6. Calculate s^2 (variance) for each group:

$$s_A^2 = \frac{\Sigma X_{iA}^2}{N_A} - \overline{X}_A^2 = 758.20 - 729 = 29.20.$$

$$s_B^2 = \frac{\Sigma X_{iB}^2}{N_B} - \overline{X}_B^2 = 385.57 - 361 = 24.57.$$

Step 7. Calculate t by using the formula

$$t = \frac{\overline{X}_A - \overline{X}_B}{\sqrt{\left(\dfrac{N_A s_A^2 - N_B s_B^2}{N_A + N_B - 2}\right)\left(\dfrac{1}{N_A} + \dfrac{1}{N_B}\right)}},$$

where $\overline{X}_A$ is the mean of scores, Group A; $\overline{X}_B$ is the mean of scores, Group B; N_A is the number of subjects in Group A; N_B is the number of subjects in Group B; s_A^2 is the variance of scores in Group A; and s_B^2 is the variance of scores in Group B.

$$t = \frac{27 - 19}{\sqrt{\left(\dfrac{(5)(29.2) + (7)(24.57)}{5 + 7 - 2}\right)\left(\dfrac{1}{5} + \dfrac{1}{7}\right)}}$$

$$= \frac{27 - 19}{\sqrt{\left(\dfrac{146 + 171.99}{10}\right)\left(\dfrac{12}{35}\right)}} = \frac{8}{3.29} = 2.43.$$

The t value is 2.43, $df = 10$.

A p p e n d i x   D

Step-By-Step Computation of Pearson Product-Moment Correlation Coefficient

Note. The following scores were obtained from two separate administrations of a test to the same group of students. The scores on the test-retest will be correlated to arrive at an estimate of test reliability.

Table D.1

Subject (Ss)	1st testing Score X	2nd testing Score Y
1	50	70
2	60	58
3	65	78
4	47	59
5	58	68
6	74	80
7	50	40
8	52	64
9	45	51
10	58	77
11	56	58
12	80	85
13	63	90
14	55	76
15	69	80

Enter the scores of both tests for each individual as shown on Table D.1. Then prepare a table like Table D.2. Computational steps 1 to 5 are reflected in this table.

Table D.2 Computation of Steps 1 to 5

X	X^2	Y	Y^2	XY
50	2500	70	4900	3500
60	3600	58	3364	3480
65	4225	78	6084	5070
47	2209	59	3481	2773
58	3364	68	4624	3944
74	5476	80	6400	5920

Table D.2 *(Continued)*

X	X²	Y	Y²	XY
50	2500	40	1600	2000
52	2704	64	4096	3328
45	2025	51	2601	2295
58	3364	77	5929	4466
56	3136	58	3364	3248
80	6400	85	7225	6800
63	3969	90	8100	5670
55	3025	76	5776	4180
69	4761	84	7056	5796
882	53258	1038	74600	62470

Step 1. Sum all X scores: $\Sigma X = 882$.

Step 2. Square each X score, then sum square of scores: $\Sigma X^2 = 53258$.

Step 3. Sum all Y scores: $\Sigma Y = 1038$.

Step 4. Square each Y score, then sum square of scores: $\Sigma Y^2 = 74600$.

Step 5. Multiply each XY score, then sum all products: $\Sigma XY = 62470$.

Step 6. Compute

$$\overline{X} = \frac{\Sigma X_i}{N} = \frac{882}{15} = 58.8$$

and

$$\overline{X}^2 = (58.8)^2 = 3457.44.$$

Step 7. Compute standard deviation of X scores:

$$SD_x = \sqrt{\frac{\Sigma X^2}{N} - \overline{X}^2} = \sqrt{\frac{53258}{15} - 3457.44} = 9.65.$$

Step 8. Compute

$$\overline{Y} = \frac{\Sigma Y_i}{N} = \frac{1038}{15} = 69.2$$

and

$$\overline{Y}^2 = (69.2)^2 = 4788.64.$$

Step 9. Compute standard deviation of Y scores:

$$SD_y = \sqrt{\frac{\Sigma Y^2}{N} - \bar{Y}^2} = \sqrt{\frac{74600}{15} - 4788.64} = 13.59.$$

Step 10. Compute the reliability coefficient

$$r = \frac{\dfrac{\Sigma XY}{N} - (\bar{X})(\bar{Y})}{(SD_x)(SD_Y)}$$

$$= \frac{\dfrac{62470}{15} - (58.8)(69.2)}{(9.65)(13.59)}$$

$$= \frac{4164.67 - 4068.96}{131.14}$$

$$= \frac{95.71}{131.14}$$

$$= .73.$$

The test reliability would be $r = .73$.

One-Way ANOVA Procedures for Test Responses of Children Trained Under Four Different Teaching Methods

Group 1		Group 2		Group 3		Group 4	
X_1	X_1^2	X_2	X_2^2	X_3	X_3^2	X_4	X_4^2
24	576	8	64	8	64	28	784
24	576	16	256	36	1296	8	64
16	256	8	64	16	256	20	400
12	144	28	784	20	400	8	64
32	1024	24	576	24	576	8	64
		48	2304				
108	2576	132	4048	104	2592	72	1376

$\Sigma X_{\text{Tot}} = \Sigma X_{i1} + \Sigma X_{i2} + \Sigma X_{i3} + \Sigma X_{i4} = 108 + 132 + 104 + 72 = 416.$

$\Sigma X_{\text{Tot}}^2 = \Sigma X_{i1}^2 + \Sigma X_{i2}^2 + \Sigma X_{i3}^2 + \Sigma X_{i4}^2 = 2576 + 4048 + 2592 + 1376 = 10592.$

$N_{\text{Tot}} = N_1 + N_2 + N_3 + N_4 = 5 + 6 + 5 + 5 = 21.$

Calculation:

1. Sum of squares for total equals sum of squares minus the mean of the total sum of squares:

$$SS_{\text{Tot}} = \sum_{\text{Tot}} X^2 - \frac{(\Sigma X_{\text{Tot}})^2}{N_{\text{Tot}}}$$

$$= 10592 - \frac{(416)^2}{21}$$

$$= 10592 - 8240.76$$

$$= 2351.24.$$

2. Sum of squares between groups equals mean of squared score of each group minus the mean of the total score squared:

$$SS_{bg} = \sum_g \left[\frac{(\Sigma X_g)^2}{N_g} \right] - \frac{(\Sigma X_{Tot})^2}{N_{Tot}}$$

$$= \frac{(108)^2}{5} + \frac{(132)^2}{6} + \frac{(104)^2}{5} + \frac{(72)^2}{5} - \frac{(416)^2}{21}$$

$$= 8436.80 - 8240.76 = 196.04.$$

3. Sum of squares within groups equals total sum of squares minus sum of squares between groups:

$$SS_{wg} = SS_{Tot} - SS_{bg}$$

$$= 2351.24 - 196.04$$

$$= 2155.2.$$

4. Degrees of freedom and mean squares:
    (a) df between groups = classes − 1 = 4 − 1 = 3.
    (b) df within groups = N_{Tot} − classes = 21 − 4 = 17.
    (c) Mean square between groups = $MS_{bg} = \dfrac{SS_{bg}}{df_{bg}} = \dfrac{196.04}{3} = 65.35.$
    (d) Mean square within groups = $MS_{wg} = \dfrac{SS_{wg}}{df_{wg}} = \dfrac{2155.20}{17} = 126.78.$

5. F equals the ratio of mean square between groups and the mean square within groups:

$$F = \frac{MS_{bg}}{MS_{wg}} = \frac{65.35}{126.78} = .52.$$

6. Determine the significance of F by looking at F table (see statistics books) with df 3 and 17. F value must be greater than 3.20 at the 5% level in order to indicate significance of differences between groups.

Decision: The null hypothesis is not rejected. There are no statistically significant differences between groups that were exposed to differing methods of instruction.

7. Presentation of Results.

Summary Table for One-Way ANOVA

Source of variation	SS	df	MS	F	P
Between groups	196.04	3	65.35	.52	>.05
Within groups	2155.20	17	126.26		
Total	2351.24	20			

Appendix F

3 × 2 ANOVA Design

First Level of Computation: Step-by-Step Computational Procedure (Data from Table 10.4)

	Fourth grade scores			Sixth grade scores		
	Low	Average	High	Low	Average	High
1	13	21	24	16	22	32
2	19	14	15	14	19	27
3	21	16	22	21	16	25
4	16	21	19	19	20	27
5	11	13	17	23	29	21

Step 1. Place data in a two-way table. Leave space for squaring scores and for summing totals in rows and columns.

Fourth Grade

Low		Average		High	
X	X^2	X	X^2	X	X^2
13	169	21	441	24	576
19	361	14	196	15	225
21	441	16	256	22	484
16	256	21	441	19	361
11	121	13	169	17	289
$\Sigma = 80$	$\Sigma X^2 = 1348$	$\Sigma = 85$	$\Sigma X^2 = 1503$	$\Sigma X = 97$	$\Sigma X^2 = 1935$

Sixth Grade

16	256	22	484	32	1024
14	196	19	361	27	729
21	441	16	256	25	625
19	361	20	400	27	729
23	529	29	841	21	441
$\Sigma = 93$	$\Sigma X^2 = 1783$	$\Sigma = 106$	$\Sigma X^2 = 2342$	$\Sigma X = 132$	$\Sigma X^2 = 3548$

Step 2. Square all scores, then sum all X and X^2 scores.

Step 3. Total all scores and squared scores:

$\Sigma X = 80 + 85 + 97 + 93 + 106 + 132 = 593.$

$\Sigma X^2 = 1348 + 1503 + 1935 + 1783 + 2342 + 3548 = 12459.$

Step 4. Place all data in a summary table:

Summary Table

	L	M	H	
Fourth grade	$\Sigma X = 80$ $N = 5$	$\Sigma X = 85$ $N = 5$	$\Sigma X = 97$ $N = 5$	$\Sigma X_{\text{Tot}} = 262$ $N = 15$
Sixth grade	$\Sigma X = 93$ $N = 5$	$\Sigma X = 106$ $N = 5$	$\Sigma X = 132$ $N = 5$	$\Sigma X_{\text{Tot}} = 331$ $N = 15$
Total	$\Sigma X = 173$ $N = 10$	$\Sigma X = 191$ $N = 10$	$\Sigma X = 229$ $N = 10$	$\Sigma X_{\text{Tot}} = 593$ $N_{\text{Tot}} = 30$

This summary displays the total of the sum (Σ) of raw scores by rows and columns as well as the total of the rows and columns. The ANOVA deals with the ratio of the variance regarding all parameters, rows, columns, cells, and the total.

Second Level of Computation

We will use the summary figures to compute what is called the sum of squares total. The figures used are the total sum of scores (593), the totals $\Sigma X^2 = 12459$, and the N of 30. This will be used to determine total variance.

Step 1.

$$SS_{\text{Tot}} = (\Sigma X^2_{\text{Tot}}) - \frac{(\Sigma X)^2}{N_{\text{Tot}}}$$

$$= 12459 - \frac{(593)^2}{30} = 12459 - 11721.63$$

$$= 737.37.$$

Step 2. Break down the variance into two components—the sum of squares between groups and the sum of squares within groups:

$$SS_{\text{bg}} = \Sigma_g \left[\frac{(\Sigma X_g)^2}{N_g} \right] - \frac{(\Sigma X^2_{\text{Tot}})}{N_{\text{Tot}}}$$

$$= \frac{(80)^2}{5} + \frac{(85)^2}{5} + \frac{(97)^2}{5} + \frac{(93)^2}{5} + \frac{(106)^2}{5} + \frac{(132)^2}{5} - \frac{(593)^2}{30}$$

$$= 12068.60 - 11721.6 = 346.97.$$

Step 3. Because the sum of squares of the total group is known (737.37) and because we know the SS_{bg}, we can find the next needed figures, the sum of squares within groups, by subtraction:

$$SS_{wg} = SS_{Tot} - SS_{bg}$$

$$= 737.37 - 346.97 = 390.40.$$

This represents the variability that exists within each cell in the summary table (Table 10.5). They will be used to assess later the main effects of the variables.

Third Level of Computation

Break down the sum of squares by groups (Step 3, Level 2) into the sources of variability—the columns and rows and the interaction of the two. This is done by testing the column conditions (*L, M, H*) and testing the rows conditions (fourth and sixth grades):

Step 1.

$$SS_A = \frac{(\Sigma X_{AI})^2}{N_{AI}} + \frac{(\Sigma X_{AII})^2}{N_{AII}} + \frac{(\Sigma X_{AIII})^2}{N_{AIII}} - \frac{(\Sigma X_{Tot})^2}{N_{Tot}}$$

$$= \frac{(173)^2}{10} + \frac{(191)^2}{10} + \frac{(229)^2}{10} - \frac{(593)^2}{30}$$

$$= 11855.10 - 11721.63$$

$$= 163.47.$$

Step 2.

$$SS_B = \frac{(\Sigma X_{BI})^2}{N_{BI}} + \frac{(\Sigma X_{BII})^2}{N_{BII}} - \frac{(\Sigma X_{Tot})^2}{N_{Tot}}$$

$$= \frac{(262)^2}{15} + \frac{(331)^2}{15} - \frac{593}{30}$$

$$= 158.7.$$

Step 3. As in Step 3, Level 2, knowing SS_A and SS_B we can calculate the interaction $SS_{A \times B}$ by subtraction.

$$SS_{A \times B} = SS_{bg} - SS_A - SS_B$$

$$= 349.97 - 163.47 - 158.7$$

$$= 24.8.$$

Fourth Level of Computation

To compute the degrees of freedom:

A = columns. There are three columns in the design: therefore, $df = A - 1 = 3 - 1 = 2$.

B = rows. There are two rows; therefore $df = B - 1 = 2 - 1 = 1$.

df for interaction: $A \times B = (A - 1)(B - 1) = (2)(1) = 2$.

df within groups: $N - (A)(B) = 30 - (3)(2) = 30 - 6 = 24$.

To obtain mean squares:

$$MS_A = \frac{SS_A}{df_A} = \frac{163.47}{2} = 81.74.$$

$$MS_B = \frac{SS_B}{df_B} = \frac{158.70}{1} = 158.70.$$

$$MS_{A \times B} = \frac{SS_{A \times B}}{df_{A \times B}} = \frac{24.80}{2} = 12.40.$$

$$MS_{wg} = \frac{SS_{wg}}{df_{wg}} = \frac{390.4}{24} = 16.27.$$

Table 10.6 and the following pages in the chapter provide the calculation procedures for determining the F values.

Selected Bibliography

Selected Bibliography

Note. This bibliography includes important source materials *not* listed either in the chapter references or in the suggested readings.

Akers, W. G. (1974). Implications of Stephen C. Pepper's aesthetic theories for music education (Doctoral dissertation, University of Southern Mississippi). *Dissertation Abstracts International, 35* (5), 2744A.

Almack, J. C. (1930). *Research and thesis writing.* Boston: Houghton Mifflin.

Altick, R. D. (1982). *The art of literary research* (3rd ed.). New York: Norton.

American Association of Colleges of Teacher Education (1972). *Performance-based teacher education: An annotated bibliography.* Washington, D.C.: American Association of Colleges for Teacher Education.

Ary, D., Jacobs, L. C., & Kazavieh, A. (1979). *Introduction to research in education* (2nd ed.). New York: Holt, Rinehart and Winston.

Asch, S. E. (1952). *Social psychology.* Englewood Cliffs, NJ: Prentice-Hall.

Asher, J. W. (1976). *Educational research and evaluation methods.* Boston: Little, Brown.

Ausubel, D. P. (1968). *Educational psychology: A cognitive view.* New York: Holt, Rinehart and Winston.

Bababie, E. (1985). *The practice of social research* (5th. ed) Belmont, CA: Wadsworth.

Beardsley, M. C. (1981). *Aesthetics: Problems in the philosophy of criticism* (2nd ed.). Indianapolis: Hackett Publishing Co.

Beardsley, M. C., & Schueller, H. M. (1967). *Aesthetic inquiry: Essays on art criticism and the philosophy of art.* Belmont, CA: Dickenson.

Beittel, K. R. (1973). *Alternatives for art education research.* Dubuque, IA: William C. Brown.

Berlyne, D. E. (Ed.) (1965). *Structure and direction in thinking.* New York: John Wiley.

Berlyne, D. E. (1974). *Studies in the new experimental aesthetics: Steps toward an objective psychology of aesthetic appreciation.* Washington, D.C.: Hemispheric Publishing. New York: Halsted Press.

Bernstein, A. L. (1964). *A handbook of statistics solutions for the behavioral sciences.* New York: Holt, Rinehart and Winston.

Best, J. W., & Kahn, J. V. (1986). *Research in education* (5th ed.), Englewood Cliffs, NJ: Prentice-Hall.

Beveridge, W. I. B. (1960). *The art of scientific investigation.* New York: Random House.

Beyer, L. E. (1981). Aesthetics and the curriculum: Ideological and cultural form in school practice (Doctoral dissertation, University of Wisconsin-Madison), *Dissertation Abstracts International, 43* (1), p. 61A.

Bogdan, R. C., & Bikleman, S. K. (1982). *Qualitative research for education: An introduction to theory and methods.* Boston: Allyn and Bacon.

Books in print: An author-title series index to the publisher's trade list annual (1948-). New York: R. R. Bowker.

Borg, W. R., & Gall, M. D. (1983). *Educational research: An introduction* (4th ed.) New York: Longman.

Bowles, E. A. (Ed.) (1967). *Computers in humanistic research.* Englewood Cliffs, NJ: Prentice-Hall.

Brennan, J. G. (1967). *The meaning of philosophy* (2nd ed.) New York: Harper and Row.

Brickman, W. W. (1973). *Research in educational history.* Norwood, PA: Folcroft Library Editions.

Burke, A. J., & Burke, M. A. (1967). *Documentation in education* (4th rev. ed.). New York: Teachers College Press.

Butler, J. D. (1951). *Four philosophies.* New York: Harper and Brothers.

Camp, J. B. (1964). Epistemological change as a basis for interpreting contemporary Western culture, particularly in the arts of painting and music (Doctoral dissertation, Florida State University). *Dissertation Abstracts International, 25* (9), 5200A.

Cassirer, E. (1966). *The logic of the humanities* (C. S. Howe, Trans). New Haven: Yale University Press.

Chancellor, G. R. (1974). Aesthetic value in music: Implications for music education from the classic literature of the field (Doctoral dissertation, Northwestern University). *Dissertation Abstracts International, 35* (10), 6493A.

Chromister, F. B. (1969). The practical significance of Susanne Langer's views on the emotion-intellect dilemma in music education: A philosophical analysis and appraisal (Doctoral dissertation, University of Kansas). *Dissertation Abstracts International, 30* (6), 2414A.

Cohen, J. (1977). *Statistical power analysis for the behavioral sciences* (rev. ed.). New York: Academic Press.

Coker, W. W. (1965). The roots of musical meaning with special reference to Leonard B. Meyer's theory (Doctoral dissertation, University of Illinois). *Dissertation Abstracts International, 26* (6), 3388.

Collins, T. C. (1967). *A survey of music education materials and the compilation of an annotated bibliography.* (U.S. Office of Education Cooperative Research Project 5-13341). (ERIC Document Reproduction Service No. ED 020 194.)

Colwell, R. J. (1969). *A critique of research studies in music education.* (U.S. Office of Education Research Project 6-10-245). (ERIC Document Reproduction Service No. 035 100.)

Cook, D. R., & LaFleur, N. K. (1975). *A guide to educational research* (2nd ed.). Boston: Allyn and Bacon.

Culbertson, J. A., & Hencley, S. P. (Eds.) (1963). *Educational research: New perspectives.* Danville, IL: Interstate Printers and Publishers.

Delpaz, A. L. (1974). The nature of the aesthetic experience in the philosophies of Dewey and Collingwood and its implications for music education (Doctoral dissertation, Pennsylvania State University). *Dissertation Abstracts International, 36* (3), 1363A.

Dewey, J. (1933). *How we think.* Boston: D.C. Heath.

Dipert, R. R., & Whelden, R. M. (1976). Set-theoretical music analysis. *Journal of Aesthetics and Art Criticism, 35,* (Fall), 15–22.

Dennis, L. J. W. (1968). The implications of Dewey's esthetics for the teaching of music (Doctoral dissertation, Southern Illinois University). *Dissertation Abstracts International, 29* (7), 2145A.

Dixon, W., & Massey, F. J., Jr. (1969). *Introduction to statistical analysis* (3rd ed.). New York: McGraw-Hill.

Documentary report of the Ann Arbor symposium: Applications of psychology to the teaching and learning of music **(1981).** Reston, VA: Music Educators National Conference.

Documentary report of the Ann Arbor symposium session III: Applications of psychology to the teaching and learning of music **(1983).** Reston, VA: Music Educators National Conference.

Documentary report of the Wesleyan symposium on the application of social anthropology to the teaching and learning of music **(1985).** Reston: VA: Music Educators National Conference.

Doe, P. (Ed.) (1965). *R.M.D. research chronicle no. 3.* Birmingham, England: Royal Music Association.

Drew, C. J. (1980). *Introduction to designing research and evaluation* (2nd ed.). St. Louis: C.V. Mosby.

Duckles, V. (1974). *Music reference and research materials* (3rd ed.). New York: Free Press.

Durham, R. F. (1977). Aesthetic development in adolescence (Doctoral dissertation, University of Utah). *Dissertation Abstracts International, 38* (11), 6597A.

Ecker, D. W. (Ed.) (1981). *Qualitative evaluation in the arts.* New York: New York University Press.

Ecker, D. W., & Kaelin, E. F. (1972). The limits of aesthetic inquiry: A guide to educational research. In *Seventy-first yearbook of the national society for the study of education* (pp. 258–286). Chicago: University of Chicago Press.

Edwards, A. L. (1984). *Experimental design in psychological research* (5th ed.). New York: Holt, Rinehart and Winston.

Farmer, E. R. (1974). The development of sensuous/aesthetic perception for affective learning (Doctoral dissertation, Pennsylvania State University). *Dissertation Abstracts International, 36* (3), 1250A.

Ferguson, D. N. (1973). *Music as metaphor.* (Reprint of 1960 ed.) Minneapolis: University of Minnesota Press.

Fischer, D. H. (1970). *Historian's fallacies: Toward a logic of historical thought.* New York: Harper and Row.

Floyd, S. A. (1969). The implications of John Dewey's theory of appreciation for the teaching of music education (Doctoral dissertation, Southern Illinois University). *Dissertation Abstracts International, 30* (10), 4476A.

Fowler, Ch. B. (1964/1965). A reconstructionist philosophy of music education

(Doctoral dissertation, Boston University). *American Doctoral Dissertations,*
13, 168.

Gage, N. L. (Ed.) (1963). *Handbook of research on teaching.* Chicago: Rand
McNally.

Garrett, A. M. (1958). *An introduction to research in music.* Washington, D.C.:
Catholic University of America Press.

Gay, L. R. (1981). *Educational research: Competencies for analysis and application*
(2nd ed.). Columbus, OH: Charles E. Merrill.

George, W. E. (1980). Measurement and evaluation of musical behavior. In
D. Hodges (Ed.), *Handbook of music psychology* (pp. 291–391). Lawrence, KS:
National Association of Music Therapy.

Ghiselin, B. (Ed.) (1952). *The creative process.* New York: Mentor Books.

Gilbert, J. V. (Ed.) (1984). *Qualitative evaluation in the arts.* (Vol. II). New York:
New York University Press.

Goldstone, J. A. (1979). A general mathematical theory of expectation models
of music (Doctoral dissertation, University of Southern California). *Disser-*
tation Abstracts International, 39 (11), 6387A.

Good, C. V. (1966). *Essentials of educational research.* New York: Appleton-
Century-Crofts.

Goodman, H. A. (1982). *Music education: Perspectives and perceptions.* Dubuque,
IA: Kendall/Hunt.

Gordon, E. (1970). *Iowa tests of music literacy.* Iowa City: University of Iowa
Bureau of Educational Research and Service.

Gorovitz, S., Hintikka, M., Provence, D., & Williams, R. G. (1979).
Philosophical analysis: An introduction to its language and technique (3rd ed.).
New York: Random House.

Gottschalk, L. (1969). *Understanding history* (2nd ed.). New York: Knopf.

Gribenski, J. (1979). *Thèses de doctorat en langue française relatives a la musique:*
Bibliographie commentée. New York: Pendragon Press. [French language dissertations in music: An annotated bibliography].

Hardyck, C., & Petrinovich, L. F. (1975). *Understanding research in the social*
sciences. Philadelphia: W.B. Saunders.

Hegel, G. W. F. (1920). *The philosophy of fine arts* (F.P.B. Osmaston, Trans.).
London: G. Bell and Sons.

Heller, G. N. (1985). *Historical research in music education: A bibliography.* Lawrence, KS: The University of Kansas.

Hildebrand, J. W. (1975). A critical analysis of Bennett Reimer's philosophy
of music education (Doctoral dissertation, University of North Dakota). *Dis-*
sertation Abstracts International, 37 (2), 857A.

Hilgard, E. L., & Bower, G. H. (1981). *Theories of learning* (5th ed.). Englewood
Cliffs, NJ: Prentice-Hall.

Hill, W. F. (1977). *Learning: A survey of psychological interpretations* (3rd. ed.).
New York: Harper and Row.

Hillman, H., & Natale, K. (1977). *The art of winning government grants.* New
York: Vanguard.

Hillway, T. (1964). *Introduction to research* (2nd ed.). Boston: Houghton Mifflin.

Hockett, H. C. (1955). *The critical method in historical research and writing.* New York: Macmillan.

Hodges, D. (Ed.) (1980). *Handbook of music psychology.* Lawrence, KS: National Association of Music Therapy.

Hopkins, C. D. (1980). *Understanding educational research: An inquiry approach* (2nd ed.). Columbus, OH: Charles E. Merrill.

Hospers, J. (1967). *An introduction to philosophical analysis* (2nd ed.). Englewood Cliffs, NJ: Prentice-Hall.

Hunt, D. E. & Sullivan, E. V. (1974). *Between psychology and education.* Hinsdale, IL: Dryden Press.

Immroth, J. P. (1971). *A guide to the Library of Congress classifications* (2nd ed.). Littleton, CO: Libraries Unlimited.

Irvine, D. B. (1968). *Writing about music. A style book for reports and theses* (2nd ed., rev.). Seattle: University of Washington Press.

Jacobs, J. E. (1977). Toward an ontology of musical works of art (Doctoral dissertation, University of Chicago). *Dissertation Abstracts International, 38* (12), 7379A.

Johnston, M. A. (1977). An investigation into the possibility of cognitive-developmental stages of the aesthetic experience of children (Doctoral dissertation, University of Utah). *Dissertation Abstracts International, 38* (11), 6435A.

Jones, B. J., & McFee, B. K. (1986). Research on teaching arts and aesthetics. In M. C. Wittrock (Ed.), *Handbook of research on teaching* (3rd ed.) (pp. 906–916). (A project of the American Educational Research Association). New York: Macmillan; London: Collier Macmillan.

Jones, R. H. (Ed.) (1973). *Methods and techniques of educational research.* Danville, IL: Interstate Printers and Publishers.

Jones, W. J. (1973). A study of values in music education, 1950–1970 (Doctoral dissertation, University of the Pacific, Stockton, CA). *Dissertation Abstracts International, 34,* 1313A.

Kacanek, H. S. (1983). A descriptive analysis of Wisconsin music educators' agreement with Bennett Reimer's *A Philosophy of Music Education* (Doctoral dissertation, University of Kansas, 1982). *Dissertation Abstracts International, 43* (8), 2589A.

Kainz, F. (1962). *Aesthetics: The science.* (Trans. and Intro, H. M. Schueller). Detroit: Wayne State University Press.

Kaplan, M. (1966). *Foundations and frontiers of music education.* New York: Holt, Rinehart and Winston.

Keene, J. A. (1982). *A history of music education in the United States.* Hanover, NH: University Press of New England.

Keppel, G. (1982). *Design and analysis: A researcher's handbook* (2nd ed.). Englewood Cliffs, NJ: Prentice-Hall.

Kerlinger, F. N. (1979). *Behavioral research: A conceptual approach.* New York: Holt, Rinehart and Winston.

Kneller, G. F. (1971). *Introduction to the philosophy of education* (2nd ed.) New York: John Wiley.

Kneller, G. F. (1958). *Existentialism and education.* New York: Philosophical Library.

Koeffod, P. E. (1964). *The writing requirements for graduate degrees.* Englewood Cliffs, NJ: Prentice-Hall.

Kostka, S. M. (1974). *A bibliography of computer applications in music.* Hackensack, NJ: Joseph Boonin.

Kovach, F. J. (1974). *Philosophy of beauty.* Norman, OK: University of Oklahoma Press.

Krummel, D. W., Geil, J., Doyen, D. J., & Root, D. L. (1981). *Resources of American music history.* Urbana, IL: University of Illinois Press.

Kwalwasser, J. (1955). *Exploring the musical mind.* Boston: Coleman-Ross.

Labovitz, S., & Hagedorn, R. (1981). *Introduction to social research* (3rd ed.). New York: McGraw-Hill.

Langer, S. K. (1953). *Feeling and form: A theory of art.* New York: Scribner.

Langer, S. K. (1957). *Philosophy in a new key* (3rd ed.). Cambridge: Harvard University Press.

Langer, S. K. (1967). *Mind: An essay on human feeling.* Baltimore: Johns Hopkins Press.

LaRue, J. (1971). *Guidelines for style analysis.* New York: W.W. Norton.

Lebaron, B. V. (1976). Helen M. Hosmer's philosophy of music education and its implementation (Doctoral dissertation, University of Florida). *Dissertation Abstracts International, 38* (2), 689A.

Lehman, P. R. (1968). *Tests and measurements in music.* Englewood Cliffs, NJ: Prentice-Hall.

Lewin, K. (1951). *Field theory in social science.* New York: Harper and Brothers.

Lewis, D. R. (1973). Implications of music education from Susanne K. Langer, Abraham Maslow, Marshall McLuhan, Jerome S. Bruner, Max Kaplan, and Jean Piaget (Doctoral dissertation, University of Mississippi, 1972). *American Doctoral Dissertations,* X1973.

Lincoln, H. B. (Ed.) (1970). *The computer and music.* Ithaca, NY: Cornell University Press.

Long, N. H. (1967). *Indiana-Oregon music discrimination test.* Bloomington, IN: Midwest Music Tests.

Madeja, S. S. (Ed.) (1977). *Arts and aesthetics: An agenda for the future.* St. Louis: CEMREL.

Madeja, S. S. & Onuska, S. (1977). *Through the arts to aesthetics.* St. Louis: CEMREL.

Madeja, S. S. (Ed.) (1978). *The arts, cognition, and basic skills.* St. Louis: CEMREL.

Mark, M. (1986). *Contemporary music education* (2nd ed.). New York: Schirmer.

Mason, E. J., & Bramble, W. (1977). *Understanding and conducting research: Applications in education and the behavioral sciences.* New York: McGraw-Hill.

Manual of Music Librarianship (1966). Ann Arbor, MI: Music Library Association.

McAshan, H. H. (1963). *Elements of educational research.* New York: McGraw-Hill.

McClelland, D. (1955). *Studies in motivation.* New York: Appleton-Century-Croft.

McGrath, G. D., Jelinek, J., & Wochner, R. E. (1963). *Educational research methods.* New York: Ronald Press.

McMillan, J. H. & Schumacher, S. (1984). *Research in education: A conceptual approach.* Boston: Little, Brown.

Mead, H. (1952). *An introduction to aesthetics.* New York: Ronald Press.

Mehrens, W. A. & Lehmann, I. J. (1980). *Standardized tests in education* (3rd ed.). New York: Holt, Rinehart and Winston.

Mellem, R. I. (1974). Definitions comprising a concept analysis and theoretical model of "good musical taste" (Doctoral dissertation, Columbia University). *Dissertation Abstracts International, 35* (2), 866A.

Meyer, L. B. (1959). Some remarks on value and greatness in music. *Journal of Aesthetics and Art Criticism, 17,* (6), 486–500.

Mill, J. S. (1919). *A system of logic: Ratiocinative and inductive.* London: Longmans, Green.

Miller, D. C. (1983). *Handbook of research design and social measurement* (4th ed.). New York: David McKay.

Morton, B. N. (1972). Some problems in the philosophy of music (Doctoral dissertation, University of Rochester). *Dissertation Abstracts International, 33* (1), 316A.

Mouly, G. J. (1970). *The science of educational research* (2nd ed.). New York: Van Nostrand Reinhold.

Mueller, J. H. (1958). Music education: A sociological approach. In H. Nelson (Ed.), *Basic concepts in music education* (pp. 88–122). Chicago: National Society for the Study of Education.

Munro, T. (1956). *Toward science in aesthetics: Selected essays.* Indianapolis: Bobbs-Merrill.

Munro, T. (1928). *Scientific method in aesthetics.* New York: W. W. Norton.

Murphy, J., & Sullivan, G. (1968). *Music in American society.* Washington, D.C.: Music Educators National Conference.

Murphy, J., & Jones, L. (1978). *Research in arts education.* Washington, D.C.: U.S. Department of Health, Education, and Welfare.

Music and music education: Data and information (1984). Reston, VA: Music Educators National Conference.

National Assessment of Education Progress (1970). *Music objectives.* Ann Arbor, MI: National Assessment of Educational Progress.

Nevins, A. (1962). *The gateway to history* (rev. ed.). Garden City, NY: Anchor Books.

Orlich, D. C. (1977). *The art of writing successful R&D proposals.* Pleasantville, NY: Redgrave.

Piaget, J. (1970). *Science of education and the psychology of the child* (D. Coltman, Trans.). New York: Orion Press.

Polanyi, M. (1962). *Personal knowledge.* Chicago: University of Chicago Press.

Polya, G. (1945). *How to solve it: A new aspect of mathematical method.* Princeton, NJ: Princeton University Press.

Prall, D. W. (1929). *Aesthetic judgment.* New York: Thomas Y. Cromwell.

Quattlebaum, M. V. (Ed.) (1966). *Subject headings* (7th ed.). Washington, D.C.: Library of Congress.

Regelski, T. A. (1975). *Principles and problems of music education.* Englewood Cliffs, NJ: Prentice-Hall.

Research in the arts and aesthetic education. A directory of investigators and their fields of inquiry **(1977).** Project coordinators R. A. Smith and C. M. Smith. (Prepared for the National Institute of Education by the Research Program for the Study of the Arts and Aesthetic Education). St. Louis: CEMREL.

Revesz, G. (1953). *Introduction to the psychology of music* (G. I. C. deCourcy, Trans.). London: Longmans, Green.

Ridell, K. J. (1972). An evaluation of selected humanistic art concepts and art values (Doctoral dissertation, University of Northern Colorado). *Dissertation Abstracts International, 33* (11), 6392–6393A.

Rosen, F. B. (1968). *Philosophic systems and education.* Columbus, OH: Charles E. Merrill.

Rosenshine, B., & Furst, N. (1971). Research on teacher performance criteria. In B. O. Smith (Ed.), *Research in teacher education* (pp. 31–72). Englewood Cliffs, NJ: Prentice-Hall.

Ross, J. (1963). The development of a comprehensive philosophy for music in elementary education (Doctoral dissertation, New York University). *Dissertation Abstracts International, 24* (3), 1100.

Rummel, J. F. (1964). *An introduction to research procedures in education* (2nd ed.). New York: Harper and Row.

Runkel, P. J., & McGrath, J. E. (1972). *Research on human behavior.* New York: Holt, Rinehart and Winston.

Russell, C. T. (1972). The analysis and evaluation of music: A philosophical inquiry. *The Musical Quarterly, 58* (2), 161–184.

Schaal, R. (1974). *Verzeichnis deutsch-sprachiger musikwissenschaftlicher Dissertationen, 1881–1960.* [Index of musicological dissertations in the German language]. Kassel: Bärenreiter.

Scheid, P., & Eccles, J. C. (1975). Music and speech: Artistic functions of the human brain. *Psychology of Music, 3* (1), 21–35.

Schneider, E. H., & Cady, H. L. (1965). *Evaluation and synthesis of research studies related to music education.* (U.S. Office of Education Cooperative Research Project E-016). (ERIC Document Reproduction Service No. ED 010 298).

Schoen, M. (1940). *The psychology of music.* New York: Ronald Press.

The school music program: Description and standards **(1974).** Reston, VA: Music Educators National Conference.

Seashore, C. E. (1919). *Seashore measures of musical talents.* New York: Columbia Phonograph Company.

Seashore, C. E., Lewis, L., & Saetveit, J. G. (1960). *Seashore measures of musical talents.* New York: The Psychological Corporation.

Sellars, R. W. (1932). *The philosophy of physical realism.* New York: Macmillan.

Shafer, R. J. (Ed.) (1980). *A guide to historical method* (3rd. ed.). Homewood, IL: Dorsey Press.

Shank, W., & Engelbrecht, L. C. (1966). Records and tapes. In *Manual of Music Librarianship*. Ann Arbor, MI: Music Library Association.

Shuter, R. (1981). *The psychology of musical ability* (2nd ed.). London: Methuen.

Simon, J. L. (1978). *Basic research methods in social science: The art of empirical investigation* (2nd ed.). New York: Random House.

Skaife, A. M. (1966). The role of complexity and deviation in changing musical taste (Doctoral dissertation, University of Oregon). *Dissertation Abstracts International, 27* (11), 3696A.

Smith, H. L. (1944). *Educational research, principles and practices.* Bloomington, IN: Educational Publications.

Smith, P. L. (1980). On the distinction between quantitative and qualitative research. *CEDR Quarterly, 13* (Fall), 3–6.

Solie, R. A. (1977). Metaphor and model in the analysis of melody (Doctoral dissertation, University of Chicago). *Dissertation Abstracts International, 38* (3), 1109A.

Sowell, E. J., & Casey, R. J. (1982). *Research methods in education.* Belmont, CA: Wadsworth.

Sprinthall, R. C., & Sprinthall, N. A. (1977). *Educational psychology* (rev. ed.). Reading, MA: Addison-Wesley.

Stanton, H. (1935). *Measurement of musical talent: The Eastman experiment.* (University of Iowa Studies in the Psychology of Music, No. 2). Iowa City: University of Iowa Press.

Strong, E. K. (1966). *Strong vocational interest blank for men and women.* New York: Consulting Psychologists Press.

Stroud, J. B. (1946). *Psychology in education.* New York: Longmans, Green.

Strunk, W., Jr., & White, E. B. (1979). *The elements of style* (3rd ed.). New York: Macmillan.

Tait, M. J. (1963). The significance of musical understanding in music education (Doctoral dissertation, Columbia University). *Dissertation Abstracts International, 25* (1), 528.

Tellstrom, A. T. (1971). *Music in American education: Past and present.* New York: Holt, Rinehart and Winston.

Travers, R. M. W. (1978). *An introduction to educational research* (4th ed.). New York: McGraw-Hill.

Tuckman, B. W. (1978). *Conducting educational research* (2nd ed.). New York: Harcourt Brace Jovanovich.

Van Dalen, D. B. (1979). *Understanding educational research: An introduction* (4th ed.). New York: McGraw-Hill.

Venable, T. C., & Alger, S. (1973). Trend studies and curriculum research. In R. H. Jones (Ed.), *Methods and techniques of educational research.* Danville, IL: Interstate Printers and Publishers.

Villeman, F. T. (1953). *Philosophic research in education.* New York: New York University Press.

Vincent, J. M. (1934). *Aids to historical research.* New York: Appleton-Century-Crofts.

Vockell, E. L. (1983). *Educational research.* New York: Macmillan.

Walker, H. M. (1951). *Mathematics essential for elementary statistics.* (Rev ed.). New York: Holt, Rinehart and Winston.

Ward, D. (1983). *Perception and imagination in music: A philosophical and psychological investigation.* Unpublished doctoral dissertation, University of London, Institute of Education.

Warren, F. (1966). A history of the Music Education Research Council and *The Journal of Research in Music Education* of the Music Educators National Conference. (Doctoral dissertation, University of Michigan). *Dissertation Abstracts International, 27,* 2172A. University Microfilms no. LC-66-14612.

Watanabe, R. T. (1967). *Introduction to music research.* Englewood Cliffs, NJ: Prentice-Hall.

Webb, E. J., Campbell, D. T., Schwartz, R. D., & Sechrest, L. (1966). *Unobtrusive measures: Nonreactive research in the social sciences.* Chicago: Rand McNally.

Westby, B. M. (1982). *Sears list of subject headings.* (12th ed.). New York: H. W. Wilson.

Whitehouse, P. G. (1976). The limited application of Dewey's *Art as Experience* to esthetic education (Doctoral dissertation, Southern Illinois University). *Dissertation Abstracts International, 37* (6), 3497A.

Whitney, F. L. (1950). *The elements of research.* (3rd ed.). Englewood Cliffs, NJ: Prentice-Hall.

Whybrew, W. E. (1971). *Measurement and evaluation in music.* (2nd ed.). Dubuque, IA: William C. Brown.

Wiersma, W. (1985). *Research methods in education.* (3rd ed.). Newton, MA: Allyn and Bacon, Inc.

Wirtala, A. E. (1954). Taste in the arts: Its nature, formation, and development (Doctoral dissertation, University of Florida). *Dissertation Abstracts International, 14,* 811.

Wise, J. E., Nordberg, R.B., & Reitz, D. J. (1967). *Methods of research in education.* Boston: D.C. Heath.

Wry, O. E. (1976). The implications of Merleau-Ponty's theory of the body-subject as the basis for a philosophy of music education (Doctoral dissertation, Temple University). *Dissertation Abstracts International, 37* (8), 4691A.

Indexes

Name Index

Note: This index includes all names cited in the text and all authors referenced in the chapters, in the suggested reading lists, and in the selected bibliography. Boldface numbers indicate the page where full bibliographical information for a source is given for the first time. The same publication is not listed twice.

Lovejoy, A.O., 5, **20**
Luckman, T., 9, **19**
Ludlow, H.G., **225**
Lukacs, G., 144, **159**
Lundin, R.W., **18**
Lysenko, T., 8

Madeja, S.S., **156, 306**
Madsen, C.H., Jr., **195,** 217–18, **227**
Madsen, C.K., **195,** 217–18, **227**
Mainwaring, J., 24, 27, **34**
Mandelbaum, M., 128–131, 136, **159**
Margolis, J., 3, **20,** 129
Mark, M., 154, **159, 310**
Martin, E., 114, **126**
Maslow, A., 154
Mason, E.J., **310**
Mason, J., **156**
Massey, F.J., **307**
Mauk, F.H., **157**
McAshan, H.H., **310**
McClain, E.G., 3, **19**
McClelland, D., **311**
McFee, J.K., **309**
McGrath, G.D., **311**
McGrath, J.E., **312**
McKay, G., **157**
McMillan, J.H., **311**
McMurray, F., **157**
Mead, H., **311**
Medley, D.M., 213, **227**
Mehrens, W.A., **311**
Mellem, R.I., **311**
Meske, E., 60
Meyer, L.B., 154, **157, 308**
Mill, J.S., **311**
Miller, D.C., **311**
Miller, R.F., **18**
Mitchell, A., 112
Mitzel, H.E., 213, **227**
Moore, B.C.J., 16, **20**
Moore, D.S., 163, 170, 174, **195,** 204, 237
Moore, R.P., **225**
Moore, R.S., 217, **227**
Morgan, R., 120
Morgenbesser, S., 129, **159**
Morris, B., 136, **159**
Morton, B.N., **311**
Mouly, G.J., **311**
Mountford, R., 60

Mueller, F.L., 165, **195**
Mueller, J.H., **157, 311**
Munro, T., **311**
Murphy, J., **311**

Nagel, E., **156**
Natale, K., **308**
Nehrich, R.B., 5, **19**
Nelson, D., 16, **20,** 60
Nevins, A., 114, **311**
Newell, R.W., 128, 136, **159**
Newman, E., 31, **34**
Newmark, J., **258**
Newton, Sir Isaac, 7
Newton, W.J., 30, **34**
Nitko, A.J., **195**
Nordberg, R.B., **314**
Northrop, F.S.C., **157**
Nozick, R.W., 136, **160**
Nunnally, J.C., 210, **227**

Onuska, S., **310**
Oppenheim, A., 116, **127,** 200–205
Orlich, D.C., **311**

Parker, C.A., **270**
Partchey, K.C., 16, **19,** 60
Paul, S.J., **33**
Payne, D.A., **225**
Perelman, C., 144, **166**
Perkins, D., **156**
Peters, G.D., **18**
Peters, J., 30, **34**
Petrinovich, L.F., **308**
Petrie, R.G., **82**
Petzold, R.G., **82**
Pfrogner, H., 3, **19**
Phelan, C.M., **157**
Phelps, R., 16, **19,** 47, 131
Piaget, J., 24–25, **82, 311**
Pierce, J.R., 16, **20**
Pike, A., 153, **159**
Pirsig, R.M., **18**
Plank, M., 7
Plato, 3
Plomp, R., **82**
Polanyi, M., **311**
Polya, G., **311**
Popper, K.R., 5, **20,** 140, **160**
Prall, D.W., **312**

Subject Index

Note: Boldface numbers indicate the page on which—if applicable—the full bibliographical information pertaining to a particular subject heading or the title of a referenced publication is given.